NETWORK ADMINISTRATION

UNIX SVR4.2

Edited by John A. Van Dyk

UNIX
Press

Published by Prentice-Hall, Inc.
A Simon & Schuster Company
Englewood Cliffs, New Jersey 07632

IMPORTANT NOTE TO USERS

While every effort has been made to ensure the accuracy and completeness of all information in this document, USL assumes no liability to any party for any loss or damage caused by errors or omissions or by statements of any kind in this document, its updates, supplements, or special editions, whether such errors, omissions, or statements result from negligence, accident, or any other cause. USL further assumes no liability arising out of the application or use of any product or system described herein; nor any liability for incidental or consequential damages arising from the use of this document. **USL disclaims all warranties regarding the information contained herein, whether expressed, implied or statutory, including implied warranties of merchantability or fitness for a particular purpose.** USL makes no representation that the interconnection of products in the manner described herein will not infringe on existing or future patent rights, nor do the descriptions contained herein imply the granting of any license to make, use or sell equipment constructed in accordance with this description.

USL reserves the right to make changes to any products herein without further notice.

TRADEMARKS

Datakit is a registered trademark of AT&T.
Epson FX-86e is a trademark of Epson America, Inc.
Ethernet is a trademark of Xerox Corporation.
HP and LaserJet are registered trademarks of Hewlett-Packard Company.
MS-DOS is a registered trademark of Microsoft Corporation, Inc.
PostScript is a registered trademark of Adobe Systems, Inc.
Proprinter is a trademark of International Business Machines.
UNIX is a registered trademark of UNIX System Laboratories, Inc. in the USA and other countries.
VMS is a registered trademark of Digital Equipment Corporation.
XENIX is a registered trademark of Microsoft Corporation.

10 9 8 7 6 5 4 3 2 1

ISBN 0-13-017633-8

P R E N T I C E   H A L L

ORDERING INFORMATION

UNIX® SYSTEM V RELEASE 4.2 DOCUMENTATION

To order single copies of UNIX® SYSTEM V Release 4.2 documentation, please call (515) 284-6761.

ATTENTION DOCUMENTATION MANAGERS AND TRAINING DIRECTORS:
For bulk purchases in excess of 30 copies, please write to:

Corporate Sales Department
PTR Prentice Hall
113 Sylvan Avenue
Englewood Cliffs, N.J. 07632

or

Phone: (201) 592-2863
FAX: (201) 592-2249

ATTENTION GOVERNMENT CUSTOMERS:

For GSA and other pricing information, please call (201) 461-7107.

Prentice-Hall International (UK) Limited, *London*
Prentice-Hall of Australia Pty. Limited, *Sydney*
Prentice-Hall Canada Inc., *Toronto*
Prentice-Hall Hispanoamericana, S.A., *Mexico*
Prentice-Hall of India Private Limited, *New Delhi*
Prentice-Hall of Japan, Inc., *Tokyo*
Simon & Schuster Asia Pte. Ltd., *Singapore*
Editora Prentice-Hall do Brasil, Ltda., *Rio de Janeiro*

Contents

1 **Introduction**
About This Book 1-1

Part 1 - Setting Up a Network

2 **Network Services**
An Overview of Network Administration 2-1
Network Selection 2-10
Name-to-Address Mapping 2-17
The Connection Server 2-22
cr1 Bilateral Authentication Scheme 2-31
ID Mapping 2-41
Basic Networking Utilities 2-64
REXEC 2-132

Part 2 - Setting Up TCP/IP

3 **Introduction to Administering TCP/IP Networks**
About TCP/IP Administration 3-1
Introducing the Internet Protocol Suite 3-2

4 **Setting Up TCP/IP**
Overview of Setting Up TCP/IP 4-1
Obtaining an Internet Network Number 4-2

Assigning IP Addresses to Your Network Hosts 4-3
Establishing a Domain 4-5
Installing Network Media 4-10
Installing TCP/IP Software 4-11
Modifying the Startup Script 4-12
Setting Up TCP/IP Files 4-13
Setting Up the Listener 4-19
Setting Up TCP/IP As the Preferred Network 4-24
Starting TCP/IP 4-25

5 Maintaining Security in a TCP/IP Environment
Granting Access to Network Machines 5-1
Administering the host.equiv and .rhosts Files 5-2
Security Issues 5-6

6 Expanding Your TCP/IP Network
Introduction 6-1
Hardware Devices for Expanding the Local Network 6-2
Creating an Internetwork 6-4
Setting Up Subnets 6-23

7 Using Domain Name Service with TCP/IP
An Overview of the Domain Name Service 7-1
Setting Up DNS on a Client 7-8
Setting Up DNS on a Name Server 7-11
A Practical Example 7-35

8 Troubleshooting TCP/IP
Troubleshooting Commands 8-1
Running Software Checks 8-10
Restarting TCP/IP 8-12

Improving System Performance 8-13
Logging Network Problems 8-14

9 Guidelines for Completing the IP Number Registration Form
Guidelines for Completing the IP Number Registration Form 9-1

10 Guidelines for Completing the Domain Registration Form
Guidelines for Completing the Domain Registration Form 10-1

Part 3 - Setting Up DFS

11 Introduction to Distributed File System (DFS) Administration
About DFS Administration 11-1
System V File Sharing 11-3
RFS vs. NFS 11-5
An Overview of DFS Administration 11-9

12 Setting Up DFS Administration
DFS Administration Setup 12-1
Installing the Software 12-2
Changing the File Sharing Package Default 12-3
Starting Distributed File System Operation 12-4

13 Using DFS Commands and Files
Sharing and Unsharing Resources 13-1
Mounting and Unmounting Remote Resources 13-6
Displaying Information 13-11

14 DFS sysadm Interface

Introduction 14-1
The DFS Management Menu Tree 14-2
DFS Menu Options 14-3

Part 4 - Setting Up RFS

15 RFS Introduction

About RFS Administration 15-1
Introduction to RFS 15-2

16 RFS sysadm Interface

Overview of RFS sysadm 16-1
Procedure 1: Set Up Remote File Sharing 16-3
Procedure 2: Start/Stop Remote File Sharing 16-5
Procedure 3: Local Resource Sharing 16-6
Procedure 4: Remote Resource Mounting 16-7
Procedure 5: Change RFS Configuration 16-8

17 RFS Command Interface

Setting Up RFS 17-1
Starting/Stopping RFS 17-25
Sharing RFS Resources 17-32
Mapping Remote Users 17-43
RFS Domain Name Servers 17-54
Monitoring 17-58
Parameter Tuning 17-70

Part 5 - Setting Up NFS

18 NFS Introduction

About NFS Administration 18-1
Introduction to NFS 18-3
An Overview of NFS Administration 18-6

19 Setting Up NFS

Introduction 19-1
Starting and Stopping NFS Operation 19-2
Setting Up Automatic Sharing 19-3
Setting Up Automatic Mounting 19-5

20 Sharing and Mounting NFS Resources Explicitly

Sharing and Unsharing Resources 20-1
Mounting and Unmounting NFS Resources 20-4

21 Obtaining NFS Information

Obtaining Information About NFS Resources 21-1
Browsing Available Resources with the dfshares Command 21-2
Displaying Shared Local Resources with the share Command 21-3
Monitoring Shared Local Resources with the dfmounts Command 21-4

22 Handling NFS Problems

NFS Troubleshooting 22-1
An Overview of the Mount Process 22-2
Determining Where NFS Service Has Failed 22-4
Fixing Hung Programs 22-9

23 Setting Up Secure NFS

Introduction to Secure NFS 23-1
An Overview of Secure RPC 23-2
Administering Secure NFS 23-7
Important Considerations 23-9

24 Using the NFS Automounter

The NFS Automounter 24-1
How the Automounter Works 24-2
Preparing the Automounter Maps 24-3
Invoking the Automounter 24-14
Updating the Mount Table 24-16
Modifying the Maps 24-17
Troubleshooting the Automounter 24-18

25 The NFS Network Lock Manager

An Overview of the Network Lock Manager 25-1

26 Using the NFS sysadm Interface

NFS sysadm Interface 26-1
Procedure 1: Set Up Network File System 26-2
Procedure 2: Start/Stop Network File System 26-3
Procedure 3: Local Resource Sharing 26-4
Procedure 4: Remote Resource Mounting 26-5

Part 6 - Setting Up RPC

27 RPC Administration

Introduction to RPC Administration 27-1
RPC Administration Files 27-2
Secure RPC Overview 27-4
Secure RPC Administration 27-6

Part 7 - Setting Up NIS

28 Network Information Service

Introduction to NIS 28-1
Implementing the NIS 28-7
Administering NIS Maps 28-21
Adding a New NIS Server to the Original Set 28-28
Summary of NIS-Related Commands 28-31
Fixing NIS Problems 28-33
Turning off NIS 28-40

GL Glossary

Glossary GL-1

IN Index

Index IN-1

Figures and Tables

Figure 2-1: A Diagram of the Networking Applications Architecture 2-2
Figure 2-2: Network Services Management Menu 2-9
Figure 2-3: Network Selection Management Menu 2-10
Figure 2-4: Sample netconfig File 2-15
Figure 2-5: Machine and Service Address Management Menu 2-17
Figure 2-6: Sample `/etc/hosts` File 2-19
Figure 2-7: Sample `/etc/services` File 2-19
Figure 2-8: Sample `/etc/net/`*transport*`/hosts` File 2-20
Figure 2-9: Sample `/etc/net/`*transport*`/services` File 2-21
Figure 2-10: Sample `/etc/iaf/serve.allow` File 2-24
Figure 2-11: Example of a Small Authentication File 2-28
Figure 2-12: Sample Output from a Connection Server Log File 2-29
Figure 2-13: Sample Output from a Connection Server Debug File (`cs -d`) 2-30
Figure 2-14: cr1 Menu 2-35
Figure 2-15: SAF Menu 2-36
Figure 2-16: Name Mapping Menu 2-42
Figure 2-17: `mappings` sub-menu for Name Mapping Administration 2-43
Figure 2-18: Attribute Mapping Menu 2-44
Figure 2-19: `mappings` sub-menu for Attribute Mapping Administration 2-45
Figure 2-20: Sample Output from `idadmin -c` 2-53
Figure 2-21: Sample `uidata` File 2-54
Figure 2-22: Example of a GID Map 2-58
Figure 2-23: Sample Output from `attradmin -A` *attrname* `-c` 2-63
Figure 2-24: The Basic Networking Utilities Management Menu 2-64
Figure 2-25: Basic Networking Process Diagram 2-66
Figure 2-26: Sample `Systems` File 2-92
Figure 2-27: Sample `Devices` file 2-92
Figure 2-28: Sample `Dialers` File Entries 2-100
Figure 2-29: Basic Networking System Management Menu 2-102
Figure 3-1: Sender/Receiver Interaction 3-4
Figure 4-1: A Typical Internet Domain Hierarchy 4-6
Figure 4-2: Sample `/etc/networks` File 4-16
Figure 4-3: Sample `/etc/ethers` File 4-17
Figure 4-4: Sample `/etc/protocols` File 4-17
Figure 4-5: Excerpt from a Typical `/etc/services` File 4-18

Figure 6-1: Sample `/etc/confnet.d/netdrivers` File for Two Network Cards 6-8
Figure 6-2: Sample Unmodified `/etc/confnet.d/inet/interface` File 6-9
Figure 6-3: Sample List of Network Cards (Devices) Available for Configuration 6-10
Figure 6-4: Help Message from `configure -i` 6-10
Figure 6-5: Selecting the (1st) Device to be Configured 6-11
Figure 6-6: Choosing the IP Host Name for the (1st) Device Being Configured 6-11
Figure 6-7: Choosing the IP Address for the (1st) Device Being Configured 6-11
Figure 6-8: Choosing the `ifconfig` Options for the (1st) Device Being Configured 6-12
Figure 6-9: Informational Message regarding the `ifconfig` Options 6-12
Figure 6-10: Partially Configured `/etc/confnet.d/inet/interface` File 6-13
Figure 6-11: Partially Configured `/etc/confnet.d/netdrivers` File 6-13
Figure 6-12: Selecting a Network Card (Device) to be Configured 6-13
Figure 6-13: Selecting the (2nd) Device to be Configured 6-14
Figure 6-14: Choosing the IP Host Name for the (2nd) Device Being Configured 6-14
Figure 6-15: Choosing the IP Address for the (2nd) Device Being Configured 6-14
Figure 6-16: Configured `/etc/confnet.d/inet/interface` File 6-15
Figure 6-17: Configured `/etc/confnet.d/netdrivers` File 6-16
Figure 6-18: Configuring the Machine to Act as a Gateway 6-16
Figure 6-19: Network Mask 6-24
Figure 7-1: Administrative Zones 7-3
Figure 7-2: Sample `/etc/resolv.conf` File 7-9
Figure 7-3: Boot File and Data Files 7-13
Figure 7-4: Sample Boot File for a Primary Master Server 7-14
Figure 7-5: Sample Boot File for a Secondary Master Server 7-15
Figure 7-6: Sample Boot File for a Caching Only Server 7-17
Figure 7-7: Sample hosts File 7-18
Figure 7-8: Sample named.local File 7-19
Figure 7-9: Sample hosts.rev File 7-20
Figure 7-10: Sample named.ca File 7-21
Figure 7-11: Format for a Start of Authority Resource Record 7-26
Figure 7-12: Sample SOA Resource Record 7-27
Figure 7-13: Format for a Name Server Resource Record 7-27
Figure 7-14: Sample NS Resource Record 7-27
Figure 7-15: Format for an Address Resource Record 7-28
Figure 7-16: Sample Address Resource Record 7-28
Figure 7-17: Format for a HINFO Resource Record 7-28
Figure 7-18: Sample HINFO Resource Record 7-29
Figure 7-19: Format for a WKS Resource Record 7-29
Figure 7-20: Sample WKS Resource Record 7-29
Figure 7-21: Format for a CNAME Resource Record 7-30
Figure 7-22: Sample CNAME Resource Record 7-30
Figure 7-23: Format for a PTR Resource Record 7-30
Figure 7-24: Sample PTR Resource Record 7-31
Figure 7-25: Format for an MX Resource Record 7-31
Figure 7-26: Sample MX Resource Record 7-32

Figure 7-27: An Imaginary Network 7-36
Figure 8-1: Sample Output from `ping -s elvis` 8-2
Figure 8-2: Sample Output from `ifconfig -a` 8-3
Figure 8-3: Sample Output from `netstat -s` 8-4
Figure 8-4: Sample Output from `netstat -i` 8-5
Figure 8-5: Sample Output from `netstat -r` 8-6
Figure 8-6: Sample Output from `netstat -rs` 8-7
Figure 8-7: Sample Output from `ps -ef | grep inetd` 8-11
Figure 15-1: Example — Sharing Resources 15-3
Figure 17-1: ID Mapping Components 17-13
Figure 17-2: ID Mapping Files 17-14
Figure 17-3: Example `uid.rules` File 17-18
Figure 17-4: Sample Output from `idload -n` 17-19
Figure 17-5: Format of `uid.rules` and `gid.rules` Files 17-46
Figure 17-6: `uid.rules` File: Setting Global Defaults 17-49
Figure 17-7: `uid.rules` File: Global Mapping by Remote ID 17-50
Figure 17-8: `uid.rules` File: Host Mapping by Remote ID 17-50
Figure 17-9: `uid.rules` File: Mapping by Name with map all 17-51
Figure 17-10: `uid.rules` File: Mapping Specific Users by Name 17-51
Figure 17-11: Sample Output from `idload -n` 17-52
Figure 17-12: Sample Output from `idload -k` 17-53
Figure 17-13: Sample Output from `sar -Dc` 17-59
Figure 17-14: Sample Output from `sar -x` 17-60
Figure 17-15: Sample Output from `sar -Du` 17-62
Figure 17-16: Sample Output from `sar -Db` 17-64
Figure 17-17: Sample Output from `sar -C` 17-65
Figure 17-18: Sample Output from `sar -S` 17-66
Figure 17-19: Sample Output from `fusage` 17-68
Figure 17-20: Sample Output from `df` 17-69
Figure 17-21: RFS Tunable Parameter Settings 17-73
Figure 18-1: Mounting a Remote Resource 18-4
Figure 25-1: Architecture of the Locking Service Over NFS 25-3
Figure 28-1: Relationships between Master, Slave(s) and Client(s) Machines 28-4
Figure 28-2: Sample `chkey` Session 28-10
Figure 28-3: Typical `auto.master` Map 28-11
Figure 28-4: Typical `auto.home` Map 28-11
Figure 28-5: Typical `/etc/auto.direct` Map 28-12
Table 2-1: Command Alternatives to the Network Selection Management Menu 2-11
Table 2-2: Fields in netconfig Entries 2-12
Table 2-3: Shell Commands for Name-to-Address Mapping 2-17
Table 2-4: Command Alternatives to the cr1 Menu 2-35
Table 2-5: Command Alternatives to the Name Mapping Menu 2-43
Table 2-6: Command Alternatives to the Second-Level Name Mapping Menu 2-44
Table 2-7: Command Alternatives to the Attribute Mapping Menu 2-45
Table 2-8: Command Alternatives to the Second-Level Attribute Mapping Menu 2-46

Table 2-9: Summary of BNU Log Files 2-129
Table 3-1: TCP/IP Protocol Layers 3-3
Table 4-1: Network Address Structure 4-4
Table 6-1: Choices for Setting the `ifconfig` Options with `configure -i` 6-6
Table 6-2: Choices for Setting up a Machine As a Gateway with `configure -i` 6-7
Table 7-1: Common Types of Resource Records 7-24

1 Introduction

About This Book 1-1

About This Book

Network Administration is directed to system administrators who are setting up and maintaining UNIX® System V Release 4.2 file sharing capabilities.

File sharing refers to the process of making file resources on your local system available to remote systems via a network, and conversely, to accessing file resources on remote systems from your local system. UNIX SVR4.2 offers two file sharing packages, also called "distributed file systems." These are Remote File Sharing (RFS) and Network File System (NFS).

This manual tells you how to set up and administer both RFS and NFS, and how to set up and use Distributed File System Administration (DFS), a software package that provides a common interface to both RFS and NFS.

Also included in this volume is documentation that tells you how to set up TCP/IP, a family of network protocols that determines how data is transferred across network media. TCP/IP supports both RFS and NFS, and is provided in UNIX SVR4.2 as the TCP/IP Internet package. It is not necessary that you install TCP/IP to run RFS. RFS can run over any network protocol that conforms to the Transport Level Interface (TLI). NFS, however, requires UDP/IP as its transport. UDP/IP are protocols at the transport layer in the TCP/IP protocol family.

Included in TCP/IP at the application layer are a number of commands and programs that allow users to perform remote operations. These, too, are documented in this manual.

This manual is not intended to be an introduction to networking, nor to all the networking features of UNIX SVR4.2.

Because you may be setting up network services using a mix and match of applications and protocols, this document has been organized into the major topics listed below.

- Basic Network Administration

  The major sections of the "Network Services" chapter include an overview of networking for SVR4.2, how to select a network, setting up name-to-address mapping, the connection server (which establishes connections for network services that communicate over TLI connection-oriented and dialup connections), using authentications schemes (for additional system security), setting up and administering ID mappings (for users on remote systems), administering and using the Basic Networking Utilities (BNU) (for communicating to other systems that support the Basic Networking Utilities), and interactive remote execution (REXEC) utilities (to allow remote administration of a machine).

- TCP/IP Network Administration

  Although TCP/IP can be used on a local area network to provide remote services and to support file sharing applications, it was originally developed by the Department of Defense to support the ARPANET, a packet switching wide area network. Today, the ARPANET is part of a wider public network, called the Internet. In addition to telling you how to set up and maintain TCP/IP software on your network machines, instructions are also included that tell you how to join the Internet. TCP/IP Network Administration is covered in the following chapters: "Introduction to Administering TCP/IP Networks", "Setting Up TCP/IP", "Maintaining Security in a TCP/IP Environment", "Expanding Your TCP/IP Network", "Using Domain Name Service with TCP/IP", "Troubleshooting TCP/IP", "Guidelines for Completing the IP Number Registration Form", and "Guidelines for Completing the Domain Registration Form".

- Distributed File System Administration

  The Distributed File System (DFS) Administration chapters, describe a command interface common to both RFS and NFS. Because both RFS and NFS are provided in UNIX SVR4.2, one set of commands is provided with which an administrator can administer both packages. For example, the DFS software provides you with the **share** command, which allows you to share a resource on your system using either RFS or NFS. The Distributed File System Administration chapters are directed to administrators who are running both RFS and NFS on their systems. The commands described in the DFS guide are described in the RFS and NFS guides as well, but the RFS and NFS guides describe package-specific options only. DFS Administration is covered in the following chapters: "Introduction to Distributed File System (DFS) Administration", "Setting Up DFS Administration", "Using DFS Commands and Files", and "DFS sysadm Interface".

- Remote File Sharing Administration

  The Remote File Sharing (RFS) Administration chapters tell you how to set up and maintain RFS on your system, including how to share resources with remote systems and how to mount remote resources on your machine. RFS Administration is covered in the following chapters: "RFS Introduction", "RFS sysadm Interface", and "RFS Command Interface".

- Network File System Administration

  The Network File System (NFS) Administration chapters tell you how to set up and maintain NFS on your system, including how to share and mount resources, how to mount resources automatically using a feature called the automounter, and how to set up Secure NFS. NFS Administration is covered in the following chapters: "NFS Introduction", "Setting Up NFS", "Sharing and Mounting NFS Resources Explicitly", "Obtaining NFS Information", "Handling NFS Problems", "Setting Up Secure NFS", "Using the NFS Automounter", "The NFS Network Lock Manager", and "Using the NFS sysadm Interface".

- Remote Procedure Call

  This chapter tells what administration files that are used by RPC and how to set up and establish secure RPC domains.

- Network Information Service

  This chapter explains how to setup, administer, and update NIS.

- Glossary

  Contains definitions for terms used throughout this book.

Setting Up a Network

2 Network Services

An Overview of Network Administration 2-1
A Model of Network Administration 2-1
UNIX System V Networking Facilities 2-2
Procedural Overview of BNU and REXEC Administration 2-5
- Step 1: Set Up Network Selection 2-5
- Step 2: Set Up Name-to-Address Mapping 2-6
- Step 3: Set Up the listen Port Monitor 2-6
- Step 4: Set Up the Connection Server 2-7
- Step 5: Set Up the cr1 Authentication Scheme 2-7
- Step 6: Setting Up ID Mapping 2-8
- Step 7: Set Up BNU 2-8
- Step 8: Set up REXEC 2-8

Using the sysadm Menu Interface 2-9

Network Selection 2-10
Network Selection Overview 2-11
The /etc/netconfig File 2-12
The NETPATH Environment Variable 2-16

Name-to-Address Mapping 2-17
Setting Up the Name-to-Address Mapping Libraries 2-18
- The tcpip.so Library 2-18
- The resolv.so Library 2-19
- The straddr.so Library 2-20

The Connection Server 2-22

The Connection Server Application Interface 2-23

Connection Server Administration 2-23

- Server Machine Administration 2-23
- Client Machine Administration 2-24
- The reportscheme Service 2-25
- The Connection Server Authentication Scheme File 2-27
- The Connection Server Log File 2-28
- The Connection Server Debug File 2-29

cr1 Bilateral Authentication Scheme 2-31

An Overview of cr1 Administration 2-33

Registering cr1 with a Port Monitor 2-36

Registering cr1 with the Connection Server 2-37

Managing the Daemon and the Master Key 2-37

- Starting and Stopping the Daemon 2-38
- Creating a Master Key 2-38

Setting Up the Key Database 2-39

ID Mapping 2-41

Setting Up Login Maps 2-46

- Administering an idata File 2-47
- Administering a uidata File 2-54

Setting Up Attribute Maps 2-58

- Setting Up an Attribute Map 2-59
- Adding an Entry to an Attribute Map 2-60
- Deleting an Entry in an Attribute Map 2-61
- Deleting an Attribute Map 2-62
- Checking Files and Fixing File Inconsistencies 2-62
- Displaying Information 2-63

Basic Networking Utilities 2-64

Overview of BNU 2-64

- What BNU Does 2-64
- BNU Components 2-67
- BNU Administration 2-71

Database Support Files 2-78
- The Permissions File 2-78
- The Devconfig File 2-88
- The Sysfiles File 2-88
- The Limits File 2-89
- The Config File 2-90
- The Devices File 2-91
- The Dialers File 2-99
- The Systems File 2-102
- The Dialcodes File 2-110
- The Poll File 2-110
- The Grades File 2-111

Administrative Support Files 2-113
Log Files 2-116
- Command Log 2-116
- System History Log 2-116
- Error Log 2-117
- Transfer Log 2-118
- Accounting Log 2-119
- Security Log 2-120
- Performance Log 2-122
- Foreign Log 2-124

Adding uucp Logins 2-125
BNU Maintenance 2-125
- Automated Networking Maintenance (cron) 2-126
- Manual Maintenance 2-128

BNU Debugging 2-129
- Check Basic Information 2-129
- Check for Faulty ACU/Modem 2-130
- Check Systems File 2-130
- Debug Transmissions 2-130

REXEC 2-132
Overview of REXEC Administration 2-133
Registering REXEC with a Port Monitor 2-134
Adding and Removing Services 2-135
- Adding a Service 2-136
- Removing a Service 2-137

Listing Defined Services 2-138
Linking Services to REXEC 2-138

An Overview of Network Administration

This section provides a brief overview to networking in UNIX SVR4.2. This section is not intended to be a networking primer. Instead, it places the features of UNIX System V in the context of a general network administration model and presents an overview of the tasks involved in the administration of UNIX System V user-level services.

A Model of Network Administration

The network facilities provided in UNIX System V are built on the client/server model. A "client" is a networked machine that uses the resources of another machine on the network. A "server" is a system that provides resources to other systems on the network. A system can be both a client, utilizing another system's resources, and a server, making local resources available to other systems.

Typically, the steps involved in setting up a networked machine are the following:

1. Making the physical connection to the network and installing any software that drives the network hardware.
2. Installing the network software, which packages data according to a set of protocols. The network software includes a transport provider, which manages the transfer of data across the network connection.
3. On the server side, setting up continuous processes, called daemons, that listen for connection requests from other network machines.
4. On the client side, creating an address database that contains the addresses of all machines and services on the network to which the client can connect. The client consults the database before it sends a connection request to another network machine.
5. Setting up security. Typically, each network application has its own mechanism for performing a minimum of authentication.

The following section describes the network facilities in UNIX System V and explains how they fit into the general model of network administration.

UNIX System V Networking Facilities

UNIX System V includes a number of network facilities that give the administrator flexibility in building a network. Several facilities relieve the application of the need to know the underlying characteristics of the network. Thus, the application can run on different networks, and still present a consistent interface to the user.

Two distinct styles of network service provision are supported. One is the Berkeley style, implemented as "r-commands" (such as **`rlogin`**), which is described in *User's Guide*. The other style is the new Networking Applications Architecture (NAA), which is depicted in Figure 2-1 and described in the following list.

Figure 2-1: A Diagram of the Networking Applications Architecture

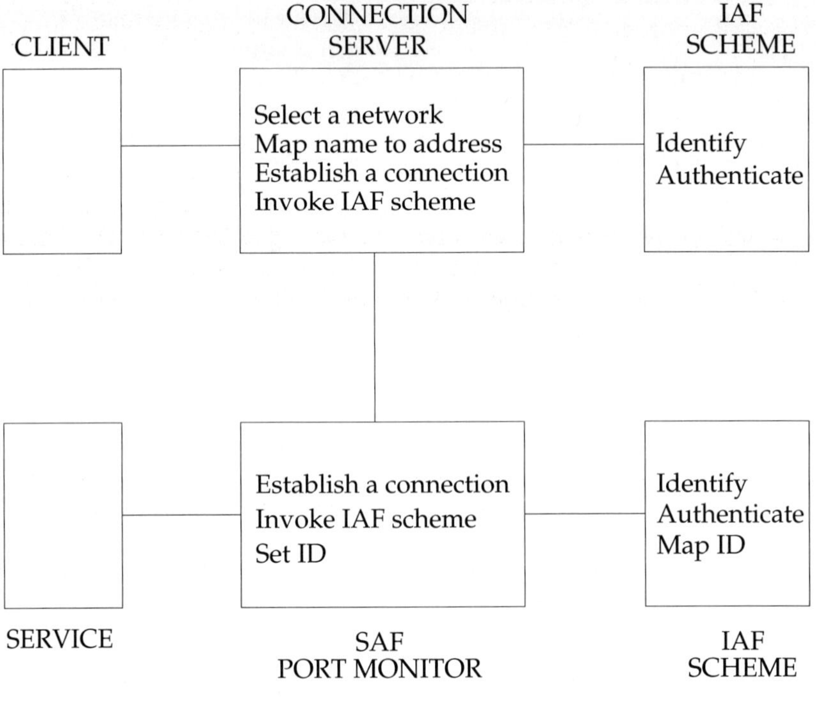

- The listen Port Monitor
  A port monitor is a continuous process, called a daemon, that listens to a given physical port or on a network address for connection requests. **`listen`**, also called the listener, is a network port monitor. It listens on

addresses associated with a connection-oriented transport network. There may be multiple **listen** port monitors on the system, each monitoring multiple addresses.

The listener listens on the server for incoming connection requests, accepts the requests, and starts services that have been requested. If a service is protected by an authentication scheme, the listener invokes the authentication scheme. If the authentication protocol completes successfully, the client user's identity is mapped to an identity on the server; then, the port monitor starts the requested service.

All port monitors, including **listen**, are managed by the Service Access Facility (SAF). The SAF generalizes service access procedures so login access on the local system and network access to local services are managed in similar ways. This means, from the system administrator's perspective, that local and network access are managed similarly, as is access over different networks. (For more information, see "Managing Ports" in *Advanced System Administration*.)

- The Connection Server
  The Connection Server can be viewed as a counterpart on the client to the server's listener. The Connection Server uses Network Selection to determine which network to use, and Name-to-Address Mapping to determine the address of the requested service on the requested host. The Connection Server sends a connection request to the server, manages the client's role in establishing the connection, and invokes the appropriate authentication scheme. If the scheme completes successfully, the Connection Server turns over the connection to the client process.

- Identification and Authentication Facility
  The Identification and Authentication Facility (IAF) authenticates network connections independently of the network application. It consists of three components—an invocation function, the cr1 and login authentication schemes, and the ID Mapping facility. The cr1 schemes, see "cr1 Bilateral Authentication Scheme", and ID Mapping, see "ID Mapping", are discussed as separate features.

  Following the establishment of a connection, the Connection Server and the port monitor each invoke an authentication scheme. Once the client scheme has succeeded, the Connection Server passes the connection to the client application. Once the server scheme has succeeded, it searches the ID Mapping database to determine how the user on the client should be mapped to a user on the server. Minimally, the database consists of a map file that maps user logins on client systems to user logins on the server. Once the scheme maps the client user's identity into a local identity, the port monitor invokes the requested service.

Authentication schemes are invoked by the IAF. The release of UNIX System V contains the cr1 authentication scheme. By default, cr1 uses DES encryption, and can also be referenced as **`cr1.des`**. Because of export restrictions on DES, cr1 can also use ENIGMA encryption. When using ENIGMA encryption, cr1 is referenced as **`cr1.enigma`**. Other than the underlying encryption algorithm used, all cr1 schemes behave identically. The cr1 schemes operate as follows: The client and server schemes exchange a sequence of encrypted messages. Each system uses a secret key, which it retrieves from its local cr1 key database, to encrypt its own messages and decrypt the other's messages. (A secret key is a bit string known only to the client and server.) By successfully decrypting the other's messages, each machine authenticates the other's identity. The client scheme informs the server scheme of its user's identity.

- Network Selection
  Network Selection is a facility that generalizes the way an application chooses a network. It allows an administrator or a user to specify an order of preference among available transport providers. When a user attempts to access a remote service, the system first attempts to make the connection over the primary network; if that attempt fails, it tries each network in order of preference until the connection is made.

- Name-to-Address Mapping
  Name-to-Address Mapping is a feature that allows applications to obtain transport-specific addresses in a transport-independent manner. The administrator maintains a configuration file with records describing each transport provider available to be used by applications. One of the fields in each record is the name of the shared library to use for the transport provider being described in the record. This library contains name-to-address mapping routines specific to the transport protocol. When a new transport protocol is being installed, a new entry in the configuration file is made, allowing network applications to make use of the new protocol without being changed.

- User-Level Services
  UNIX System V facilities that provide services to end-users include the Basic Networking Utilities (BNU) and REXEC. BNU provides basic network communication (such as queued remote execution and file transfer capabilities) and REXEC is an interactive remote execution facility. Whereas many network packages provide remote execution capabilities, BNU and REXEC provide file transfer and remote execution independent of the transport provider. Both BNU and REXEC take advantage of the features of the Network Application Architecture (NAA) described in the previous sections.

In addition to BNU and REXEC, UNIX System V includes two distributed file system packages, Remote File Sharing (RFS) and Network File System (NFS). Both packages provide the user with access to resources on other machines on the network. RFS provides access to data files, executables, applications, and peripheral hardware on a network of UNIX System V machines. NFS provides access to files and directories across a network of machines running different operating systems. In addition, TCP/IP includes a number of application level services in its protocol suite.

BNU and REXEC are described in this chapter. Distributed File Systems are described in "Introduction to Distributed File System (DFS) Administration", "Setting Up DFS Administration", "Using DFS Commands and Files", and "DFS sysadm Interface". The user services that are provided by TCP/IP are discussed in *User's Guide*.

The following section leads you step-by-step through administration of BNU and REXEC.

Procedural Overview of BNU and REXEC Administration

Ultimately, the network administrator's objective is to provide services to users of networked machines. This section presents a high-level procedure for setting up REXEC and BNU, as well as all the network services on which they depend. The administration of each component mentioned in the following procedure is described in more detail later in the chapter.

This procedure makes the following assumptions:

1. Your network hardware and software have been installed and any administration specific to the network package has been completed.
2. Applications are to be set up to take advantage of the IAF in UNIX SVR4.2. For compatibility, BNU can be configured as it was on previous versions of UNIX SVR4. However, this section assumes BNU connections will be configured using enhanced authentication procedures (primarily cr1).

Step 1: Set Up Network Selection

Network Selection consists of the following elements:

- **netconfig**, a network configuration file [see **netconfig**(4)]
- **NETPATH**, an environment variable

To set up Network Selection, you need to create an entry in the **netconfig** file for each network available to the local system.

Any user, including the administrator, may use the **NETPATH** variable to modify the default order in which networks are tried by an application seeking a network connection. If a user does not set the **NETPATH** variable, networks are used in the order specified in **netconfig**.

For more information see "Network Selection".

Step 2: Set Up Name-to-Address Mapping

Name-to-Address Mapping consists of routines that application programs can call to determine the addresses of services and machines on the network. These routines are combined into libraries, with one library associated with each available transport provider. For every network available to the local system, the network administrator must create and maintain the following files used by the library routines:

- the **hosts** file, which lists the addresses of machines on the network
- the **services** file, which lists the port numbers of services available across the network

The files that support TCP/IP must be located in **/etc**. The files that support other networks must be located in **/etc/net/***transport*, where *transport* is the name of the transport provider.

For more information, see "Name-to-Address Mapping".

Step 3: Set Up the listen Port Monitor

The listener is a port monitor under the control of the Service Access Controller (SAC), a daemon process that provides a consistent interface to all services, whether the user's connection to the system is local or across a network. (Because the purpose of the SAC is not limited to managing network access, it is not documented in this chapter. For more information about the SAC and setting up the listener, see the See "Managing Ports" in *Advanced System Administration*.) To set up the listener, do the following:

1. Add a **listen** port monitor to the Service Access Controller's administrative file, using **sacadm** [see **sacadm**(1M)].

2. Set up the port monitor's administrative file, using **pmadm** [see **pmadm**(1M)]. Setting up the file involves

   - adding one or more services to the listener's administrative file
   - enabling the service on a port that the listener is monitoring
   - associating an authentication scheme with a service

Step 4: Set Up the Connection Server

The Connection Server is a daemon process running on the client that makes network connections. Applications obtain network connections by calling library routines that access the daemon. An error reporting routine (**cs_perror**), an associated service (**reportscheme**), and three optional administrative files are available. To set up the Connection Server, do the following:

1. Optionally, on the client, set up the file **serve.allow**. The **serve.allow** file enforces authentication, in the event the service is not protected by an authentication scheme on the server side.
2. Optionally, on the client, set up the file **serve.alias**. The **serve.alias** file maps aliases to service names, making it possible to register a service under two names with different authentication schemes associated with each name.
3. Optionally, on the client, set up the authentication file, **auth**. This file lists network services and their associated authentication schemes.
4. Add an entry for **reportscheme** to the port monitor's administrative file on each server to which the Connection Server should be able to connect.

For more information about Connection Server administration, see the "The Connection Server".

Step 5: Set Up the cr1 Authentication Scheme

To set up cr1, do the following:

1. Start the **keymaster** daemon process [see **keymaster**(1M)].
2. Administer individual keys using **cryptkey** [see **cryptkey**(1)].

If you intend to set up REXEC or BNU, you need to add keys shared by a client machine and the server machines. Each client and server pair must share identical keys.

For more information, including detailed procedures, see "cr1 Bilateral Authentication Scheme".

Step 6: Setting Up ID Mapping

cr1 maps remote user identities to the local system using map files that are administered under the ID Mapping facility.

On a server, to set up ID Mapping to support cr1, do the following:

- Use the **idadmin** command [see **idadmin**(1M)] to install cr1 name mapping. Instructions for setting up ID mapping appear in "ID Mapping".

Step 7: Set Up BNU

The Basic Networking Utilities package is a collection of programs and support files that provide network communication services such as file transfer capabilities and remote execution. All BNU support files are located in **/etc/uucp**.

To set up BNU, do the following:

1. Create BNU logins.
2. On the server side, for every transport provider on which BNU will be supported, use **pmadm** to add the **uucico** service and associate the cr1 authentication scheme with the service.
3. Create or modify the BNU database files as needed. See the "Database Support Files" section.

Step 8: Set up REXEC

To set up REXEC, do the following:

1. Register REXEC with a network port monitor (the listener) under the Service Access Facility, specifying an associated authentication scheme that uses ID Mapping, that is, cr1.
2. Set up the file **/etc/rexec/services** on the server.

The **services** file is a database containing all the services on the server system that are available to remote users through REXEC. Typically, the list of available services consists of the pre-defined REXEC services **rl**, **rx**, and **rquery**.

For more information, see "REXEC".

Using the sysadm Menu Interface

Any of the functions associated with Network Services may be performed by selecting the appropriate "task" from a series of menus provided for administration. To access the system administration menu for using Network Services, type: **`sysadm network_services`** The following menu will appear on your screen:

Figure 2-2: Network Services Management Menu

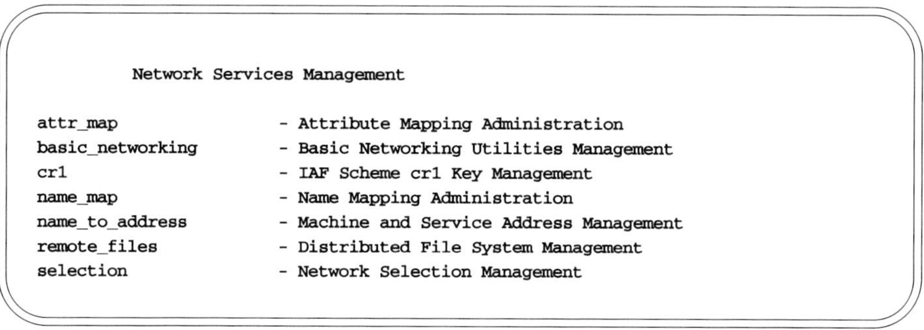

```
        Network Services Management

attr_map            - Attribute Mapping Administration
basic_networking    - Basic Networking Utilities Management
cr1                 - IAF Scheme cr1 Key Management
name_map            - Name Mapping Administration
name_to_address     - Machine and Service Address Management
remote_files        - Distributed File System Management
selection           - Network Selection Management
```

NOTE The **`Distributed File System Management`** option is described in the *UNIX® Software Development Tools*.

When you have chosen an option, self-explanatory submenus and instructions will be displayed on the screen to lead you through the appropriate procedures.

Network Selection

In order for network applications to be portable to different environments, the application process must have a standard interface into the various transport providers available in any current environment. Network Selection provides a simple and consistent interface that allows user applications to select networks (at the transport level), enabling applications to be protocol- and media-independent. System V Networking Services applications that allow a user to influence the choice of transports use the standard interface outlined here.

Tasks associated with Network Selection administration may be performed either by using the menu system or by entering shell commands on the command line. The screen below is the top-level menu for Network Selection. It can be brought up on the screen by typing **sysadm selection**.

Figure 2-3: Network Selection Management Menu

```
            Network Selection Management

display     - Display Network Selection Configuration
modify      - Modify Network Selection Configuration
```

When you select an option, self-explanatory submenus and instructions lead you through the appropriate procedures.

You can also bypass the menu system by issuing commands directly to the shell. Where these commands involve editing sensitive system files, be sure to keep a backup copy of the file you are editing. When you have finished editing the file, use **diff** [see **diff**(1)] on the edited file and the backup copy to verify that only the changes you want have been made.

Table 2-1: Command Alternatives to the Network Selection Management Menu

Task Description	Menu Item	Shell Command
Display the contents of the **netconfig** file; display the entry for network *netid*	**display**	**cat /etc/netconfig** **grep** *netid* **/etc/netconfig**
Change a **netconfig** entry	**modify**	**vi /etc/netconfig**

If you want to add networks to the network configuration database, you need to edit **/etc/netconfig**, and add the appropriate entries. To remove networks from the network configuration database, you need to edit **/etc/netconfig**, and delete the appropriate entries.

Network Selection Overview

The UNIX System V Network Selection component is built around:

- a network configuration database (the **/etc/netconfig** file) that contains entries for each network available to the system, and
- an optional **NETPATH** environment variable, set by a user or the system administrator and containing an ordered list of network identifiers. These network identifiers match the **netconfig** *network ID* field and are used as links to the records in the **netconfig** file.

The Network Selection application programming interface consists of a set of network configuration database access routines. One group of these library routines accesses only the **netconfig** entries identified by the **NETPATH** environment variable; another group of routines accesses **netconfig** directly. The routines are described in *Network Programming Interfaces*. The first group is also described in detail in **getnetpath**(3N). The second group is described in **getnetconfig**(3N).

Applications should use the routines that access **NETPATH**. They allow users to influence the selection of transports used by the application. If an application does not want the user to influence its decision, then the routines that access the **netconfig** database directly should be used.

The **netconfig** file, on which the Network Selection library routines depend, is maintained by the system administrator. The **NETPATH** environment variable is typically set or modified by application programmers and users, depending on the needs of their applications, but it may also be set by the system administrator in response to the needs of administrative applications.

The /etc/netconfig File

The system administrator is responsible for maintaining the network configuration database file **/etc/netconfig**. Entries in the **netconfig** file contain the following fields in the order shown. A sample **netconfig** file is shown in Figure 2-4.

Table 2-2: Fields in netconfig Entries

network_id	*semantics*	*flags*	*protofamily*	*protoname*	*device*	*nametoaddr_libs*

The fields correspond to elements of the **netconfig** structure. Pointers returned by Network Selection library routines are pointers to **netconfig** entries in **netconfig** format. See **netconfig**(4) for more information. The **netconfig**(4) manual page also describes the elements of the **struct netconfig** structure. All symbolic names, structure definitions, and constant values for the Network Selection feature are defined in the header files **/usr/include/netconfig.h**, **/usr/include/sys/netconfig.h**, and **/usr/include/netdir.h**.

netconfig fields are defined as follows:

network_id — A string used to identify a transport provider. *network_id* consists of non-NULL characters, and has a length of at least 1. No maximum length is specified. This name space is locally significant and the local system administrator is the naming authority responsible for ensuring that all *network_id*s on a system are unique.

semantics — A string that identifies the "semantics" of the transport provider, that is, the set of services it supports, by identifying the service interface it provides. This is closely related to, but not identical with, the API (Application Programming Interface) with which applications are "supposed" to access the network. Typically, an application will specify its API by pushing an appropriate STREAMS module (such as **timod**) and using an appropriate user-level library (such as the TLI library). The *semantics* field is mandatory. The following semantics are recognized.

`tpi_clts`	Transport Provider Interface, connectionless
`tpi_cots`	Transport Provider Interface, connection-oriented
`tpi_cots_ord`	Transport Provider Interface, connection-oriented and supports orderly release
`tpi_raw`	Transport Provider Interface, raw

flags

The *flags* field contains two-valued ("true" and "false") attributes of transport providers. *flags* is a string of characters, each of which specifies the value of the corresponding attribute. If the character is present, the attribute is "true." If the character is absent, the attribute is "false." A hyphen (-) indicates no attributes are present. The characters currently recognized are:

`v` Visible network. Used to establish a default list of networks to search when the environment variable **NETPATH** is *unset*. See "The NETPATH Environment Variable", for a description of how the **v** flag is used.

`b` Enable RPC broadcast. Used by **rpc_broadcast**() [see **rpc_clnt_calls**(3N)].

protofamily

The *protofamily* and *protoname* fields are provided for protocol-specific applications. The *protofamily* field contains a string that identifies a protocol family. The *protofamily* identifier follows the rules for *network_ids*: It is a string of non-NULL characters with a length of at least `1`. No maximum length is specified.

A hyphen (-) in the *protofamily* field indicates that none of the available protocol family identifiers applies, that is, the transport provider is experimental. An application that wants to have family characteristics can match on the *protofamily* field when selecting a network. (For example, an application can search for an "osi" family.) In this case, the application is not protocol independent, since it has searched only for OSI entries. The following are examples of protocol family identifiers:

`loopback`	Loopback (local to host)
`inet`	Internetwork: UDP, TCP, and so on.
`implink`	ARPANET imp addresses

`pup`	PUP protocols: for example, BSP
`chaos`	MIT CHAOS protocols
`ns`	XEROX NS protocols
`nbs`	National Bureau of Standards (NBS) protocols
`ecma`	European Computer Manufacturers Association
`datakit`	Datakit protocols
`ccitt`	CCITT protocols, X.25, and so on.
`sna`	IBM SNA
`decnet`	DECNET
`dli`	Direct data link interface
`lat`	LAT
`hylink`	NSC Hyperchannel
`appletalk`	Apple Talk
`nit`	Network Interface Tap
`ieee802`	IEEE 802.2; also ISO 8802
`osi`	Umbrella for all families used by OSI
`x25`	CCITT X.25 in particular
`osinet`	AFI = 47, IDI = 4
`gosip`	U.S. Government OSI

protoname

The *protoname* field contains a string that identifies a protocol. This field is currently used only for the **`inet`** family. For any other family, the protocol name field contains a hyphen (–). The *protoname* identifier follows the same rules as *network_ids*: The string consists of non-NULL characters and has a length of at least `1`. No maximum length is specified.

The *protoname* field may contain:

`icmp`	Internet Control Message Protocol
`tcp`	Transmission Control Protocol
`udp`	User Datagram Protocol

device The *device* is the full pathname of the device used to connect to the remote machine via the transport provider. Typically, this device will be in the **/dev** directory. The *device* must be specified.

nametoaddr_libs The *nametoaddr_libs* support a "directory service" (that is, a Name-to-Address Mapping service) for the network. This service is implemented by the UNIX System V Name-to-Address Mapping feature. If a transport is not provided with such a library, that is, if the *nametoaddr_libs* field in the **netconfig** file contains only a hyphen, the Network Selection request will fail.

The *nametoaddr_libs* field consists of a comma-separated list of full pathnames to dynamically linked libraries.

Literal commas may be embedded as "**\,**"; backslashes as "****." Lines in **/etc/netconfig** that begin with a pound sign (**#**) in the first column are comments.

The system administrator determines the order of the entries in the **netconfig** database. Because the Network Selection library routines that access **netconfig** directly return entries in order, beginning at the top of the **/etc/netconfig** file, the order in which networks are entered in the file by the system administrator becomes the default search path for applications choosing networks to which they will connect.

Figure 2-4: Sample netconfig File

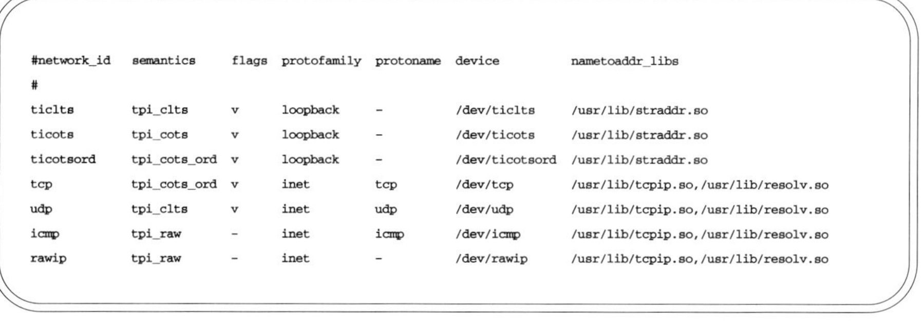

```
#network_id  semantics     flags  protofamily  protoname  device           nametoaddr_libs
#
ticlts       tpi_clts      v      loopback     -          /dev/ticlts      /usr/lib/straddr.so
ticots       tpi_cots      v      loopback     -          /dev/ticots      /usr/lib/straddr.so
ticotsord    tpi_cots_ord  v      loopback     -          /dev/ticotsord   /usr/lib/straddr.so
tcp          tpi_cots_ord  v      inet         tcp        /dev/tcp         /usr/lib/tcpip.so,/usr/lib/resolv.so
udp          tpi_clts      v      inet         udp        /dev/udp         /usr/lib/tcpip.so,/usr/lib/resolv.so
icmp         tpi_raw       -      inet         icmp       /dev/icmp        /usr/lib/tcpip.so,/usr/lib/resolv.so
rawip        tpi_raw       -      inet         -          /dev/rawip       /usr/lib/tcpip.so,/usr/lib/resolv.so
```

The NETPATH Environment Variable

In most cases a user isn't interested in which transport provider handles a network operation, and the default network search path established by the system administrator (the **netconfig** file) is used to locate a transport provider available for connection. However, if a user or the system administrator wants to influence the choices made by applications, the search path can be modified using a new standard shell variable, **NETPATH**. **NETPATH** is similar to the **PATH** variable.

NETPATH consists of a colon-separated list of network IDs. Each network ID corresponds to the *network_id* field of a record in the **netconfig** database. A literal colon can be embedded as "**\:**" and a literal backslash as "****." An empty component in **NETPATH** (signified by a beginning colon, an ending colon, or two successive colons) is not a valid entry because the empty string is not a valid network ID. **NETPATH** is described in **environ**(5).

The **NETPATH** environment variable is not set in **/etc/profile**. It can, however, be set in a user's *$HOME*/**.profile**.

Both users and system administrators should be aware that the set of "default" networks is different for routines that access **netconfig** directly and routines that access **netconfig** via the **NETPATH** environment variable. For routines that access **netconfig** directly [see **getnetconfig**(3N)], the set of default networks is the entire **netconfig** file; the set of "default" networks for the routines that access **netconfig** via **NETPATH** is the visible networks in the **netconfig** file [see **getnetpath**(3N)]. A network is "visible" if the system administrator has included a **v** flag in the flag field. If **NETPATH** is unset, these visible networks are the default search path for this second group of access routines.

Name-to-Address Mapping

The Name-to-Address Mapping feature allows an application to obtain the address of a service on a specified machine in a transport-independent manner.

Tasks associated with Name-to-Address Mapping administration may be performed using the menu system or shell commands entered on the command line. The screen below is the top-level menu for Name-to-Address Mapping. It can be brought up on the screen by typing **sysadm name_to_address**.

Figure 2-5: Machine and Service Address Management Menu

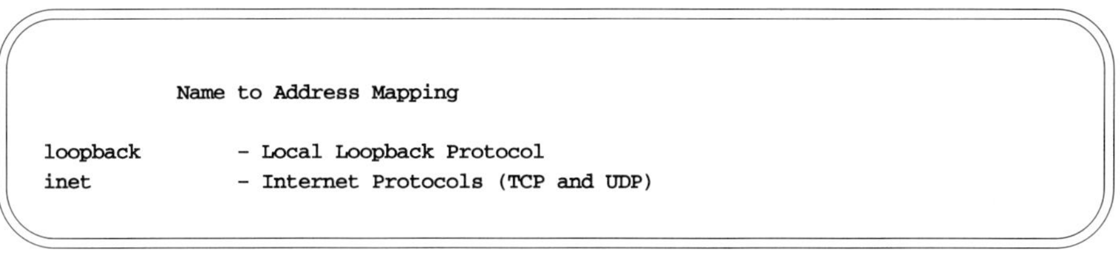

```
            Name to Address Mapping

loopback        - Local Loopback Protocol
inet            - Internet Protocols (TCP and UDP)
```

NOTE The menu screen may be different on your machine. The actual menu selections depend on the software packages and protocols installed on your system.

When you have selected the option you want, self-explanatory submenus and instructions will be displayed on the screen to lead you through the appropriate procedures.

If you want to bypass the menu system, you may issue commands directly to the shell, as shown in Table 2-3.

Table 2-3: Shell Commands for Name-to-Address Mapping

Task Description	Menu Item	Shell Command
Local Loopback Protocol	**loopback**	**vi /etc/net/***transport***/hosts** **vi /etc/net/***transport***/services**
Internet Protocols (TCP and UDP)	**inet**	**vi /etc/hosts** **vi /etc/services**

Name-to-Address Mapping consists of routines for use by application programs.

These routines [described on **netdir**(3N)] are used to obtain addresses of services on given hosts. All routines are combined into a library, one for each transport provider address management mechanism. The library to use for a specific transport provider is named in the **/etc/netconfig** file. A call to any of these routines by an application dynamically links the library named in the *nametoaddr_libs* field of the **/etc/netconfig** file.

The functions described on **netdir**(3N) take a pointer to a **netconfig** structure and returns a list of addresses of the service and host names over a given transport provider.

The following libraries provide the routines shown on **netdir**(3N):

tcpip.so contains the **/etc/hosts** Name-to-Address Mapping routines for the TCP/IP protocol suite

resolv.so contains the Domain Name Server (DNS) Name-to-Address Mapping for the TCP/IP protocol suite

straddr.so contains the Name-to-Address Mapping routines for any protocol that accepts strings as addresses. The loopback driver is an example.

Setting Up the Name-to-Address Mapping Libraries

Files for each of the libraries must be created and maintained by the system administrator.

The tcpip.so Library

The routines in this dynamic library create addresses from the **/etc/hosts**(4) and **/etc/services**(4) files available with the TCP/IP package. The **/etc/hosts** file contains the machine's IP address as the first field followed by any number of machine names separated by white space. For example:

Figure 2-6: Sample /etc/hosts File

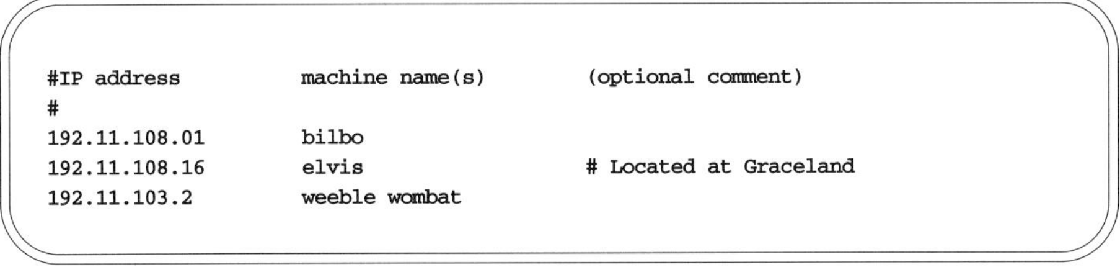

```
#IP address          machine name(s)        (optional comment)
#
192.11.108.01        bilbo
192.11.108.16        elvis                  # Located at Graceland
192.11.103.2         weeble wombat
```

The **/etc/services** file contains three fields, service name, port/protocol (with one of two protocol specifications either **tcp** or **udp**), and aliases. For example:

Figure 2-7: Sample /etc/services File

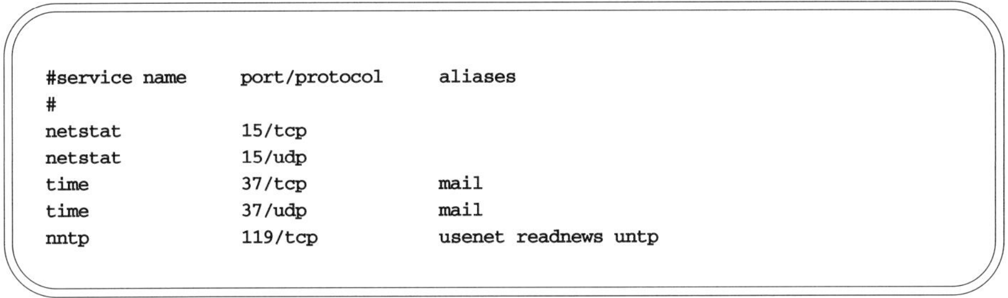

```
#service name     port/protocol     aliases
#
netstat           15/tcp
netstat           15/udp
time              37/tcp            mail
time              37/udp            mail
nntp              119/tcp           usenet readnews untp
```

For an application to use this library to request the address of a service on a particular host, the host name must appear in the **/etc/hosts** file and the service name must appear in the **/etc/services** file. If one or the other does not appear, an error will be returned by the name-to-address mapping routines.

The resolv.so Library

The routines in this dynamic library create addresses similar to the **tcpio.so** file, except that it uses Domain Name Service (DNS), (see "Using Domain Name Service with TCP/IP") instead of **/etc/hosts** to provide similar features.

The straddr.so Library

The routines in this dynamic library create addresses from files that have the same format as the **tcpip.so** file described above. The **straddr.so** files are **/etc/net/***transport***/hosts** and **/etc/net/***transport***/services**. *transport* is the local name of the transport provider that accepts string addresses (specified in the *network_id* field of the **/etc/netconfig** file). For example, the host file for **ticlts** would be **/etc/net/ticlts/hosts**, and the service file for **ticlts** would be **/etc/net/ticlts/services**. For **ticots**, the files would be **/etc/net/ticots/hosts** and **/etc/net/ticots/services**.

Even though most string addresses do not distinguish between "host" and "service," separating the string into a host part and a service part provides consistency with other transport providers. The **/etc/net/***transport***/hosts** file will therefore contain a string that is considered to be the machine address, followed by the machine name. For example:

Figure 2-8: Sample /etc/net/*transport*/hosts **File**

```
#machine addr  machine name
#
bilboaddr      bilbo
elvisaddr      elvis
frodoaddr      frodo
```

The **/etc/net/***transport***/services** file contains a service name followed by a string identifying the service port. For example:

Figure 2-9: Sample `/etc/net/`*transport*`/services` File

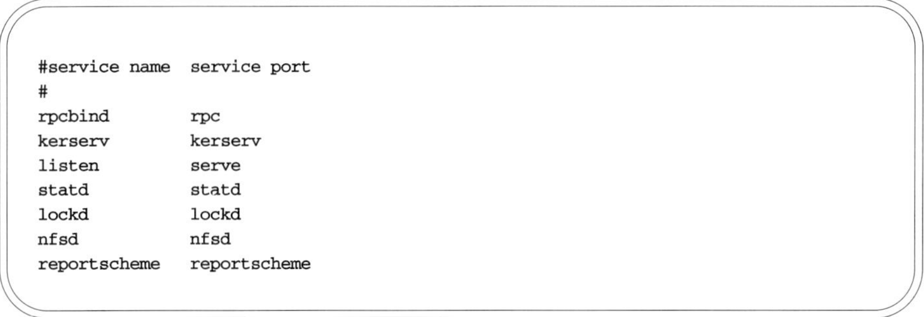

```
#service name  service port
#
rpcbind        rpc
kerserv        kerserv
listen         serve
statd          statd
lockd          lockd
nfsd           nfsd
reportscheme   reportscheme
```

The routines create the full string address by combining the "host address" and the "service port," separating the two with a dot (.). For example, the address of the "listen" service on **`bilbo`** would be **`bilboaddr.serve`** and the address of the "rpcbind" service on **`bilbo`** would be **`bilboaddr.rpc`**.

When an application requests the address of a service on a particular host on a transport provider that uses this library, the host name must appear in **`/etc/net/`***transport***`/hosts`** and the service name must appear in **`/etc/net/`***transport***`/services`**. If one or the other does not appear, the Name-to-Address Mapping routines return an error.

The Connection Server

The Connection Server [see **cs**(1M)] is a standing process or daemon that runs on all client machines. It is used to establish connections for all network services that communicate over TLI connection-oriented and dialup connections. The Connection Server is started automatically (from **/etc/dinit.d/S80cs**) during initialization when the system goes to multi-user state. It receives requests for network services from client machine applications, establishes connections to the server-machine ports associated with the requested services, and passes the connections back to the application. Before passing a connection to an application, the Connection Server may invoke an authentication scheme.

The Connection Server is made up of the following components:

- An application interface to the standing server. The interface consists of library routines that make the connection over connection-oriented networks or using dialup connections, and an error reporting routine. The use of the application interface routines is described in "The Connection Server", *Network Programming Interfaces*, and on **cs_connect**(3N) and **dial**(3N).

- An **/etc/iaf/serve.allow** file, maintained on the client machine. **/etc/iaf/serve.allow** contains a list of network services that client applications expect to use and the acceptable authentication scheme or schemes for each service. This file is not needed if client applications do not authenticate server identities, that is, if client applications will accept any authentication scheme imposed by server machines. **/etc/iaf/serve.allow** is described below.

- An optional file, **/etc/iaf/serve.alias**, also maintained on the client machine. **/etc/iaf/serve.alias** contains a list of server names, network service names and their aliases. The file is described below.

- A non-standing network service, **reportscheme**, that tells client machine applications what authentication scheme to use for a requested network service. The **reportscheme** service must exist on each port monitor that offers network services if the server is to enforce authentication scheme invocation. **reportscheme** is described throughout this section, in *Network Programming Interfaces*, and on **reportscheme**(1M).

- A Connection Server log file.

In addition, the Connection Server may make use of the Service Access Facility's administrative command, **pmadm** [see **pmadm**(1M)], to install authentication schemes.

The Connection Server Application Interface

The application interface to the Connection Server consists of the library routines **cs_connect()**, **cs_perror()**, and **dial()**. They are described in *Network Programming Interfaces* and on **cs_connect**(3N) and **dial**(3N).

Connection Server Administration

An authentication scheme is a program called by **listen** on the server machine and by the Connection Server on the client machine. It is called after physical connection takes place and before the connection is handed over to the service. An authentication program allows client and server machines to verify each other's identities.

Authentication scheme administration is performed on both client and server machines.

Server Machine Administration

Registering Authentication Schemes

The authentication scheme for a network service is registered using the port monitor administrative command, **pmadm** [see **pmadm**(1M)]. Each network service under the Service Access Facility is associated with a port under a given port monitor. The port monitor administrative command adds, removes, and maintains services by adding, removing, or changing lines in a port monitor's administrative file. (See "Managing Ports" in *Advanced System Administration* and **pmadm**(1M) for more information.)

The system administrator must "register" the authentication scheme for a service. If the service exists on the system, this is done using the port monitor administrative command, **pmadm**, with the **-c** and **-S** *scheme* options. If an authentication scheme has been associated with the service, *scheme* will be entered in the *scheme* field of the port monitor's administrative file. If an authentication scheme has already been associated with the service, the same command will replace the existing scheme with *scheme*. A **pmadm** command line in the following form will remove an authentication scheme for a service:

pmadm -c -S "" -s *svctag* **-p** *pmtag*

If the service does not yet exist, the name of the authentication scheme associated with it may be included on the command line that adds the service. In this case, **-S** *scheme* is included as one of the arguments on the **pmadm -a** command line.

After the authentication scheme name has been included in the *scheme* field of the port monitor's administrative file, it is available to the Connection Server on the client machine by way of the **reportscheme** service.

Client Machine Administration

If the administrator of the client machine wants to enforce the use of a given authentication scheme or schemes for a particular service and machine, the **/etc/iaf/serve.allow** file must be administered. If the **serve.allow** file is not administered, any authentication scheme specified by the server machine is used; if no scheme is specified, the NULL scheme is assumed. Any scheme named in the **serve.allow** file thus serves to enforce the type of authentication specified.

Maintaining the /etc/iaf/serve.allow File

The **/etc/iaf/serve.allow** file lists the names of the network services the client machine expects to use and the names of the authentication schemes acceptable to the client machine for use with each service. The system administrator is responsible for creating and maintaining the **/etc/iaf/serve.allow** file on the client machine. Each line in the file contains the name of a server machine, a network service name, and a comma-separated list of scheme names. The three fields are separated by white space.

Figure 2-10: Sample /etc/iaf/serve.allow File

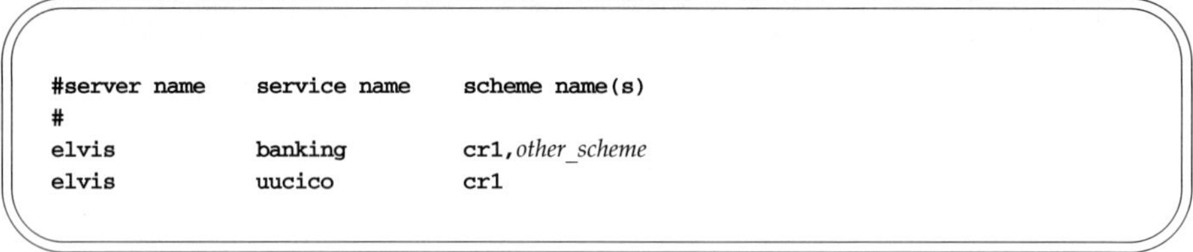

```
#server name    service name    scheme name(s)
#
elvis           banking         cr1,other_scheme
elvis           uucico          cr1
```

In the example, **elvis** is a server machine name, **banking** is a network service name, and **cr1** is the name of authentication scheme acceptable to the client machine for the **banking** service on **elvis**. *other_scheme* could be any other secure authentication scheme (for example, **kerberos**). It must be registered with the **banking** service on the server machine for an application on the client machine to be able to access the service. If there is no entry in the **serve.allow** file for a network service, the client machine accepts any authentication scheme the server machine specifies for the service.

The system administrator maintains the **/etc/iaf/serve.allow** file using an editor such as **vi**.

Maintaining the /etc/iaf/serve.alias File

Before Name-to-Address Mapping is invoked, the Connection Server consults the **/etc/iaf/serve.alias** file, if it exists, to find out if the service requested by an application should be requested under another name. If the service name is found in the file, the Connection Server substitutes its alias for the name given by the application.

The administrator of a server machine may register a service under two names with two different authentication schemes to implement a gradual migration from one authentication scheme to another. For example, a server machine may register a new authentication scheme, **newauth**, with one of its network services, **date**. Not all client machines that use the server machine's **date** command have installed the **newauth** scheme. In this case the administrator of the server machine will add a **date.old** line to the service line in the appropriate port monitor administrative file and enter the old authentication scheme name, **ns**, in the *scheme* field. A client machine that wants to continue using the **ns** authentication scheme will add

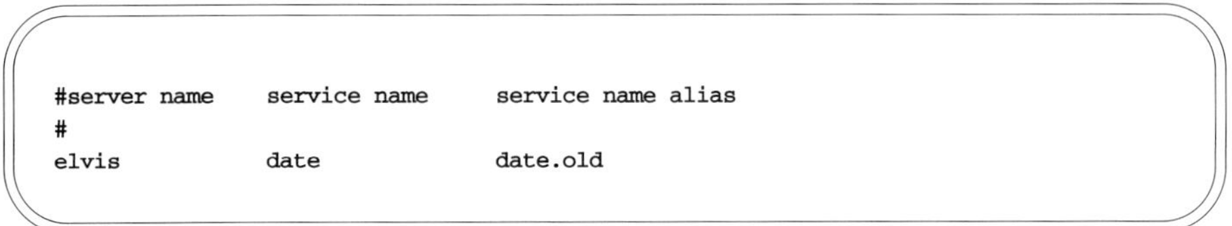

```
#server name    service name    service name alias
#
elvis           date            date.old
```

to its **/etc/iaf/serve.alias** file.

In the example, the first field is the name of the server machine, **elvis**; the second field is the network service as it is known to the application. Field three is the network service's alias. The Connection Server will translate the application's request for the **date** command to a request for **date.old** and the **ns** authentication scheme will be used.

The **/etc/iaf/serve.alias** file is updated using one of the text editors such as **vi**.

The reportscheme Service

reportscheme(1M) is a network service invoked by the Connection Server to determine what authentication scheme is associated with a given service on the server machine. If the server is to enforce authentication scheme invocation, a **reportscheme** line must appear in the port monitor administrative file for every port monitor that offers network services. If the **reportscheme** service is not entered in a port monitor's administrative file, applications on client machines cannot successfully query scheme information and will assume a NULL authentication scheme is associated with the service to which they are trying to connect.

The **reportscheme** entry itself must not have an authentication scheme associated with it.

The following is a sample **reportscheme** entry in the port monitor administrative file **/etc/saf/tcp/_pmtab**. The entry is a single line. It is shown wrapped around for readability.

```
reportscheme::root:reserved:reserved::\x00020AD0C00B02510000000000000000::c::
/usr/sbin/reportscheme#reportscheme service - no authentication scheme
```

There must also be a **reportscheme** entry in the **/etc/services** file:

```
#service name       port number/transport
#
reportscheme        2768/tcp
```

with the following entry in **/etc/hosts**:

```
#host address       host name
#
192.11.2.81         elvis
```

A **reportscheme** entry in the **ticots** port monitor administrative file **/etc/saf/ticots/_pmtab** will look like this:

```
reportscheme::root:reserved:reserved::elvis.reportscheme::c::/usr/sbin/reportscheme
#reportscheme service - no authentication scheme
```

In this case, the entry in the **/etc/net/ticots/services** file will be:

```
#service name      service port
#
reportscheme       reportscheme
```

The entry in the `/etc/net/ticots/hosts` file will be:

```
#machine addr      machine name
#
elvis              elvis
```

The Connection Server Authentication Scheme File

The Connection Server authentication file or `/etc/cs/auth` is an optional file, maintained by the system administrator, that lists the authentication scheme and role associated with a particular host, service, network tuple. The system administrator does not need to (and in most cases will not) put information into this file. Typically, the Connection Server obtains the initial authentication information about a particular host, service, network tuple from the **reportscheme** service. The Connection Server retains this data in an internal cache so the **reportscheme** service will not be called in subsequent network requests for the same host, service, network tuple.

If, for any reason, the system administrator does not want the **reportscheme** service to be called for a particular host, service, network tuple, the authentication scheme information can be stored in `/etc/cs/auth`. When the Connection Server is started, it uses the information in `/etc/cs/auth` to initialize its internal cache.

The Connection Server authentication file is read only once when the Connection Server is started up. If the system administrator changes the file while the Connection Server is running, the command

```
cs -x
```

must be issued from the command line to tell the Connection Server to read the authentication file again. See **cs**(1M) for further information on **cs**.

Administrators of server machines that do not offer the **reportscheme** service must inform administrators of client machines of changes to the authentication scheme of a service from NULL to another scheme, such as cr1. Then client machine administrators must either update the **/etc/cs/auth** file with the new scheme information and execute the **cs -x** command, or kill the **cs** daemon and then restart it so the internal cache will be rebuilt with the correct information.

To change the Connection Server authentication file, the system administrator should edit the file manually. The format of the file, which consists of one line and the fields are separated by tabs, is:

host service transport authentication scheme imposer role

When no scheme is required (sometimes referred to as a NULL scheme), the administrator indicates this by putting a dash (-) in the authentication scheme field. The "role" field indicates the client will act as either the responder (**r**) to the authentication process or as the imposer (**i**).

An example of a small authentication file is shown in Figure 2-11:

Figure 2-11: Example of a Small Authentication File

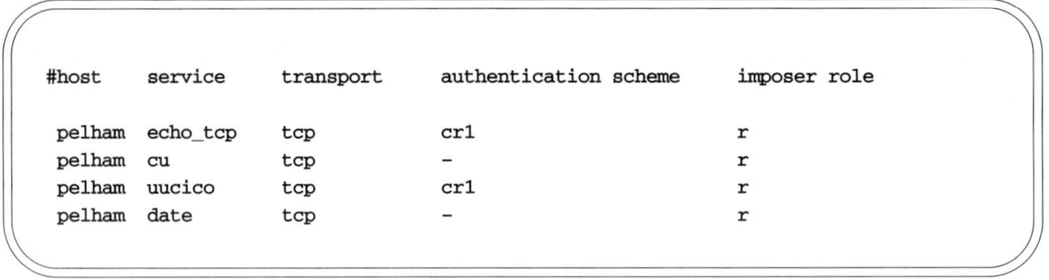

```
#host   service    transport   authentication scheme   imposer role

 pelham echo_tcp   tcp         cr1                     r
 pelham cu         tcp         -                       r
 pelham uucico     tcp         cr1                     r
 pelham date       tcp         -                       r
```

For more information on imposer role and authentication schemes, see "cr1 Bilateral Authentication Scheme".

The Connection Server Log File

The Connection Server logs information in the file **/var/adm/log/cs.log** on the client machine. A message is logged on startup.

Any time a connection request fails, the reason for failure is written to the log file. In addition, for each connection requested through **cs_connect**() or **dial**(), a message is logged containing the following data: time, date, user ID, group ID, network service requested, name of server machine, and status of request (success or failure). For example:

Figure 2-12: Sample Output from a Connection Server Log File

```
05/13/92 13:07:45;   229; *** CONNECTION SERVER starting ***
05/13/92 13:09:16;   313; Request by process uid<0> gid<5>
05/13/92 13:09:16;   313;   for service<cu> on host<hulk> FAILED
05/13/92 13:09:38;   468; Request by process uid<0> gid<5>
05/13/92 13:09:38;   468;   for service<cu> on host<hulk> SUCCEEDED
```

The number immediately following each date and time (such as **468** in the last line) is the process ID of the process that the Connection Server daemon spawned to handle the connection request.

The Connection Server Debug File

If the Connection Server is invoked with the debug option, the Connection Server daemon will write debug information to **/var/adm/log/cs.debug**. See **cs**(1M) for further information on **cs**. The command line used is:

```
/usr/sbin/cs -d
```

A sample output file is shown in Figure 2-13.

Figure 2-13: Sample Output from a Connection Server Debug File (`cs -d`)

```
10:40:58;  4404; cs: Debugging turned on
10:40:58;  4404; cs: chdir to ROOT
10:40:58;  4404; gs: reading schemes from /etc/cs/auth
10:40:58;  4404; cs: created CS pipe: /etc/.cs_pipe
10:41:08;  4404; cs: conn done; client talks to server
10:41:08;  4404; cs: fd to read request from: 3
10:41:08;  4412; cs: connection server child forked
10:41:08;  4412; cs: request-type: DIAL_REQUEST
10:41:08;  4412; cs: fd to read from <3>
10:41:08;  4412; sr: netpath<NULL>
10:41:08;  4412; cs: dial Call structure set up as follows:
10:41:08;  4412; cs: baud<-1>
10:41:08;  4412; cs: speed<-1>
10:41:08;  4412; cs: modem<-1>
10:41:08;  4412; cs: dev_len<-1>
10:41:08;  4412; cs: c_iflag<6182>
10:41:08;  4412; cs: c_oflag<6148>
10:41:08;  4412; cs: c_cflag<445>
10:41:08;  4412; cs: c_lflag<48>
10:41:08;  4412; cs: c_line<0>
10:41:08;  4412; cs: line<NULL>
10:41:08;  4412; cs: telno<sfsup>
10:41:08;  4412; cs: service<cu>
10:41:08;  4412; cs: class<NULL>
10:41:08;  4412; cs: protocol<NULL>
```

cr1 Bilateral Authentication Scheme

cr1 is an identification and authentication scheme that protects a system from unauthorized access. By default, cr1 uses DES encryption, and can also be referenced as **cr1.des**. Because of export restrictions on DES, cr1 can also use ENIGMA encryption. When using ENIGMA encryption, cr1 is referenced as **cr1.enigma**. Other than the underlying encryption algorithm used, all cr1 schemes behave identically.

The cr1 scheme is bilateral, which means it authenticates both client and server identities. Generally, it authenticates a connection established by a Connection Server on the client side and a port monitor on the server. When a cr1 exchange is complete, the client, as well as the server, can be certain of the other party's identity.

cr1 requires a system to store a cryptographic key for every protected system with which it needs to communicate. The key is a bit string known only to the principals in the exchange (the client and server); the string is used to encrypt and decrypt messages passed between the two principals. Typically, when a remote client attempts to access a local service protected by cr1, the cr1 scheme on the server engages the client in a sequence of exchanges involving the shared cryptographic key and one-time challenges. If the remote client responds appropriately to the server's challenge, the server can be certain that the remote client is authorized to access the service. If the server does not engage the client in the exchange, the client can engage the server. If the server responds appropriately to the client's challenge, the client can be certain that it is connecting to the desired server, not an imposter.

cr1 consists of the following components:

- an executable program, **/usr/lib/iaf/cr1/scheme**
- the **/etc/iaf/cr1/keys** file, which is a database of shared keys, optionally encrypted with a master key
- **keymaster**, a daemon process that manages the key database
- **/var/iaf/cr1**, containing the log file **log**

The cr1 privileged user can create a key to be shared by the local system and any remote machine on the network. The privileged user is the owner of the **keys** file. Once a shared key is created for the two principals, the key management daemon stores the key in the key database, then uses a cryptographic key—called the master key—to encrypt the keys in the database. The keys in the database are re-encrypted every time a new key is added.

Shared keys can also be created for users. For example, **bob** on **system1** can share a key with **system2** or with user **joe** on **system2**. When a key is created for a user, the name of the client user and the system to which the user wants access must be specified. The privileged user can create a shared key for any local user. A non-privileged user can create shared keys for their individual login name.

When a user attempts to run a service on the client, the command that executes the service initiates the following sequence of actions:

1. The Connection Server on the client requests the **reportscheme** service from the port monitor on the server. **reportscheme** is an internal service that determines the scheme that is protecting a service, then passes the information to the client.
2. The **reportscheme** service returns a message informing the Connection Server that the service is protected by cr1.

Once the client receives the name of the scheme, it caches the information for future use, so **reportscheme** need not be called every time the Connection Server requests a connection to the service.

3. The Connection Server then requests a connection to the service from the port monitor on the server.
4. Both the Connection Server and the port monitor invoke cr1. On the client, the Connection Server calls cr1 to play the role of the "responder" in the authentication exchange. (cr1 on a client is called the responder because it responds to the server's requirement that cr1 be used.) On the server, the port monitor calls cr1 to play the role of the "imposer." (cr1 on the server is called the imposer because it protects a local service by imposing the use of the cr1 protocol on the client machine.)
5. The responder searches various local databases and sends pertinent information to the server. Included in that information is the responder's effective identity (that of the local user) and the name of the client machine. Also included in the message is a unique token, which the responder sends as a challenge to cr1 on the server.
6. The responder's message is received by cr1 on the server (the imposer). After the imposer receives the responder's message, it retrieves the shared key from its key database, and verifies that the key properly decrypts the message. It then sends the responder a message that includes the responder's token; by returning the token, the imposer proves its identity to the responder. The imposer's message also includes another unique token, which the imposer sends to challenge the responder.

7. The responder receives the message and validates its contents, proving that the sender properly decrypted the first message using the key known only to the two parties. The responder then sends a third message that includes the unique token provided by the imposer.
8. The imposer receives the third message and verifies that the token it included in the previous message was successfully decrypted and returned, proving that the responder is an active participant in the conversation.

When the authentication exchange is successfully completed, the user on the client connects to the service on the server.

An Overview of cr1 Administration

cr1 works with a number of facilities and databases to provide an authenticated connection between client and server. These facilities and databases must be administered prior to creating a shared key for two principals in a cr1 exchange. The following is an overview of setting up a cr1-protected service, first on the client side, then on the server side. This overview assumes a TLI connection.

To administer cr1 for a service on the client side, you must do the following:

1. Set up **/etc/net/***transport***/hosts** to include the remote system's name and address. If the connection is over TCP/IP, use the **/etc/hosts** and the **/etc/services** files.
2. Set up **/etc/net/***transport***/services**.
    a. Add the service and its port address.
    b. Add **reportscheme** and its address.

For information about the **hosts** and **services** files, see **hosts**(4) and **services**(4).

If the connection is not over TLI, the Connection Server searches for the address of the service in the BNU **Systems** and **Devices** files. See the discussion of BNU files later in this chapter.

3. Make sure the Connection Server and the key management daemon are running.

An initialization script starts both the Connection Server and the key management daemon. If the Connection Server has been stopped manually, use the `cs` command to restart it. For more information about starting and stopping the Connection Server, see "The Connection Server". Starting and stopping the key management daemon is described later in this section.

4. Add a shared key for the server to the client's key database.

To set up cr1 to protect the service on the server side, you must do the following:

1. Set up the port monitor's **_pmtab** file.

    a. Create an entry for the service and specify

        cr1 -s *servicetag*

        in the *scheme* field.

    b. Create an entry for **reportscheme**. Leave the *scheme* field empty to mean the **NULL** scheme.

2. Set up ID mapping to include a database entry that maps the name of the user on the client to a local name. The command lines are as follows:

    idadmin -S cr1 -I M1@M2 (to initialize the scheme)

    idadmin -S cr1 -a -r *@client -l %1 (transparent mapping)

For information about administration of the ID mapping databases, see "ID Mapping".

3. Add the shared key to the server's key database.

The following tasks are specifically part of cr1 administration:

1. Setting up the key database initially and managing shared keys
2. Creating and managing the master key
3. Stopping and starting the key management daemon
4. Optionally, adding cr1 to the Connection Server's **serve.allow** file on the client

All administrative tasks can be performed through the system administration menu interface. When you select an option from a menu, self-explanatory submenus and instructions lead you through the appropriate procedures.

Most tasks can be done from the cr1 menu. The screen below is the top-level cr1 menu. It can be displayed by typing the following command:

```
sysadm network_services/cr1
```

Figure 2-14: cr1 Menu

```
          IAF Scheme cr1 Key Management

add       - Add an Entry to the Key File
modify    - Modify an Entry in the Key File
remove    - Remove an Entry from the Key File
set       - Set the Master Key for the Key File
start     - Start the Keymaster Daemon
stop      - Stop the Keymaster Daemon
```

The command alternatives to the cr1 menu interface are listed in the following table.

Table 2-4: Command Alternatives to the cr1 Menu

Task Description	Menu Item	Shell Command
Add shared keys to the **keys** file.	**add**	**cryptkey -a**
Modify a **keys** entry.	**modify**	**cryptkey -c**
Remove a **keys** entry.	**remove**	**cryptkey -d**
Set a master key.	**set**	**keymaster -c**
Start the **keymaster** daemon.	**start**	**keymaster**
Stop the **keymaster** daemon.	**stop**	**keymaster -k**

Registering the scheme with a port monitor is done through the top-level Service Access Facility menu, shown below. It can be reached by typing the following command:

```
sysadm ports
```

Figure 2-15: SAF Menu

```
          Service Access Management

port_monitors      - Port Monitor Management
port_services      - Port Service Management
quick_terminal     - Quick Terminal Setup
tty_settings       - Terminal Line Setting Management
```

You can bypass the menu system by issuing commands directly to the shell. The command alternative to editing the **_pmtab** file through the SAF menu is **pmadm** [see **pmadm**(1M)].

Instructions for administering facilities with which cr1 interfaces, such as the Connection Server and ID Mapping can be found in "The Connection Server" and "ID Mapping", respectively. Because the menu interface is self-explanatory, the following instructions assume you are administering cr1 using shell commands.

Registering cr1 with a Port Monitor

To protect a local service with cr1, you must instruct the port monitor associated with the service to use cr1 to authenticate any remote client attempting to gain access. To do this, you must add **cr1** to the *scheme* field of the service's entry in the port monitor's **_pmtab** file.

To specify **cr1** in the *scheme* field of a file entry, enter the **pmadm** command and include

-S "cr1 -s *servicetag***"**

on the command line.

For more information about port monitors and the **_pmtab** file, see **pmadm**(1M) and "Managing Ports" in *Advanced System Administration*. This chapter includes specific instructions for editing **_pmtab** using the **pmadm** command.

Typically, cr1 in the role of the imposer is invoked with the **-s** option; however, a number of options are supported. For a complete list of options, see **cr1**(1M).

Registering cr1 with the Connection Server

Nothing needs to be done on the client side to register cr1. Once the cr1 executable program is installed, the Connection Server automatically invokes **cr1** with the **-r** option whenever it receives a message from the server that cr1 is protecting the requested service. The **-r** option tells the program on the client that it is to play the role of the responder in the authentication exchange.

When cr1 on the client is called, it searches local databases and sends pertinent information to the server, which the port monitor passes as arguments to the server's local cr1. Included in the arguments are the name of the user on the remote system and the remote system's machine name, which cr1 uses to locate the shared key in its key database. Setting up the key database is described in ''Setting Up the Key Database''.

Although cr1 does not need to be administered on the client, the client administrator has the option to specify a list of acceptable schemes in the Connection Server's **serve.allow** file. If cr1 is specified, the Connection Server will fail the connection request if the use of cr1 is not mandated by the server. By forcing the server to use cr1, the client can verify the server's identity.

Instructions for setting up the **serve.allow** file can be found under ''The Connection Server''.

Managing the Daemon and the Master Key

Before you can administer the key database, the key management daemon must be running. Typically, the daemon is started by default when you boot the system.

When you administer the key database—whether to add a new shared key to the **keys** file, delete a key that is no longer needed, or modify an existing key—the command you enter calls the key management daemon, which performs the requested operation. If you are supplying a new shared key, for example, the daemon takes the shared key from the **cryptkey** command [see **cryptkey**(1)] and stores it in the **keys** file. The daemon then uses the master key to encrypt the keys in the **keys** file. Every time the daemon modifies the **keys** file, it re-encrypts the keys—using the master key.

Both the key management daemon and the master key are managed using the **keymaster** command [see **keymaster**(1M)], as described in the following sections.

Starting and Stopping the Daemon

The key management daemon is started automatically through an initialization script whenever you boot the system; however, you can do this only if there is no master key.

If you have a master key, the **keymaster** daemon cannot be started automatically at boot time; **keymaster** must be started manually. You must also edit the **init** script **/etc/dinit.d/S69keymaster** and comment out the line which reads **keymaster -n**.

If your system needs to be re-booted frequently, and you are unable to attend the system during a re-boot, you may want to store the **keys** file in unencrypted form. To store the **keys** file in unencrypted form, you need to change the master key to NULL.

In certain circumstances—if there is a problem with the **keys** file, for example—you may want to stop the daemon manually. Enter the **keymaster** command as follows to stop the daemon:

```
keymaster -k
```

No key is required to stop the daemon; however, the operation fails if you are not the privileged user (the owner of the **keys** file).

To re-start the daemon, enter the **keymaster** command.

Creating a Master Key

When cr1 is first installed and the system is booted, an initialization script runs the **keymaster** command, which starts the key management daemon. Because the **keys** file is empty at this point, the master key is NULL.

To create the master key, simply enter the following command:

```
keymaster -n -c
```

keymaster prompts you for the key, which can be any alphanumeric string between zero and eight characters in length.

When you enter the key, the **keymaster** command does not echo it on the screen. Instead, **keymaster** prompts you to enter the key a second time. If the first and second entries match, the daemon stores the master key. If the entries do not match, the operation fails and the master key remains unchanged.

Once you create a master key, the daemon takes it and stores it. (For security reasons, it stores the key in cleartext in its process address space, not in a file. An encrypted copy of the master key is stored in the **keys** file.) The daemon then uses the master key to encrypt the shared keys in the **keys** file and to re-encrypt them every time the file is modified.

To change a master key once you have created it, enter

```
keymaster -c
```

The system then prompts you to enter the old master key. Once you enter the old master key, it prompts you to enter, and then re-enter the new master key. If the entries do not match, the operation fails and the master key remains unchanged.

Setting Up the Key Database

As described earlier, shared keys are stored in a **keys** file, which is set up and maintained by the cr1 administrator. Whenever you administer the **keys** file, the key management daemon must be running.

Shared keys are stored in **keys** files on both the client and server machines. The cr1 administrator of the client must enter a key to be shared by the local and remote systems. The cr1 administrator of the server machine must enter the same key into its key database. The database entry and the syntax of the command used to create the entry differ on the client and server machines; however, the entry always includes the names of the two principals in the exchange and, of course, the shared key. The key must be entered into both the client and server databases locally; there is no service available to propagate cr1 keys on the network.

Typically, authentication is done at the system level. Authorization of individual users is managed locally. If there is a need to deny a user access to a service on a machine, the user is denied access locally, through the standard permissions mechanism.

Although we recommend restricting access through cr1 at the system level, access by individual users can be controlled through cr1, as well. Shared keys can be entered into the key database for individual users. If access is controlled through cr1 at the user level, users can enter and maintain their own keys, in the same way that they maintain their own login passwords in **/etc/shadow** [see **shadow**(4)].

The interface to the **keys** file is the **cryptkey** [see **cryptkey**(1)] command. The **cryptkey** command allows privileged and non-privileged users to add, delete, and modify a key shared by two principals in a cr1 authentication exchange. A non-privileged user must be the local principal for whom the key is being added, deleted, or modified. The privileged user is the owner of the **keys** file. A privileged user can create, delete, or modify keys for any user on the local system.

The **cryptkey** command has the following syntax:

cryptkey [-a | -c | -d] [*local_principal*] *remote_principal*

For further information on the options, see **cryptkey**(1).

If **cryptkey** is entered without options, the **-c** option is assumed and an existing key shared by the principals is modified.

When a user enters the command to add or change a key, he or she is prompted to enter a new key; the key can be any alphanumeric string between zero and eight characters in length.

When a non-privileged user is deleting an old key, he or she is prompted to enter the old key. When changing a key, a non-privileged user is prompted to enter the old key, followed by the new key.

As with passwords, an administrator may need to change keys for users who do not remember their old keys, or remove keys belonging to users who no longer have access to the system. Therefore a privileged user is not required to supply the old key when changing or deleting a key.

Assume you want to create a shared key for **adam** on your system, named **eden**, and for **tom** on a remote host named **utopia**. You want to enter **serpent** as the key. On the client, you must do the following:

1. Enter

   ```
   cryptkey -a adam utopia!tom
   ```

   The system then prompts you to enter a key.

2. In response to the prompt, type **serpent**. The system then prompts you to enter the key a second time.

3. Enter **serpent** a second time. If the first and second entries match, the key is added to the database. If they fail to match, the operation quits.

To add the key into the server's key database, you would do the following:

1. Access the server and enter

   ```
   cryptkey -a tom eden!adam
   ```

   Again, the system prompts you to enter a key.

2. Enter the same key that was added to the client's database—in this case, **serpent**.

   The system then prompts you to enter the key a second time.

3. Enter the key a second time. When you enter the key a second time, and the first and second entries match, the key is added to the server's key database.

Now the two principals have a shared key.

ID Mapping

UNIX System V ID Mapping is a facility that can be used to establish local identities for users on remote systems. It provides a common mechanism through which applications can identify remote users and control remote access to local resources.

The ID Mapping module consists of two routines that map remote users into local identities, plus a database from which the routines retrieve the relevant mapping information. The ID Mapping database includes two types of map files. One type contains entries that map user logins; the other contains entries that map the values of user attributes, such as UIDs and GIDs.

When a remote user attempts to access a service on your system, the port monitor receives the connection request. It uses an authentication scheme to validate the user; the scheme then calls the ID Mapping routines. One routine checks the login maps associated with the ID Mapping scheme, then maps the user to a login on the local system. The other routine checks the local system's attribute maps, then maps the values of user attributes on the remote system to the specified local values.

Both login mapping and attribute mapping are provided in System V as part of a general mapping facility. Some applications may require that users be mapped both by login and by attribute; other applications may require that they be mapped only by attribute. Typically, however, users are mapped only by login; when users are mapped by login, the administrator controls a remote user's local environment by associating attributes with the user's login in the local system's **/etc/passwd** file [see **passwd**(4)].

ID Mapping administration entails setting up and maintaining the ID Mapping database; however, before you set up the database, it is assumed you have installed the authentication schemes you intend to use.

The cr1 authentication scheme is the only authentication scheme provided with System V Release 4.2 at this time—with the exception of the traditional login/password scheme, which doesn't rely on ID Mapping. Unless otherwise stated, examples throughout the discussion of ID Mapping assume cr1 is the authentication scheme.

We recommend you administer your system in the following sequence:

1. Check that authentication scheme executable programs are installed in the proper directories; **cr1** should be installed in **/usr/lib/iaf/cr1**.

2. Set up the ID Mapping database, following instructions in this section.
3. Register services with port monitors and associate them with authentication schemes through the Service Access Facility. See "Managing Ports" in *Advanced System Administration* for more information on registering services.
4. Update the ID Mapping database as needed.

If you enable a facility called "user-controlled mapping," non-privileged users can help you maintain login maps. When user-controlled mapping is enabled, a user with logins on both the local and a remote system can access the local system and add a database entry that maps their own remote login to a local login. User-controlled mapping is described in "Enabling and Disabling User-Controlled Mapping".

The administrator of user-controlled mapping databases must be in group **sys**.

Administering the ID Mapping database can be done using either the **sysadm** command or ID Mapping commands. When you use **sysadm**, self-explanatory submenus and instructions lead you through the appropriate procedures. The screen below is the top-level Name Mapping menu. It can be displayed on the screen by typing **sysadm name_map**.

Figure 2-16: Name Mapping Menu

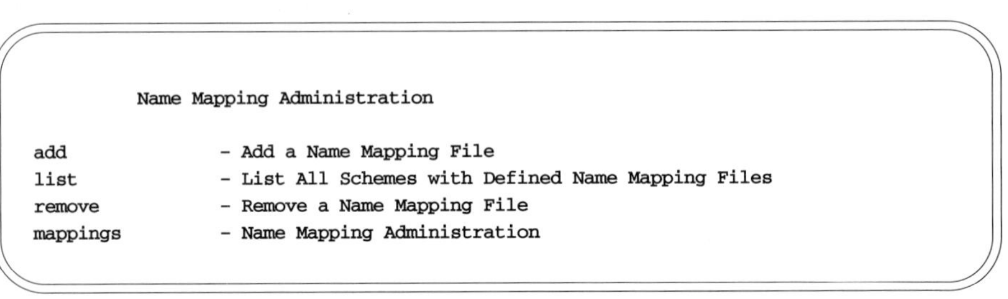

```
          Name Mapping Administration

add             - Add a Name Mapping File
list            - List All Schemes with Defined Name Mapping Files
remove          - Remove a Name Mapping File
mappings        - Name Mapping Administration
```

You can bypass the menu system by issuing commands directly to the shell. The command alternatives to the name mapping menu options are listed below:

Table 2-5: Command Alternatives to the Name Mapping Menu

Task Description	Menu Item	Shell Command
Add a new name mapping file.	**add**	**idadmin -S** *scheme* **-I** *descr*
List all schemes with defined name-mapping files.	**list**	**idadmin**
Remove a name-mapping file.	**remove**	**idadmin -S** *scheme* **-D**

When you select **mappings** from the menu, the following sub-menu is displayed:

Figure 2-17: `mappings` sub-menu for Name Mapping Administration

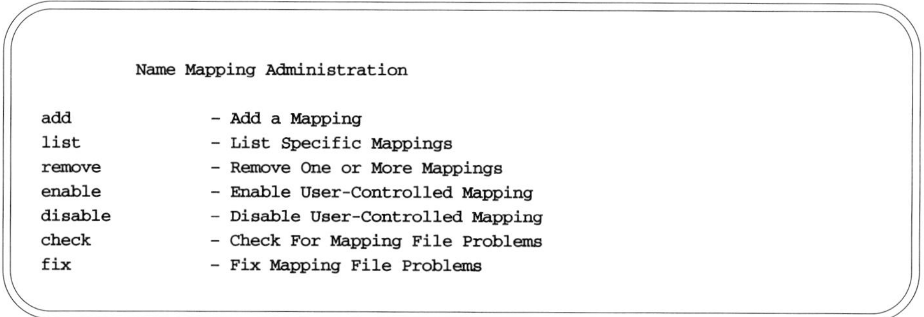

```
          Name Mapping Administration

add              - Add a Mapping
list             - List Specific Mappings
remove           - Remove One or More Mappings
enable           - Enable User-Controlled Mapping
disable          - Disable User-Controlled Mapping
check            - Check For Mapping File Problems
fix              - Fix Mapping File Problems
```

Command alternatives to the second-level menu options are listed in the following table:

Table 2-6: **Command Alternatives to the Second-Level Name Mapping Menu**

Task Description	Menu Item	Shell Command
Add a name mapping to a file.	**add**	**idadmin -S** *scheme* **-a -l** *logname* **-r** *g_name*
Check mapping consistency.	**check**	**idadmin -S** *scheme* **-c**
Fix mapping inconsistencies.	**fix**	**idadmin -S** *scheme* **-f**
List entries in a map.	**list**	**idadmin [-S** *scheme* **[-l** *logname***]]**
Disable user-controlled mapping.	**disable**	**idadmin -S** *scheme* **-s**
Remove a specific map entry.	**remove**	**idadmin -S** *scheme* **-d -l** *logname* **[-r** *g_name***]**
Enable user-controlled mapping.	**enable**	**idadmin -S** *scheme* **-u**

Attribute mapping is done from a separate menu and submenu. The top-level attribute mapping menu can be displayed by typing **sysadm attr_map**.

The following is the top-level attribute mapping menu:

Figure 2-18: Attribute Mapping Menu

```
          Attribute Mapping Administration

add              - Add an Attribute Mapping File
list             - List All Attributes with Defined Attribute Mapping Files
remove           - Remove an Attribute Mapping File
mappings         - Attribute Mapping Administration
```

Command alternatives to the attribute mapping menu options appear below:

Table 2-7: Command Alternatives to the Attribute Mapping Menu

Task Description	Menu Item	Shell Command
Create a new attribute map file.	**add**	**attradmin -A** *attrname* **-I** *descr*
List all attribute mapping files.	**list**	**attradmin**
Delete an attribute map file.	**remove**	**attradmin -A** *attrname* **-D**

When you select **mappings** from the menu, the following sub-menu is displayed:

Figure 2-19: `mappings` sub-menu for Attribute Mapping Administration

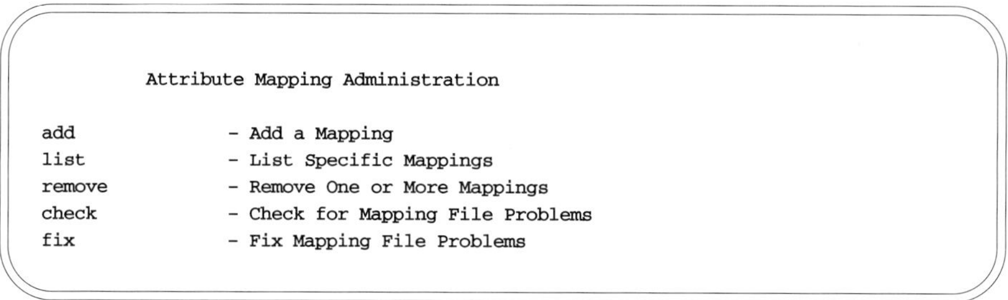

```
          Attribute Mapping Administration

add             - Add a Mapping
list            - List Specific Mappings
remove          - Remove One or More Mappings
check           - Check for Mapping File Problems
fix             - Fix Mapping File Problems
```

Command alternatives to the second-level menu options are listed in the following table:

Table 2-8: Command Alternatives to the Second-Level Attribute Mapping Menu

Task Description	Menu Item	Shell Command
Add an entry to an attribute map file.	**add**	**attradmin -A** *attrname* **-a -l** *localval* \ **-r** *remoteval*
Check mapping consistency.	**check**	**attradmin -A** *attrname* **-c**
Fix mapping inconsistencies.	**fix**	**attradmin -A** *attrname* **-f**
List entries in a map.	**list**	**attradmin [-A** *attrname* **[-l** *localval***]]**
Remove a specific map entry.	**remove**	**attradmin -A** *attrname* **-d -l** *localval* \ **[-r** *remoteval***]**

Because menus are self-explanatory, instructions in this guide for setting up and maintaining the ID Mapping database assume the use of shell commands.

Setting Up Login Maps

There are two types of login maps: one that contains map entries specified by the system administrator, and one that contains user-specified entries.

It is conceivable that you might have two or more sets of login maps on your system. Authentication schemes require a specific ID Mapping scheme. What this means, essentially, is that entries in maps that support a particular authentication scheme must have a specific format, which is dictated by the authentication scheme. If your system supports two authentication schemes, for example, and each scheme requires map entries to have a unique format, you will need to have two administrator-controlled login maps on your system.

The term "ID Mapping scheme" refers to the format of a set of maps. Generally, there is a one-to-one correspondence between ID Mapping schemes and authentication schemes, such that one set of maps supports one authentication scheme. When there is a one-to-one correspondence, the name of the ID mapping scheme and the name of the authentication scheme can be the same.

At the present time, cr1 is the only authentication scheme provided as part of UNIX SVR4.2—with the exception of the traditional login/password scheme, which doesn't rely on ID Mapping. The ID Mapping scheme that supports the cr1 authentication scheme is also called cr1.

Administrator-specified map files are named **idata**. User-specified map files are named **uidata**. Both login map files are stored in the **/etc/idmap** directory, in a subdirectory named for the ID Mapping scheme. Below are the full pathnames of the map files that support cr1.

```
/etc/idmap/cr1/idata
/etc/idmap/cr1/uidata
```

The name of the ID Mapping scheme is hard coded in the authentication scheme. If, in the future, your system supports an authentication scheme in addition to cr1, check the documentation that accompanies the scheme software to determine the name you need to assign to the maps that support the scheme.

Examples throughout the discussion of ID Mapping assume you are setting up maps to support cr1.

The following sections describe setting up and maintaining **idata** and **uidata** map files.

Administering an idata File

Each entry in **idata** maps a user login on a remote system to a login on the local system. Below is a sample **idata** file:

```
!M1@M2.M3.M4.M5
root@joker.sf.buu.com root
*@*.sf.buu.com %1
*@*.tm.buu.com guest
ilya@*.*.*.* ilya
```

Note that the example includes regular expressions, which are used to map remote users transparently or to map multiple users to a general login. The use of regular expressions in the **idata** file is explained in detail in "Adding an Entry to an idata File".

All entries in an **idata** file are specified by the system administrator. When a remote user has an entry in **idata**, he or she can access a service on the local system and assume the user identity defined by the administrator.

The **idadmin** command is the command interface to **idata**. It allows a privileged user to do the following:

- create and delete an **idata** file for a particular ID Mapping scheme
- add and delete user entries in an **idata** file
- display information about the **idata** files
- check the consistency of file entries and fix inconsistencies
- enable and disable user-controlled mapping.

The **idadmin** command has the following syntax:

```
idadmin [-S scheme [-l logname]]
idadmin -S scheme -a -l logname -r g_name
idadmin -S scheme -d -l logname [-r g_name]
idadmin -S scheme -I descr
idadmin -S scheme [-Duscf]
```

See **idadmin**(1M) for an explanation of the options accepted by the **idadmin** command.

The options and command syntax required to execute a particular operation are described in the following sections.

Setting Up the idata File

When you want to set up an **idata** map file for a particular ID Mapping scheme, you must enter the **idadmin** command with the ID Mapping scheme name and specify the format that the global name should take in all file entries.

The **idadmin** command has the following syntax when used to set up a new file:

```
idadmin -S scheme -I descr
```

where *scheme* is the name of the ID Mapping scheme, and *descr* is a string called a format descriptor. The string specifies the form that the name of the remote user must take in the **idata** map file.

For example, **cr1** expects global names to consist of the user's login, followed by the character **@**, then the system name. The global name of a user with the login **jeff** on a machine called **moon** would be

```
jeff@moon
```

The format descriptor itself consists of field numbers, the letter M, indicating the fields are mandatory, and the character(s) that are used as field separators.

The file descriptor you would enter to set up an **idata** file for **cr1** would be

```
M1@M2
```

The field numbers indicate the order of significance of the fields, where higher numbered fields are more significant. In the example, **M2** means that the entity to be specified in the second field is of greater significance on the network than the entity specified in the first field. In this case, the system is of greater significance than the user. The letter **M** indicates that the fields are required when specifying **g_name**.

Assume that BNU services are registered with the authentication scheme **cr1**. To set up an **idata** file that would map remote users to the local system and give them access to BNU, you would enter the following command:

```
idadmin -S cr1 -I M1@M2
```

When the **idadmin** command in the example is executed, it creates the file **/etc/idmap/cr1/idata**. The first line of the file consists of the format descriptor. Except for the format descriptor, the file is empty until user entries are added, as described in the following section.

Adding an Entry to an idata File

To map a remote user to a login on the local system, add an entry for the remote user to the appropriate **idata** file. The local login must be in the **/etc/passwd** file on the local system.

When you add a user entry to **idata**, **idadmin** has the syntax

idadmin -S *scheme* **-a -l** *logname* **-r** *g_name*

where *scheme* is the name of the ID mapping scheme, *g_name* is the global name of the remote user, and *logname* is the local login. For example, given the format descriptor **M1@M2**, the following entry maps **jeff** on machine **moon** to the local login **guest**:

```
idadmin -S cr1 -a -l guest -r jeff@moon
```

You can set up transparent mapping of logins by using regular expressions in the *g_name* field and the **%** character in the *logname* field. The special characters supported by the **idadmin** command are explained on **idadmin**(1M).

File entries are sorted so that an entry that maps a login explicitly is found in a search before entries that implement transparent mapping. Likewise, entries that map logins transparently are sorted based on the position of the regular expression in the global name. Entries with a regular expression in place of a remote user login appear in the file before entries with a regular expression in place of a system name.

Examples

Assume the ID Mapping scheme is **idmp** and *g_name* has the form **M1@M2.M3**, where **M1** indicates the user's login. The following command line transparently maps all users on the remote system **man** in the domain **moon**. All users are mapped to the local login **guest**.

```
idadmin -S idmp -a -l guest -r "*@man.moon"
```

To protect characters that are meaningful to the shell, enclose global names in quotes.

If you enter ***** in place of the remote user name and **%1** in place of *logname* on the **idadmin** command line, you map all remote logins to the same values indicated in **M1**. Assume the authentication scheme is called cr2 and the format descriptor is **M2:M1**. If you want to map all logins on **pluto** to identical logins on your machine, you would enter

```
idadmin -S cr2 -a -l %1 -r "pluto:*"
```

In this example, user **bob** on the remote system would be mapped to **bob** on the local system; **johnd** on the remote system would be mapped to **johnd**, and so on.

In the next example, assume you want to map all logins on remote system **mars** to identical logins on your system, with the exception of the remote login **guest**. Assuming cr1 is the authentication scheme, the map must contain the following pair of entries:

```
guest@mars %i
*@mars %1
```

To add the entries to the map, first enter

```
idadmin -S cr1 -a -l %i -r guest@mars
```

Then enter

```
idadmin -S cr1 -a -l %1 -r "*@mars"
```

These entries could have been added in reverse order. The **idadmin** command ensures that the most specific entry appears first in the file. If you enter **%i** in place of *logname* on the **idadmin** command line, the remote user specified by the **-r** would be rejected.

Other characters can appear in a field containing an asterisk. For example, all remote system names beginning with **ux** will match the pattern **ux***. The following command adds transparent mapping for all users on machines with names being with **ux**.

```
idadmin -S cr1 -a -l %1 -r "*@ux*"
```

In addition, to exclude all **guest** users on these remote systems, enter

```
idadmin -S cr1 -a -l %i -r "guest@ux*"
```

The contents of an **idata** file with these four entries would be

```
M1@M2
guest@mars %i
*@mars %1
guest@ux* %i
*@ux* %1
```

When an **idata** file is searched for a global name, it is scanned sequentially. Therefore the ordering of global names in this file is critical.

Global names are sorted on the highest numbered field first. Entries with explicit values in this field appear first in the file. Entries with regular expressions in this field appear next and are sorted from most specific to least specific. For example, the remote system name **ux*** is more specific than the remote system name **u*** and therefore would appear first in the file.

If two or more entries are equally specific, the specificity of the next lower numbered field is examined. Fields are examined from highest to lowest until the global names can be differentiated.

Remote IDs should not be mapped to **uucp**. Instead, they should be mapped to **nuucp** or some other login used exclusively for data transfer.

Deleting an Entry in an idata File

To delete an entry in **idata**, enter **idadmin** with the following syntax:

idadmin -S *scheme* **-d -l** *logname* **[-r** *g_name***]**

where *scheme* is the name of the ID mapping scheme, *g_name* is the global name of the remote user, and *logname* is the local login.

The use of **-r** is optional. If you enter the command without the **-r** option, every entry associated with the local login is deleted. If **g_name** is specified with the **-r** option, only the entry that maps the specified remote user to the specified local login is deleted.

For example, to delete all entries in **/etc/idmap/cr1/idata** that map remote users to the local login **guest**, you would enter

```
idadmin -S cr1 -d -l guest
```

Deleting the idata and uidata Files

To delete the **idata** and **uidata** files (removing a *scheme*), enter the **idadmin** with the syntax

idadmin -S *scheme* **-D**

where *scheme* is the name of the ID Mapping scheme to be deleted. This command removes the following files:

```
/etc/idmap/cr1/idata
/etc/idmap/cr1/uidata
```

Checking Files and Fixing File Inconsistencies

Periodically you should run a check on the **idata** files and correct any problems that might exist. The **idadmin** command provides options that allow you to check a file, correct entries with syntax errors, sort entries that are out of order, and delete entries for unknown local logins.

Deleting an entry does not necessarily invalidate the remote user login. The remote login might be matched by a regular expression in another entry further down in the file. To insure that the remote login is invalidated, change the local name to **%i**.

If you use the ID Mapping commands to update the mapping databases, inconsistencies will occur only if the ID Mapping files get out of sync with the password file.

To check the consistency of the file, enter the **idadmin** command with the **-c** option, as follows:

idadmin -S *scheme* **-c**

where *scheme* is the name of the ID Mapping scheme.

The report generated by the **idadmin -c** is shown in Figure 2-20.

Figure 2-20: Sample Output from `idadmin -c`

```
Error on line number 2: Mandatory field missing
Error on line number 4: Duplicate entry
Error on line number 5: Line out of order
Error on line number 7: Mandatory field missing
Error on line number 8: Line out of order
Error on line number 9: Line out of order
Error on line number 10: Bad transparent mapping
Error on line number 15: Line out of order
Error on line number 18: Unknown mapped user
9 error(s) was (were) found in system map
```

To correct problems (such as the ones shown above) in the file, enter the command with the **-f** option, as in the following syntax line:

> **idadmin -S** *scheme* **-f**

When **-f** is entered, the command gives you the option to delete, skip, or change invalid entries. It also sorts entries in the file that are out of order. By entering the **idadmin** command with the **-c** option again will allow you to verify that all changes were made correctly.

Displaying Information

idadmin can be used to display information about the **idata** files on the system, or about the entries in a particular **idata** file. When used to display information, the command has the following syntax:

> **idadmin [-S** *scheme* **[-l** *logname***]]**

where *scheme* is the name of the ID Mapping scheme, and *logname* is a local login.

If **idadmin** is entered without options, it displays the names of all the ID Mapping schemes on the system.

If you enter **idadmin** with a scheme name only, the command displays the scheme's **idata** file. If you enter **idadmin** with a scheme name and a local login, the command displays all the entries that map to that particular login.

Administering a uidata File

Like an **idata** file, a **uidata** file maps remote user logins to local logins; however, entries in a **uidata** file are specified by users themselves, not the system administrator.

A sample **uidata** file is shown in Figure 2-21.

Figure 2-21: Sample `uidata` File

```
!M1@M2
joe@ulysses jfl
mike@alpha mickey
mike@beta mickey
```

NOTE Unlike **idata**, the administrator-controlled login map file, **uidata**, cannot be used to set up transparent mapping; the use of regular expressions in **uidata** entries is not permitted.

When you enable user-controlled mapping, a user with logins on both a remote system and the local system can access the local system and make an entry in **uidata** that maps his or her remote login to a local login. By enabling user-controlled mapping and instructing users to update the database, an administrator can distribute the workload and minimize the administrative overhead. For more information about user-controlled mapping, see ''Enabling and Disabling User-Controlled Mapping''.

The **uidadmin** command is the command interface to **uidata**. When entered by a user, assuming user-controlled mapping is enabled, the non-privileged user can do the following:

- add and delete his or her entries
- display his or her entries.

An administrator can use the **uidadmin** command to

- display all the entries in a **uidata** file
- check the consistency of file entries and fix inconsistencies
- add or delete an entry on behalf of a non-privileged user

The administrator of user-controlled mapping must be in group **sys**. This is required whether or not the Enhanced Security Utilities are installed and running.

The **uidadmin** command has the following syntax:

uidadmin [-S *scheme* **[-l** *logname***]]**
uidadmin -S *scheme* **-a [-l** *logname***] -r** *g_name*
uidadmin -S *scheme* **-d -l** *logname* **[-r** *g_name***]**
uidadmin -S *scheme* **[-cf]**

See **uidadmin**(1) for an explanation of the options accepted by the **uidadmin** command.

The options and command syntax required to execute a particular operation are described in the following sections.

Setting Up the uidata File

A **uidata** file is set up for a particular authentication scheme when you set up the scheme's **idata** file, using the **idadmin** command. For example, to set up an **idata** file for **cr1**, you enter the following:

```
idadmin -S cr1 -I M1@M2
```

When the command executes, a **uidata** file is created in **/etc/idmap/cr1**, along with an **idata** file; however, users cannot add entries to the file, nor will the name mapping function attempt to read the file, until user-controlled mapping is enabled, as described in the following section.

Enabling and Disabling User-Controlled Mapping

When user-controlled mapping is disabled, every time a remote user attempts to access the local system, an internal routine searches the appropriate **idata** file for a map entry for that user. When user-controlled mapping is enabled, the **uidata** file is searched first. Because any entry in **uidata** relevant to the remote user is found before an entry in **idata**, the entry in **uidata** takes precedence over the **idata** entry. In this way, the user-specified mapping overrides an administrator-specified mapping for that user. When user-controlled mapping is disabled, **uidata** is not searched at all.

Whenever maps for a new ID Mapping scheme are set up, user-controlled mapping is disabled. Before enabling user-controlled mapping, create local logins for your remote users.

To enable user-controlled mapping for a particular authentication scheme, you enter **idadmin** with the **-u** option, as in the following syntax line:

```
idadmin -S scheme -u
```

where *scheme* is the name of the ID Mapping scheme. This command activates the **USER** mode of the authentication scheme.

To disable user-controlled mapping, you enter **idadmin** with the **-s** option, as in the following line:

```
idadmin -S scheme -s
```

This command activates the **SECURE** mode of the authentication scheme. When **idadmin** is entered without options, it lists all schemes and indicates whether each is in **USER** or **SECURE** mode. A scheme in **SECURE** mode has user-controlled mapping disabled.

Adding an Entry to a uidata File

When user-controlled mapping is enabled, non-privileged users with logins on the local system can map their own logins on a remote system to their own local logins. A non-privileged user cannot add entries for other users.

When used to add an entry to a **uidata** file, the **uidadmin** command has the syntax

```
uidadmin -S scheme -a [-l logname] -r g_name
```

where *scheme* is the name of the ID mapping scheme, *g_name* is a global name that includes the remote login, and *logname* is the local login. A non-privileged user is permitted to map a remote login only to his or her local login; if the **-l** option is omitted, the user's local login is assumed.

If the administrator enters the **uidadmin** command to add an entry on behalf of a non-privileged user, the **-l** option is required.

In the following example, a user named Mike has logins on two systems. His login on a machine called **wizard** is **michael**; his login on a machine called **zooey** is **mike**. Mike wants to map his login on **wizard** to his login on **zooey**. The service he wants to access on **zooey** is associated with the **cr1** authentication scheme. To set up mapping from **wizard** to **zooey**, Mike would access **zooey** and enter the following command:

```
uidadmin -S cr1 -a -r michael@wizard
```

Deleting an Entry in a uidata File

When user-controlled mapping is enabled, any non-privileged user may choose to delete an entry mapping his or her login; however, a non-privileged user cannot delete entries made by another user.

If a user also has a map entry in the administrator-controlled **idata** file, he or she will be mapped to the login specified in that entry once the **uidata** entry has been deleted.

When used to delete an entry, the **uidadmin** command has the following syntax:

uidadmin -S *scheme* **-d -l** *logname* **[-r** *g_name***]**

where *scheme* is the name of the ID Mapping scheme, and *logname* is the local login.

The use of *g_name* is optional. If *g_name* is omitted, every entry that maps a remote login to the specified local login is deleted from the **uidata** file. If *g_name* is specified, only the entry that maps that global name to the local login is deleted.

If user Mike wants to delete the entry that maps his login **michael** on **wizard** to **mike** on **zooey**, he would enter the following:

```
uidadmin -S cr1 -d -l mike -r michael@wizard
```

Checking Files and Fixing File Inconsistencies

Because there is no need for your users to edit the **uidadmin** file directly, there is little danger that the file will become cluttered with entries containing syntax errors; however, you should run a check on the file periodically and correct any problems that might exist. The **uidadmin** command provides options that allow an administrator to check the file, correct entries with syntax errors, and delete entries that map to unknown logins.

To check the consistency of the file, enter **uidadmin** with the following options:

uidadmin -S *scheme* **-c**

where *scheme* is the name of the ID Mapping scheme.

To correct the problems in the file, enter the command with the following options:

uidadmin -S *scheme* **-f**

When the **-f** option is entered, **uidadmin** gives you the opportunity to replace entries that contain syntax errors and to delete entries associated with logins that do not exist in **/etc/passwd**. It then sorts entries that are out of order. Entering **uidadmin** with the **-c** option again will verify that all changes were done correctly.

Displaying Information

uidata file, displaying information Both the system administrator and a non-privileged user may use the **uidadmin** command to display information. When used to display information, the command has the following syntax:

uidadmin [-S *scheme* **[-l** *logname***]]**

where *scheme* is the name of the ID Mapping scheme, and *logname* is a local login.

If **uidadmin** is entered without options, it displays the names of all the ID Mapping schemes on the system. If an administrator enters **uidadmin** with a scheme name only, the command displays the **uidadmin** file associated with the specified scheme. If the administrator enters **uidadmin** with a scheme name and a local login, the command displays all entries that map remote logins to the specified local login.

If a non-privileged user enters **uidadmin** with only a scheme name, the command displays only the entries in **uidata** associated with his or her local login.

Setting Up Attribute Maps

Attribute map files map the values of user attributes on a remote system to attribute values on the local system. Most likely, an authentication scheme that maps user attributes will map such attributes as UID and GID.

Attribute maps are created in the **/etc/idmap/attrmap** directory. Generally, you'll name each file for the attribute it maps.

The names of the attribute map files must match the name used in the authentication scheme. If your system supports an application that uses attribute mapping, check the documentation that accompanies the scheme software to determine the names you should give the map files.

An example of a GID map is shown in Figure 2-22.

Figure 2-22: Example of a GID Map

```
M1:M2
10:sysA 20
1:sysB 1
```

Each entry in the map file maps one value to another. Note that the first entry in the sample file maps the GID value of 10 to the value of 20 on the local system. With this entry in the file, any user with GID 10 on a remote system who accesses a service on the local system remotely is mapped to GID 20 on the local system.

Attribute maps support transparent mapping. By using regular expressions when specifying attribute values, an administrator can set up transparent mapping such that a number of attribute values on the remote system are mapped with a single file entry. Transparent mapping is described in detail in "Adding an Entry to an Attribute Map".

The **attradmin** command is the command interface to the attribute maps. It allows a privileged user to do the following:

- create and delete an attribute map file
- add and delete map entries in a file
- display file contents
- check the consistency of file entries and fix inconsistencies

The **attradmin** command has the following syntax:

attradmin [**-A** *attrname* [**-l** *localval*]]
attradmin -A *attrname* **-a -l** *localval* **-r** *remoteval*
attradmin -A *attrname* **-d -l** *localval* [**-r** *remoteval*]
attradmin -A *attrname* **-I** *descr*
attradmin -A *attrname* [**-Dcf**]

See **attradmin**(1M) for an explanation of the options accepted by the **attradmin** command.

The options and command syntax required to execute a particular operation are described in the following sections.

Setting Up an Attribute Map

If you want to set up an attribute map file, you must enter the **attradmin** command with the attribute map filename and specify the format the remote value should take in all map entries.

When the **attradmin** command is used to set up a new file, it has the following syntax:

attradmin -A *attrname* **-I** *descr*

where *attrname* is the name of the attribute, and *descr* is a string called a format descriptor. The format descriptor specifies the format in which the remote attribute value must be entered when a map entry is created.

If you're using cr1 as your authentication scheme, the format descriptor you need to enter is **M1@M2**.

At this time, the cr1 authentication scheme is the only authentication scheme provided with System V—with the exception of the traditional login/password scheme, which doesn't rely on ID Mapping. Unless otherwise stated, examples throughout the discussion of ID Mapping assume cr1 as the authentication scheme.

Field numbers indicate the order of significance of the fields. Higher numbered fields are the more significant. **M2** in the descriptor **M1@M2** means that the second field contains an entity of greater significance on the network than does the first field. The letter **M** indicates that the fields are required. The **@** symbol is a field separator. For example, given the format descriptor **M1@M2**, UID 104 on the remote system **venus** would be specified as **104@venus**.

To set up a map file that maps UIDs on remote systems to UIDs on the local system, you might enter the following command line:

```
attradmin -A uid -I M1@M2
```

Once the command executes, the file **uid.map** appears in **/etc/idmap/attrmap**, and the format descriptor appears in the first line of the file.

Adding an Entry to an Attribute Map

To add an entry that maps a remote attribute value to a local value, you enter **attradmin** with the syntax

attradmin -A *attrname* **-a -l** *localval* **-r** *remoteval*

where *attrname* is the name of the attribute, *remoteval* is the combination of an attribute value on the remote system and the remote system name, and *localval* is the attribute value on the local system. For example, the following command line maps GID 10 on the remote system **moon** to a GID 20 on the local system:

```
attradmin -A gid -a -l 20 -r 10@moon
```

Once the command executes, any user with a GID of 10 on **moon** has a GID of 20 on the local system.

You can set up transparent mapping of attributes by using regular expressions in the *remoteval* and special characters in the *localval* field. The characters supported by the **attradmin** command are explained on **attradmin**(1M).

File entries are sorted so an entry that maps a value explicitly is found in a search before entries that implement transparent mapping. Likewise, entries that map values transparently are sorted based on the position of the regular expression in *remote_attr*. Entries with a regular expression in place of a remote attribute value appear in the file before entries with a regular expression in place of a system name.

The **attradmin** command sorts entries containing regular expressions in *remote_attr* in the same way the **idadmin** command sorts entries containing regular expressions in the global name, with one addition: fields with regular expressions containing brackets, **[ ]**, are considered more specific than fields with an asterisk and therefore will precede fields containing an asterisk. See "Adding an Entry to an idata File".

Examples

The following command line transparently maps all GIDs on the remote system **mars** to GID 10 on the local system.

```
attradmin -A gid -a -l 10 -r "*@mars"
```

To protect characters that are meaningful to the shell, enclose *remoteval* in quotes.

Given the format descriptor **M1@M2**, the following command line maps all UID values on the remote system **mars** to identical values on the local system.

```
attradmin -A uid -a -l %1 -r "*@mars"
```

In this example, UID 101 on **mars** is mapped to UID 101 on the local machine, UID 102 is mapped to UID 102, and so on.

By using a regular expression in place of a remote machine name, you can map values on every machine on the network with access to your system to identical local values. The following command line maps all remote UIDs to the same UIDs on the local system:

```
attradmin -A uid -a -l %1 -r "*@*"
```

Deleting an Entry in an Attribute Map

To delete an entry in an attribute map, enter **attradmin** with the syntax

attradmin -A *attrname* **-d -l** *localval* **[-r** *remoteval***]**

where *attrname* is the name of the attribute, *remoteval* is the combination of an attribute value on the remote system and the remote system name, and *localval* is the attribute value on the local system.

The use of **-r** is optional. It you enter the command without the **-r** option, every entry that maps a value to the specified local value is deleted. If you include the **-r** option, only the entry that maps the specified remote value to the specified local value is deleted.

To delete an entry that maps GID 10 on a remote system **moon** to GID 20 on the local system, you might enter the following command line:

```
attradmin -A gid -d -l 20 -r 10@moon
```

Deleting an entry does not necessarily invalidate the remote user login. The remote login might be matched by a regular expression in another entry further down in the file. To insure that the remote login is invalidated, change the local name to `%i`.

Deleting an Attribute Map

To delete an attribute map, enter **attradmin** with the syntax

attradmin -S *attrname* **-D**

where *attrname* is the name of the attribute to be deleted.

Checking Files and Fixing File Inconsistencies

Periodically you should run a check on the attribute map files and correct any problems that might exist. The **attradmin** command provides options that allow you to check a file, correct entries with syntax errors, and sort entries that are out of order.

`attradmin` does not check the validity of the attributes it maps.

To check the consistency of the file, enter **attradmin** with the following syntax:

attradmin -A *attrname* **-c**

where *attrname* is the name of the attribute.

If the file contains errors, the command displays output similar to the output shown in Figure 2-23:

Figure 2-23: Sample Output from `attradmin -A` *attrname* `-c`

```
Error on line number 2: Mandatory field missing
Error on line number 4: Duplicate entry
Error on line number 5: Line out of order
Error on line number 7: Mandatory field missing
Error on line number 8: Line out of order
Error on line number 9: Bad transparent mapping
Error on line number 10: Bad transparent mapping
Error on line number 15: Line out of order
8 error(s) found in attribute map
```

To correct the problems in the file, enter the command with the `-f` option, as in the following syntax line:

`attradmin -A` *attrname* **`-f`**

When the `-f` option is entered, **`attradmin`** gives you the opportunity to replace entries that contain syntax errors. It then sorts entries that are out of order.

Entering **`attradmin`** with the `-c` option again will verify that all errors were fixed correctly.

Displaying Information

`attradmin` can be used to display information about all the attribute map files on the system, as well as the contents of a specific map file.

When used to display information, **`attradmin`** has the following syntax:

`attradmin` `[-A` *attrname* `[-l` *localval*`]]`

If **`attradmin`** is entered without options, it displays the names of the attribute map files on the system.

If you enter **`attradmin`** with an attribute map filename only, it displays the contents of the file. If you enter **`attradmin`** with an attribute map filename and a local attribute value, the command displays all file entries that map the values of the specified remote attribute to the specified local value.

Basic Networking Utilities

The Basic Networking Utilities package (BNU) allows any computer running the UNIX operating system to communicate with any other computer that supports the Basic Networking Utilities. This includes non-UNIX systems as well as systems running any release of the UNIX operating system. The Basic Networking Utilities range from programs used to copy files between computers (**uucp** and **uuto**) to routines used for remote login and command execution (**cu**, **ct**, and **uux**).

Most tasks associated with Basic Networking Utilities administration may be performed using either the menu system or shell commands entered on the command line. The screen below shows the top-level BNU menu. It can be brought up on the screen by typing **sysadm basic_networking**.

Figure 2-24: The Basic Networking Utilities Management Menu

```
          Basic Networking Utilities Management

devices - Adding, Listing, and Removing Networking Devices
polling - Adding, Listing, and Removing Systems to Be Polled
systems - Adding, Listing, and Removing Remote Systems
```

When you have selected the option you want, self-explanatory submenus and instructions are displayed on the screen to lead you through the appropriate procedures.

Overview of BNU

What BNU Does

The following is a general description of the BNU process. The component parts of this process are described either later in this chapter or in the places indicated. The phases are marked on the diagram that follows.

Phase A — A user on the local machine issues a command requesting file transfer or remote execution communication with a remote computer (phase **A**). Several BNU database support files are read to determine if the remote computer is accessible by the local computer and the priority of the user's request compared to other users' requests. This phase ends by queuing the user's request in a spool area on the local machine and triggering the next phase.

Phase B — The **uucico** routine is triggered automatically (phase **B**). It reads several BNU database support files to determine when the remote computer can be reached, how to establish the link to the remote computer, how to handle data flow between the local and remote computers, and the maximum number of simultaneous requests for communication to the remote computer.

Phase B′ — The **uucico** routine calls the connection routine, **dial** [see **dial**(3N)], and passes the request and associated information to the server.

Phases C and C′ — The **uucico** routine on the remote computer is triggered automatically when a call for communication is received from the local computer (phase **C**). In this phase, the remote **uucico** routine reads BNU database support files on its computer to determine if the calling computer is allowed access, and what action to take if the calling computer is not allowed access (phase **C'**). For calling computers that are allowed access to the remote computer, the level of access is determined in this phase.

Phase D — Requests initiated on the local computer may contain commands to be executed on the remote computer (phase **D**). When these commands arrive on the remote computer, they are stored in a spool area. During this phase, the remote **uuxqt** routine runs these commands on the remote computer.

Figure 2-25: Basic Networking Process Diagram

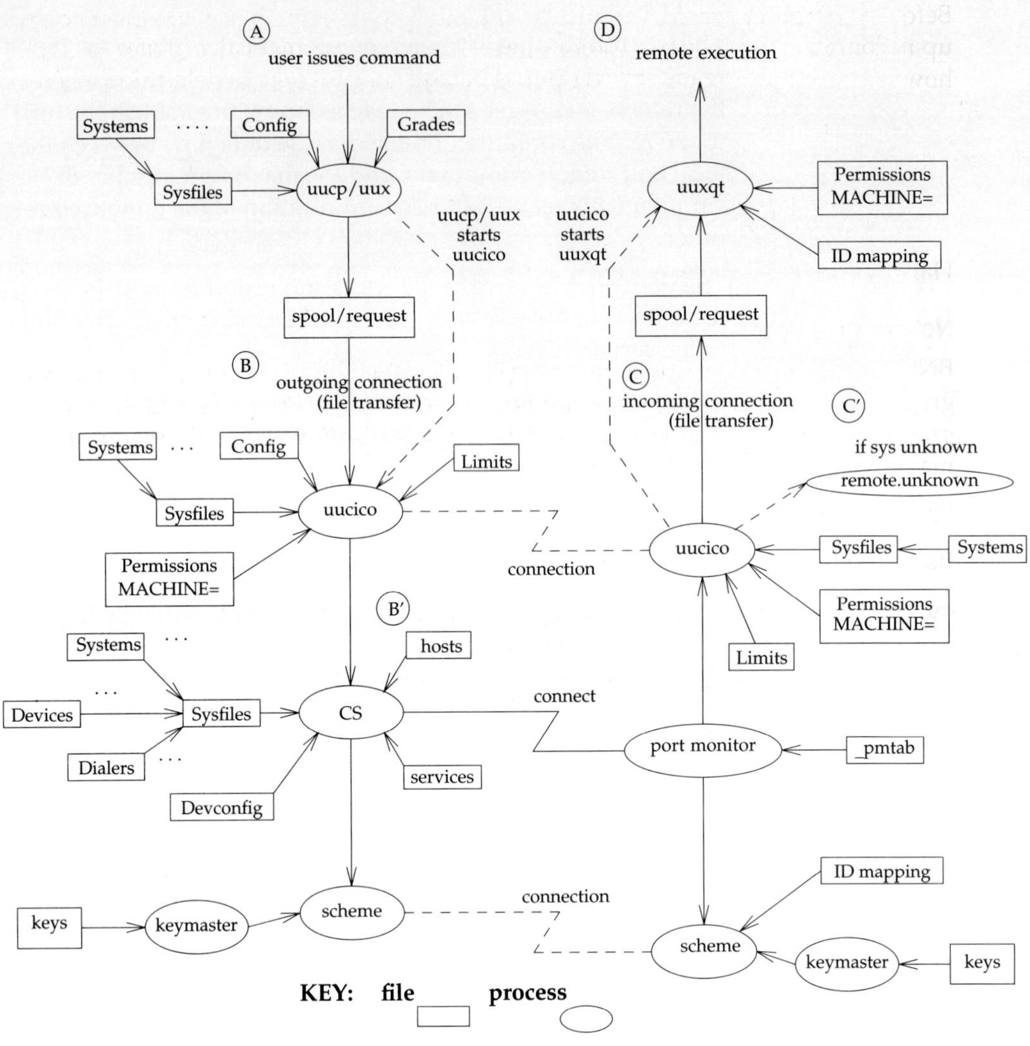

BNU Components

Networking Hardware

Before a computer can communicate with other computers, hardware must be set up to complete the communications link. The hardware needed will depend on how you want to connect the computers. Computers may be connected using

- direct links
- telephone lines
- local area networks

Hardware installation is not the subject of this chapter.

Networking Programs

BNU is made up of programs and support files. BNU programs include user programs, administrative programs, and daemons. These three types of BNU programs are described in this section. They are described briefly with pointers to the manual pages that describe them in detail.

BNU support files are described in detail in the next section.

User Programs The Basic Networking Utilities user programs are:

`cu` — Calls another UNIX system, a terminal, or possibly a non-UNIX system and manages an interactive conversation with possible transfers of files. See **cu**(1C) for more information.

`ct` — Dials the telephone number of a modem that is attached to a terminal and spawns a login process to that terminal. See **ct**(1C) for more information.

`uucp` — Copies files from a local UNIX machine to a destination either on the same machine or on a remote UNIX machine. **uucp** may also be used to copy files from a remote computer to another remote computer, to copy files from one location to another on a given remote computer, and to copy files from a remote computer to a local computer. Some remote copies will be restricted by the administrator of the remote machine. See **uucp**(1C) for more information.

`uuto` — Uses the **uucp** facility to send files to *PUBDIR* on another system. See **uuto**(1C) for more information.

`uupick` — Accepts or rejects files transmitted to a user. Specifically, **uupick** searches *PUBDIR* for files destined for the user. **uupick** is described on **uuto**(1C).

uux Gathers files from various systems, executes a command on a named system and then sends the output to a file on another named system. See **uux**(1C) for more information.

uustat Displays the status of, or cancels, previously specified **uucp** commands; provides remote system performance information; and provides remote status of **uucp** connections to other systems. See **uustat**(1C) for more information.

uulog Queries log files of **uucp** and **uuxqt** transactions. **uuxqt** is also described in "Networking Daemons". **uulog** is described on **uucp**(1C).

uuglist Prints the list of service grades available on a system for use with the **-g** option of **uucp** and **uux**. See **uuglist**(1C) for more information.

uuname Lists the names of systems known to **uucp**. **uuname** is described on **uucp**(1C).

uuencode Converts a binary file into an ASCII-encoded file that can be transmitted using **mail** [see **mail**(1)]. See **uuencode**(1C) for more information.

uudecode Reads an encoded file, strips off any leading and trailing lines added by mailer programs, and recreates the original binary data. See **uuencode**(1C) for more information.

The BNU user programs are located in **/usr/bin**. The BNU user programs are described in their respective manual pages. No special permissions are needed to use these programs.

Administrative Programs The Basic Networking Utilities include the following three administrative programs:

uucheck Checks for the presence of the **uucp** system-required files and directories. **uucheck** also checks the **/etc/uucp/Permissions** file for errors. See **uucheck**(1M) for more information.

uucleanup Scans the spool directories for old files and removes them. The default values for file aging can be changed by command line options. An option also exists to restrict **uucleanup**'s action to the **system** spool directory. See **uucleanup**(1M) for more information.

Uutry **Uutry** is a shell used to invoke **uucico** when calling a remote site. Debugging is initially turned on and the debugging output is put in a file. See **Uutry**(1M) for more information.

The BNU administrative programs are in **/usr/lib/uucp**, along with Basic Networking shell scripts. All Basic Networking Utilities administrative commands are fully described in their respective manual pages.

Since **uucp** owns the Basic Networking and spooled data files, the **uucp** login ID should be used only for BNU administration. The home directory for the **uucp** login is **/usr/lib/uucp**. Another Basic Networking login ID, **nuucp**, is used by remote computers to access the local machine. Calls to **nuucp** are answered by **uucico**.

Networking Daemons The Basic Networking Utilities package includes three daemons. A daemon is a standing server or a routine that runs as a background process and performs system-wide public functions. The BNU daemons handle both file transfers and command execution. They may be invoked from the shell.

uucico Checks permissions, transfers files (if requested), logs results, and notifies the user (by **mail**) of transfer completion. When the local **uucico** daemon calls a remote computer, it invokes the **dial** routine [see **dial**(3N)], which then obtains authenticated connections from the Connection Server.

uucico is executed by the **uucp**, **uuto**, and **uux** programs, after all the required files have been created, to contact the remote computer. It is also executed by **uusched** and **Uutry**. See **uucico**(1M) for more information.

uuxqt Executes remote execution requests. **uuxqt** searches the spool directory for execute files (always named **X.***file*) that have been sent from a remote computer. When an execute file is found, **uuxqt** opens it to get the list of data files required for the execution. It then checks to see if the required data files are available and accessible. If the files are present and can be accessed, **uuxqt** checks the **Permissions** file to verify that it has permission to execute the requested command. **uuxqt** is executed by the **uudemon.hour** shell script, which is started by **cron**. See **uuxqt**(1M) for more information.

uusched Schedules the queued work in the spool directory. Before starting **uucico**, **uusched** randomizes the order in which remote computers will be called. **uusched** is executed by the shell script **uudemon.hour**, which is started by **cron**. See **uusched**(1M) for more information.

The remote.unknown File The **remote.unknown** file is a binary program that executes when a machine not found in any of the **Systems** files starts a conversation. It will log the conversation attempt and drop the connection. Its function is similar to that of a daemon.

If you change the permissions of the `remote.unknown` file so it cannot execute, your system will accept connections from any system.

Networking Support Files

There are three types of BNU support files: database files, administrative files, and log files.

- Database Files BNU database files are located in `/etc/uucp`. They are responsible for much of the actual networking activity associated with the Basic Networking Utilities package. In general, they determine which computers your computer will communicate with, the devices over which the communication will take place, and the protocols for communicating with remote computers.

BNU database support files used with previous releases of the UNIX operating system are compatible with the current release and may be used without alteration.

The following list describes each of the database support files and its function briefly. These files are described in detail in the "Database Support Files" section below.

`Config` Contains a list of variable parameters within BNU. The administrator can set these parameters to configure the network manually.

`Devconfig` This file is used to configure network connections on TCP/IP or some other network provider.

`Devices` Contains information concerning the location and line speed of automatic call units, direct links, and network devices.

`Dialcodes` Contains dial-code abbreviations that may be used in the *telephone number* field of the **`Systems`** and **`Dialers`** files.

`Dialers` Contains character strings required to communicate with network devices, automatic calling units, and direct links.

`Grades` Used to define the job grades, and the permissions associated with each job grade, that users may specify to queue jobs to a remote computer.

Limits Defines the maximum number of simultaneous **uucico**s, **uuxqt**s, and **uusched**s permitted on a machine.

Permissions Defines the levels of access granted to remote computers when they attempt to transfer files or execute remote commands on the local computer.

Poll Defines computers that are to be polled by the local system and when they are polled.

Sysfiles Assigns different or multiple files to be used as **Systems**, **Devices**, and **Dialers** files by various services (such as **uucico** and **cu**).

Systems Contains information needed by the **uucico** daemon and the **cu** program to establish a link to a remote system such as the name of the remote system, the name of the connecting device associated with the remote system, when the system can be reached, a telephone number or network address, login ID, and password.

The **Systems** file is also used by the client machine to verify that the client is allowed to connect to the server and by the server machine to verify that the server may accept calls from the client.

- Administrative Files BNU administrative files are created in spool directories by network processes to hold temporary data or store information about remote transfers and command executions. They are described in detail in "Administrative Support Files".
- Log Files BNU log files keep track of overall statistics for the computer network, particularly in the areas of security and accounting. The structure of each of the BNU log files is described in "Log Files".

BNU Administration

This section outlines the steps a system administrator must take before using the Basic Networking Utilities and indicates where to find the information required to administer BNU once it has been set up.

NOTE BNU database support files used with previous releases of the UNIX operating system are compatible with the current release and may be used without alteration.

Briefly, BNU administration involves the following procedures:

Setup — BNU setup is described in detail in the "BNU Setup Procedures".

Maintenance — Basic Networking Utilities maintenance involves updating BNU database support files when necessary, tracking BNU transactions, and cleaning up BNU administrative and log files. BNU Maintenance is discussed in "BNU Maintenance".

Debugging — BNU debugging procedures help identify and correct common problems in BNU operation and administration. BNU debugging procedures are discussed in "BNU Debugging".

BNU Setup Procedures

This section describes the steps in the BNU setup procedure. These steps fall into three groups:

- The steps required in every case; see section **(1)**, below.
- The additional steps required if you are using the new CS dialer type (the Connection Server); see sections **(2a)** and **(2b)**, below.
- The additional steps required if you are *not* using the new CS dialer type; see sections **(3a)** and **(3b)**, below.

BNU setup thus always requires the steps in section **(1)** and, in addition, will require the steps in *either* section **(2)** *or* section **(3)**.

Sections **(2)** and **(3)** are divided into client and server machine subsections; **(2a)** and **(3a)** describe client machine administration and **(2b)** and **(3b)** describe server machine administration. Each subsection presents essential steps first, followed by optional or conditional steps.

(1) For All Types of Connection

- To use BNU, you must set up the necessary BNU database support files. This is true whether you are using the Connection Server or not. The following database files must be modified for your system or you must determine that the delivered default files are appropriate. If these files exist and were used on your system with a previous release, you may use the existing files without alteration.

- □ **Sysfiles**
- □ **Systems**
- □ **Devices**
- □ **Dialers**
- □ **Devconfig**
- □ **Config**

There can be multiple **Systems**, **Devices**, and **Dialers** files registered in the **Sysfiles** file.

(2a) For Connections That Use the New CS Dialer Type – the Client Machine

Essential Steps

- Set up **hosts** and **services** files. These files are needed to perform the authentication required by the server machine. See "Name-to-Address Mapping" for a description of how to administer the **hosts** and **services** files.

Optional or Conditional Steps

- Set up a **serve.allow** file. Set up an **/etc/iaf/serve.allow** file that includes a line associating an authentication scheme with the **uucico** network service. The **serve.allow** file allows the administrator of the client machine to enforce the use of specific authentication schemes for specific services and machines. The following line from a sample **/etc/iaf/serve.allow** file associates the **cr1** bilateral authentication scheme with the **uucico** network service.

```
# machine   service   scheme

elvis       uucico    cr1
```

Without this entry, any authentication scheme specified by the server will be accepted. This may result in the transmission of sensitive data (passwords) across the network in clear text.

See "The Connection Server" for a description of the **serve.allow** file.

- Specify authentication for **uux**. If you want to use the new features of the **uux** command, specify the authentication you want performed by making the appropriate entries in the **Config** file. For example:

  ```
  AUTH=req KEYS=cr1
  ```

  For the current release, **cr1** key management is the only key management mechanism available to BNU for use in authenticating remote execution requests.

  BNU uses the **KEYS=** and **AUTH=** values in the **Config** or **Permissions** files. If **uux** can obtain a key for the user, it spools a request including all the necessary authentication information. If it cannot obtain a key and the value of **AUTH** is **opt** or **no**, it spools the request without authentication information. Otherwise, the request fails.

- Perform **cr1** key administration. If you are using **cr1** as your authentication scheme or for **uux** key management, you must perform **cr1** key administration. See "cr1 Bilateral Authentication Scheme".

(2b) For Connections That Use the New CS Dialer Type – the Server Machine

Essential Steps

- Register services. Set up the **_pmtab** files for port monitors that expect requests for network services. The **_pmtab** files are administered using the **pmadm** [see **pmadm**(1M)] command. Two services in particular must be registered on the server machine: **uucico** and **reportscheme**. See "Managing Ports" in *Advanced System Administration* for a description of registering services and "The Connection Server" in this chapter for a description of the **reportscheme service**.

- Register **uucico** services. A system that expects to be a server in BNU transactions must register a **uucico** service for each port monitor that receives BNU service requests. Each **uucico** service registered should include an authentication scheme name in the *scheme* field of the port monitor administrative file for the port.

  The **uucico** service is added using the **pmadm** command. **pmadm** is described in detail in "Managing Ports" in *Advanced System Administration* and on **pmadm**(1M). The following **pmadm** command adds a line for **uucico** to the port monitor's **_pmtab** file. In this case, the port monitor is **tcp**.

```
pmadm -a -p tcp -s uucico -m "`nlsadmin -c \"/usr/lib/uucp/uucico -r 0 \
-A Addr\"`" -v `nlsadmin -V` -S "cr1 -suucico" -y"uucp"
```

NOTE Replace *Addr* in the example with the address on which the `uucico` service will be offered.

- Register `reportscheme` services. Add a `reportscheme` service entry to the appropriate port monitor administrative files for each transport on which you want to support BNU. See "The Connection Server" and `reportscheme`(1M) for a description of the `reportscheme` service.

Optional or Conditional Steps

- Perform `cr1` key administration. If you are using the `cr1` authentication scheme, you must perform `cr1` key administration. See "cr1 Bilateral Authentication Scheme".
- Perform ID mapping. See "ID Mapping".

NOTE Remote IDs should not be mapped to `uucp`. Instead, they should be mapped to `nuucp` or some other login used exclusively for data transfer.

- Specify authentication for `uux`. If you want to use the new features of the `uux` command, specify the authentication you want performed by making the appropriate entries in the `Config` file. For example,

  ```
  AUTH=req KEYS=cr1
  ```

  For the current release, the `cr1` authentication scheme is the only scheme available to BNU for authenticating remote command execution.

  BNU looks for the `KEYS` entry in the `Config` file, then gets the key for the user from `cr1`. If `KEYS` has no assigned value, or if `uux` fails to get a key and `AUTH=yes` or `AUTH=req`, `uux` will fail. Otherwise `uux` will proceed without the key, although the results on the remote system may not be the same.

(3a) For Connections That Do Not Use the CS Dialer Type – the Client Machine

Optional or Conditional Steps

- Include an *invoke-scheme* Pair. Include an *invoke-scheme* pair in the appropriate **Systems** or **Dialers** file entry. For example:

```
#Systems file
#
sysa Any DK speed sysa INVOKE "cr1 -r"
sysb Any DKcr1 speed sysb
```

```
#Devices file
#
DK term/11 - Any datakit \D
DKcr1 term/11 - Any datakitcr1 \D
```

```
#Dialers file
#
datakit ""         "" \d TION:--TION: \D
datakitcr1 ""      "" \d TION:--TION: \D INVOKE "cr1 -r"
```

  Whether calling **sysa** or **sysb**, a Datakit® VCS connection will be made and the **cr1** authentication scheme will be invoked in the responder role. See "The Dialers File" and "The Systems File" below for field definitions.

- Specify authentication for **uuxqt**. If you want to allow the use of the new features of the **uux** facility, you must perform this step. For the current release, **cr1** key management is the only key management scheme available to BNU for use in authenticating remote execution requests.

  BNU uses the **KEY=** and **AUTH=** values in the **Config** or **Permissions** files. If **uuxqt** can obtain and successfully decode the authentication information supplied with a request, the request is executed *as the mapped user*. (See "ID Mapping".) If no authentication information is supplied and the value of **AUTH** is **opt** or **no**, **uuxqt** will execute the request as it did in previous releases. If either the decoding of authentication information fails or no authentication was attempted, and the value of **AUTH** is **req** or **yes**, the request will be rejected.

- Perform **cr1** key administration. If you are using the **cr1** authentication scheme, you must perform **cr1** key administration. See "cr1 Bilateral Authentication Scheme".

(3b) For Connections That Do Not Use the CS Dialer Type – the Server Machine

Optional or Conditional Steps

- Register **uucico** services. A system that expects to be a server in BNU transactions must register a **uucico** service for each port monitor that receives BNU service requests. Each **uucico** service registered should include an authentication scheme name in the *scheme* field of the port monitor administrative file for the port.

  The **uucico** service is added using the **pmadm** command. **pmadm** is described in detail in "Managing Ports" in *Advanced System Administration* and on **pmadm**(1M). The following **pmadm** command adds a line for **uucico** to the port monitor's **_pmtab** file. In this case, the port monitor is **tcp**.

```
pmadm -a -p tcp -s uucico -m "`nlsadmin -c \"/usr/lib/uucp/uucico -r 0 \
-A Addr\"`" -v `nlsadmin -V` -S "cr1 -suucico" -y"uucp"
```

  In the example above, replace *Addr* with the address on which the **uucico** service will be offered.

NOTE When using cr1 on serial connections, you should configure the port to start on carrier (that is, -c). This is necessary because the responder sends no data until the imposer indicates it is ready to start the protocol. For this reason, autobaud will not work on parts protected by cr1.

Database Support Files

Setting up the Basic Networking Utilities involves configuring the database support files. This section describes these files and their structure in detail. Some of the database support files are delivered with the system. In some cases these default files can be used without modification. In other cases they cannot. Each of the file descriptions below indicates whether the default file may be used and, if not, what changes must be made. BNU support files are in the **/etc/uucp** directory.

BNU database support files used with previous releases of the UNIX operating system are compatible with the current release and may be used without alteration.

Wherever possible, changes to the database support files should be made by using the system administration menus (accessed through the **sysadm** command). The BNU setup procedure provides the steps for initializing the BNU database files. This procedure uses the **sysadm** subcommands and a text editor.

Begin by typing **sysadm basic_networking**. This will give you the starting menu. From this point, you can begin setting up (initializing) the various database files. To get help along the way, press the HELP function key. This will give you a detailed description of a menu selection. Pressing the CANCEL function key exits help mode.

Setting up the **Permissions**, **Devconfig**, **Sysfiles** and **Limits** files, and adding **uucp** logins are principal functions in the initial Basic Networking setup process.

The permissions on networking devices should be 0600, with the owner set to **root**.

The Permissions File

A default **/etc/uucp/Permissions** file is delivered with the system and contains the following entry, which provides maximum security:

```
LOGNAME=nuucp
```

/etc/uucp/Permissions specifies the permissions that remote computers have with respect to login, file access, and command execution. There are options that restrict the remote computer's ability to request files and its ability to receive files queued by the local site. Another option is available that specifies the commands that a remote site can execute on the local computer.

Changing this value is discouraged, as it may have an adverse affect on other system utilities.

READ and **WRITE**

These options specify the various parts of the file system that **uucico** can read from or write to. The **READ** and **WRITE** options can be used with either **MACHINE** or **LOGNAME** entries.

The default for both the **READ** and **WRITE** options is the **PUBDIR** directory, which would be equivalent to the following entries:

```
READ=/var/spool/uucppublic
WRITE=/var/spool/uucppublic
```

The strings

```
READ=/ WRITE=/
```

specify permission to access any file that can be accessed by a local user whose access permissions are set to "other."

The value of these entries is a colon separated list of pathnames. The **READ** option is for requesting files, and the **WRITE** option for depositing files. One of the values must be a component of any full pathname of a file coming in or going out. To grant permission to deposit files in **/usr/news** as well as the public directory, the following values would be used with the **WRITE** option:

```
WRITE=/var/spool/uucppublic:/usr/news
```

It should be pointed out that if the **READ** and **WRITE** options are used, all pathnames must be specified because the pathnames are not added to the default list. For instance, if the **/usr/news** pathname was the only one specified in a **WRITE** option, permission to deposit files in the public directory would be denied.

You should be careful what directories you make accessible for reading and writing by remote systems. For example, you probably wouldn't want remote computers to be able to write over your **/etc/passwd** file, so **/etc** shouldn't be open to writes.

NOREAD and **NOWRITE**

The **NOREAD** and **NOWRITE** options specify exceptions to the **READ** and **WRITE** options or defaults. The strings

```
READ=/ NOREAD=/etc WRITE=/var/spool/uucppublic
```

would permit reading any file except those in the **/etc** directory (and its subdirectories—remember, these are prefixes) and writing only to the default **/var/spool/uucppublic** directory. **NOWRITE** works in the same manner as the **NOREAD** option. The **NOREAD** and **NOWRITE** can be used in both **LOGNAME** and **MACHINE** entries.

DIRECT This option specifies whether files that have been received can be placed into a directory into the destination directory. If the value of **DIRECT** is no, files that are received are put into **uucp**'s private spool directory, and then copied to the destination directory. If the value of **DIRECT** is yes, files that are received are directly put into the destination directory. The default value for **DIRECT** is no.

CALLBACK The **CALLBACK** option is used in **LOGNAME** entries to specify that no transaction will take place until the calling system is called back. **CALLBACK** can be used in the following two examples. From a security standpoint, if you call back a machine, you can be fairly certain it is the machine it says it is. If you are doing long data transmissions, you can choose the machine that will be billed for the longer call.

The string

```
CALLBACK=yes
```

specifies that your computer must call the remote computer back before any file transfers will take place.

The default for the **COMMAND** option is

```
CALLBACK=no
```

The **CALLBACK** option is rarely used. Note that if two sites have this option set for each other, a conversation will never get started and no transfers will occur between them.

KEYS The **KEYS=** entry defines the key management facility that obtains keys used in the authentication of remote command execution requests. This option provides an override capability for the global value specified in the **Config** file. At present, **cr1** is the only key management facility available to BNU. There is no default key management facility. To specify the **cr1** key management facility, the string

```
KEYS=cr1
```

must be entered in the **Permissions** file.

CRYPT This option specifies the encryption type to use when authenticating remote execution requests generated by the **uux** command. The default value is **des**. The value **enigma** may be used if the export controlled Encryption Utilities Package is not available. This option provides an override capability for the global value specified in the **Config** file.

AUTH The **AUTH=** entry determines whether authentication is required for remote requests. This option provides an override capability for the global value specified in the **Config** file. If either of the strings

```
AUTH=yes
```

or

```
AUTH=req
```

is included in the **Permissions** file, no remote command request will be accepted without authentication. When authenticated requests are executed, they are executed under the mapped id of the originator and all commands are allowed, that is, the **COMMANDS** value is ignored.

Either of the strings

```
AUTH=opt
```

or

```
AUTH=no
```

indicates that authentication is not required for remote command execution. In this case, commands are executed as in previous releases, limited by the **COMMANDS** value.

If authentication is attempted but *fails*, the request will be rejected, regardless of the value of **AUTH**.

COMMANDS

The **COMMANDS** option can compromise the security of your system. Use it with extreme care.

The **COMMANDS** option is used only for unauthenticated remote command execution requests. See **KEYS** and **AUTH**, above, for use with authenticated remote command execution requests.

The **uux** program will generate remote execution requests and queue them to be transferred to the remote computer. Files and a command are sent to the target computer for remote execution. The **COMMANDS** option can be used in **MACHINE** entries to specify the commands that a remote computer can execute on the local computer. Note that **COMMANDS** is not relevant in a **LOGNAME** entry; **COMMANDS** in **MACHINE** entries define command permissions whether we call the remote system or it calls us.

The string

```
COMMANDS=rmail
```

specifies the default commands that a remote computer can execute on your computer. If a command string is used in a **MACHINE** entry, the default commands are overridden. For instance, the entry

```
MACHINE=owl:raven:hawk:dove \
COMMANDS=rmail:rnews:lp
```

overrides the **COMMANDS** default so that the computers **owl**, **raven**, **hawk**, and **dove** can now execute **rmail**, **rnews**, and **lp** on your computer.

In addition to the names as specified above, there can be full path names of commands. For example,

```
COMMANDS=rmail:/usr/lbin/rnews:/usr/local/lp
```

specifies that the command **rmail** uses the default path. The default path for remote execution is **/usr/bin**. When the remote computer specifies **rnews** or **/usr/lbin/rnews** for the command to be executed, **/usr/lbin/rnews** will be executed regardless of the default path. Likewise, **/usr/local/lp** is the **lp** command that will be executed.

Including the **ALL** value in the list means that any command from the remote computer(s) specified in the entry will be executed. If you use this value, you give the remote computer full access to your computer. Be careful. This allows far more access than normal users have.

The string

```
COMMANDS=/usr/lbin/rnews:ALL:/usr/local/lp
```

illustrates two points:

- The **ALL** value can appear anywhere in the string.

- The pathnames specified for **rnews** and **lp** will be used (instead of the default) if the requested command does not contain the full pathnames for **rnews** or **lp**.

If commands are executed using the authenticated remote execution feature, the **COMMANDS** list is ignored and all commands are available to the authenticated user, as if the user had logged in directly.

The **VALIDATE** option described below should be used with the **COMMANDS** option whenever potentially dangerous commands like **cat** and **uucp** are specified with the **COMMANDS** option. Any command that reads or writes files is potentially dangerous to local security when executed by the **uucp** remote execution daemon (**uuxqt**).

VALIDATE The **VALIDATE** option is used in conjunction with the **COMMANDS** option when specifying commands that are potentially dangerous to your computer's security. It is used to provide a certain degree of verification of the caller's identity. The use of the **VALIDATE** option requires that privileged computers have a unique login/password for **uucp** transactions. An important aspect of this validation is that the login/password associated with this entry be protected. If an outsider gets that information, that particular **VALIDATE** option can no longer be considered secure. **VALIDATE** is merely an added level of security on top of the **COMMANDS** option (though it is a more secure way to open command access than **ALL**).

Careful consideration should be given to providing a remote computer with a privileged login and password for **uucp** transactions. Giving a remote computer a special login and password with file access and remote execution capability is like giving anyone on that computer a normal login and password on your computer. Therefore, if you cannot trust users on the remote computer, do not provide that computer with a privileged login and password.

The **LOGNAME** entry

```
LOGNAME=uucpfriend VALIDATE=eagle:owl:hawk
```

specifies that if one of the remote computers that claims to be eagle, owl, or hawk logs in on your computer, it must have used the login **uucpfriend**. If an outsider gets the **uucpfriend** login/password, masquerading is trivial.

But what does this have to do with the **COMMANDS** option, which only appears in **MACHINE** entries? It links the **MACHINE** entry (and **COMMANDS** option) with a **LOGNAME** entry associated with a privileged login. This link is needed because the execution daemon is not running while the remote computer is logged in. In fact, it is an asynchronous process with no knowledge of what computer sent the execution request. Therefore, the real question is: How does your computer know where the execution files came from?

Each remote computer has its own "spool" directory on your computer. These spool directories have write permission given only to the UUCP family of programs. The execution files from the remote computer are put in its spool directory after being transferred to your computer. When the **uuxqt** daemon runs, it can use the spool directory name to find the **MACHINE** entry in the **Permissions** file and get the **COMMANDS** list, or a default list will be used if the computer name does not appear in the **Permissions** file.

The following example shows the relationship between the **MACHINE** and **LOGNAME** entries:

```
MACHINE=eagle:owl:hawk REQUEST=yes \
COMMANDS=rmail:/usr/lbin/rnews \
READ=/  WRITE=/

LOGNAME=uucpz VALIDATE=eagle:owl:hawk \
REQUEST=yes SENDFILES=yes \
READ=/  WRITE=/
```

The value in the **COMMANDS** option means that remote mail and **/usr/lbin/rnews** can be executed by remote users.

In the first entry, you must make the assumption that when you want to call one of the computers listed, you are really calling either **eagle**, **owl**, or **hawk**. Therefore, any file put into one of the **eagle**, **owl**, or **hawk** spool directories is put there by one of those computers. If a remote computer logs in and says that it is one of these three computers, its execution files will also be put in the privileged spool directory. You therefore have to validate that the computer has the privileged login **uucpz**.

MACHINE Entry for "Other" Systems

You may want to specify different option values for the computers your computer calls that are not mentioned in specific **MACHINE** entries. This may occur when there are many computers calling in and the command set changes from time to time. The name **OTHER** for the computer name is used for this entry as shown below:

```
MACHINE=OTHER \
COMMANDS=rmail:rnews:/usr/lbin/Photo:/usr/lbin/xp
```

All other options available for the **MACHINE** entry may also be set for the computers that are not mentioned in other **MACHINE** entries.

Combining MACHINE and LOGNAME Entries

It is possible to combine **MACHINE** and **LOGNAME** entries into a single entry where the common options are the same. For example, the two entries

```
MACHINE=eagle:owl:hawk REQUEST=yes \
  READ=/  WRITE=/
```

and

```
LOGNAME=uucpz REQUEST=yes SENDFILES=yes \
  READ=/  WRITE=/
```

share the same **REQUEST**, **READ**, and **WRITE** options. These two entries can be merged as shown below:

```
MACHINE=eagle:owl:hawk REQUEST=yes \
LOGNAME=uucpz SENDFILES=yes \
  READ=/  WRITE=/
```

As can be seen, the default entry

```
LOGNAME=nuucp
```

provides maximum security since it is equivalent to

```
LOGNAME=nuucp \
     MACHINE=OTHER \
     REQUEST=no \
     SENDFILES=call \
     READ=/var/spool/uucppublic \
     WRITE=/var/spool/uucppublic \
     AUTH=no \
     COMMANDS=rmail
```

Because **KEYS** is not specified, no keys will be available to authenticate requests. Attempts will therefore fail. Only **rmail** will be available, as it was in previous releases.

The Devconfig File

The **/etc/uucp/Devconfig** file is used if you are using BNU over a TCP network or some other TLI-conformant provider. **Devconfig** entries define the STREAMS modules that are used for a particular device. (The **push=** variable shows the modules and the order in which they are pushed onto a stream.) Different modules and devices can be defined for **cu** and **uucico** services.

Entries in the **Devconfig** file have the format:

service=*x***[:***x***...] device=***y* **push=***z***[:***z***...]**

where *x* can be **cu**, **uucico**, or both separated by a colon; *y* is the name of a network and must match an entry in the **Devices** file; and *z* is replaced by the names of STREAMS modules in the order in which they are to be pushed onto the Stream. Different modules and devices can be defined for **cu** and **uucico** services.

If you are using TCP/IP, the two entries shown below are all you need in this file.

```
service=cu       device=TCP  push=ntty:tirdwr
service=uucico   device=TCP  push=ntty:tirdwr
```

In the example, first **ntty** in pushed, then **tirdwr**. **ntty** is a hardware emulation module.

You must also create an entry for TCP in the **Devices** file. Descriptions in the **Devices** file define Transport Interface devices.

The **Devconfig** file cannot be modified using the **sysadm** menu interface. If you want to change the contents of the file, you must use a text editor.

The Sysfiles File

/etc/uucp/Sysfiles allows you to break the logical **Systems**, **Devices**, and **Dialers** files into multiple physical files. This makes it possible for different files to be used by **uucp** and **cu** as **Systems**, **Devices**, and **Dialers** files. These files may be useful in the following cases:

- You may want different **Systems** files so requests for **cu** services can be made to different addresses than the addresses used for **uucico** services.
- You may want different **Dialers** files to use different chat scripts for **cu** and **uucico**.
- You may want to have multiple **Systems**, **Dialers**, and **Devices** files. The **Systems** file in particular may become large, making it convenient to split it into several smaller files.

The format of the **Sysfiles** file is

```
service=w[:w...]  systems=x[:x...] \
        dialers=y[:y...] \
        devices=z[:z...]
```

where *w* is replaced by **uucico**, **cu**, or both, separated by a colon; *x* is one or more files to be used as the **Systems** file, with each file name separated by a colon and read in the order presented; *y* is one or more files to be used as the **Dialers** file; and *z* is one or more files to be used as the **Devices** file. Each file is assumed to be relative to the **/etc/uucp** directory, unless a full path is given. A backslash (\) can be used to continue an entry on to the next line.

The following is an example of a **Sysfiles** file.

```
service=uucico  systems=Systems.cico:Systems\
                dialers=Dialers.cico:Dialers\
                devices=Devices.cico:Devices
service=cu      systems=Systems.cu:Systems\
                dialers=Dialers.cu:Dialers\
                devices=Devices.cu:Devices
```

When different systems files are defined for **uucico** and **cu** services, your machine will store two different lists of systems. To print the **uucico** list, use the **uuname** command; to print the **cu** list, use the **uuname -c** command.

The Limits File

The **/etc/uucp/Limits** file is used to limit the maximum number of simultaneous **uucicos**, **uuxqts**, and **uuscheds** that are running on your machine.

The format of the **Limits** file is

```
service=x  max=y
```

where *x* can be **uucico**, **uuxqt** or **uusched**, and *y* is the limit permitted for that service.

The fields are order insensitive and lowercase.

The following entries should most commonly be used in the file:

```
service=uucico max=5
service=uuxqt max=2
service=uusched max=2
```

The example allows five **uucicos**, two **uuxqts**, and two **uuscheds** to run simultaneously.

The **Limits** file cannot be modified using the system administration menus (accessed through the **sysadm** command). If you want to change the contents of the file, you must use one of the UNIX system text editors.

The Config File

The **/etc/uucp/Config** file allows the administrator to override certain parameters within BNU by specifying global BNU options.

Each entry in the **Config** file has the following format:

parameter=value

Where *parameter* is one of the configurable parameters and *value* is the value to be assigned to that parameter. See the **Config** file provided with your system for a complete list of configurable parameter names.

The following **Config** file entry sets the default protocol ordering to "**Gge**" and changes the "**G**" protocol defaults to 7 windows and 512-byte packets. See "Protocols" under "The Devices File".

```
Protocol=G(7,512)ge
```

If the system administrator requires authentication of **uux** requests for all or some systems, the entry

```
AUTH=yes
```

or

```
AUTH=req
```

can be included in the **Config** file. This establishes a global value for BNU. To override the global values specified in the **Config** file, entries may be included in the **/etc/uucp/Permissions** file for specific machines. See the section on the **Permissions** file.

If the **AUTH** option is not included, **AUTH** defaults to optional (**AUTH=opt** or **AUTH=no**).

To specify a key management mechanism, a line of the form

    KEYS=name

can be included in the **Config** file. *name* is the name of the key management mechanism. For example, to specify that the **cr1** key management mechanism is to be used, the entry

    KEYS=cr1

should be included in the **Config** file.

The Devices File

The **Devices** file (**/etc/uucp/Devices**) contains information for all the devices that may be used to establish a link to a remote computer. Provisions are made for several types of devices, such as automatic call units, direct links, and network connections.

> **NOTE** This file works closely with the **Dialers**, **Systems**, and **Dialcodes** files. Before you make changes in any of these files, you should be familiar with them all. A change to an entry in one file may require a change to a related entry in another file.

Each entry in the **Devices** file has the following format:

Type Line Line2 Class Dialer-Token-Pairs

These fields are defined as:

Type This field contains the device name. The device name can be a name of the user's choosing, but it must match the name in the third field of the **Systems** file. The two names **Direct** and **ACU** are reserved. Generally the *Type* field is the name of a particular computer directly linked to the computer on which the **Devices** file in question is located (to differentiate it from other directly linked computers) or the name of a network accessible to the computer on which the **Devices** file is located (to differentiate it from other accessible networks).

Direct Indicates a Direct Link to another computer or a switch.

ACU Specifies that the link to a remote computer is made through an automatic call unit (Automatic Dial Modem). This modem may be connected either directly to your computer or indirectly through a Local Area Network (LAN) switch.

LAN_Switch The name of the LAN or switch. For instance, **TCP** could be the name for the TCP/IP network.

Sys-Name Specifies a direct link to a particular computer. (*Sys-Name* is replaced by the name of the computer.) This naming scheme is used to convey the fact that the line associated with this **Devices** entry is for a particular computer in the **Systems** file.

CS TLI LAN-type connection with authentication scheme invocation.

The keyword used in the *Type* field is matched against the third field of **Systems** file entries, as shown in these sample files.

Figure 2-26: Sample `Systems` File

```
#Systems file
#
eagle Any ACU  1200 3251        ogin: nuucp ssword: XXXXXX
sys1  Any CS -    sys1,uucico
sys2  Any CS -
sys3  Any CS -    sys3,login  in:--in nuucp word:XX
sys4  Any DK   9600 sys4        INVOKE "cr1 -r"
sys5  Any DK   9600 sys5        in:--in nuucp word:XX
sys6  Any LAN - network_address
```

Figure 2-27: Sample `Devices` file

```
#Devices file
#
ACU term/11 - 2400 att4024
Direct term/12 - Any direct
sysb term/13 - Any uudirect
CS - - - CS
LAN,eg tcp - - TLI \D
```

The protocol to use for a device can be designated within the *Type* field. See the "Protocols" section at the end of the description of the **Devices** file.

Line This field contains the device name of the line (port) associated with the **Devices** entry. For instance, if the Automatic Dial Modem for a particular entry is attached to the **/dev/term/11** line, the name entered in the *Line* field will be **term/11**. There is an optional modem control flag, **M**, that can be used to indicate that the device should be opened without waiting for a carrier. The modem control flag is separated from the device name by a comma. For example,

```
term/11,M
```

CS entries must contain a hyphen (-) in the *Line* field.

Line2 If the keyword **ACU** is used in the *Type* field and the ACU is an 801-type dialer, *Line2* will contain the device name of the 801 dialer. Since 801-type ACUs do not contain a modem, separate modems are required and are connected to a different line, defined in the *Line* field. This means that one line will be allocated to the modem and another to the dialer. Non-801 dialers will not normally use this configuration. Although non-801 dialers therefore ignore the *Line2* field, it must contain a hyphen (-) as a placeholder. **CS** entries must also contain a hyphen in the *Line2* field.

Class If the **ACU** or **Direct** keywords are used in the *Type* field, the *Class* field need include only the speed of the device. It may, however, contain a letter and a speed, for example, C1200 (Centrex), or D1200 (Dimension PBX). This allows large organizations that have more than one type of telephone network to differentiate between classes of dialers. One network may be dedicated to serving only internal office communications, for example, while another handles external communications. In this case, it is necessary to distinguish which line(s) should be used for internal communication and which should be used for external communication. The keyword used in the *Class* field of the **Devices** file is matched against the fourth field of **Systems** file entries as shown in the **Devices** and **Systems** file lines below.

```
#Devices file
#
ACU tty11 - D1200 penril
```

```
#Systems file
#
eagle Any ACU D1200 3251 ogin: nuucp ssword: XXXXXX
```

Some devices can be used at any speed. In this case, the keyword **Any** may be entered in the *Class* field. If **Any** is used, the line will match any speed requested in a **Systems** file entry. However, if the **Devices** file *Class* field contains **Any** *and* the **Systems** file *Class* field contains **Any**, the speed defaults to 1200 bps.

Dialer-Token-Pairs

This field contains pairs of dialers and tokens. The *Dialer* portion of a dialer-token pair may be the name of an automatic dial modem, a LAN switch, or it may be **direct** or **uudirect** for a Direct Link device. The *Token* portion of a dialer-token pair may be entered immediately following the *Dialer* portion, or, if it is not present, it will be taken from a related entry in the **Systems** file. There may be any number of dialer-token pairs.

This field has the format:

dialer token [*dialer token*]

where the last pair may or may not be present, depending on the associated device (dialer). In most cases, the last pair contains only a *dialer* portion and the *token* portion is retrieved from the *Phone* field of the **Systems** file entry.

A valid entry in the *dialer* portion may be defined in the **Dialers** file or may be one of several special dialer types. These special dialer types are compiled into the software and are therefore available without having to be entered in the **Dialers** file.

CS — A request for a TLI network. The specific network is chosen from the networks available to the system on which the requested service is available. Generally, the network connection returned supports **t_snd**(3N) and **t_rcv**(3N) semantics but may be modified using the **Devconfig** file.

801 — Bell 801 auto dialer

TLI/TLIS — Transport Level Interface Network. Generally, the network connection returned supports **t_snd**(3N) and **t_rcv**(3N) semantics but may be modified to support **read**(2) and **write**(2), using the **Devconfig** file.

The *Dialer-Token-Pairs* field may be structured differently, depending on the device associated with the entry:

- If an automatic dialing modem is connected directly to a port on your computer, the *Dialer-Token-Pairs* field of the associated **Devices** file entry will only have one pair. This pair will normally be the name of the modem and is used to match the **Devices** file entry with an entry in the **Dialers** file. The *dialer* field must therefore match the first field of a **Dialers** file entry as shown below:

```
#Devices file
#
ACU term/11 - 1200 att2212c
```

```
#Dialers file
#
att2212c =+-, "" atzod,o12=y,o4=n\r\c \
        \006 atT\T\r\c ed
```

  Notice that only the *dialer* portion (**att2212c**) is present in the *Dialer-Token-Pairs* field of the **Devices** file entry. This means that the *token* to be passed to the dialer (in this case the phone number) is taken from the *Phone* field of a **Systems** file entry. (**\T** is implied; backslash sequences are described below.)

- If a direct link is established to a given computer, the *Dialer-Token-Pairs* field of the associated entry will contain the keyword **direct** or **uudirect**. This is true for both types of direct link entries, **Direct** and *System-Name* (see the discussion of the *Type* field).

- If you want to communicate with a computer that is on the same local network switch as your computer, your computer must first access the switch and the switch can make the connection to the other computer. In this type of entry, there is only one pair. The *dialer* portion is used to match a **Dialers** file entry as shown below:

```
#Devices file
#
Datakit term/13 - 9600 datakit
```

```
#Dialers file
#
datakit ""          "" \d TION: - - :TION \D
```

In the example, the *token* portion is left blank. This indicates that it is retrieved from the **Systems** file. The **Systems** file entry for this particular computer will contain the token in the *Phone* field, which is normally reserved for the telephone number of the computer (see the discussion of the *Phone* field in the section "The Systems File". This type of dialer-token pair contains an escape character (**\D**), to ensure that the contents of the *Phone* field will not be interpreted as a valid entry in the **Dialcodes** file.

- If an automatic dialing modem is connected to a switch, your computer must first access the switch and the switch will make the connection to the automatic dialing modem. This type of entry requires two dialer-token pairs. The *dialer* portion of each pair (the fifth and seventh fields of the entry) will be used to match entries in the **Dialers** file:

```
#Devices file
#
ACU term/14 - 1200 datakit dial att2212c
```

```
#Dialers file
#
datakit ""          "" \d TION: - - :TION \D
att2212c =+-, "" atzod,o12=y,o4=n\r\c \006 atT\T\r\c ed
```

In the first pair, **datakit** is the dialer and **dial** is the token that is passed to the Datakit® switch to tell it which device (auto dial modem) to connect to your computer. This token will be unique for each LAN switch since each switch may be set up differently. Once the modem has been connected, the second dialer-token pair is accessed. The second dialer is **att2212c**; the token is retrieved from the **Systems** file.

There are two escape characters that may appear in a **Dialer-Token-Pairs** field:

\T Specifies that the *Phone* (*token*) field should be translated using the **Dialcodes** file. This escape character is normally placed in the **Dialers** file for each caller script associated with an automatic dial modem. The translation will not therefore take place until the caller script is accessed.

\D Indicates that the *Phone* (*token*) field should not be translated using the **Dialcodes** file. A **\D** is also used in the **Dialers** file with entries associated with network switches (develcon and micom).

If the dialer is an internal dialer, **\T** is the default. Otherwise, **\D** is the default.

Protocols

You can choose the protocol to use with each device. Usually, it is not needed since you can use the default. If you do specify the protocol, you must do so in the form *Type*,*Protocol*[(*parameters*)] (for example, **TCP,eg**). Available protocols are:

g Generic packet protocol. It provides error detection and retransmission intended for use over potentially noisy lines. By its nature, it is relatively slow. Two parameters characterize the **g** protocol, *windows* and *packetsize*. *windows* indicates the number of packets which may be transmitted without waiting for an acknowledgement from the remote host. *packetsize* indicates the number of data bytes in each packet. *windows* value is set at 7, and *packetsize* is set at 64 bytes.

G Identical to the **g** protocol in that it provides the same error detection and retransmission. However, in addition, the **G** protocol allows the number of windows and the packet size to be varied to match the characteristics of the transmission medium. When properly configured, performance can be significantly better than the **g** protocol. *windows* may range from 1 to 7, and *packetsize* may range from 32 to 4096 bytes, in powers of 2 (that is, 32, 64, 128, 256, 512, 1024, 2048, 4096).

e Assumes error-free transmission and performs no error checking or retransmission. It is therefore the fastest of the three protocols. It should be used for reliable local area networks. There are no parameters to be tuned within the **e** protocol.

The following example uses the **e** protocol over a TCP/IP local area network. If the **e** protocol is not available, **g** will be used.

```
TCP,eg tcp - - TLIS \D
```

This example uses the **G** protocol on a high-speed modem. The number of windows is set to 7, and the packet size is 512 bytes. If the **G** protocol is unavailable, the standard **g** protocol will be used.

```
ACU,G(7,512)g term/11 - 9600 att2296a
```

Presumably, seven windows with a packet size of 512 bytes will provide optimum throughput for the specified device.

For incoming connections, the preferred protocol priority and parameters may be specified in the **Config** file using the *Protocol* parameter.

A default **Devices** file containing only comment lines is delivered with the system. The system administrator must modify the **Devices** file if BNU is to be used.

Serial cu Connections and the Devices File

When **cu** is used with a serial connection, the following must be done:

- Add an entry in the **Devices** file for **uudirect**.
- Add an entry in the **Systems** file for each system that will be called. See "Serial cu Connections and the Systems File" for further information.
- Verify that the **ttymon** or **uugetty** port monitor(s) are in bi-directional mode. See **ttymon**(1M), **uugetty**(1M), and "Managing TTY Ports" in *Advanced System Administration* for further information.

When using **cu** with a serial connection, the **uudirect** dialer must be used. The following line is the format for the **uudirect** dialer in the **/etc/uucp/Devices** file:

UUDirect *Line Line2 Class* **uudirect**

See the above discussion for appropriate values for the *Line*, *Line2*, *Class* fields.

TCP/IP cu Connections and the Devices File

When using **cu** over TCP/IP, the comment character (#) needs to be deleted from the following line in the **/etc/uucp/Devices** file:

```
# CS   - - - CS
```

so the line now reads,

```
CS   - - - CS
```

An entry must be added to the **Systems** file for each system that will be called. See "TCP/IP cu Connections and the Systems File" for further information.

The Dialers File

The **Dialers** file (**/etc/uucp/Dialers**) specifies the initial conversation that must take place on a line before it can be made available for transferring data. This conversation is usually a sequence of character strings that is transmitted and expected, and it is often used to dial a telephone number using an Automatic Call Unit.

This file works closely with the **Devices**, **Systems**, and **Dialcodes** files. Before you make changes in any of these files, you should be familiar with them all. A change to an entry in one file may require a change to a related entry in another file.

The fifth and subsequent odd numbered fields in the **Devices** file are indexes into the **Dialers** file or internal list of special dialer types (CS, 801, TLI, or TLIS). If a match is found, the **Dialers** entry is interpreted to perform the dialer conversation.

Each entry in the **Dialers** file has the following format:

dialer substitutions expect-send . . .

The *dialer* field matches the fifth and additional odd numbered fields in the **Devices** file. The *substitutions* field is a translate string: the first of each pair of characters is mapped to the second character in the pair. This is usually used to translate = and - into whatever the dialer requires for "wait for dial tone" and "pause."

The remaining *expect-send* fields are character strings. Figure 2-28 shows some character strings distributed with BNU in the **Dialers** file.

Figure 2-28: Sample Dialers File Entries

```
att2212C =+-, "" atzod,o12=y,o4=n\r\c \006 atT\T\r\c ed
att2212c =+-, "" atzod,o12=y,o4=n\r\c \006 atT\T\r\c ed
att2224 =+-, "" \r\c :--: T\T\r\c red
att2224B =+-, "" atT\T\r\c ed
att2224CEO =+-, "" atzod,o12=y,o4=n,\\n3\\c1\\j0\\q0\\g0\r\c \006 atT\T\r\c Connected
att2224G =+-, "" atzod,o12=y,o4=n,o1=n\r\c \006 atz\\n3\\c1\\j0\\q0\\g0\r\c
   "" \datT\T\r\c Connected
att2224b =+-, "" atT\T\r\c ed
att2224ceo =+-, "" atzod,o12=y,o4=n,\\n3\\c1\\j0\\q0\\g0\r\c \006 atT\T\r\c Connected
att2224g =+-, "" atzod,o12=y,o4=n,o1=n\r\c \006 atz\\n3\\c1\\j0\\q0\\g0\r\c
   "" \datT\T\r\c Connected
att2248A =+-, "" atzod,o12=y\r\c \006 atT\T\r\c Connected
att2248a =+-, "" atzod,o12=y\r\c \006 atT\T\r\c Connected
att2296A =+-, "" atzod,o12=y,o50=y,o51=n,o55=n,o69=n\r\c \006 atz\\n3\\c1\\j0\\q0\\g0
   \r\c "" \datT\T\r\c Connected
att2296a =+-, "" atzod,o12=y,o50=y,o51=n,o55=n,o69=n\r\c \006 atz\\n3\\c1\\j0\\q0\\g0
   \r\c "" \datT\T\r\c Connected
att4000 =,-, "" ATZ\r\p\p OK\r ATZ\r OK\r\c \EATDT\T\r\c CONNECT
att4024 =+-, "" atzod,o12=y,o4=n\r\c \006 atT\T\r\c ed
datakit "" "" \d TION:--TION: \D
develcon "" "" \pr\ps\c est:\007 \E\D\e \n\007
direct
direct_cr1 "" "" \r\d INVOKE "cr1 -r"
direct_modem "" "" \M\d
hayes =,-, "" \M\dAT\r\c OK\r \EATDT\T\r\c CONNECT \r\m\c
HayesSmartm1200 =,-, "" \M\dAT\r\c OK\r ATZ\r\c OK\r ATM0\r\c OK\r ATE1\r\c OK\r
   ATS0=2\r\c OK\r \EATDT\T\r\c CONNECT \r\m\c
HayesSmartm1200B =,-, "" \M\dAT\r\c OK\r ATZ\r\c OK\r ATM1\r\c OK\r ATE1\r\c OK\r
   ATS0=2\r\c OK\r ATC1\r\c OK\r \EATDT\T\r\c CONNECT \r\m\c
HayesSmartm2400 =,-, "" \M\dAT\r\c OK\r AT&F\r\c OK\r ATZ\r\c OK\r ATM0\r\c OK\r
   AT&D2\r\c OK\r AT&C1\r\c OK\r ATS0=1\r\c OK\r \EATDT\T\r\c 00 \r\m\c
HayesSmartm2400B =,-, "" \M\dAT\r\c OK\r AT&F\r\c OK\r ATZ\r\c OK\r
   ATM0\r\c OK\r AT&D2\r\c OK\r AT&C1\r\c OK\r ATS0=1\r\c OK\r \EATDT\T\r\c 00 \r\m\c
micom "" "" \s\c NAME? \D\r\c GO
Multimodemv29 =w-, "" \MAT&F OK\r AT$BA0&D3&E1&E5&E7$F0&R1$SB19200X4S0=1S11=55\r\c
   OK\r AT&W0 OK\r AT&E2 OK\r ATDT\T\r\c CONNECT \m\c
Multinormalv29 =w-, "" \MAT&F OK\r AT$BA0&D3&E1&E5&E7$F0&R1$SB19200X4S0=1S11=55\r\c
   OK\r AT&W0 OK\r AT&E0 OK\r ATDT\T\r\c CONNECT \m\c
nls.cu "" "" NLPS:000:001:cu\N\c
nls.uucico "" "" NLPS:000:001:10103\N\c
penril =W-P "" \d > Q\c : \d- > s\p9\c )-W\p\r\ds\p9\c-) y\c : \E\TP > 9\c OK
rixon =&-% "" \r\r\d $ s9\c )-W\r\ds9\c-) s\c : \T\r\c $ 9\c LINE
safari =,-, "" \M\dATZ\r\c OK\r ATM0\r\c OK\r AT&D2\r\c OK\r AT&C1\r\c OK\r
   ATS0=1\r\c OK\r \EATDT\T\r\c CONNECT \r\m\c
tb =W-, "" A\pA\pA\pT OK AT~&F0S0=1S52=2S54=3S110=1S111=30DT\T "CONNECT"\s""
tbq =W-, "" A\pA\pA\pT OK AT~&F0S0=1S52=2S54=3S110=1S111=30M0DT\T "CONNECT"\s""
telebit =W-, "" A\pA\pA\pT OK ats50=255DT\T CONNECT\sFAST
telebit12 =W-, "" A\pA\pA\pT OK ats50=2DT\T CONNECT\s1200
telebit24 =W-, "" A\pA\pA\pT OK ats50=3DT\T CONNECT\s2400
```

(continued on next page)

Figure 2-28: Sample `Dialers` File Entries (continued)

```
telebitlong =W-, "" A\pA\pA\pT OK ats7=250 OK ats50=255DT\T CONNECT\sFAST
telebitmnp =W-, "" A\pA\pA\pT OK ats95=2 OK ats50=3DT\T CONNECT
uudirect "" "" \r\d in:--in:--in: \d
vadic =K-K "" \005\p *-\005\p-*\005\p-* D\p BER? \E\T\e \r\c LINE
ventel =&-% "" \r\p\r\c $ <K\T%%\r>\c ONLINE!
```

The escape characters (those beginning with "\") used in the **`Dialers`** are explained in the following section, "The Systems File".

The **`att2212c`** entry in the **`Dialers`** file is processed in two steps. First, the telephone number argument is translated as follows:

- Any equals sign (`=`) is replaced by a plus sign (`+`)
- Any minus sign (`-`) is replaced by a comma (,)

The plus sign and comma in the translated telephone number argument have the following values:

+	Wait for dial tone.
,	Pause.

Second, the handshake given by the remainder of the line is interpreted as follows:

`""`	Wait for nothing, that is, proceed to the *expect-send* string.
`atzod`	Enter command mode, reset modem, set options to default.
`o12=y`	Set option **`12`** to **`y`** (transparent data mode).
`o4=n\r\c`	Set option **`4`** to **`n`** (don't disconnect on received spaces). Terminate with a carriage return but no newline.
`\006`	Wait for acknowledge signal (ACK).
`atT\T\r\c`	Enter command mode. Use tone dialing. Translate the phone number and terminate with a carriage return, but no newline.
`ed`	Expect "**`ed`**" (as in the last two letters of answer*ed*).

The Systems File

The **Systems** file (**/etc/uucp/Systems**) must contain an entry for each system BNU is allowed to communicate with. Each entry in the file represents a computer that can be called by the local machine in its role as client machine and contains the information the **Connection Server** daemon needs to establish a communication link. The Basic Networking software is configured to prevent any remote system not included in the local machine's **Systems** file from logging in. That is, the local machine can not communicate with any machine that is not listed in its **Systems** file, either in the role of client machine or server machine. See the section on the **remote.unknown** file. There may be more than one entry for a particular computer. The additional entries represent alternative communication paths that will be tried in sequential order.

Systems files from previous releases may be installed without change. This provides backward compatibility without the administrative overhead involved in setting up the Connection Server and **cr1**.

The **Systems** file works closely with the **Devices**, **Dialers** and **Dialcodes** files. Before you make changes in any of these files, you should be familiar with them all. A change to an entry in one file may require a change to a related entry in another file.

The BNU System Management Menu, below, can be brought up on the screen by typing **sysadm systems**.

Figure 2-29: Basic Networking System Management Menu

```
           Adding, Listing, and Removing Remote Systems
add    - Adds Systems to the Basic Networking Database
list   - Lists Systems Known to Basic Networking
remove - Removes Systems from the Basic Networking Database
```

If the remote machine supports machine authentication and is connected via a non-Connection Server connection, the entry in the **Systems** file must include the appropriate **INVOKE**-*scheme* pair or pairs to enforce the use of an authentication scheme. For the current release, if the **cr1** authentication scheme is not included in the **Systems** file, passwords will be passed between machines in clear text. In this case, the entry in the **Systems** file will be:

```
INVOKE "cr1 -r"
```

NOTE More than one file can be defined as a **Systems** file by using the **Sysfiles** file. See the description of the **Sysfiles** file for details.

Each entry in the **Systems** file has the following format:

System-Name Time Type Class Phone Login

These fields are defined as:

System-name Contains the node name of the remote computer.

Time Specifies when the remote system can be used. *Time* is a string that specifies both the day of the week and the time of day when the remote system can be called. The format of the *Time* field is:

daytime[;*retry*]

day may be a list containing some of the following:

Su Mo Tu We Th Fr Sa
for individual days

Wk for any weekday (Mo Tu We Th Fr)

Any for any day

Never for a passive arrangement with the remote computer. If the *Time* field is **Never**, the local computer will never initiate a call to the remote computer. The call must be initiated by the remote computer. In other words, the local computer is passive with respect to the remote computer. (See "The Permissions File".)

time should be a range of times specified in 24-hour notation, for example 0800-1230 for "8:30 A.M. to 12:30 P.M." If no *time* portion is specified, any time of day is assumed to be allowed for the call. A time range that spans 0000 is permitted. For example, **0800-0600** means all times are allowed other than times between 6 A.M. and 8 A.M.

An optional subfield, *retry*, is available to specify the minimum time (in minutes) before a retry, following a failed attempt. The default wait is five minutes. The subfield separator is a semicolon (;). For example, **Any;9** is interpreted as call any time, but wait at least nine minutes before retrying after a failure occurs. The following is a sample *time* entry:

```
Wk1700-0800,Sa,Su
```

The example allows calls from 5:00 P.M. to 8:00 A.M., Monday through Friday, and calls any time Saturday and Sunday. In this example, calls are allowed only when telephone rates are low.

Any and **Never** are the most common entries in the *Time* field.

Type

The *Type* field contains the device type used to establish a communication link with a remote computer. It is used to access the entry in the **Devices** file. The **Systems** file *Type* entry is matched against the first field of the **Devices** file entries.

The protocol used to contact the system can be defined by adding the protocol identifier to the *Type* field. If the *Type* is **CS** and the protocol string in the **Devices** file specified that the **e** or **g** protocol should be used, the string entered in the *Type* field of the **Systems** file could be **CSeg**. The use of the protocol information from the **Devices** file as part of the *Type* entry in the **Systems** file is optional but it is often included to make these files easier to understand. The device type and the protocols must be comma separated. In the **Systems** file example below, the protocol **g** is attached to the device type **ACU**. See "Protocols" under "The Devices File".

```
#Systems file
#
eagle Any ACU,g D1200 3251 ogin: nuucp ssword: XXXXXX
```

NOTE Replace **XXXXXX** in the examples with the appropriate password.

```
#Devices file
#
ACU tty11 - D1200 penril
```

Class

Specifies the transfer speed of the device used in establishing the communication link. It may contain a letter and speed (for example, C1200, D1200) to differentiate between classes of dialers (see the discussion of the *Class* field under "The Devices File"). Some devices can be used at any speed. In this case the keyword **Any** may be used. The *Class* field in the **Systems** file must match the *Class* field in the associated **Devices** file entry. For example:

```
#Systems file
#
eagle Any ACU D1200 NY3251 ogin: nuucp ssword: XXXXXX
```

```
#Devices file
#
ACU tty11 - D1200 penril
```

If information is not required for this field, a – should be placed in the file as a placeholder for the field.

Phone Specifies the telephone number or network address of the remote computer. A telephone number is made up of an optional alphabetic abbreviation and a numeric part. If an abbreviation is used, it must be one that is listed in the **Dialcodes** file. For example:

```
#Systems file
#
eagle Any ACU D1200 NY3251 ogin: nuucp \
          ssword: XXXXXX
```

```
#Dialcodes file
#
NY 9=1212555
```

In this string, an equal sign (=) tells the ACU to wait for a secondary dial tone before dialing the remaining digits. A dash (–) in the string instructs the ACU to pause four seconds before dialing the next digit.

If your computer is connected to a LAN switch, you may access other computers that are connected to that switch. The **Systems** file entries for these computers will not have a telephone number in the *Phone* field. Instead, this field will contain the token that must be passed to the switch so it will know which computer your computer wishes to communicate with (this is usually just the system name). The associated **Devices** file entry should have a **\D** at the end of the entry to ensure that this field is not translated using the **Dialcodes** file.

If the *Type* entry is **CS**, any information in the *Phone* field is passed to the **dial**() routine. In this case, the *Phone* field may consist of *system,service*, where either or both may be "**-**" or the *Phone* field may contain a single "**-**" character. If neither *system* nor *service* is specified, the *machine-name* (the first field in the line) and the *service-name* (**uucico** or **cu**) will be passed as parameters to **dial**().

Login This field contains login information given as a series of fields and subfields of the format:

expect send

where *expect* is the string that is received and *send* is the string that is sent when the *expect* string is received.

The *expect* field may be made up of subfields of the form:

expect[-*send*-*expect*] . . .

where the *send* is sent if the prior *expect* is not successfully read and the *expect* following the *send* is the next expected string. For example, with **ogin:--ogin:**, **uucp** will expect **login**. If **uucp** gets **ogin:**, it will go on to the next field. If it does not get **ogin:**, it will send nothing followed by a newline, then look for **ogin** again. If no characters are initially expected from the remote computer, the characters **""** (null string) should be used in the first *expect* field. Note that all *send* fields will be sent followed by a newline unless the *send* string is terminated with a **\c**.

The "l" and other initial characters are often omitted from chat scripts since chat scripts are case-sensitive. Some systems capitalize the first letter of prompts while others do not.

Here is an example of a **Systems** file entry that uses an expect-send string:

```
owl Any ACU 1200 Chicago6013 "" \r ogin:-BREAK-ogin: \
uucpx word: xyzzy
```

This example says don't wait, just send a carriage return and wait for **ogin:** (for **Login:**). If you don't get **ogin**, send a **BREAK**. When you do get **ogin:** send the login name **uucpx**, then when you get **word:**
(for **Password**:), send the password **xyzzy**.

There are several escape characters that cause specific actions when they are a part of a string sent during the login sequence. The following escape characters are useful when using BNU communications:

\b	Send or expect a backspace character
\c	If at the end of a string, suppress the newline that is normally sent. Ignored otherwise.
\d	Delay two seconds before sending or reading more characters
\p	Pause for approximately ¼ to ½ second
\E	Start echo checking. (From this point on, whenever a character is transmitted, it will wait for the character to be received before doing anything else.)
\e	Echo check off
\M	Turn on **CLOCAL** flag
\m	Turn off **CLOCAL** flag
\n	Send a newline character
\r	Send or expect a carriage-return
\s	Send or expect a space character
\t	Send or expect a tab character
\\	Send or expect a \ character
BREAK	Send or expect a BREAK character
\D	Telephone number or token without **Dialcodes** translation

EOT	Send or expect EOT newline twice
\K	Same as BREAK
\N	Send or expect a null character (ASCII NUL)
\T	Telephone number or token with **Dialcodes** translation
\ddd	Collapse the octal digits (ddd) into a single character
~*nn*	Specify the timeout by appending *nn* to the expect string, where *nn* is the timeout time in seconds.

The *Login* field may contain the keyword **INVOKE** followed by white space followed by the name of an authentication scheme. This pair may appear several times in the *Login* field of a **Systems** file entry if more than one authentication step is expected to take place. The following is an example of a **Systems** file entry that specifies more than one authentication step:

```
systemX Any ACU 1200 95551234 INVOKE "inap -r" \
        INVOKE "cr1 -r"
```

systemX is understood to be a valid system name.

If the **expect** string consists of the keyword **ABORT**, then the string after it is used to arm an abort trap. If that string is subsequently received any time prior to the completion of the entire **expect/send** script, then **uucico** aborts, as it would if the script had timed out. This is useful for trapping error messages—such as **Host Unavailable** or **System is Down**— from port selectors or front-end processors. Note that in an **expect/send** script, the format in which the **ABORT** appears is backward: **ABORT expect** instead of **expect ABORT**.

The entire *Login* field is ignored for **cu** and **ct** service requests since the user is expected to enter the proper connect sequence manually. This means that *Login* chat scripts that include an **INVOKE** statement will also be ignored when the service being requested is **cu** or **ct**.

The system administrator must create the entries in the **Systems** file. A **Systems** file is delivered with the system but contains only comment lines.

The Systems File and Pre-UNIX SVR4.0 Systems

When using TCP/IP with machines that are pre-UNIX SVR4.0, the **/etc/uucp/Systems** file requires updating. In a UNIX SVR4.0 (and later) machine, the port number **0ACE** is used by default, whereas the port number **0401** is used in pre-UNIX SVR4.0 machines.

If you are going to be communicating with a pre-UNIX SVR4.0 system, you must change that system's address in **/etc/uucp/Systems** so that the **0401** port number is used. For example, if you had the following entry for machine **downtown** in your **/etc/uucp/Systems** file:

```
downtown Any TcpCico10103 - \x00020aceAE026e50
```

and **downtown** was running pre-UNIX SVR4.0, you would have to change the entry for **downtown** to the following:

```
downtown Any TcpCico10103 - \x00020401AE026e50
```

Serial cu Connections and the Systems File

When **cu** is used with a serial connection, the following must be done:

- Add an entry in the **Devices** file for **uudirect**. See "Serial cu Connections and the Devices File"
- Add an entry in the **Systems** file for each system that will be called.
- Verify that the **ttymon** or **uugetty** port monitor(s) are in bi-directional mode. See **ttymon**(1M), **uugetty**(1M), and "Managing TTY Ports" in *Advanced System Administration* for further information.

When using **cu** with a serial connection, the **uudirect** dialer must be used.

System-Name *Time* **UUDirect** *Class* **Phone** **Login**

See the above discussion for appropriate values for the *System-Name*, *Time*, *Class*, *Phone*, and *Login* fields.

TCP/IP cu Connections and the Systems File

When using **cu** over TCP/IP, an entry for each system that is to be called must be added to the **Systems** file. The entry has the following format:

System-Name *Time* **CS - -,listen:cu**

See the above discussion for appropriate values for the *System-Name* and *Time* fields.

The **Devices** file must also be modified to support **cu** over TCP/IP. See "TCP/IP cu Connections and the Devices File" for further information.

The Dialcodes File

The **Dialcodes** file (**/etc/uucp/Dialcodes**) contains the dial-code abbreviations that can be used in the *Phone* field of the **Systems** file.

The **Dialcodes** file works closely with the **Devices**, **Dialers** and **Systems** files. Before you make changes in any of these files, you should be familiar with them all. A change to an entry in one file may require a change to a related entry in another file.

Each **Dialcodes** entry has the format:

abb dial-seq

where *abb* is the abbreviation used in the **Systems** file *Phone* field and *dial-seq* is the dial sequence that is passed to the dialer when that particular **Systems** file entry is accessed.

The entry

```
jt 9=555-
```

would be set up to work with a *Phone* field in the **Systems** file such as `jt7867`. When the entry containing `jt7867` is encountered, the sequence 9=555–7867 would be sent to the dialer if the token in the dialer-token pair is **\T**.

The default **Dialcodes** file delivered with the system is empty. It is not necessary for the system administrator to do anything to the file.

The Poll File

The **Poll** file (**/etc/uucp/Poll**) contains information for polling remote computers. Each entry in the **Poll** file contains the name of a remote computer to call, followed by a tab character (a space won't work), and finally the hours the computer should be called.

The format for entries in the **Poll** file is:

sys-name<tab>*hour* . . .

For example the entry:

```
eagle   0       4       8       12      16      20
```

polls the computer **eagle** every four hours.

The **uudemon.poll** script does not actually perform the poll. It merely sets up a polling work file (always named C.*file*) in the spool directory. **uudemon.hour** starts the scheduler; it is the scheduler that examines all work files in the spool directory and does the polling.

A default **Poll** file is delivered with the system and does not need to be modified.

The Grades File

The **Grades** file (**/etc/uucp/Grades**) contains the definitions for the job grades that may be used to queue jobs to a remote computer. It also contains the permissions for each job grade. Each entry in this file represents a definition of an administrator defined job grade that allows users to queue jobs.

Each entry in the **Grades** file has the following format:

User-job-grade System-job-grade Job-size Permit-type ID-list

Each entry in this file contains fields that are separated by white space. The last field in the entry is made up of sub-fields that are also white space separated. If a entry takes up more than one physical line, then a backslash (\) is used to continue the entry onto the following line. Comment lines begin with a pound sign (**#**) and occupy the entire line. Blank lines are always ignored. Here is a description of each field:

User-job-grade — This field contains an administrative defined user job grade name of up to 64 characters.

System-job-grade — This field contains a one character job grade to which *User-job-grade* will be mapped. The valid list of characters is A–Z, a–z, with A having the highest priority and z the lowest.

Job-size — This field specifies the maximum job size that can be entered in the queue. *Job-size* is measured in bytes and may be a list of the following:

- *nnnn* — where *nnnn* is an integer that specifies the maximum job size for this job grade
- *n***K** — where *n* is a decimal number that represents the number of kilobytes and **K** is an abbreviation for kilobyte
- *n***M** — where *n* is a decimal number that represents the number of megabytes and **M** is an abbreviation for megabyte
- **Any** — a keyword to specify that there is no maximum job size

Here are some examples:

`5000`	represents 5000 bytes
`10K`	represents 10 kilobytes
`2M`	represents 2 megabytes

Permit-type This field contains a keyword that denotes how to interpret the ID list. The following list contains the keywords and their meanings:

`User`	ID list contains the login names of users permitted to use this job grade.
`Non-user`	ID list contains the login names of users not permitted to use this job grade.
`Group`	ID list contains the group names whose members are permitted to use this group.
`Non-group`	ID list contains the group names whose members are not permitted to use this job grade.

ID-list This contains a list of login names or group names that are to be permitted or denied queuing to this job grade. The list of names are separated by white space and terminated by a newline character. The keyword **`Any`** is used to denote that anyone is permitted to queue to this job grade.

The user job grade may be bound to more than one system job grade. It is important to note that the **`Grades`** file will be searched sequentially for occurrences of a user job grade. Therefore, any multiple occurrences of a system job grade should be listed according to the restriction on the maximum job size.

While there is no maximum number for the user job grades, the maximum number of system job grades allowed is 52. The reason is that more than one *User-job-grade* can be mapped to a *System-job-grade*, but each *User-job-grade* job grade must be on a separate line in the **`Grades`** file. For example:

```
mail      N    Any    User    Any
netnews   N    Any    User    Any
```

Given this configuration in a **`Grades`** file, these two *User-job-grade* grades will share the same *System-job-grade*. Since the permissions for a *Job-grade* are associated with a *User-job-grade* and not a *System-job-grade*, it is even possible for two *User-job-grades* to share the same *System-job-grades* and have two different sets of permissions for each one.

Default Grade

The binding of a default *User-job-grade* to a system job grade can be defined by the administrator. The administrator must use the keyword **`default`** as user job grade in the *User-job-grade* field of the **`Grades`** file and the system job grade that it is bound to. The restrictions and ID fields should be defined as **`Any`** so that any user and any size job can be queued to this grade. Here's an example:

```
default   a      Any      User      Any
```

If the default user job grade is not defined by the administrator, then the built-in default grade, **`Z`**, will be used. Because it is assumed that the restriction field is **`Any`**, multiple occurrences of the default grade are not checked.

The **`Grades`** file delivered with the system contains the following three default grades:

```
high     F      Any      User      Any
medium   S      Any      User      Any
low      n      Any      User      Any
```

The file must be administered only if you are using grades. If you are not using grades, it is not necessary to modify the file.

Administrative Support Files

The Basic Networking administrative files are described below. These files are created in spool directories to hold temporary data or store information about remote transfers or executions.

`TM.` (temporary data file)

These data files are created by Basic Networking processes under the spool directory (that is, **`/var/spool/uucp/`***X*) when a file is received from another computer. The directory *X* has the same name as the remote computer that is sending the file. The names of the temporary data files have the format:

`TM.`*pid.ddd*

where *pid* is a process-ID and *ddd* is a sequential three-digit number starting at 0.

When the entire file is received, the **`TM.`***pid.ddd* file is moved or copied to the pathname specified in the **`C.`***sysnxxxx* file (discussed below) that caused the transmission. If processing is abnormally terminated, the **`TM.`***pid.ddd* file may remain in the *X* directory. These files should be automatically removed by **`uucleanup`**.

P. (checkpoint file)

A checkpoint file is created when processing terminates abnormally. Unlike the **TM.***pid.ddd* file, it is not removed. Therefore, when the transfer session is re-established, the length of the *checkpoint* file serves as an appropriate place to restart the transfer of the file, instead of restarting from the beginning. When checkpointing is specified for a file being transferred from another computer, the checkpoint file is used instead of a **TM** file. *checkpoint* files are created in the spool directory. Checkpointing occurs only between two systems that have the BNU enhancements introduced in System V Release 4. The names of the checkpoint files have the following format:

P.*systmxxxxyyy*

where *systm* is the first five characters in the name of the remote computer, *xxxx* is a four-digit job sequence number assigned by **uucp**. The four digit job sequence number may be followed by a sub-sequence number, *yyy*, which is used when there are several **P.** files created for a work (**C.**) file. When the entire file is received, the **P.***systmxxxxyyy* file is moved to the pathname specified in the **C.***sysnxxxx* file (discussed above) that caused the transmission.

LCK. (lock file)

These lock files prevent duplicate conversations and transfers. The names have the form:

LCK.*system.grade*

where *system* is the name of the remote system and *grade* is the *System-Job-grade* being processed. The lock file contains the process ID of the process holding the lock. This process ID remains valid as long as the process is active.

C. (work file)

Work files are created in a spool directory when work (file transfers or remote command executions) has been queued for a remote computer. The names of work files have the format:

C.*sysnxxxx*

where *sys* is the name of the remote computer, *n* is the ASCII character representing the grade (priority) of the work, and *xxxx* is the four digit job sequence number assigned by **uucp**. Work files contain the following information:

- Type of request, `S` (send) or `R` (receive)
- Pathname of the file to be sent or received
- Pathname of the destination or user file name
- User login name
- List of options
- Name of associated data file in the spool directory. If the **uucp -c** or **uuto -p** option was specified, a dummy name may be used
- Mode bits of the source file
- Remote user's login name to be notified upon completion of the transfer

`D.` (data file)
: Data files are created when it is specified in the command line to copy the source file to the spool directory. The names of data files have the following format:

  `D.`*systmxxxxyyy*

  where *systm* is the first five characters in the name of the remote computer and *xxxx* is a four-digit job sequence number assigned by **uucp**. The four digit job sequence number may be followed by a sub-sequence number, *yyy*, which is used when there are several **D.** files created for a work (**C.**) file.

`D.` (Authentication file)
: The authentication file is an encrypted (that is, non-readable) file that contains information needed for the authentication and identification of remote users making **uux** requests. The file is interpreted by **uuxqt**.

X. (**Execute** file)
: **Execute** files are created in the spool directory prior to remote command executions. The names of **Execute** files have the following format:

  `X.`*sysnxxxx*

  where *sys* is the name of the remote computer, *n* is the character representing the grade (priority) of the work, and *xxxx* is a four digit number assigned by **uucp**. **Execute** files contain the following information:

  - requester's login and computer name

- name of file(s) required for execution
- input file to be used as the standard input to the command string
- computer and file name to receive standard output and standard error from the command execution
- command string
- option lines for return status requests

Log Files

The BNU commands provide eight logs, some of which are optional. They are described below.

Command Log

The command log contains the commands issued by the user, the administrator, and the operator. It can help the system administrator in trouble-shooting. The full path name of the command log is **/var/spool/uucp/.Admin/command**. The format of each entry is as follows:

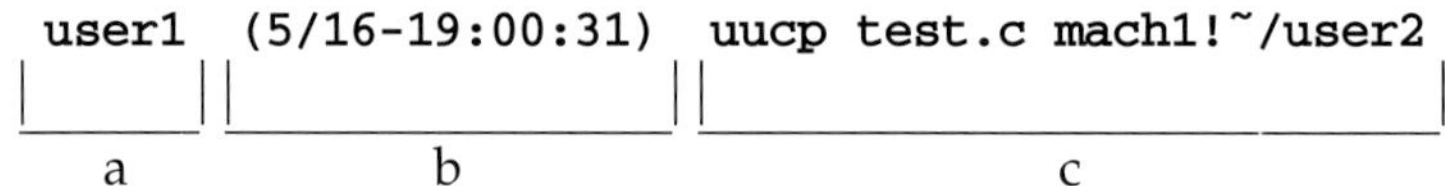

KEY:

a user login name
b date and time the command was issued
c command line

System History Log

The system history log contains a record of each action that alters the state of the system and queue. The system history log can be generated by **uucp**, **uucico**, **uux**, or **uuxqt** programs and put into the **uucp**, **uucico**, **uux**, **uuxqt** subdirectories of the **/var/spool/uucp/.Log** directory. Below is a sample entry that **uucico** writes into **/var/spool/uucp/.Log/uucico/mach1**.

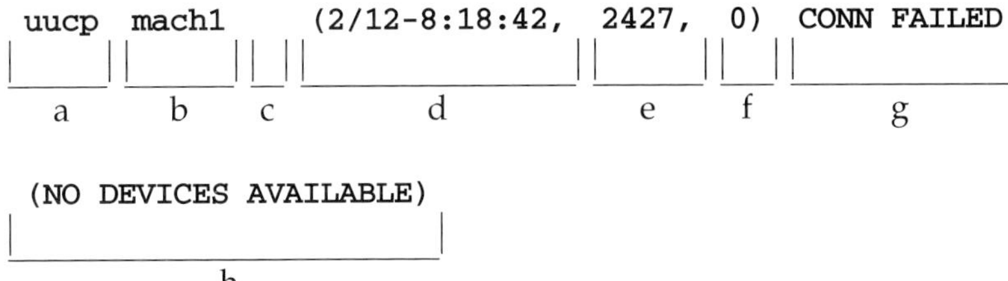

KEY:

- **a** user who submitted the job
- **b** name of the remote machine
- **c** job ID if a job is currently being processed; otherwise null, as in this line
- **d** date and time that the entry was written to the file
- **e** process ID of **uucico** in this example
- **f** file transfer sequence number within the current invocation of **uucico**
- **g** status message
- **h** status message elaboration

Error Log

The error log contains the error messages in the network. Error messages appear in the **/var/spool/uucp/.Admin/errors** file. When the errors occur, the program aborts. In most cases, this results from file-system problems. A typical entry is as follows:

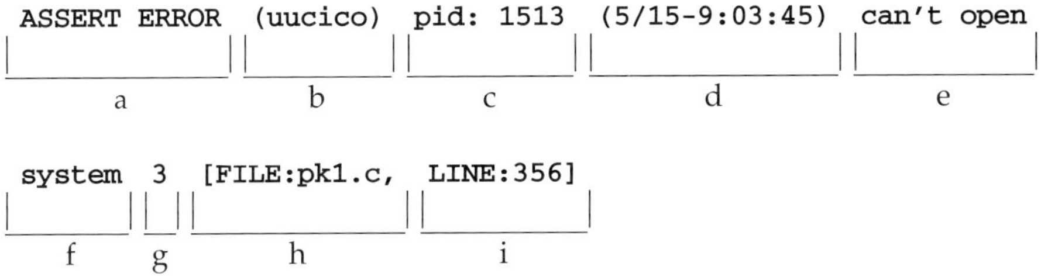

KEY:

- **a** error type
- **b** program name
- **c** process ID
- **d** date and time that this entry was written to the file
- **e** error message part 1
- **f** error message part 2

g error number
h name of calling module
i line of calling module where the error occurred

Transfer Log

The transfer log contains information pertaining to file transfer. For example, it shows the number of bytes transferred and how long the transfer took. After both **uucicos** (master and slave) agree on the protocol, the transfer information of each file is written into **/var/spool/uucp/.Admin/xferstats**. A typical entry is as follows:

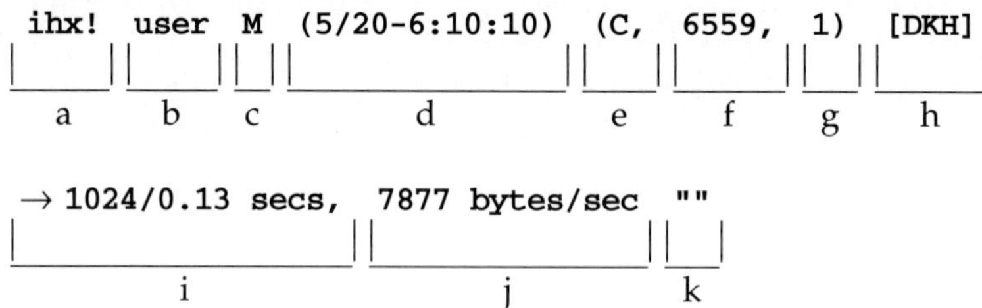


```
→ 1024/0.13 secs,  7877 bytes/sec  ""
```

i j k

KEY:

a name of remote system
b user login
c M=master, S=slave
d date and time that entry was written to log
e C=uucico, U=uucp, X=uux, Q=uuxqt
f process ID of **uucico**, **uucp**, **uux**, or **uuxqt**
g sequential number for each file transferred in a session
h device name of media
i direction and data bytes / clock time to transfer
j transfer rate (bytes/sec)
k **"PARTIAL FILE"** if the file was not completed because of transmission error; **""** if the file was transmitted completely (as in this record)

Report Statistics of File Transfer

By specifying the **-s***file* option with **uucp**, you can have the statistics of your file transfer reported to *file*. For each file transfer request, *file* will contain three lines. For multiple file transfer requests, the size of *file* increases accordingly. A typical entry is:

First line:

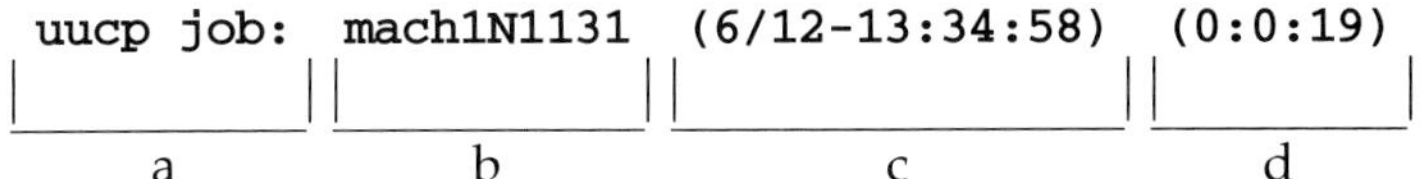

KEY:

- **a** message header (always the same)
- **b** job ID assigned by **uucp**
- **c** date and time the file transfer completed
- **d** *hh:mm:ss* of elapsed time between time of creation of queue file and completion of the file transfer

Second Line:

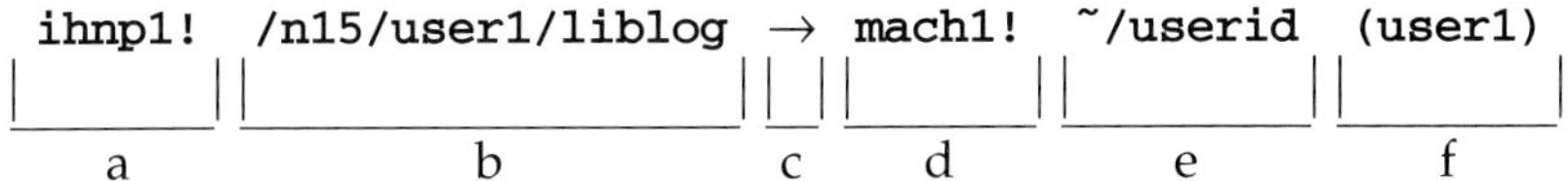

KEY:

- **a** sender node name
- **b** source file name
- **c** direction (always the same)
- **d** receiver node name
- **e** destination directory/file name
- **f** requester login ID

Third line (status):

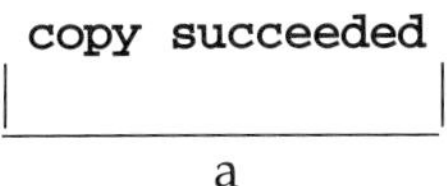

KEY:

- **a** a message

Accounting Log

The accounting log contains information needed for network charging. Upon completing a successful job transaction, accounting information is written to file **/var/spool/uucp/.Admin/account**. If the job transaction is a file transfer, then accounting information is written to file **/var/spool/uucp/.Admin/account** on the requesting site. If the job transaction is a remote execution, then accounting information is written to file **/var/spool/uucp/.Admin/account** on the executing (target) site.

Accounting is optional. Accounting information is collected only if an account file exists and is writable by **uucp**; the file is not created automatically. The system administrator can therefore start or stop accounting by creating or removing the accounting log.

The following is a typical accounting log entry:

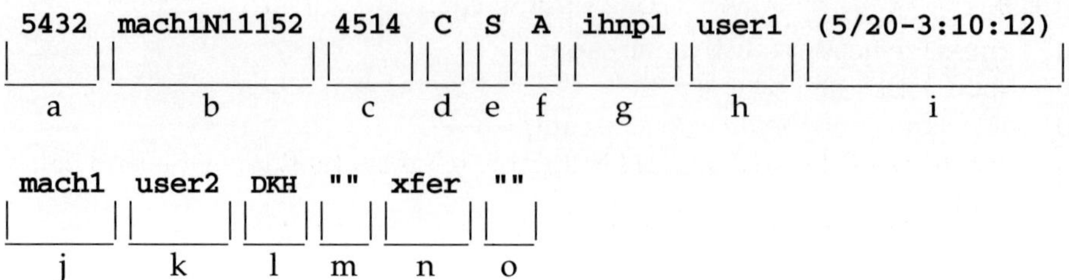

KEY:

- `a` user ID
- `b` job ID assigned by **uucp**
- `c` size of job in bytes if the job transaction is a file transfer; time of job in seconds if the job transaction is a remote execution
- `d` C = job completed. P = partial job completed.
- `e` service class of the job, namely: premium, standard, or economy. At present, only "standard" service class is supported.
- `f` job grade identification
- `g` originating system's name
- `h` originator's login name
- `i` date and time the job originated
- `j` destination system's name
- `k` destination user's login name
- `l` device name of media
- `m` ID of physical network (always `""`)
- `n` type of transaction: xfer = file transfer, rexe = remote execution.
- `o` The command if the job transaction is a remote execution.

Security Log

The security log contains the job transactions that attempt to violate system and user security measures. It is used to aid in detecting attacks on the systems. An attempted security violation is detected when the requester fails to pass the security checks specified in the **/etc/uucp/Permissions** file or tries to access a protected source or destination file. The occurrence is logged for further analysis in the **/var/spool/uucp/.Admin/security** file. Two different entries can appear in the security log.

xfer file transfer
rexe remote execution

Their formats are as follows:

File Transfer (xfer) Security Log

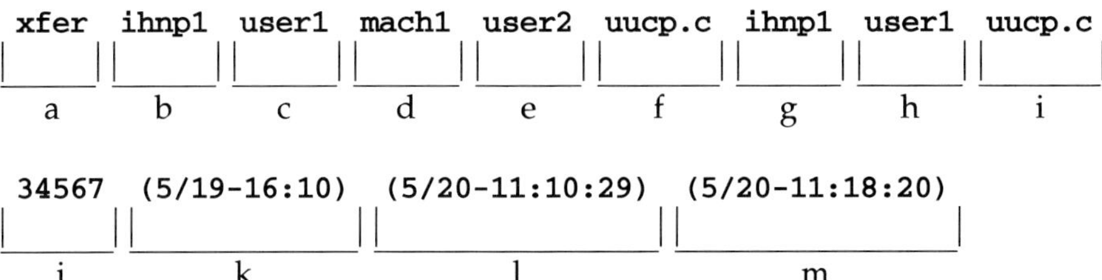

KEY:

- **a** record type (always **xfer**)
- **b** requester node name
- **c** requester user login
- **d** destination node name
- **e** destination user login
- **f** destination file name
- **g** source node name
- **h** source file owner login
- **i** source file name
- **j** source file size in bytes
- **k** modification date and time of source file
- **l** date and time that transfer started
- **m** date and time that transfer completed

Remote Execution (rexe) Security Log

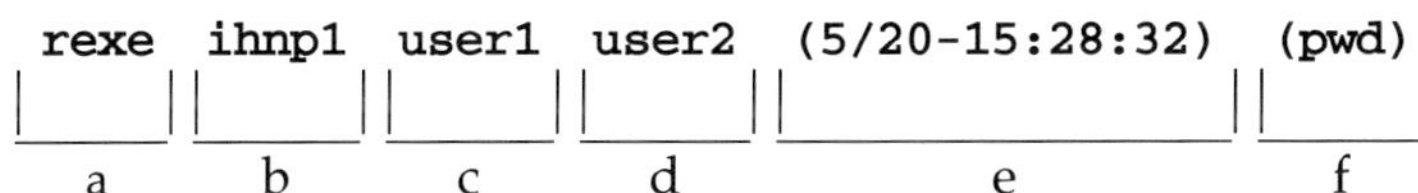

KEY:

- **a** record type (always rexe)
- **b** client (requesting) node name
- **c** client (requesting) user login
- **d** server (destination) user login
- **e** date and time that command was executed by server
- **f** command name and options

Performance Log

The performance log contains statistics about the operation of **uucico**. **uucico** writes the log entries to **/var/spool/uucp/.Admin/perflog**. Statistics are collected only if **perflog** exists when **uucico** starts and is writable by **uucico**. The **perflog** file is not created automatically. The system administrator can therefore start or stop the collection of performance statistics by creating or removing the performance log file, or by making it writable or not writable by **uucico**. In processing terms, if the performance log file can be opened for writing, logging is performed; if the file cannot be opened for writing, logging is not performed. In either case, processing continues.

Two types of records are written to the file; each is identified by a mnemonic type at the beginning of the record. The fields of a record are separated by the "|" character. The record types are:

conn contains statistics about the successful establishment of a connection

xfer contains statistics about a file transfer

> **NOTE** Fields that are not applicable or unknown are marked by double quotes ("").

Their formats are as follows:

Connection (conn) Performance Log

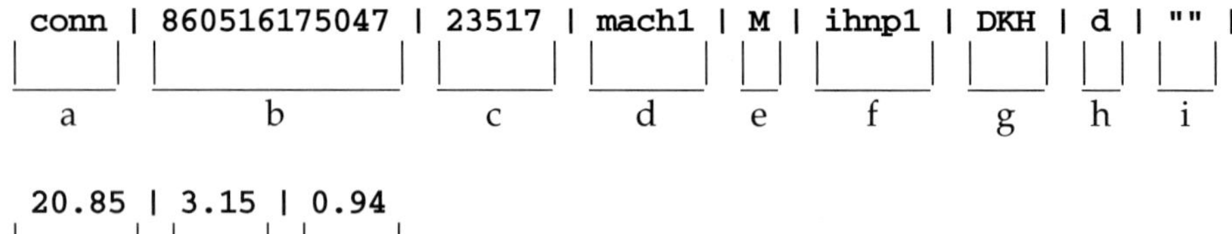

KEY:

- **a** record type (always conn)
- **b** time stamp *YYMMDDhhmmss* for sorting
- **c** **uucico**'s process ID
- **d** the name of the machine where the record was written
- **e** M = master, S = slave

- `f` name of remote system
- `g` device name of media
- `h` the protocol that was used for communications
- `i` physical network ID (always `""`)
- `j` real time to connect
- `k` user time to connect
- `l` system (kernel) time to connect

File Transfer (xfer) Performance Log

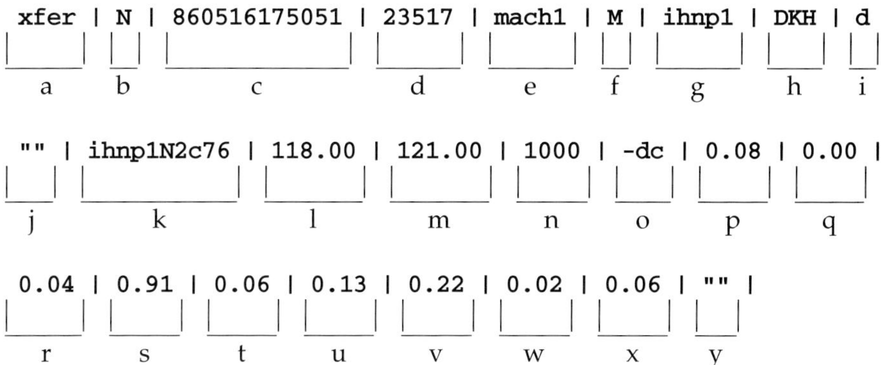

KEY:

- `a` record type (always **`xfer`**)
- `b` job grade ID
- `c` time stamp (*YYMMDDhhmmss*) for sorting
- `d` **`uucico`**'s process ID
- `e` the name of the machine where the record was written
- `f` M = master, S = slave
- `g` name of remote system
- `h` device name of media
- `i` the protocol that was used for communications
- `j` physical network ID (always `""`)
- `k` job ID if master, `""` if slave
- `l` time in seconds that job was in queue if master, `""` if slave
- `m` turn around time in seconds if master, `""` if slave
- `n` size of the file that was actually transferred successfully or partially because of transmission error
- `o` command line options if master, `""` if slave
- `p` real time to start up transfer

- `q` user time to start up transfer
- `r` system (kernel) time to start up transfer
- `s` real time to transfer file
- `t` user time to transfer file
- `u` system (kernel) time to transfer file
- `v` real time to terminate the transfer
- `w` user time to terminate the transfer
- `x` system (kernel) time to terminate the transfer
- `y` **"PARTIAL FILE"** if the file was not completed because of transmission error; **""** if the file was transmitted completely (as in this record)

Fields that are not applicable or unknown are marked by double quotes ("").

Start-up time includes the time for the master to search the queues for the next job, for the master and slave to exchange work vectors, and the time to open files.

Transfer time is the time it takes to transfer the data, close the file, and exchange confirmation messages.

Termination time is the time it takes to send mail notifications and write status files.

Turnaround time is the difference between the time that the job was queued and the time that the final notification was sent.

Foreign Log

The foreign log is a list of unknown systems that attempted to connect to the current machine. The list appears in the **/var/spool/uucp/.Admin/Foreign** file. The format produced by **remote.unknown** is as follows:

Wed Jan 16 15:44:20 1987: **call from system** *machine* **login** *logname*

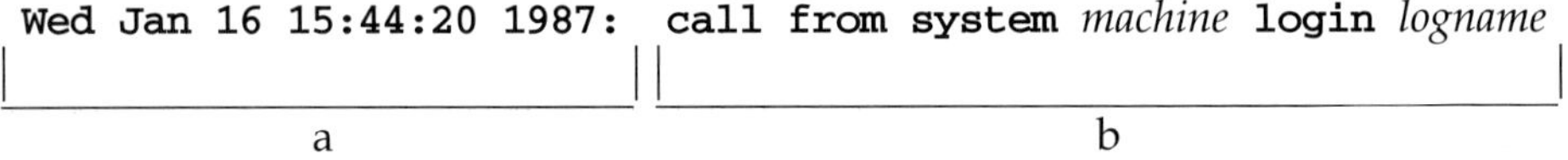

KEY:

- `a` date and time that the entry was written to the file
- `b` the message logged by **remote.unknown**

Adding uucp Logins

You may add one or more logins to your system so incoming **uucp** (**uucico**) requests from different remote machines can be handled differently. Each remote machine should have an entry in its **Systems** file for your machine that contains the login ID and password that you add to your **/etc/passwd** file.

The default entry in the **/etc/passwd** file is shown below.

```
uucp:x:5:5:0000-uucp(0000):/usr/lib/uucp
nuucp:x:10:10:0000-uucp(0000):/var/spool/uucppublic:/usr/lib/uucp/uucico
```

This entry shows that a login by **nuucp** is answered by **/usr/lib/uucp/uucico**. The home directory is **/var/spool/uucppublic**. The *x* indicates that the encrypted password is stored in **/etc/shadow**.

Notice that the standard shell is not given to the **nuucp** login. The shell that **nuucp** receives is the **uucico** daemon that controls the conversation when a remote machine logs in to your machine.

The assigning of passwords for the **uucp** and **nuucp** logins is left up to the administrator. The passwords should be at least six to eight characters. Only the first eight characters of the passwords are significant. If the password for the access login is changed for security reasons, make certain that the remote machines that are a part of your network are properly notified of the change.

The **uucp** login is for local administration only. The password should *not* be given to remote administrators.

BNU Maintenance

Maintenance involves modifying BNU database support files when necessary, tracking transactions, and cleaning up BNU administrative and log files. Maintenance may be automatic or manual.

The following four shell scripts are delivered as part of the BNU software:

```
uudemon.poll
uudemon.hour
uudemon.admin
uudemon.clean
```

These scripts poll remote machines, reschedule transmissions, and clean up old log files and unsuccessful transmissions. They should be run regularly. Normally, they are run automatically by **cron** [see **cron**(1M)] although they can also be run manually.

Automated Networking Maintenance (cron)

BNU is delivered with entries for shell scripts in the **/var/spool/cron/crontabs/uucp** file. These entries will automatically handle some BNU administrative tasks for you. The shell scripts are in **/usr/lib/uucp**.

In multi-user state, tasks scheduled by the **crontab** command are automatically performed by cron. The **crontab** file for **uucp** is now used to schedule regular BNU maintenance using the following shell scripts:

uudemon.poll

The **uudemon.poll** shell script delivered with the system does the following:

- Reads the **Poll** file (**/etc/uucp/Poll**).
- If any of the machines in the **Poll** file is scheduled to be polled, places a work file (**C.sysnxxxx**) in the **/var/spool/uucp/***nodename* directory (*nodename* is the name of the machine being polled).

By default, the shell script is scheduled to run twice an hour, just before **uudemon.hour**, so the work files will be there when **uudemon.hour** is called. The following is the default **uucp crontab** entry for **uudemon.poll**:

```
1,30 * * * * $TFADMIN /usr/lib/uucp/uudemon.poll > /dev/null
```

uudemon.hour

The **uudemon.hour** shell script delivered with the system does the following:

- Calls the **uusched** program to search the spool directories for work files (**C.***files*) that have not been processed and schedules these files for transfer to a remote machine.
- Calls the **uuxqt** daemon to search the spool directories for execute files (**X.***files*) that have been transferred to your computer and were not processed at the time they were transferred.

The following is the default **uucp crontab** entry for **uudemon.hour**:

```
41,11 * * * * $TFADMIN /usr/lib/uucp/uudemon.hour > /dev/null
```

On the system as delivered, **uudemon.hour** is run twice an hour. You may want it to run more often if you expect high failure rates.

uudemon.admin

The **uudemon.admin** shell script delivered with the system does the following:

- Runs the **uustat** command with the **-p** and **-q** options. The **-q** option reports on the status of work files (**C.***files*), data files (**D.***files*), and execute files (**X.***files*) that are queued. The **-p** option prints process information for networking processes listed in the lock files (**/var/spool/locks**).
- Sends the resulting status information to the **uucp** administrative login via **mail** [see **mail**(1)].

There is no default **crontab** entry for **uudemon.admin**. To set up administrative reporting it is recommended that the following line be entered in the **uucp crontab** file.

```
48 8,12,16 * * * $TFADMIN /usr/lib/uucp/uudemon.admin > /dev/null
```

uudemon.clean

The delivered **uudemon.clean** shell script does the following:

- Takes log files for individual machines from the **/var/spool/uucp/.Log** directory, merges them, and places them in the **/var/spool/uucp/.Old** directory with other old log information. If log files become large, the **ulimit** parameter may need to be increased.
- Removes work files (**C.***files*) seven days old or older, data files (**D.***files*) seven days old or older, and execute files (**X.***files*) two days old or older from the spool directory.
- Returns mail that cannot be delivered to the sender.
- Mails a summary of the status information gathered during the current day to the **uucp** administrative login.

The following is the default **uucp crontab** entry for **uudemon.clean**:

```
45 23 * * * $TFADMIN /usr/lib/uucp/uudemon.clean > /dev/null 2>&1
```

uudemon.clean is described in detail in "Cleaning Up Log Files".

NOTE If your system handles a heavy **uucp** load, it may be necessary to run **uudemon.clean** with an increased **ulimit**. For example:

```
45 23 * * * ulimit 5000; $TFADMIN /usr/bin/su uucp -c \
"/usr/lib/uucp/uudemon.clean" > /dev/null 2>&1
```

Manual Maintenance

Some files may grow indirectly from **uucp** and other Basic Networking activities. The following file should be checked and deleted if it has become too large:

/usr/lib/cron/log	This file is a log of **cron** activities. While it grows with use, it is automatically truncated when the system goes to the multi-user state.

Cleaning Up Log Files

uudemon.clean is a shell script that should be invoked daily by **cron** to clean up **uucp**'s spool directory and to consolidate and dispose of the log files that currently exist for **uucp**. Currently, **uudemon.clean** uses two techniques to clean up the log files:

1. The *Multi-day* (multi) technique. Three days of logs are kept in files called **Old-1**, **Old-2**, and **Old-3**. Whenever **uudemon.clean** is run, **Old-2** is renamed **Old-3**, **Old-1** is renamed **Old-2**, and the current log is renamed **Old-1** and stored in **/var/spool/uucp/.Old/Old-1**.

2. The *Single-day* (single) technique. The current log is moved to **/var/spool/uucp/.Old**. This means that the log is preserved for one day only (assuming that **uudemon.clean** is run daily).

Although **uudemon.clean** does take care of removing old log entries, as an administrator, you should monitor the size of the log files. The exact procedure **uudemon.clean** uses to remove old log entries varies according to the type of log file. Here's a description of how the **uucp** log files will be cleaned up.

Table 2-9: Summary of BNU Log Files

File Use	File Name (beginning with **/var/spool/uucp**)	Cleanup Technique
Command	**.../.Admin/command**	single
History	**.../.Log/[uucp|uucico|uux|uuxqt]/system**	multi
Foreign	**.../.Admin/Foreign**	single
Error	**.../.Admin/errors**	single
Transfer	**.../.Admin/xferstats**	single
Accounting	**.../.Admin/account**	multi
Security	**.../.Admin/security**	multi
Performance	**.../.Admin/perflog**	single

BNU Debugging

The *Debug* procedures are intended to help identify and correct common problems in Basic Networking operations and administration. The following monitoring tools are available for detecting and solving Basic Networking problems:

uustat(1C)
cu(1C)
Uutry(1M)
uuname [see **uucp**(1C)]
uulog [see **uucp**(1C)]
uucheck(1M)

Check Basic Information

There are several commands you can use to check for Basic Networking information.

uuname Lists the machines your machine can contact.

uulog Displays the contents of the log directories for particular hosts.

uucheck -v Run to check for the presence of files and directories needed by **uucp**. **uucheck** also checks the **Permissions** file and provides information on the permissions you have set up.

Check for Faulty ACU/Modem

You can check if the automatic call units or modems are not working properly in several ways.

- Run **uustat -q**. This will give counts and reasons for contact failure.
- Run **cu -d -l***line*. This will let you call over a particular communications line and print debugging information on the attempt. If the communications line, *line*, is connected to an autodialer, you must add a telephone number at the end of the command line you execute. Otherwise, *line* must be defined as **direct** in the **Devices** file.

cs must be in debug mode. See "The Connection Server" for more information

Check Systems File

Check that you have up-to-date information in your systems file if you are having trouble contacting a particular machine. Some things that may be out of date for a machine are its:

- phone number
- login
- password

Debug Transmissions

If you cannot contact a machine, check communications to that machine with **Uutry** and **uucp**. For a listing of the options accepted by **Uutry** and **uucp**, see **Uutry**(1M) and **uucp**(1C), respectively.

Step 1: Simply to try to make contact, run:

/usr/lib/uucp/Uutry -r *machine*

where *machine* is replaced with the node name of the machine you are having problems contacting. This command will:

1. Start the transfer daemon (**uucico**) with debugging. You will get more debugging information if you are **root**.

2. Direct the debugging output to `/tmp/`*machine*,

3. Print the debugging output to your terminal, using **`tail -f`**. When the conversation has completed, the **`tail -f`** process is killed.

You can copy the output from `/tmp/`*machine* if you want to save it.

Step 2: If **`Uutry`** doesn't isolate the problem, try to queue a job by running:

`uucp -r` *file machine*`!`*/dir/file*

where *file* is replaced by the file you want to transfer, *machine* is replaced by the machine you want to copy to, and *dir/file* is where the file will be placed on the other machine. The **`-r`** option will queue a job but not start the transfer.

Now use **`Uutry`** again. If you still cannot solve the problem, you may need to call support personnel. Save the debugging output; it will help diagnose the problem.

NOTE Since the connection phase is now performed by the Connection Server, information previously found in **`/tmp/machine`** is now maintained in the Connection Server debug log (if it is enabled). For more information, see "The Connection Server".

REXEC

Many commercially available transport protocols provide remote execution capabilities that are tied to the protocols. In UNIX SVR4.2, the **rlogin** command, for example, allows remote users to log into a host on a TCP/IP network. REXEC is a remote execution facility that is independent of transport protocol. It allows a user to execute a process on a remote host, independent of the transport provider.

From the user perspective, remote execution of a process through REXEC is transparent. Once the user executes a process on a remote machine, the user interfaces with the process as if it were running locally. However, all files referenced by a remote command are relative to the server. If a user executes the **who** command remotely, for example, a list of users logged in to the remote machine is displayed, not a list of users on the local machine.

For the system administrator, REXEC makes it possible to administer a set of machines remotely from a single location, without the overhead of logging in to the remote machines. REXEC gives administrators the ability

- to monitor the system activity of several machines from a single machine
- to stop and start network applications, such as RFS
- to tune the performance of a set of machines by specifying that certain processes are to execute on a less active system.

REXEC is service-based. A server defines services that a client can execute remotely. By default, when REXEC is first installed, a server has the following standard services defined:

rx — A service that allows a user on a client to execute a command or shell script on the server.

rl — A service that allows a user on a client to log in to the server.

rquery — A service that allows a client user to list the services available on a server for remote execution.

General instructions for invoking an REXEC service, as well as specific instructions for using the standard services, appear in *User's Guide* and on **rexec**(1).

Overview of REXEC Administration

Although REXEC is independent of other network applications, it utilizes components of the Network Applications Architecture, specifically ID Mapping and the Service Access Facility on the server side, the Connection Server on the client side, and an IAF authentication scheme on both the server and client. The client also utilizes Name-to-Address Mapping.

This section first describes the components of the Network Applications Architecture that need to be administered before you set up REXEC. It then gives an overview of the steps that are specifically part of REXEC administration.

Prior to setting up REXEC on the server, you must

1. Install an authentication scheme.
2. Set up ID Mapping.
3. Set up the Connection Server.

The authentication scheme, cr1, will be used to protect the REXEC service from unauthorized remote access. Setting up the authentication scheme will include the use of the cr1 administrative commands to control the key management daemon, and to administer the key database.

Using the ID Mapping facility, map the logins of users on a client to logins on the server. Before client logins can be mapped, the server logins to which client logins will be mapped must exist on the server system with valid entries in the server's **/etc/passwd** file. When this is done, use the ID Mapping administrative commands with a cr1 mapping scheme specification to complete the set up of the facility.

Currently, cr1 is the only authentication provided with System V Release 4.2 that uses ID Mapping. cr1 administration involves setting up and maintaining the cr1 key database, as described in "cr1 Bilateral Authentication Scheme".

Setting up the Connection Server on the server will include the installation of the **reportscheme** service for each port monitor being used to offer the **rexec** service.

Before you use REXEC from a client, you must do the following:

1. Set up a host address database.
2. Install the same authentication scheme used on the server to protect REXEC.
3. Set up the Connection Server.

How you set up a host address database depends on your network. Host addresses are stored in any of several databases, depending on the type of network connection the client has to the server. If a client can reach a server over a TCP/IP transport, for example, then that client should have the server's name and address in its `/etc/hosts` file. See "Name-to-Address Mapping" for information about setting up a host address database for your network.

Setting up the authentication scheme on the client will include the use of the cr1 administration command **`cryptkey`** to specify the key to be shared between the server and the client.

Setting up the Connection Server on the client will include the specification of the authentication scheme to be used. For example, cr1 needs to be specified in `/etc/iaf/serve.allow`. This will help ensure enforcement of bilateral authentication.

Instructions for setting up and administering Name-to-Address Mapping, the cr1 Bilateral Authentication Scheme, ID Mapping, and the Connection Server appear in preceding sections of this chapter, and should be consulted for more details.

Once you've set up the network services on which REXEC depends, you're ready to set up REXEC itself. Administering the REXEC facility on a server involves the following tasks:

1. Registering REXEC with a port monitor under the Service Access Facility.
2. Maintaining a database of services available for remote execution through REXEC.

Administering REXEC on a client is just a matter of installing the REXEC software. However, the client administrator may choose to create links from REXEC services to the REXEC command interface to improve the ease with which local users can execute remote services.

The following sections describe REXEC administrative tasks.

Registering REXEC with a Port Monitor

As with any service, you must register REXEC with a port monitor under the Service Access Facility (SAF). By registering the service with a port monitor, you associate the service with a specific port and an authentication scheme. When a client machine attempts to access the service, it calls the port monitor, which informs the client that the service is protected by the scheme. If the client supports the scheme, it begins the authentication process.

The authentication scheme authenticates the user on the client machine and maps the user's login to a local login before REXEC is invoked. REXEC obtains the information established by the authentication scheme and sets up the environment of the mapped user before executing the requested service.

As explained earlier, cr1 is the only authentication scheme provided with System V Release 4.2 that uses ID Mapping. It is assumed throughout the REXEC documentation that your authentication scheme is cr1.

To register REXEC with a port monitor and protect it with the cr1 authentication scheme, you must add REXEC to the port monitor's **_pmtab** file. If the port monitor is **tcp**, the **rexec** service is added to the **_pmtab** file by using the command:

```
pmadm -a -p tcp -s rexec -f u \
-m "`nlsadmin -c /usr/lib/rexec/rxserver -p tirdwr`" \
-v `nlsadmin -V` -S "cr1 -srexec" -y "remote execution"
```

The port monitor-specific command, the **-m** operand, specifies the server **rxserver** to be executed and the module to be pushed on the Stream. **rxserver** is invoked by a network listener process after a connection has been established between a client and the server's port associated with the **rexec** service, and performs REXEC server functions.

The **-S** operand of the **pmadm** command specifies the authentication scheme to be associated with the service tag **rexec**.

For more information about registering services under the SAF, see "Managing Ports" in *Advanced System Administration* for more information. For additional information about cr1, see "cr1 Bilateral Authentication Scheme".

Adding and Removing Services

The server administrator controls which local services are available for remote execution by adding and removing services from the REXEC database **/etc/rexec/services**.

Although REXEC is installed with three standard services defined, these services can be removed from the REXEC database at any time. In addition, the server administrator can add other services to the database and make them available to clients for remote execution.

You don't need to edit **/etc/rexec/services** explicitly; instead, the **rxservice** command is provided as an interface to the file. **rxservice** allows a privileged user to add and remove services from the REXEC database.

Adding a Service

To make a service on your machine available to remote users through REXEC, you add the service to the REXEC database, using the **rxservice** command.

The syntax of the **rxservice** command, when used to add a service, is as follows:

rxservice -a *servicename* **[-d** *description***] [-u]** *servicedef*

See **rxservice**(1M) for an explanation of the options accepted by the **rxservice** command.

The REXEC facility defines the following macros, which can be used by any service. When you specify any of the following macros, REXEC substitutes appropriate values for the macros when a remote user makes a request for the service. The remote user is not required to enter the information as arguments to the invoking command.

%m The address of the client machine.

%t The name of the transport provider used to connect to the server.

%s The mapped user's shell, obtained from the **/etc/passwd** file on the server.

If the value of a macro cannot be obtained, the macro is expanded to a dash (–).

Examples

Assume you want to define the **shutdown** command so that it can be used remotely. The syntax of **shutdown** is as follows:

shutdown [-y] [-g *grace_period***] [-i** *init_state*]

Let's call the remote shutdown service **rshutdown**. If you want **rshutdown** to support all the parameters to **shutdown** and in the same way (as options), then you would define **rshutdown** as follows:

```
rxservice -a rshutdown -d "rshutdown usage: rshutdown \
        shutdown_options" 'cd/;/sbin/shutdown %*'
```

The macro **%*** means that **rshutdown** supports all options to **shutdown**. Suppose you were to define the **rshutdown** service as follows:

```
rxservice -a rshutdown -d "rshutdown usage: rshutdown \
        minutes initstate" 'cd/;/sbin/shutdown -g%1 -i%2'
```

When defined this way, the macros indicate that the **-g** and **-i** operands (that is, values for **%1** and **%2**, respectively) are required. If the remote user fails to supply a grace period operand or an init state operand, the **rshutdown** command will fail. Note that the service definition omits the **-y** option. Because the option has been omitted in the service definition, the **rshutdown** user cannot by-pass the prompt that asks him or her to confirm that the system should be shut down.

The following command line defines a service called **rlookup**, which accesses a local database via a command called **dblook**:

```
rxservice -a rlookup -d 'Remote database lookup' \
      '/usr/bin/dblook %*'
```

The following command line defines a service called **rsetup**, which modifies database tables via a local command called **setdb**. The **setdb** command takes the address of the client machine as a parameter.

```
rxservice -a rsetup -d 'remote setup service' \
      '/usr/bin/setdb %m'
```

Removing a Service

To disable a service so that it is no longer available for remote execution, you remove the service from the REXEC database. In addition to providing a means to add services to the database, the **rxservice** command allows you to remove services.

The syntax of the **rxservice** command when used to remove a service is

rxservice -r *servicename* **. . .**

where *servicename* can be one or more service names.

Example

To remove the services **rshutdown**, **rsetup**, and **rlookup** from the REXEC database, enter the following command line:

```
rxservice -r rshutdown rsetup rlookup
```

NOTE If you want to remove a service temporarily, you can remove the service's execute permissions.

Listing Defined Services

As a system administrator, you may need to view the contents of **/etc/rexec/services** from time to time, to remind yourself which services you have made available for remote execution. To display the **services** file, enter the **rxservice** command with the **-l** option, as follows:

```
rxservice -l
```

In addition to providing an option to **rxservice** that allows the administrator to display **/etc/rexec/services**, REXEC installs a command on the server that allows a remote user to display the file. When a remote user displays the file, however, only the services available to that user are displayed.

The command on the server that allows remote users to display the **services** file is the **rxlist** command. Remote users use the standard REXEC service **rquery** to run **rxlist** remotely.

If the **rxlist** command is removed from the server, client users cannot determine which services are available to them for remote execution; however, they can still invoke those services, provided they already know the names of the services and have appropriate permissions.

Instructions for using **rquery** appear in *User's Guide* and on **rexec**(1).

Linking Services to REXEC

Administration of REXEC on a client machine is simply a matter of installing the REXEC software.

You may choose, however, to create links from the **rexec** command to the REXEC services defined on a remote machine. The **rexec** command is the user interface to the REXEC facility. When you link services to **rexec**, your users can enter abbreviated commands to invoke a remote service.

The standard REXEC services are linked to the **rexec** command by default when the software is installed. If a user wants to run **rquery** on a server named **sftig**, for example, the user enters

```
rquery sftig
```

With the link removed, the user enters

```
rexec sftig rquery
```

For information about creating and removing hard or symbolic links, see **ln**(1).

Setting Up TCP/IP

3 Introduction to Administering TCP/IP Networks

About TCP/IP Administration 3-1
Organization 3-1

Introducing the Internet Protocol Suite 3-2
Physical Layer 3-5
Data Link Layer 3-5
Network Layer 3-5
Transport Layer 3-6
Application Layer 3-6

About TCP/IP Administration

The TCP/IP administration chapters explain how to set up and administer a network built on the TCP/IP Internet protocol family, as provided in UNIX SVR4.2. The administrative steps needed are simple and few—once you understand the concepts underlying them. Therefore, this guide concentrates on the concepts that will allow you to install the most appropriate network for your particular needs.

Organization

The TCP/IP administration chapters are organized as follows:

- "Introduction to Administering TCP/IP Networks", which introduces basic concepts relating to TCP/IP and describes the tasks which an administrator must perform when dealing with a TCP/IP network.
- "Setting Up TCP/IP", in which various aspects of the network software are discussed. Also covered are the procedures you follow to obtain a network number, register a domain, set up administration files, and boot TCP/IP on network hosts.
- "Maintaining Security in a TCP/IP Environment" which explains the effects of the **hosts.equiv**, and **.rhosts** files, as well as the implications that these files have on security issues.
- "Expanding Your TCP/IP Network", which describes the hardware you need to expand your network and presents procedures for creating an internetwork, setting up a router, setting up subnets, and how to configure multiple networking boards.
- "Using Domain Name Service with TCP/IP", which tells you how to take advantage of Domain Name Service, a name service at the application layer of TCP/IP.
- "Troubleshooting TCP/IP", in which various commands that help you diagnose problems on the network are discussed.
- "Guidelines for Completing the IP Number Registration Form", which contains information you need to register your network with SRI-NIC.
- "Guidelines for Completing the Domain Registration Form", which contains information you need to register your domain with the NIC Domain Registrar.

Introducing the Internet Protocol Suite

A network is a configuration of machines that exchange information among themselves. In order for the network to function properly, the information originating at a sender must be transmitted along a communication line and delivered to the intended recipient in an intelligible form. Because different types of networking software and hardware need to interact to perform this function, network designers developed the concept of the communications protocol family (or suite). A *network protocol* is a set of formal rules explaining how software and hardware should interact within a network in order to transmit information. The Internet Protocol family is one such group of network protocols. It is centered around the Internet Protocol (IP). The other members of the Internet protocol family are Transmission Control Protocol (TCP), User Datagram Protocol (UDP), Address Resolution Protocol (ARP), Reverse Address Resolution Protocol (RARP), and Internet Control Message Protocol (ICMP).

The entire family is popularly referred to as TCP/IP, reflecting the names of the two main protocols. This is also the terminology used in this document.

TCP/IP provides service to many different types of host machines connected to heterogeneous networks. These networks may be wide area networks, such as X.25-based networks, but they may also can be local area networks, such as one you might install in a single building.

TCP/IP was originally developed by the United States Department of Defense to run on the ARPANET, a packet-switching wide area network first demonstrated in 1972. Today the ARPANET is part of a wide area network known as the DoD (Department of Defense) Internet, or, for short, the Internet. Many popular texts use the term *Internet* to describe both the protocol family and the wide area network. This text uses the term *TCP/IP* to refer to the Internet protocol suite and *Internet* when referring to the network itself.

The TCP/IP protocol structure can be conceptualized as being formed of a series of layers as shown in Table 3-1.

Table 3-1: TCP/IP Protocol Layers

Layer	Network Services
Application	Telnet, FTP
Transport	TCP, UDP
Network	IP, ICMP
Data Link	ARP, RARP, device driver (such as Ethernet®)
Physical	Cable or other device (such as an Ethernet board)

In TCP/IP jargon, a machine engaged in communication is termed either a sending or receiving host. Every protocol layer on the sending host has its peer protocol layer on the receiving host. Each layer is required by design to handle communications in a pre-determined fashion.

Each protocol formats communicated data and appends or removes information from it. Then the protocol passes the data to a lower layer on the sending host or a higher layer on the receiving host, as illustrated in Figure 3-1:

Figure 3-1: Sender/Receiver Interaction

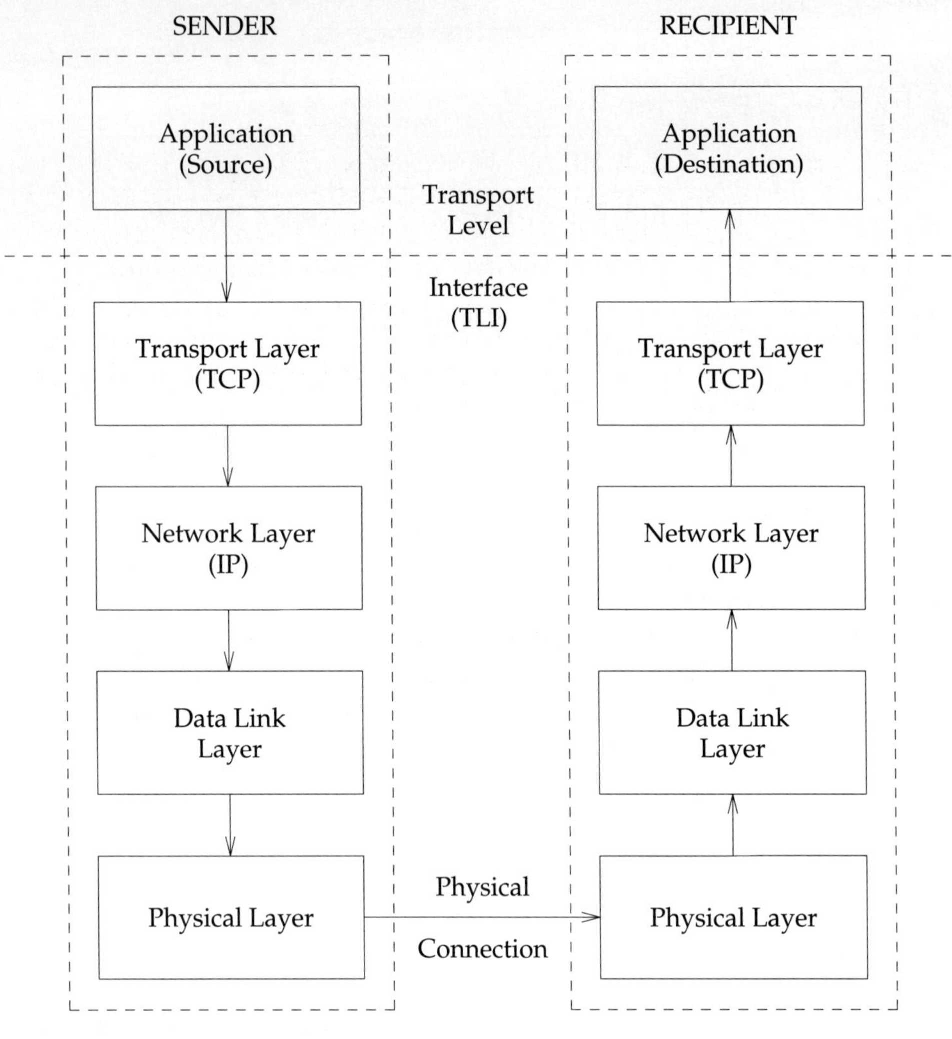

In the UNIX SVR4.2 implementation, the interface between the application and the transport layers is Transport Level Interface (TLI), an interface that eliminates the need for applications to know particulars about the transport layer. Any application written to TLI can run on a TCP/IP network. For more information about TLI, see *Network Programming Interfaces*.

The next subsections briefly explain how each protocol layer handles messages. For more detailed information, refer to the manual page for the appropriate protocol.

Physical Layer

The physical layer is the hardware level of the protocol model, which is concerned with electronic signals. Physical layer protocols send and receive data in the form of *packets*. A packet contains a source address, the transmission itself, and a destination address.

TCP/IP supports a number of physical layer protocols, including Ethernet. Ethernet is an example of a *packet switching network*; its communications channels are occupied only for the duration of the transmission of a packet. The telephone network is an example of a *circuit switching network.*

Data Link Layer

The data link layer is concerned with addressing at the physical, machine level. Protocols at this layer are involved with communications controllers, their chips, and their buffers. Ethernet is supported at this layer by TCP/IP.

Two additional TCP/IP protocols, ARP and RARP, can be viewed as existing between the network and data link layers. ARP is the Ethernet address resolution protocol. It maps known IP addresses (32 bits long) to Ethernet addresses (48 bits long).

RARP (or Reverse ARP) is the IP address resolution protocol. It maps known Ethernet addresses (48 bits) to IP addresses (32 bits), the reverse of ARP.

Network Layer

IP (Internet Protocol) and Internet Control Message Protocol (ICMP) are the protocols present at the network layer.

IP provides machine-to-machine communication. It performs transmission routing by determining the path a transmission must take, based on the receiving machine's IP address. (IP addresses are discussed in further detail in "Assigning IP Addresses to Your Network Hosts"). IP also provides transmission formatting services; it assembles data for transmission into an *internet datagram.* If the datagram is outgoing (received from the higher layer protocols), IP attaches an

IP header to it. This header contains a number of parameters, including the IP addresses of the sending and receiving hosts. Refer to **IP**(7) for more information.

ICMP sends error or control messages to other hosts. It provides communication of Internet software between machines. Refer to **ICMP**(7) for information about ICMP.

Transport Layer

The TCP/IP transport layer protocols enable communications between processes running on separate machines. Protocols at this level are TCP and UDP.

TCP (Transmission Control Protocol) enables applications to talk to one another via virtual circuits, as if connected by physical circuits. TCP is a connection-oriented, reliable delivery protocol; any data written to a TCP connection will be received by its peer in sequence, or an error indication will be returned.

UDP (User Datagram Protocol) is the alternative protocol available at the Transport layer. UDP is a connectionless datagram protocol. Datagrams are groups of information transmitted as a unit to and from the upper layer protocols on sending and receiving hosts. UDP datagrams use port numbers to specify sending and receiving processes. However, no attempt is made to recover from failure or loss; packets may be lost with no error indication returned.

Whether TCP or UDP is used depends on the network application invoked by the user. For example, if the user invokes **telnet**, that application passes the user's request to TCP. If the user's request involves the Domain Name Service, that application passes the request to UDP.

Refer to the **TCP**(7) and **UDP**(7) for more information about these protocols.

Application Layer

A variety of TCP/IP protocols exist at the application layer. Here is a description of some of the more widely used:

- `telnet`

  The Telnet protocol enables terminals and terminal-oriented processes to communicate on a network running TCP/IP. It is implemented as the program **telnet** on the local machine and the daemon **telnetd** on the remote machine. Telnet provides a user interface through which two hosts can open communications with each other, then send information on a character-by-character or line-by-line basis. The application includes a series of commands, which are documented in **telnet**(1).

The **telnetd** daemon on the remote host handles requests from the **telnet** command. For more information about **telnetd**, see **telnetd**(1M).

- **ftp**

  The File Transfer Protocol (FTP) transfers files to and from a remote network. The protocol includes the **ftp** command on the local machine and **ftpd** daemon on the remote machine. **ftp** lets you specify on the command line the host with whom you want to initiate file transfer and options for transferring the file. The **ftpd** daemon on the remote host handles the requests from your **ftp** command.

  The options to **ftp**, as well as the commands you invoke through the **ftp** command interpreter, are described on **ftp**(1).

  The services provided by the **ftpd** daemon are described on ftpd(1M).

- Domain Name Service

  The Domain Name Service (DNS) is a protocol that provides domain-name-to-address-mapping of forwarding hosts and mail recipients on a network. DNS is described on **named**(1M). See "Using Domain Name Service with TCP/IP" on how to implement the Domain Name Service on your network.

Other application layer protocols exist that are also implemented as a program on the local machine and a daemon on the remote one; examples of these are **rlogin** and **rlogind**, which permit a user to log on to a remote machine; **rsh** and **rshd**, which enable the user to spawn a shell on a remote machine, and **finger** and **fingerd**, which permit a user to obtain information about users on remote machines.

To avoid the need to have an excess of daemons running at all times, the daemon **inetd** is initiated at startup time. After consulting the **/etc/inetd.conf** file, **inetd** runs the appropriate daemons as needed. For example, the daemon **rlogind** will be run by **inetd** whenever there is a request for a remote login from another machine, and only at that time and for the duration of the remote login.

4 Setting Up TCP/IP

Overview of Setting Up TCP/IP 4-1

Obtaining an Internet Network Number 4-2

Assigning IP Addresses to Your Network Hosts 4-3

Establishing a Domain 4-5

The Organization of the Internet 4-5

Selecting a Domain Name 4-8

Registering Your Domain 4-9

Installing Network Media 4-10

Installing TCP/IP Software 4-11

Modifying the Startup Script 4-12

Setting Up TCP/IP Files 4-13

Setting Up the hosts File 4-13
Setting Up the networks File (Optional) 4-15
Setting Up the ethers File (Optional) 4-16
Additional TCP/IP-Related Files 4-17

- The protocols File 4-17
- The services File 4-18

Setting Up the Listener 4-19

Converting Your IP Address to Hexadecimal Notation 4-22

Setting Up TCP/IP As the Preferred Network 4-24

Starting TCP/IP 4-25

Overview of Setting Up TCP/IP

This chapter explains how to set up a machine to join a TCP/IP network. To set up your software, you must supply information, such as network addresses, to a number of programs and files. Setup tasks include

- Obtaining an Internet network number
- Assigning IP addresses to network hosts
- Selecting a domain name
- Installing network hardware
- Installing the TCP/IP Internet package and additional software on which TCP/IP depends
- Customizing your TCP/IP configuration
- Setting up administrative files `/etc/hosts` and `/etc/networks`
- Setting up the Listener, a network port monitor
- Setting up TCP/IP as the machine's preferred network (optional)
- Re-booting the system.

If you intend to set up a machine as a router, additional procedures are involved. Once you complete the procedures described in this chapter, and before you re-boot, see "Expanding Your TCP/IP Network" for instructions.

Obtaining an Internet Network Number

Every TCP/IP network should have an Internet network number, even if the network does not join the actual Internet. NIC at SRI International is the organization that registers TCP/IP networks and assigns network numbers.

To obtain an Internet network number, request the proper form from NIC. Instructions for requesting and completing the form appear in "Guidelines for Completing the IP Number Registration Form".

When you request a network number, you must tell NIC the classification you want for your network. The available network classifications are described below.

- Class A Network

  There are very few Class A networks, but each accommodates a large number of hosts. Typically, Class A networks belong to large organizations or universities. Class A networks are assigned numbers from 0-127.

- Class B Network

  Class B networks provide a median distribution between networks and hosts. For example, the NIC assigns Class B addresses to medium-sized companies with many hosts on their networks. Class B networks are assigned numbers from 128-191.

- Class C Network

  Class C networks are small networks with a maximum of 255 hosts on each. Class C networks are assigned numbers from 192-223.

When you choose a classification, choose the smallest that will accommodate network growth over the next few years. (The chances are slim that your network will need, or that the NIC will grant, Class A classification.) For a fairly large organization that routes together local area networks in several buildings, consider requesting a Class B address. This is a good idea, particularly if you plan to subnet part of your local networks. If your network will not conceivably support more than 255 hosts, ask for a Class C address.

Assigning IP Addresses to Your Network Hosts

Sometimes packets travel only from one host to another on the same local network. At other times, they travel from one local network to another network, going through a router. In the extreme, a packet may traverse many networks, crossing miles of routers, gateways, cabling, and telephone lines to reach its destination. A TCP/IP network routes a packet according to the destination *IP address*—an address provided by the IP protocol on the sending host.

To run TCP/IP properly, every host on the network must have an IP address. A machine's IP address consists of the following:

- the net number
- a subnet number (optional)
- a host number

The net number is the Internet network number you obtain from NIC. The host number is a number that uniquely identifies a machine on your network. You assign the host number.

A subnet number is an optional number representing the subnet to which the host is attached. This is a number that you (as opposed to the NIC) assign to the subnet when you set it up. A machine's IP address includes a subnet number only if the machine is on a subnet. (Refer to "Setting Up Subnets" in "Expanding Your TCP/IP Network" for information about subnet numbering.)

An IP address is 32 bits, divided into four 8-bit fields (octets) separated by periods. Each octet can have a value from 0 to 255. Here is a typical IP address:

129.144.50.56

All IP numbers in this document are provided as examples only. Do not use them for your own purposes.

The following table illustrates how addresses are structured:

Table 4-1: Network Address Structure

	Range	Network Address	Host Address
Class A	0-127	xxx	xxx.xxx.xxx
Class B	128-191	xxx.xxx	xxx.xxx
Class C	192-223	xxx.xxx.xxx	xxx

Once you have received your network number from the NIC, you can create IP addresses for network hosts. You may want to do this on paper, or in an ASCII file for reference, before supplying these addresses to the programs and files that use them.

The first part of the host's IP address must consist of the network number that the NIC assigned you.

You assign the host part of the IP address in the remaining octets after the network number. In the unlikely event that your hosts are on a Class A network, you have three octets for defining the host address. On a Class B network, you have two octets; on a Class C network, one.

On a class C network, you may assign values from 1-254 in the only (last) octet field allowed for the host address. On a class B network, you may assign values from 0-255 in the first octet field of the host address, and values from 1-254 in the last octet field of the host address. On a class A network, you may assign values from 0-255 in the first and second octet fields of the host address, and values from 1-254 in the last octet field of the host address.

The last assignable octet field of the host address should not contain 0 or 255, since these values are reserved for broadcasting.

If, for example, you have a Class A network where the net address is 10, a host could have the address 10.30.5.107 or 10.1.1.255, but it could not have the address 10.0.0.0 or 10.255.255.255; in the same vein, if your network is Class C, with address 192.9.90, you should not assign addresses 192.9.90.0 or 192.9.90.255 to any of its hosts.

Suppose you want to install a machine named `dancer` on your Class C network. If the Class C network has the network number 192.9.200, you might assign `dancer` the IP address

192.9.200.1

Then you might install other hosts on the same network with IP addresses such as 192.9.200.2, 192.9.200.3, and so on.

Establishing a Domain

Once you obtain a network number, assign IP addresses to all the hosts on your network, and install the software, you can establish a domain. A domain is a set of machines that are administered and maintained as a single entity. Generally, all the machines on a local network comprise a domain on the larger network; however, you may choose to break the local network into several administrative entities, called subdomains. For example, you may want all the machines in the Accounting department to comprise one subdomain, and all the machines in Marketing to comprise another.

To join the Internet, your domain must be named according to Internet naming conventions, and you must register your domain name with the NIC. Even if you do not intend to join the Internet at this time, it is recommended that you follow the Internet naming conventions and register with the NIC to avoid problems in the future, should you decide to join the network.

This section explains the Internet naming conventions, and directs you to "Guidelines for Completing the Domain Registration Form" for instructions for obtaining and completing the Internet domain registration form. If you intend to join a public network other than the Internet, such as BITNET or CSNET, contact the organization that administers the network for information about naming conventions and for a registration form.

The Organization of the Internet

The Internet consists of four levels of domain: the root level, the top level, the second level, and the local level. Each level branches from the level above it. Below the local level are hosts and, optionally, subdomains.

Figure 4-1 shows the different domain levels of the Internet and how they relate to each other.

Figure 4-1: A Typical Internet Domain Hierarchy

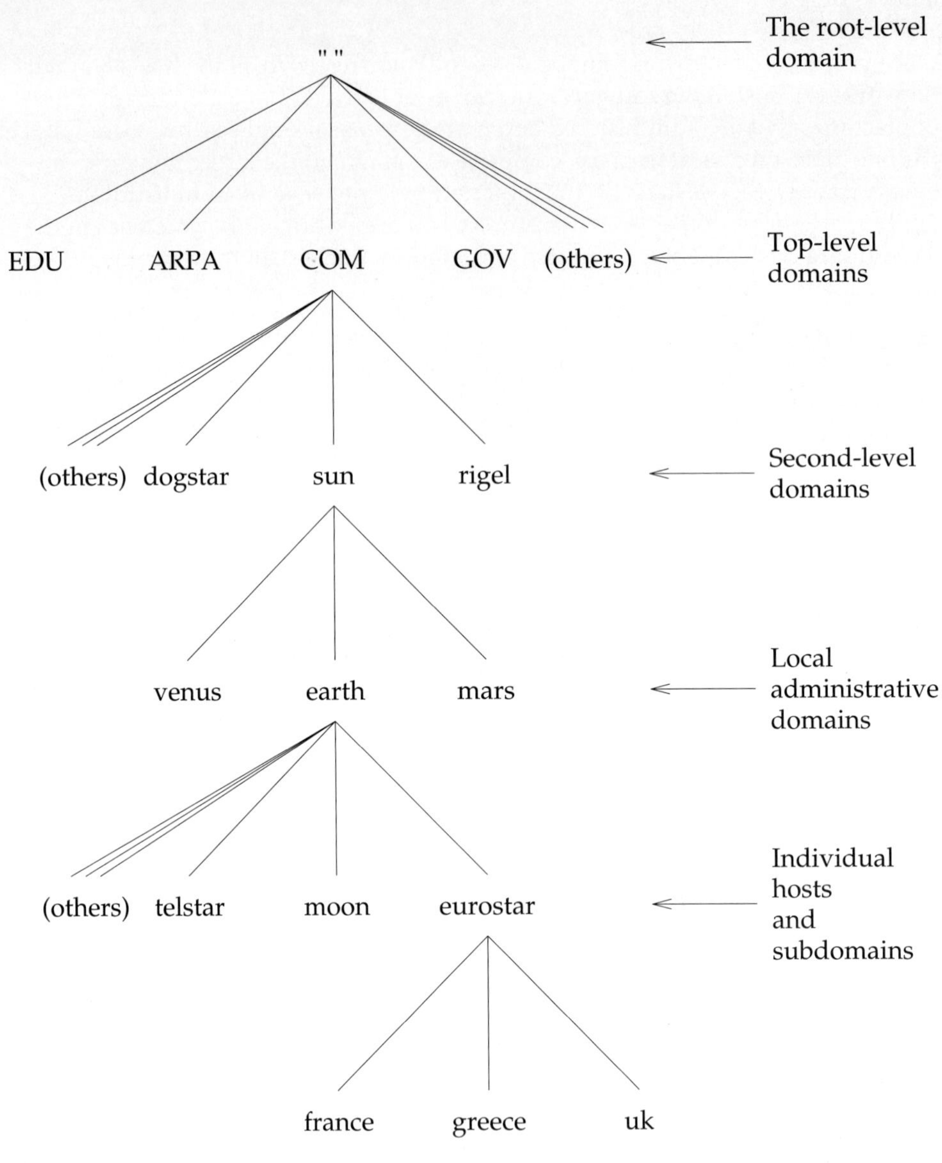

At each level of the Internet are name servers. A name server is a machine that maintains information about machines at the next lower level and facilitates name-to-address mapping.

The different levels of the Internet are described below:

- The Root-Level Domain

  The root level is the top of the entire Internet; it is maintained by the NIC. (Organizations in charge of other public networks, such as BITNET and CSNET, also administer the roots of their networks.)

  At the root level, the NIC administers *root domain name servers*, which maintain information about name servers at the next lower level.

- Top-Level Domains

  The root level branches into "top-level domains." Currently, some Internet top-level domains are EDU, ARPA, COM, GOV, MIL, NET, ORG, and US.

  The names of the top-level domains are assigned by the NIC. They reflect the types of networks that make up the domain. For example, EDU (an abbreviation of *Educational*) is a top-level domain that consists of networks administered by universities; COM (an abbreviation of *Commercial*) consists of networks belonging to business organizations.

  When you register with the NIC, it assigns your network to one of these domains, depending on your organization's function.

- Second-Level Domains

  Each top-level domain branches into second-level domains. Member organizations at the second level assign "domain administrators" to manage their name servers, and the NIC assigns a "technical contact" to coordinate administration across domains. Depending upon your site's size and requirements, you may have domain administrator responsibilities.

- Local Administrative Domains

  Within each second-level domain are local administrative domains. These are the domains you administer for your organization. A local domain can be as small as one host, or large enough to include many hosts and additional name servers. It may also have other administrative domains (called subdomains) nested within it.

For more information about name servers and administrative responsibilities, see "Using Domain Name Service with TCP/IP".

Selecting a Domain Name

The Internet is organized as a hierarchy of domains. The name space is organized as a tree according to organizational or administrative boundaries. Each node of the tree is a domain, which is given a label. The name of the domain is the concatenation of all the labels of the domain from the root to the current domain, listed from right to left and separated by dots. A host address for a host named `monet` at Podunk University might look like this:

```
monet.podunk.EDU
```

The top-level domain for educational institutions is EDU, Podunk is a subdomain of EDU, and monet is the name of the host.

When you name your domain, you must select a label that is unique within its domain. For example, you could use "podunk" as a label for a domain consisting of all machines at Podunk University, provided that another university in the domain EDU has not used this name first. The label you assign a host within your domain must be unique as well, but only within domain "podunk."

Once you choose a label, you must concatenate it with the labels of all the higher level domains to create your domain name.

Domains are not limited to any fixed number of levels. For example, the Amalgamated Widgit Company might be registered with the NIC as belonging to the domain "Widgit.COM"; it might also have a subdomain called "eng.Japan.Widgit.COM" for the engineering group within their Japan subsidiary, and another called "mktg.Japan.Widgit.COM" for marketing in Japan. However, machines at company headquarters might belong to the subdomain called "HQ.Widgit.COM."

Upper- and lower-case letters are not significant in domain names. The traditional UNIX convention is to use all lower-case; many other systems use upper-case.

At many sites, users name their individual hosts while the administrators name the servers. The administrator should ensure that there are no duplicate names within a domain by using the **nslookup** [see **nslookup**(1M)] program. This is an interactive program that you can use (among other things) either to produce a listing of all the hosts in the domain (by using the **ls** command at the **>** prompt), or to obtain information about a host. At the prompt, you enter the host's name. If the host is in the database, **nslookup** produces its address; otherwise, it informs you that the host does not exist.

Registering Your Domain

After choosing the name of your upper domain (the equivalent of ''Widgit.COM'' in the example in the preceding section), you need to register it with a higher-level domain. To do this, you should get in touch with the administrator of the higher domain. The top-level domains are administered by the NIC at SRI International.

To register a domain with NIC, request the Domain Registration Form from NIC and complete it according to the instructions in ''Guidelines for Completing the Domain Registration Form''.

Once your domain is registered, you can divide it into subdomains as the need arises.

Installing Network Media

Before you install TCP/IP, you need to install your network media. At the present time, the implementation of TCP/IP in UNIX SVR4.2 runs over Ethernet.

For information about installing Ethernet on your system, see your Ethernet documentation.

For a list of supported Ethernet interface cards, see the UNIX SVR4.2 *Installation Guide*.

Installing TCP/IP Software

Before you install the TCP/IP Internet package, you must install software on which TCP/IP depends. First, make sure the Network Support Utilities (NSU) package is installed on your system. NSU is provided as part of UNIX SVR4.2.

You also need software to drive your network media. The software you use must match the Ethernet board you have installed. For a list of supported Ethernet cards, see the UNIX SVR4.2 *Installation Guide*.

When you install the Network Support Utilities, you also must install pseudo terminal resources. At least eight pseudo-ttys should be installed, with one more for each expected simultaneous `telnet` or remote login session. For information, see the UNIX SVR4.2 *Release Notes*.

Once NSU and Ethernet drivers are installed, you can install the TCP/IP Internet package. TCP/IP Internet installation instructions also appear in the UNIX SVR4.2 *Release Notes*.

When you install TCP/IP, the installation script prompts you for the IP address of your machine and your domain name. If you have not determined your IP address, refer to "Assigning IP Addresses to Your Network Hosts".

Modifying the Startup Script

When you install TCP/IP on a host, a shell script is installed in `/etc/inet/rc.inet`. The script configures the system and starts the daemons the machine needs to run on a TCP/IP network.

The names of all TCP/IP Internet daemons include an `in.` prefix; however, names have been abbreviated throughout this guide. For example, the daemon `in.routed` is referred to as `routed`. When you specify a daemon on the command line or in the startup script, use the full name of the daemon.

All daemons are located in `/usr/sbin`.

Before you run the script, you need to edit it, and you need to set up your `/etc/hosts` and `/etc/networks` files (as described later in this chapter). This section tells you how to edit `/etc/inet/rc.inet`.

To edit the script, follow these steps:

1. If your machine will be communicating with machines that are not connected directly to the local network, locate the line

   ```
   #/usr/sbin/route add default your_nearest_gateway hops_to_gateway
   ```

   For *your_nearest_gateway*, substitute the name of the router that will be the machine's default router. For *hops_to_gateway*, substitute the number `1`. Delete the comment character (#).

   If you are unfamiliar with routers and you are unsure at this point if your local network needs a router, see "Expanding Your TCP/IP Network".

2. If your machine will only be communicating with machines that are connected to your local network, locate the line

   ```
   /usr/sbin/in.routed -q
   ```

   and insert the comment character (#). (This line starts the route daemon, which facilitates communication with subnets via a router; if your machine operates only on a local network, the route daemon is unnecessary and may degrade performance if allowed to run.)

Setting Up TCP/IP Files

There are a number of TCP/IP-related files that you, as a TCP/IP network administrator, need to set up and maintain.

`/etc/hosts` — The **hosts** [see **hosts**(4)] file maps host names to IP addresses. The file is provided by the software, and must be edited and maintained by the system administrator. Every network host must have a **hosts** file.

`/etc/networks` — The **networks** [see **networks**(4)] file maps network names to net numbers.

`/etc/ethers` — The **ethers** [see **ethers**(4)] file maps host names to their Ethernet addresses. You need to create an **ethers** file only if you are running the RARP daemon.

`/etc/protocols` — The **protocols** [see **protocols**(4)] file lists the IP protocols installed on your system and their numbers; it is created automatically when TCP/IP is installed and requires no administrative handling.

`/etc/services` — The **services** [see **services**(4)] file lists the names of reserved IP services and their port numbers; it is used by programs that call network services. **services** is created automatically when TCP/IP is installed and requires no administrative handling.

Before you run the TCP/IP startup script on a network machine, you need to set up the machine's **hosts**, **networks**, and **ethers** files. The **hosts** and **networks** files on the machine should be consistent and up-to-date with the same files that reside on the other machines on your local network.

Setting Up the hosts File

When you set up your network initially, you must make sure that all the machines know the IP addresses of all other machines on the network. To do this, you specify the IP addresses of all the machines (including the address of the host itself) in the **hosts** file.

The **hosts** file lists all machines in the local domain by IP address and name, in the following format:

IP_number host_name nickname **#***comment*

where *IP_number* is the combination net number and host number that the administrator assigns a host; *host_name* is the official name of the host machine; *nickname* is another name by which the host can receive information, such as mail or file services, over the network; and **#***comment* is any kind of note you want to append to an entry.

The following line should always be in **/etc/hosts**:

127.0.0.1 localhost

The "localhost" address is 127.0.0.1 on every machine; the address is used by programs to reach services on the same machine from which they are invoked.

Whenever you add a host to the network, you have to add its name to the **hosts** file; this means that you have to modify the **/etc/hosts** file on each machine to reflect all changes.

Example

Suppose you have a machine named **dancer** with 192.9.200.1 as the IP address for **dancer**. Next, assume you need to add three new hosts to your network—**ballet**, **raks**, and **samba**. To update the **hosts** file, you would add the following three lines to the **/etc/hosts** file on **dancer**:

```
192.9.200.2        ballet    # This is a comment
192.9.200.3        raks
192.9.200.4        samba
```

Next, edit **/etc/hosts** in each of the new machines, so that they are identical to the database on **dancer**.

At the end of the procedure, the four **/etc/hosts** files in **ballet**, **samba**, **raks**, and **dancer** should be identical (although the order of the entries may vary).

For more information about **/etc/hosts**, see **hosts**(4).

Setting Up the networks File (Optional)

The **networks** file contains the names of all TCP/IP-based networks to which your network connects, via routers. (For information about expanding your network with routers, see "Expanding Your TCP/IP Network".

The **networks** file associates a network number with a name. It should contain the names and network numbers on every network that the machine can use.

Entries in the file have the following format:

> *network_name   network_number   nickname(s)   #comments*

where *network_name* is the official name by which the network is known; *network_number* is the number assigned by the NIC; *nickname* is any other name by which the network is known; and #*comment* is any kind of note you want to append to an entry in the file.

Once you set up the **networks** file, you need to update it on the following occasions:

- Whenever you install another router, and you want to tell your server about the other network to which the router is attached.
- If you join a wide-area network, such as TELNET or BITNET, which is not listed in the file.

It is particularly important that you maintain the **networks** file, as the **netstat** program described in the section "The netstat Command" uses the information in **/etc/networks** to produce status tables.

Example

Figure 4-2 shows a sample **/etc/networks** file:

Figure 4-2: Sample `/etc/networks` File

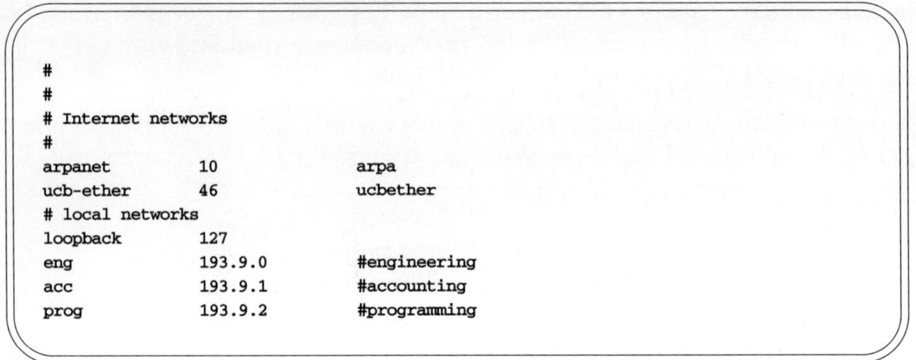

```
#
#
# Internet networks
#
arpanet         10              arpa
ucb-ether       46              ucbether
# local networks
loopback        127
eng             193.9.0         #engineering
acc             193.9.1         #accounting
prog            193.9.2         #programming
```

Setting Up the ethers File (Optional)

The **ethers** file associates host's names with their Ethernet addresses. RARP uses the file to map Ethernet addresses to IP addresses. If you are running the RARP daemon, you need to set up the **ethers** file and maintain it on all hosts to reflect changes to the network. An administrator must create an **ethers** file if it is needed, since it is not delivered with the system.

The format of the **ethers** file is as follows:

Ethernet_address host_name #comment

where *Ethernet_address* is the address of the device driver on the host; *host_name* is the official name of the host; and **#***comment* is any kind of note you want to append to an entry in the file.

The equipment manufacturer provides the Ethernet address. If a machine does not display the Ethernet address when you power up, see your hardware manuals for instructions on locating a host's address.

When adding entries to **/etc/ethers**, make sure that host names correspond to the primary names in **/etc/hosts**, not to the nicknames.

Example

Figure 4-3 shows a sample **/etc/ethers** file, such as you might have on your system. Entries, as shown in the example, should be in alphabetical order by machine name.

Figure 4-3: Sample /etc/ethers File

```
8:0:20:1:40:14  ballet
8:0:20:1:40:7   dancer     # This is a comment
8:0:20:1:40:15  raks
8:0:20:1:40:16  samba
```

Refer to the **ethers**(4) manual page for additional information.

Additional TCP/IP-Related Files

In addition to the files you need to create and maintain, TCP/IP installs two files, **protocols** and **services**, that are used by various programs. Although you do not need to handle these files, you may want to display them for information.

The protocols File

/etc/protocols contains the names of the TCP/IP protocols installed on the system. Figure 4-4 shows a sample **/etc/protocols** file:

Figure 4-4: Sample /etc/protocols File

```
#
# Internet (IP) protocols
#
ip      0       IP      # internet protocol, pseudo protocol number
icmp    1       ICMP    # internet control message protocol
ggp     3       GGP     # gateway-gateway protocol
tcp     6       TCP     # transmission control protocol
egp     8       EGP     # exterior gateway protocol
pup     12      PUP     # PARC universal packet protocol
udp     17      UDP     # user datagram protocol
hmp     20      HMP     # host monitoring protocol
xns-idp 22      XNS-IDP # Xerox NS IDP
rdp     27      RDP     # "reliable datagram" protocol
```

Refer to the **protocols**(4) manual page for more information.

The services File

/etc/services contains entries for reserved TCP/IP network services. An excerpt from a typical **/etc/services** file is shown in Figure 4-5:

Figure 4-5: Excerpt from a Typical /etc/services File

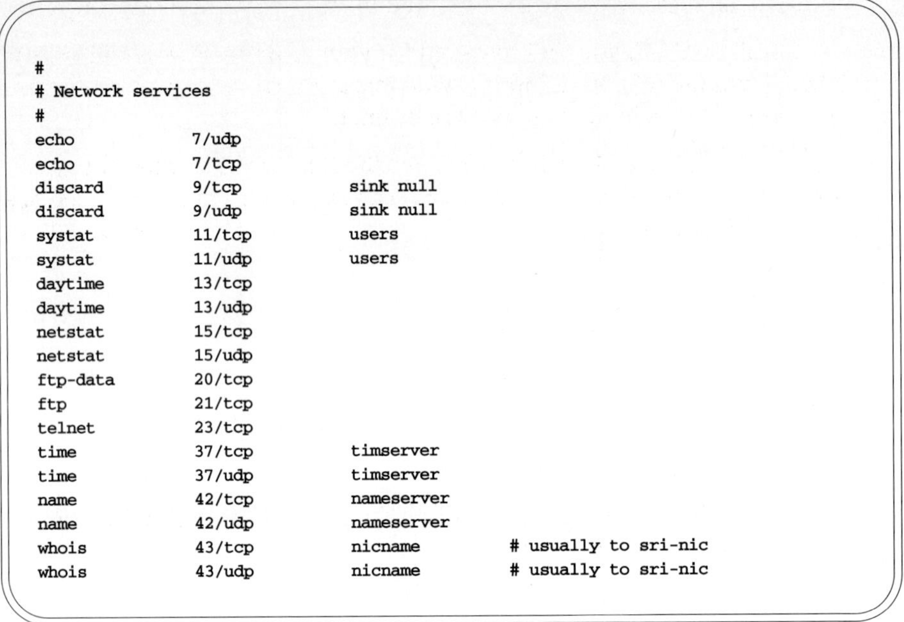

```
#
# Network services
#
echo            7/udp
echo            7/tcp
discard         9/tcp           sink null
discard         9/udp           sink null
systat          11/tcp          users
systat          11/udp          users
daytime         13/tcp
daytime         13/udp
netstat         15/tcp
netstat         15/udp
ftp-data        20/tcp
ftp             21/tcp
telnet          23/tcp
time            37/tcp          timserver
time            37/udp          timserver
name            42/tcp          nameserver
name            42/udp          nameserver
whois           43/tcp          nicname         # usually to sri-nic
whois           43/udp          nicname         # usually to sri-nic
```

Notice that various network services like **ftp** and **telnet** are listed in the first column. The second column contains the service's port number and the transport layer protocol (either TCP or UDP) that handles it. Refer to the **services**(4) manual page for more information.

Some of the reserved services may not be available on your machines; however, their port numbers must be reserved nevertheless.

Setting Up the Listener

The listener is a port monitor that listens for communication across the network. Once the listener is properly configured for TCP/IP, your system can provide network services such as Network File System (NFS) and Remote File Sharing (RFS).

When you install TCP/IP, you will be asked for your IP address as it will appear in the **/etc/hosts** file. If you do not provide this address, you will have to perform the following steps in order to use the listener.

1. Put an entry for your system in the **/etc/hosts** file if one does not exist. For the format of the entry in the **/etc/hosts** file, see "Setting Up the hosts File" and **hosts**(4).

2. Run the **listen.setup** script:

   sh /etc/inet/listen.setup

   This setup script accomplishes the following:

   1. Gets your system name via the **uname -n** command,
   2. Determines your IP address from the **/etc/hosts** file,
   3. Converts your IP address into the proper hexadecimal address for use by the **pmadm** command,
   4. Sets up the **nlps**, **rfs**, **lp**, **lpd**, **uucico**, and **cu** services.
   5. Checks and updates the appropriate system files (**/etc/uucp/Devices.tcp** and **/etc/uucp/Sysfiles**).

If, for some reason, you change your IP address, you can execute the **/etc/inet/listen.setup** script after you update the **/etc/hosts** file, and the port monitors will be updated with the new IP address.

When **listen.setup** is executed, the old port monitors (if they exist) are deleted, and the new port monitors are added via the **pmadm** command. If you had customized any of the existing services on your machine, you will have to redo the customization.

If any errors occur, an error message will be sent by mail to the appropriate user, and/or to standard error output. If the automatic setup script fails, look at the error message that is reported, correct the error, and execute the **listen.setup** script again.

If a "service" already exists and you want to change it, the existing "service" has to be removed with **pmadm** command. The format for the **pmadm** command is:

pmadm -r -p *provider* **-s** *service_tag*

where *provider* is the transport provider (for example, **tcp**) and *service_tag* is the name of the service (for example, **cu**). See **pmadm**(1M) for more information about **pmadm**.

1. Verify that your system has a valid entry in the **/etc/hosts** file
2. Convert your IP address to hexadecimal notation (see section "Converting Your IP Address to Hexadecimal Notation" for converting an IP address to hexadecimal notation.)
3. Issue the following **pmadm** command for the NLPS server:

   ```
   pmadm -a -p tcp -s 0 -i root -v `/usr/sbin/nlsadmin -V` \
          -m `/usr/sbin/nlsadmin -c /usr/lib/saf/nlps_server \
          -A \x00020ACE${ADDR}0000000000000000`
   ```

   where *${ADDR}* is the 8 hexadecimal digit host IP address. See "Converting Your IP Address to Hexadecimal Notation" for how to convert your decimal IP Address to the hexadecimal notation.
4. Issue the following **pmadm** for RFS server:

   ```
   pmadm -a -p tcp -s 105 -i root -v `/usr/sbin/nlsadmin -V` \
          -m `/usr/sbin/nlsadmin -c /usr/net/servers/rfs/rfsetup` \
          -y "RFS Server"
   ```

   For further information on other requirements for setting up RFS, see "RFS Command Interface".
5. Issue the following **pmadm** for the **lp** and **lpd** port monitors:

   ```
   pmadm -a -p tcp -s lp -i root -v `/usr/sbin/nlsadmin -V` \
          -m `/usr/sbin/nlsadmin -o /var/spool/lp/fifos/listenS5`

   pmadm -a -p tcp -s lpd -i root -v `/usr/sbin/nlsadmin -V` \
          -m `/usr/sbin/nlsadmin -o /var/spool/lp/fifos/listenBSD`
   ```

6. Issue the following **pmadm** for the **uucico** port monitor:

   ```
   pmadm -a -p tcp -s 10103 -i nuucp -v `/usr/sbin/nlsadmin -V` \
          -m "`/usr/sbin/nlsadmin -c \"/usr/lib/uucp/uucico -r 0 \
          -u nuucp -i TLI\"`" -y"uucp"
   ```

7. Issue the following **pmadm** for the **cu** port monitor:

```
pmadm -a -p tcp -s cu -i root -v `/usr/sbin/nlsadmin -V` \
      -m "`/usr/sbin/nlsadmin -c \"/usr/lib/saf/ttymon -g -h \
      -m ntty,tirdwr,ldterm\"`" -fu -y"cu"
```

You must now complete the following steps to verify that certain system files have been properly setup:

1. Verify that an entry exists for `TcpCico10103` in the `/etc/uucp/Devices.tcp` file by executing the following command:

   ```
   grep '^TcpCico10103' /etc/uucp/Devices.tcp
   ```

   You should see the following line:

   TcpCico10103,eg tcp – – TLI \D nls.uucico

   If this line doesn't exist, or is different, you must edit the `/etc/uucp/Devices.tcp` file and add the following line:

   ```
   TcpCico10103,eg tcp - - TLI \D nls.uucico
   ```

2. Verify that the service line for **uucico** is correct in `/etc/uucp/Sysfiles` by executing the following command:

   ```
   grep '^service=uucico.*systems=Systems.tcp:Systems' \
   /etc/uucp/Sysfiles
   ```

   You should see the following information:

   ```
   service=uucico systems=Systems.tcp:Systems \
         devices=Devices.tcp:Devices
   ```

   The above information may appear as shown with the ending backslashes (\) on the first line, or as one long wrap-around line without any backslashes.

   If this information doesn't exist, you must edit the `/etc/uucp/Sysfiles` file and add the following lines:

   ```
   service=uucico  systems=Systems.tcp:Systems \
         devices=Devices.tcp:Devices
   ```

The manual setup is now complete.

Converting Your IP Address to Hexadecimal Notation

Assume your IP address is 192.9.200.1. To translate the IP address to hexadecimal notation, follow these steps:

1. Enter the following shell function to convert a series of decimal numbers into hexadecimal notation:

   ```
   HEX()
   {
    for i in $*
    do echo "$i in Hex: \t\c";
    echo 16o $i p | dc;
    done ;
   }
   ```

2. When the prompt reappears, enter your IP address. Using the sample IP address, you would enter

   ```
   HEX 192 9 200 1
   ```

   The system displays

   ```
   192 in Hex:     C0
   9 in Hex:       9
   200 in Hex:     C8
   1 in Hex:       1
   ```

3. Take the digits from the display and add a zero before each single digit. Using the sample display, 9 becomes 09 and 1 becomes 01.

4. Concatenate the digits together to arrive at your IP address in hexadecimal notation. Again using the sample IP address, your hexadecimal number would be

   ```
   c009c801
   ```

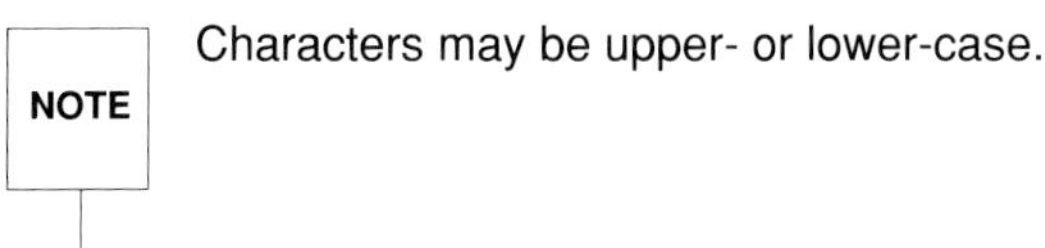

Characters may be upper- or lower-case.

5. To arrive at your listener address insert your family address, the port number of the listener, and your hexadecimal IP address into the format described in the preceding section. Then add the 16 zeros needed in the *Reserved* field.

   Given the listener port number **`0ACE`** and the sample IP address, your listener address would be

   ```
   \x00020ACEc009c8010000000000000000
   ```

Setting Up TCP/IP As the Preferred Network

When you install the TCP/IP Internet package, a file named **/etc/netconfig** is updated automatically with TCP/IP entries. **/etc/netconfig** determines what media will be used when you use a network service. The order of values in the **netconfig** file is what determines the order in which media is tried.

If you want TCP/IP to be your preferred network, edit **/etc/netconfig** and make the TCP/IP entries the first in the file.

For more information, see ''Name-to-Address Mapping'' in ''Network Services''.

Starting TCP/IP

After you install the TCP/IP Internet package, you must reboot your system. To reboot, type

```
cd /; shutdown -y -g0 -i6
```

When the system boots to multi-user state, the TCP/IP startup script runs automatically.

5 Maintaining Security in a TCP/IP Environment

Granting Access to Network Machines 5-1

Administering the host.equiv and .rhosts Files 5-2

The /etc/hosts.equiv File 5-3

The .rhosts File 5-4

Security Issues 5-6

Disabling the TCP/IP Network Service Commands 5-6

Granting Access to Network Machines

UNIX SVR4.2 includes various user programs that enable network users to perform operations on remote hosts. Some of the commands included are: **rlogin** [see **rlogin**(1)], **rsh** [see **rsh**(1)], and **rcp** [see **rcp**(1)]. **rlogin** (remote login) lets a user log in to a remote machine from his or her local machine; **rsh** (remote shell) lets a user create and use a shell on a remote machine; and **rcp** (remote copy) lets a user copy files to and from a remote machine.

Access to a machine on your local network is controlled by each machine's system administrator. Every machine's administrator determines which remote users to grant access and adds entries for those users to the machine's password files. The remote users can then log in to the machine, using the **rlogin** command, by supplying a username and a password.

NOTE

This chapter assumes you are familiar with the files **/etc/shadow**, **/etc/passwd**, and **/etc/group**. For information, see "Creating and Managing User Accounts" in *Basic System Administration* or **group**(4), **passwd**(4), and **shadow**(4) for further information.

You, as a machine's system administrator, may also want to create a home directory on your machine for each remote user to whom you grant access. If a remote user does not have a home directory on your machine and logs in, the root directory (**/**) becomes the user's home directory.

Although remote users can log in to your machine once they have entries in your password database, they cannot run a number of remote processes (such as **rsh** and **rcp**) unless their machines are listed in **/etc/hosts.equiv** or the user's **.rhosts** file, located in the user's *$HOME* directory. In addition to allowing remote users to run certain remote processes on your machine, these files grant users access to your machine without their having to supply passwords.

This chapter explains how your system uses the **hosts.equiv** and **.rhosts** files, then gives you instructions for setting up and maintaining these files.

Administering the host.equiv and .rhosts Files

On a TCP/IP-based network, security is implemented at two levels: first, at the host level, and second, at the user level.

The **/etc/hosts.equiv** file is a general database that controls access at the host level.

The **.rhosts** file controls access to your machine at the user level. It is a file located in the home directory of a specific remote user on your machine, and it is used to allow or deny access to that specific user. There may be multiple instances of **.rhosts** on your machine, one for each remote user with a home directory.

When a remote user attempts to log in to your machine, the security-checking process goes like this:

- A remote user initiates an **rlogin**, and the **rlogin** daemon on your machine checks for the user's username in the password database. If no entry is found, the remote user is denied access.
- If the remote user has an entry in your password database, the daemon next checks for the remote machine's hostname in your **/etc/hosts.equiv** file. If the hostname is found, the remote user gains access.
- If no **/etc/hosts.equiv** entry is found, the system checks for a line with the remote machine's hostname (and, optionally, the remote user's username) in the **.rhosts** file in the user's home directory on your machine. If the entry is found, the remote user gains access.
- If no entry is found for the remote machine in either your **/etc/hosts.equiv** or the remote user's *$HOME*/**.rhosts** file on your machine, the remote user can **rlogin** to the machine after giving the right password. However, the remote user will receive the message **Permission denied** when attempting to run remote processes like **rcp** or **rsh**.

By creating and maintaining a **hosts.equiv** file, you can allow everyone on a particular host to log in to your machine and run remote processes like **rcp** and **rsh**.

If you want certain users on a particular host to access your machine, but not everyone, do not include the host in your **hosts.equiv** file. Instead put the host's name in the **.rhosts** file in each remote user's home directory on your machine.

The following sections tells you how to set up **hosts.equiv** and **.rhosts** files.

The /etc/hosts.equiv File

In the simplest case, the **/etc/hosts.equiv** file is a list of machines, or hosts, from which users are permitted to log in (using **rlogin**) without supplying a password. **hosts.equiv** is a local file, pertaining only to the system in which it is found. The machine's system administrator can modify **hosts.equiv** by logging in as the superuser and using a text editor to make changes.

A typical **hosts.equiv** file has the following structure:

```
host1
host2
```

If a user attempting to log in from a remote host listed in **/etc/hosts.equiv** has an entry in the password database, he or she will be granted access without having to enter a password. If the same user attempts to log in from a host that is not listed in **hosts.equiv** or in *$HOME*/**.rhosts**, he or she will be granted access only after entering a correct password.

A single **+** on a line in a machine's **hosts.equiv** file means that all known hosts (that is, all hosts listed in the **hosts** database) are trusted.

Example

Suppose the **hosts.equiv** file on your machine looks like this (note that the file is just a list of hostnames, one per line).

```
raks
dancers
jazz
```

Now you want to allow anyone on host **ballet** to have access to your machine. Edit **/etc/hosts.equiv** and add **ballet** to the list, as follows:

```
raks
dancers
jazz
ballet
```

Now add all the users on **ballet** to your machine using **adduser** command. After you add, all users who can log in to **ballet** can also freely **rlogin** to your machine, without having to supply a password. Furthermore, users on **ballet** can remote copy from your machine and use a remote shell on your machine.

Refer to the **hosts.equiv**(4) manual page for more information.

The .rhosts File

The **.rhosts** file is located in a specific remote user's home directory on your machine; it is used to allow or deny access to that specific user.

The format of **.rhosts** is similar to that of **/etc/hosts.equiv**, that is,

```
host1
host2
```

The above entries in a user's **.rhosts** file mean that the user can log in from **host1** or **host2**, without supplying a password.

A user can allow others to log in to the remote machine using his or her login by adding usernames to the **.rhosts** file. For example, user **steve** has an **.rhosts** file on your machine that looks like this:

```
host1
host2
host1    jane
```

This means that **steve** can log in remotely to your machine as himself from **host1** and **host2**, and user **jane** can log in to your machine as **steve** from **host1**.

If your site does not require stringent security measures, the easiest way to administer machine access at the user level is to give each user an account in the password database and a home directory on your machine(s). Then ask the trusted users to create their own **.rhosts** files in their home directories on the machine(s).

Example 1

You want user **chris** to have access to your machine without restrictions. Have Chris create the file **.rhosts** in her home directory on your machine.

If Chris wants other users to have access to her login on your machine, her **.rhosts** file might look like this:

```
adams
monroe
jackson
adams       bob
jackson     jenny
```

Now user **chris** can access your machine remotely from **adams**, **monroe**, and **jackson**; **bob** can access your machine as **chris** from **adams**; and **jenny** has access as **chris** from **jackson**.

Example 2

Suppose you want only user **chris** to have access to your machine from host **samba**. To set up your machine, you would follow these steps:

1. Make sure **samba** is not in your **/etc/hosts.equiv** file.
2. Create the file **.rhosts** in **chris**'s home directory on your machine. The file should look like this:

```
samba
```

Security Issues

The only way to achieve anything resembling security in a sensitive environment is to exclude users from your password database; once someone knows a password, he or she can access your machine.

Some TCP/IP user services are especially problematic in an environment that requires strict security. For example, the **finger** command allows a user to display users on a remote host. The command starts the finger daemon **fingerd** on the remote machine, which then reports to the user the username and full name of everyone who is logged in to the machine. There is no authentication of the requestor and no auditing of the requests. Similarly, the **rwhod** daemon (on whose information **ruptime** bases its reports) freely passes around information about who is logged in to a machine.

There are no files or databases to restrict access to the information provided by these daemons; therefore, by default, they are not run. If you do not require strict security, you can run **fingerd** by deleting the comment character from the line that starts **fingerd** in **/etc/inetd.conf**(4). To start **rwhod**, add the line **/usr/sbin/in.rwhod** to the end of the startup script **/etc/inet/rc.inet**.

Disabling the TCP/IP Network Service Commands

You may want to use an application over the network and disable the TCP/IP network service commands. System administrators can configure TCP/IP solely as a transport provider and disable TCP/IP services including **telnet**, **rsh**, **rlogin**, and **rcp**. This would allow other networking services (such as RFS, RCP, and NFS) to continue to work over TCP/IP. Use the **inet.priv** shell script to disable or restore TCP/IP services as shown in the following syntax:

To disable TCP/IP services, type

```
/sbin/sh /etc/inet/inet.priv -d
```

To enable TCP/IP services, type

```
/sbin/sh /etc/inet/inet.priv -e
```

NOTE

Once disabled, TCP/IP service commands will remain disabled even after system reboots. The enable option must be run in System Maintenance Mode with privilege. The shell script must be started by the appropriate user ID with privilege.

6 Expanding Your TCP/IP Network

Introduction 6-1

Hardware Devices for Expanding the Local Network 6-2

Creating an Internetwork 6-4

Configuring a Router 6-4
- Options for the Generic configure Command 6-8
- Configuring Multiple Network Cards 6-8
- Sample Router Files 6-17
- Setting Up the Route Daemon 6-18

Setting Up Router Clients 6-19
- Specifying a Default Router 6-20
- Using Specific Routers 6-21
- Running the Route Daemon on a Client 6-22

Setting Up Subnets 6-23

Network Masks 6-23
Changing from a Non-Subnetted to a Subnetted Network 6-25
Examples of Subnets 6-25

Introduction

In time, you may need to attach more hosts to your network than you have allowable addresses, or you might want two networks in different buildings to share resources. In this chapter we first discuss generally some of the hardware that connects networks. Then we will talk about two ways you can expand your existing network:

- by connecting two or more networks to create an "internetwork."
- by creating a "subnet" on your network.

Hardware Devices for Expanding the Local Network

If your local network fails to meet your needs, you may want to expand it. Below are descriptions of the hardware devices that allow you to connect two or more local networks.

- Repeater: This is a device used at the physical layer of the network; it connects two networks together and copies each bit of a packet from one to the other.

  There are inherent limitations in the use of repeaters, given that they copy all data from one network to the other. Implementations like Ethernet, which require that data traverse the network within a specific amount of time, impose a maximum allowable length and number of repeaters.

- Bridge: This is a device used at the data link layer of the network protocol model. It selectively copies packets from one network to another.

  Bridges differ from repeaters in several ways. Because copying done by bridges is selective, this reduces traffic on the destination network. Since bridges copy whole packets, the geographical or timing constraints of the basic physical network can be extended.

  You can split a bridge as you would a repeater. Like repeaters, bridges copy raw packets, a scheme which works for all protocols above the data link layer. Since bridges copy whole packets, in theory, connections like this are "invisible" to the software on all the machines on the network.

- Router (sometimes called a "gateway"): This is a device that forwards packets of a protocol family, in this case TCP/IP, from one logical network to another. A logical network makes sense only to a particular protocol. Usually there is a one-to-one mapping between physical network and logical network, but subnets (explained in a later section) and bridges are exceptions to this rule. A collection of logical networks (all using the same protocol) connected via routers is called an "internetwork."

  The router may forward packets between different physical types of networks, for example, from an Ethernet to a ring network. It can also forward packets between two logical networks of the same type.

  During forwarding, a router looks inside the packet to find the destination address, then consults its routing table, which is normally kept up to date by having routers communicate with each other via some routing protocol. Note that it is possible to have a multilingual router—a single device that forwards packets for several protocol types, such as TCP/IP, ISO, or XNS.

- Application Gateway (sometimes called a "relay" or "forwarder"): This device and associated software enable networks using different protocols to communicate with each other. Because it translates protocols existing at all layers of the protocol model, you can use gateways to connect networks that differ on all layers from each other. You can also use an application gateway to connect parts of the same physical network that are using different protocols.

Creating an Internetwork

The TCP/IP protocol family provides intercommunication among host computers, terminal servers, and other equipment on one or more local-area or wide-area networks. A typical local network serves a limited area—within a building or between neighboring buildings. Hosts attached to the local network may function as file servers, mail servers, print servers, terminals, and workstations.

Some companies expand their networks by linking local networks together via a computer called an "IP router." A network configuration consisting of several local networks linked together by routers is often called an "internetwork."

Be careful not to confuse the term "internetwork" with the Internet. Your company can set up an internetwork if it needs to expand communications services, and you or one of your co-workers may have the responsibility of managing it. By contrast, the Internet is the name of a particular internetwork.

Configuring a Router

A TCP/IP network usually interconnects a number of hosts. Your UNIX SVR4.2 host is connected to a TCP/IP network via a hardware network interface. Individual TCP/IP networks are in turn interconnected via IP routers. IP routers forward IP packets from one TCP/IP network to another, and exchange routing information with each other to deliver packets across a number of networks. Other types of routers may forward traffic for protocol families other than TCP/IP.

If all of the hosts at your site are connected to a single TCP/IP network that is *not* interconnected with any other TCP/IP networks, an IP router is unnecessary. If your site comprises many TCP/IP networks, or if you want to interconnect your IP network with other TCP/IP networks, you must configure the interconnections with IP routers in order for all hosts to communicate.

Many types of machines may serve as IP routers. A number of vendors offer machines dedicated entirely to the function of IP routing. A system may act both as a host (offering network services such as `rlogin`) and a router.

The `routed` (routing daemon) program implements a standard routing protocol in UNIX SVR4.2. If a system has only one network interface, `routed` will passively monitor the routing traffic (if that network is a broadcast network). If a system has two or more network interfaces, the `routed` program will actively participate in the exchange of routing information with other routers.

Some simple network applications do not require the router to run **routed**. For more information about **routed**, see **routed**(1M) and "Setting Up the Route Daemon".

Assembling a router first involves setting up its hardware. Refer to the manuals that came with the router controllers for information on physical assembly. Once the router is connected to the networks it joins, you must configure the router's software.

Before actually configuring the software, make the following preparations.

- Assign the router a unique host name and a unique IP address for each network it is on. The Internet Protocol architecture requires each interface to have a unique IP address.
- Make sure you have acquired registered IP network numbers for each network the router is to connect.
- If you have not installed the TCP/IP Internet package, install it following the instructions in the SVR4.2 *Release Notes*.

Once you have TCP/IP installed, do the following in Maintenance Mode:

1. Edit **/etc/hosts**.
    a. Add the host name and IP address of each interface on the machine.
    b. Add the names and IP addresses of all the hosts that the router can reach.
2. Access **/etc/networks** and add the network names and IP addresses of all the networks that the router can reach.
3. If you have more than one network card (device) installed in your machine, you must run **/etc/confnet.d/configure -i** [see generic **configure**(1M)]. (The "generic" **/etc/confnet.d/configure** script will be referred to as **configure** in the following explanation).

    When you run **configure -i**, you are interactively configuring the device(s) in your machine. You can run the **configure** script once for each device that is installed, or you can specify the number(s) of the device(s), separated by whitespace, when you are asked which devices(s) you want to configure/reconfigure.

    Before you run **configure**, your network cards should already be installed and setup (hardware configuration).

The **configure** script runs a *protocol-specific* **configure** script (for example, **inet**, [see INET-specific **configure**(1M)]. The *protocol-specific* **configure** scripts are not meant to be run by a user.

An entry in **/etc/hosts** should be added for each network card that is installed in your machine before you run **configure -i**. If an entry does not exist for a network card in **/etc/hosts**, you will be prompted to enter a valid name and IP address for the device that is being configured.

If you populate **/etc/hosts**, one entry should be for the actual name of your machine, along with a valid IP address. Use **uname -n** to display the name of your machine. The additional entries (for multiple network cards) should be variations of **uname -n**. The entry for each networks card installed must have both a unique name and unique IP address.

The following explanations and examples will be for the **inet** protocol, since **inet** is the networking protocol supported under UNIX SVR4.2.

The INET-specific **configure** script uses the IP address from **uname -n** for the first device. For the second device, the INET-specific **configure** script defaults to **uname -n**, followed by a 2. For example, if the name of your machine is **hulk** and you have two network cards installed, the first device would default to the IP address for **hulk**, and the second device would default to the IP address for **hulk2**. You have the ability to change the defaults when you run **configure -i**.

You will then be asked to select the **ifconfig** options for the network card that is being configured. The valid choices are:

Table 6-1: Choices for Setting the `ifconfig` Options with `configure -i`

Choice	Description of ifconfig options.
yes	**-trailers**
no	Enter no options or customize the **ifconfig** options
ClassC	**netmask 0xffffff00 broadcast** *network_address*.255 **-trailers**
BerkeleyC	**netmask 0xffffff00 broadcast** *network_address*.0 **-trailers**
info	Prints informational message about common **ifconfig** options

After you chose the **ifconfig** option(s), INET-specific **interface** is updated with the information for the device being configured and the **netdrivers** file is updated by the **netinfo** command. See **netdrivers**(4) for information on **/etc/confnet.d/netdrivers**. See **netinfo**(1M) for information on **netinfo**.

When a second (or later) device is being configured, you are asked if you want to set up the machine as a **gateway**. The **IPFORWARDING** variable will be updated in the **/etc/conf/pack.d/ip/space.c** file. The valid choices are:

Table 6-2: Choices for Setting up a Machine As a Gateway with `configure -i`

Choice	Description
`yes`	If IPFORWARDING=0, change it to 1, set kernel to be rebuilt on next reboot If IPFORWARDING=1, make no changes
`no`	If IPFORWARDING=1, change it to 0, set kernel to be rebuilt on next reboot If IPFORWARDING=0, make no changes
`unchanged`	make no changes

Once you have selected the option you want, the INET-specific **configure** script will finish setting up the specified network card(s).

An example run of the generic **configure -i** script, and the resulting files, is shown in "Configuring Multiple Network Cards".

4. Change the route daemon to "active" mode by deleting the **-q** from the line

```
/usr/sbin/in.routed -q
```

so the line reads

```
/usr/sbin/in.routed
```

Once you have your router set up, add the host names and IP addresses of the router's interfaces to the **/etc/hosts** and **/etc/networks** files on each machine on your local network.

If you specified that your machine should be set up as a gateway, and the **IPFORWARDING** variable was modified by **configure**, you will see a message stating that the UNIX kernel will be rebuilt the next time you reboot your machine. If you see this message, you must reboot your machine after you are done configuring the network cards for the changes to take affect. To reboot and rebuild the UNIX kernel on your machine (if needed), enter:

```
cd /;shutdown -i6 -g0 -y
```

Your UNIX kernel will be rebuilt, and your machine will be rebooted.

Options for the Generic configure Command

The generic **configure** command has the following syntax:

> **configure [-i] [-p** *protocol* **-d** *device* **[-d** *device***...]]**
> **configure [-p** *protocol* **-d** *device***] [-O "***protocol specific opts***"]**
> **configure [-r -d** *device***] [-r -p** *protocol***] [-r -p** *protocol* **-d** *device***]**

The **-i** option runs the **configure** in the interactive mode. You can specify the *protocol* and **device**(s) that you want to configure at this time.

If you don't use the **-i** option, you must specify all of the *protocol-specific* options with the **-O** option, enclosed in a pair of double-quotes (" "). See the *protocol-specific* **configure** manual page for the options needed by the *protocol-specific* **configure** command. For example, to find out the *protocol-specific* options for **inet**, you would need to see INET-specific **configure**(1M).

The **-r** option allows you to remove a specified *device*, a specified *protocol*, or both. This command would be used if you were going to remove a *protocol* and/or *device* from the machine.

See generic **configure**(1M) for information on the **configure** command.

Configuring Multiple Network Cards

This example of **configure -i** will be for two network cards (devices), shown in the following figure, using the **inet** protocol, with the machine to be set up as a gateway. The name of the machine is **hulk**.

Figure 6-1: Sample `/etc/confnet.d/netdrivers` File for Two Network Cards

```
el16_0
wd_0
```

The above figure shows that there are two network cards installed, and that they are not mapped to any protocol.

The following figure is the unmodified INET-specific **interface** file.

Figure 6-2: Sample Unmodified /etc/confnet.d/inet/interface File

```
#version = 1.0
#Format of a 1.0 line
#       prefix:unit#:addr:device:ifconfig opts:slink opts:
#
#Field  Name            Verify  Purpose                 Default on NULL
#
#$1     prefix          string  device identifier  NONE
#       prefix is an identifier for a driver's netstat statistics
#
#$2     unit            number  device ifstats index    NONE
#       unit is the index per prefix array
#
#$3     address         NONE    IP name or address `/usr/bin/uname -n`
#       address is used by ifconfig to initialize the transport provider.
#       This may be the internet name or number.
#       Null is expanded to `/usr/bin/uname -n`
#
#$4     device          string  full device path name   NONE
#       device is the node name of the transport provider.
#       it is reserved through the generic /etc/confnet.d/configure script
#       from the generic /etc/confnet.d/netdrivers file.
#       it will be used by slink
#
#$5     ifconfig_opt    NONE    allow customized options, SLIP for example
#       ifconfig_opts is used to customize the ifconfig options used at boot time.
#       The constructed command line will take the form:
#               ifconfig prefixunit# Converted_Address ifconfig_opts up
#       Converted_Address is the /etc/inet/hosts value for the address field.
#       So ifconfig_opts has the -trailers and other options needed by
#       System V Release 4 transport providers.
#       Note that a null entry is allowed for providers like lo0 that require
#       no additional ifconfig options at boot time.
#
#$6     slink_opt NONE  allow customized options, SLIP for example
#       default: add_interface
#       The slink_opts value is used by slink to initialize the device
#       into the TCP/IP protocol stack.
#       slink_opts selects the strcf function from /etc/inet/strcf and
#       any initial arguments.
#       add_interface is the default slink_opts value; it is used with
#       Ethernet-style devices.
#       Additional arguments will be appended to slink_opt to make the final
#       form of the slink operation:
#               slink_opts ip device prefixunit#
#       Where ip will be an open file descriptor to /dev/ip and device prefix
#       and unit are defined in the current interface entry.
#       For a standard Ethernet board, slink_opts may be null; the defaults
#       will take care of all arguments.
lo:0:localhost:/dev/loop::add_loop:
```

The only entry in the **/etc/confnet.d/inet/interface** is for **lo:0** (**lo0/localhost**). **lo0/localhost** is the loopback TCP/IP software driver. **lo0/localhost** can be used as an argument to network applications without using network hardware.

After the generic **configure -i** is finished, entries are added/updated.

Configuring the First Network Device

Run the generic **configure** script in interactive mode by entering:

```
sh /etc/confnet.d/configure -i
```

The following text is the question and answer session from the generic **configure** and the INET-specific **configure** scripts, along with the resulting **netdrivers** and INET-specific **interface** files.

Figure 6-3: Sample List of Network Cards (Devices) Available for Configuration

```
These are the device(s) available on your system:
  1  el16_0
  2  wd_0
Type the number of the device(s) you wish to configure with inet [?,??,q]:
```

If you enter **?**, the following help message will be displayed.

Figure 6-4: Help Message from `configure -i`

```
Enter the number of the menu item you wish to select, or the token
which is associated with the menu item, or a partial string which
uniquely identifies the token for the menu item. Enter ?? to reprint
the menu.
```

If you enter **??**, the list of available devices will be displayed. If you enter **q**, the **configure** script will either display the next available protocol (if any are installed) or terminate execution. At this point, you can enter the number of one device, or both devices, separated by whitespace. (**configure -i** was executed for each device in this example.) For this example we will specify the 1st (**el16_0**) device.

Figure 6-5: Selecting the (1st) Device to be Configured

```
Type the number of the device(s) you wish to configure with inet [?,??,q]: 1
```

You will be prompted to enter the IP host name for **el16_0**:

Figure 6-6: Choosing the IP Host Name for the (1st) Device Being Configured

```
Please enter the IP host name for device el16_0 (default: hulk):
```

If you press return, the default name will be used. The default name is generated by the **uname -n** command. If you want to use a name other than the default, you can enter it now.

For this example, we used the default name. You are then asked for the IP address for the IP host name that was just entered. The **/etc/hosts** file is searched for the IP address for the IP host name that was specified. If a match for the specified name is found, it becomes the default entry. If a match is not found, you will be prompted to enter a valid IP address.

Figure 6-7: Choosing the IP Address for the (1st) Device Being Configured

```
Please initialize the IP address for host hulk (default: 174.2.110.56)
```

If you press return, the default IP address will be used. If you want to use an IP address other than the default, you can enter it now. If you change the IP address at this time, the change will also be made to the **/etc/hosts** file.

For this example, we used the default IP address. You are then asked for the **ifconfig** options for the device that is being configured:

Figure 6-8: Choosing the `ifconfig` Options for the (1st) Device Being Configured

```
Configure host hulk with default Ethernet™ ifconfig options?
Info message is long. (yes no ClassC BerkeleyC info; default: info):
```

For this example, we used the default, which prints the following informational message (the IP addresses shown here are specific to this example):

Figure 6-9: Informational Message regarding the `ifconfig` Options

```
The most commonly used ifconfig option list for Ethernet(TM) devices is:

     -trailers

This is the default ifconfig option list option for your network.  The
-trailers option is used to synchronize network packet trailer functionality.

Some machines need to apply 'netmask' and 'broadcast' ifconfig options to allow
routing between networks.  The netmask argument identifies the network and
machine portions of the address.  The broadcast address is usually the network
address with '255' filling in the machine address portion(s).  The 'ClassC'
option will assign the ifconfig options:

          netmask 0xffffff00 broadcast 174.2.110.255 -trailers

On Berkeley style networks, the broadcast address has '0' filling in the machine
address portion(s).  The BerkeleyC option will assign the ifconfig options:

          netmask 0xffffff00 broadcast 174.2.110.0 -trailers

Other network devices and protocols may require different ifconfig options.
Some actually require no ifconfig options.  Please refer to the ifconfig(1m)
manual page or documentation specific to your network device if you need other
options.  Answer 'no' to the prompt to customize your own ifconfig options.
```

See Table 6-1 for a summary of the **`ifconfig`** options used with **`configure -i`**. For this example, we answered **`yes`**. At this point, the INET-specific **`interface`** file is updated with the options selected with the device we configured and the **`netdrivers`** file is updated to show that the **`el16_0`** board is mapped to the **`inet`** protocol. The partially configured **`interface`** and **`netdrivers`** (for the 1st network card) are shown in the following two figures.

Figure 6-10: Partially Configured `/etc/confnet.d/inet/interface` File

```
lo:0:localhost:/dev/loop::add_loop:
el16:0::/dev/el16_0:-trailers::
```

Figure 6-11: Partially Configured `/etc/confnet.d/netdrivers` File

```
el16_0        inet
wd_0
```

Configuring the Second (or Later) Network Device

Now, we enter

`sh /etc/confnet.d/configure -i"`

again, so we can configure the second network card (device).

Figure 6-12: Selecting a Network Card (Device) to be Configured

```
These are the device(s) available on your system:
  1  el16_0
  2  wd_0
Type the number of the device(s) you wish to configure with inet [?,??,q]:
```

Please note that the first network card (`el16_0`) still appears in the list of available network cards. This allows you to reconfigure an existing network card. For this example we will specify the 2nd (`wd_0`) device.

Figure 6-13: Selecting the (2nd) Device to be Configured

```
Type the number of the devices you wish to configure with inet [?,??,q]: 2
```

You will then be prompted to enter the IP host name for **wd_0**:

Figure 6-14: Choosing the IP Host Name for the (2nd) Device Being Configured

```
Please enter the IP host name for device wd_0 (default: hulk2):
```

If you press return, the default name will be used. The default name is generated by the `uname -n` command, followed by a 2, since this is the second device that is being configured. If you want to use a name other than the default, you can enter it now.

For this example, we used the default name. You will then be asked for the IP address for the **IP host name** that you just specified. The **/etc/hosts** file will be searched for the IP address for the **IP host name** that was specified. If an IP address for the specified name is found, it will become the default entry. If a match is not found, you will be prompted to enter the IP address.

Figure 6-15: Choosing the IP Address for the (2nd) Device Being Configured

```
Please initialize the IP address for host hulk2 (default: 174.2.110.124)
```

If you press return, the default IP address will be used. If you want to use an IP address other than the default, you can enter it now. If you change the IP address at this time, the change will also be made to the **/etc/hosts** file.

For this example, we used the default IP address. You will then be asked for the **ifconfig** options for the network card the is being configured:

```
Configure host hulk with default Ethernet™ ifconfig options?
Info message is long. (yes no ClassC BerkeleyC info; default: info):
```

Since we have already seen the information message, we answered **yes**. At this point, the INET-specific **interface** file is updated with the options selected with the device we configured and the **netdrivers** file is updated to show that the **wd_0** board is mapped to the **inet** protocol.

Figure 6-16: Configured `/etc/confnet.d/inet/interface` File

```
lo:0:localhost:/dev/loop::add_loop:
el16:0::/dev/el16_0:-trailers::
wd:0:hulk2:/dev/wd_0:-trailers::
```

The fields in the **interface** file are separated by colons (:).

The first field is the identifier for the drivers **netstat**, see **netstat**(1M), statistics. The second field contains the index number for that device (the value for the first device is 0, for the second device 1, with the maximum value of 9). The third field contains either the IP host name or IP address for the device. If this field is null, the value is expanded to the system nodename. There should only be one "null" address per **interface** file. The fourth field is the device name (as it appears in the **/dev** directory) for the transport provider that is being used. The fifth field is used for customized **ifconfig** options. This field may be null, but it usually contains **-trailers** for Ethernet devices. The sixth field is used for specifying customized **ifconfig** options. This field may be null.

See INET-specific **interface**(4) for detailed information on the **/etc/confnet.d/inet/interface** file.

Figure 6-17: Configured `/etc/confnet.d/netdrivers` File

```
el16_0        inet
wd_0          inet
```

The fields in the **netdrivers** file are separated by whitespace.

The first field is the name of the network card as it appears in the **/dev** directory. The second field is the protocol that has been mapped to the device that is shown on the same line.

Configuring the 2nd (or Later) Network Device as a Gateway

Since we are configuring the second (or later) card in this machine, we are asked the following question:

Figure 6-18: Configuring the Machine to Act as a Gateway

```
Do you want to set this machine as a gateway? [y/n/unchanged]
```

For our example, we answered **y** (for yes). At this point, the INET-specific **configure** script updates the **IPFORWARDING** variable (if needed) in **/etc/conf/pack.d/ip/space.c**. If the **IPFORWARDING** variable had to be updated, the unix kernel will need to be rebuilt. You will see the following message:

```
The UNIX Operating System kernel will be rebuilt to include your
configuration changes during the next system reboot.
```

Before you make any other changes, you should reboot your system by entering the following:

```
cd /;shutdown -i6 -g0 -y
```

Your UNIX kernel will be rebuilt, and your machine will be rebooted.

Sample Router Files

Consider a router called **jekyll** that connects two Class C networks. Like all routers, **jekyll** must have two hardware network interfaces. For the network software to work properly, the router must have a unique host name in the **/etc/hosts** file for each interface.

Because the internetwork on which **jekyll** resides is a simple one, **jekyll** doesn't need to run the routing daemon. It knows about all the available hosts by virtue of being directly connected to both local networks.

Notice in the sample file that, on the second network, **jekyll** has another name—**jekyll-hyde**. (**jekyll** is the router's primary name.) For ease of administration, similar host names are used for each network. Users on both networks can address the machine by the primary name **jekyll**, while the administrator can tell the difference between the two.

Note also that **jekyll** is added with two IP addresses.

```
#
# sample hosts file
#
# 192.9.200 -- eng -- Engineering Network
#
192.9.200.1        jekyll
192.9.200.2        usher
192.9.200.3        lenore
192.9.200.5        raven
# 192.9.201 -- mktg -- Marketing Network
#
192.9.201.11       quasimoto
192.9.201.12       godzilla
192.9.201.13       rodan
192.9.201.4        jekyll-hyde
```

The following screen is an excerpt from **jekyll**'s **/etc/networks** file. The **networks** files contains just the names and IP addresses of the networks to which **jekyll** belongs.

```
#
# sample networks file
#
eng       192.9.200 # Engineering Network
mktg      192.9.201 # Marketing Network
```

Setting Up the Route Daemon

Routers manage network traffic by maintaining routing tables—tables that contain information as to which networks and hosts can be reached by which routes. A routing table can be either static or dynamic.

If a router is on a simple internetwork—one that consists of two or three local networks, for example—it can manage traffic with static routing tables. It knows how to get to every machine on the internetwork by virtue of being directly connected to the local networks.

On a more complex network—one in which a router connects a local network to other routers and gateways—the router should be configured to use dynamic routing tables. Dynamic routing tables allow the router to route traffic to the most current gateway destinations.

A router builds and maintains dynamic tables by running the routing daemon **routed**. The routing daemon manages its routing table by exchanging routing information with gateways and other routers. When **routed** runs on a router, it broadcasts its routing table and listens for broadcasts from other directly connected routers. It continually updates its routing table based on those broadcasts. A routing daemon that both broadcasts its routing tables and listens for broadcasts from other routers is called an "active" **routed**.

routed can also run on a client; however, when it runs on a client, it simply listens for broadcasts and updates its local routing table; it does not broadcast to other machines. To do this, the **-q** option is used for **routed** to be "quiet" and only listen to router information. This is called a "passive" **routed**. For information about running **routed** on a client, see **routed**(1M) and "Setting Up Router Clients".

When **routed** is first initialized on a router, it builds its table using the contents of the file **/etc/gateways**, which contains the address and distance to various networks and gateways. Once it starts to run, it immediately begins to update its table based on broadcasts from other routers and gateways.

You need to create **/etc/gateways**, using any supported text editor. The **/etc/gateways** file consists of a series of lines, each in the format

[net | host] *filename1* **gateway** *filename2 value* **[passive | active]**

where the operands have the following meanings:

net | host — **net** or **host** indicates that the route is to a network or to a specific host, respectively.

filename1 This is the name of the destination network or host. This may be a net name or host name, as specified in **/etc/networks** or **/etc/hosts**, or an IP address.

filename2 This is the name or address of the gateway to which messages should be forwarded.

value This is a number indicating the number of "hops" to the destination host or network.

passive | active
passive or active indicates that the gateway should be treated as either passive or active.

To run **routed** on a router automatically whenever TCP/IP is initialized, do the following:

1. Set up the **/etc/gateways** file. The changes will become active when you reboot your system.
2. Access the startup script **/etc/inet/rc.inet** and delete the **-q** from the following line:

   ```
   /usr/sbin/in.routed -q
   ```

   so the line now reads,

   ```
   /usr/sbin/in.routed
   ```

For more information about **/etc/gateways** and **routed**, see **routed**(1M).

Setting Up Router Clients

After you configure a router to access new networks, the clients of that router need to be informed of the path to those networks. This is done through the **route** command or by the routing daemon, **routed**.

The client uses the information you supply in the **route** command to build or update its internal routing table, or its routing daemon creates its routing table based on broadcasts from the router. The client then uses the table to find the "next hop" to the destination it is trying to reach.

Either the **route** command or **routed** must be run on the client every time TCP/IP is initialized. To ensure that either the command or the daemon is run automatically after booting, modify the client's startup script, **/etc/inet/rc.inet**. You can edit the script to specify different kinds of routing behavior, as described below:

- If there is only one router on the local network, you can set up the **rc.inet** script so that, by default, your client's attempts to reach outside the local network are directed to this router. Since there is only one router to access external networks, no additional processing is needed on the client.
- If your client has more than one router available to it on the local network, you can direct traffic to specific networks through specific routers.
- If your client is connected to a router that runs an active routing daemon, the client can take advantage of the router's dynamic routing tables by running a passive **routed -q**.

The following sections tell you how to specify the kinds of routing described above.

Specifying a Default Router

If there is only one router connected to a local network, clients should direct all external traffic through the router by default.

To specify default routing, do the following:

1. Access **/etc/inet/rc.inet** on the client and locate the line

   ```
   #/usr/sbin/route add default your_nearest_gateway hops_to_gateway
   ```

2. Enable default routing by editing the line, as follows:

   a. Delete the comment character (#).

   b. Substitute the router's host name on your local network for *your_nearest_gateway*.

   c. Substitute the argument **1** for *hops_to_gateway*.

3. Disable the route daemon by inserting the comment character (#) to the following line:

   ```
   /usr/sbin/in.routed -q
   ```

   so the line now reads,

   ```
   #/usr/sbin/in.routed -q
   ```

Using an example from a preceding section, assume that networks named **eng** and **mktg** are connected by a router. The router has two network interfaces, one for each network, and each interface has a different host name. On the network named **eng**, the router's host name is **jekyll**; on **mktg**, its name is **jekyll-hyde**.

If your client is on the network named **eng**, you would edit the **route** command in your **/etc/inet/rc.inet** to look like this:

```
/usr/sbin/route add default jekyll 1
```

If your client is on the network named **mktg**, your **route** command would look like this:

```
/usr/sbin/route add default jekyll-hyde 1
```

In both examples, the argument **default** indicates that all communication directed outside the local network from your client should be routed through the router. The argument **1** indicates that the router is connected to the local network; messages "hop" once, or go through one router, to reach their destination.

Using Specific Routers

If your machine is a client of more than one router that uses static routing tables, you may want to specify which routers should route traffic to which networks.

For example, assume your system has two routers, **barker** and **lovett,** available to it on the local network. Your system needs to communicate regularly with networks named **sales** and **adv**. You know that the router **barker** maintains information about **sales** in its routing table, and **lovett** knows how to get to **adv**. To specify that traffic from your system should follow these routes, you would edit the **route** command in **/etc/inet/rc.inet** as follows:

```
/usr/sbin/route add sales barker 1
```

Below this statement in **/etc/inet/rc.inet** you would add a second route command, as follows:

```
/usr/sbin/route add adv lovett 1
```

These commands set up the your system so that it sends messages intended for different networks through different routers, rather than sending all traffic through the same router. If all of your routes are defined in **/etc/inet/rc.inet**, you can comment out the **/usr/sbin/in.routed -q** line in **/etc/inet/rc.inet** file to improve system performance.

A powerful way to set up routing for more complex networks is to provide several specific **route add** commands for frequently used networks, as well as a **route add default** command to handle traffic to all other networks. This is particularly useful when routers, in turn, use other routers.

For more information, see the **route**(1M) manual page.

Running the Route Daemon on a Client

If your machine is a client to a router that maintains a dynamic routing table, you can set up your client to update its own tables based on the router's broadcasts.

If the router is running **`routed`**, **`routed`** listens for broadcasts from other routers and gateways and continually updates its routing tables based on the information in those broadcasts. It also broadcasts its own routing tables so that other machines can use them for updating their own routing tables. Because **`routed`** on a router both broadcasts its own routing table and listens for broadcasts from other routers, it is known as an "active" **`routed`**.

When **`routed -q`** is run on a client (a machine with only one network interface), it listens on the network and waits for the local router to broadcast its routing table. It then uses the broadcast information to update its own table. Because **`routed -q`** on a client does not broadcast its routing table, it is called a "passive" or "quiet" **`routed`**. By default, the route daemon is running in the "passive" mode.

Even if the local router uses dynamic routing tables, you can choose not to run `routed` on the client. In this case, the client's tables remain static, even though the router's are dynamic. You might choose not to run `routed` on the client if the client is on a simple internetwork, and the routes to its usual destinations do not change.

If the client's router uses static routing tables (that is, it does not run `routed`), do not run `routed` on the client.

Setting Up Subnets

Subnets are logical subsections of a single TCP/IP network. For administrative or technical reasons, many organizations chose to divide one network into several subnets.

Routing can get very complicated as the number of networks grows. For example, a small organization might give each local network a Class C number. As the organization grows, administering network numbers may get out of hand. A better idea is to allocate a few Class B network numbers for each major division in a company: one for Engineering, one for Operations, and so on. Then, divide each Class B network into physical networks using subnets. In this way, you can isolate hosts from changes you might make to the network in remote parts of the organization.

Subnets allow you more flexibility when assigning network addresses. The Internet Protocol allows 127 Class A networks with 24 bit host fields; 16,383 Class B networks with 16 bit host fields; and over two million Class C networks with eight bit host fields.

Network Masks

Typically, you create subnets by using a subnetting scheme called the "Address Mask." When setting up your network, you should select a network-wide "network mask." A network mask determines which bits in the IP address will represent the subnet number. The remaining bits represent the host within the subnet. For example, you could configure an organization's internetwork as a Class B network. Then you could assign each local subnet a subnet number within that network. The 16 bits could be allocated as eight for subnet and eight for host, or nine for subnet and seven for host, and so on. Your decision would be transparent to everyone outside that organization. Figure 6-19 illustrates the effect of the network mask:

Figure 6-19: Network Mask

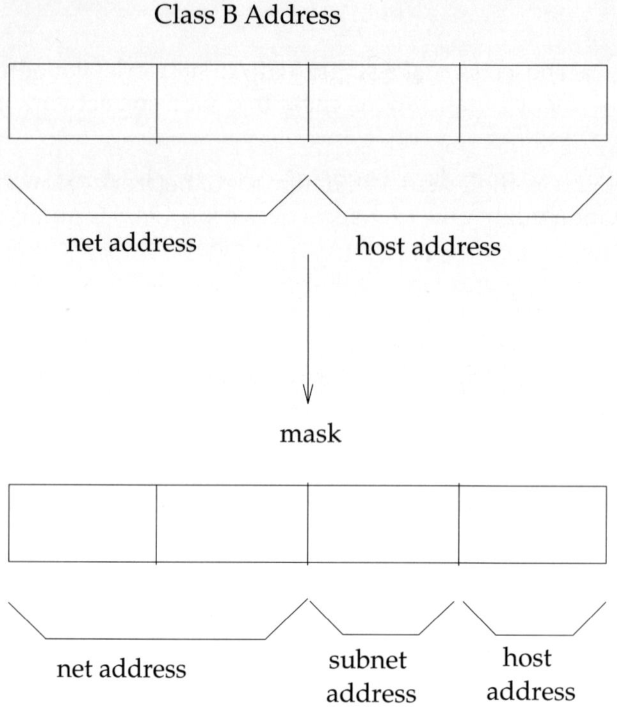

You can express network masks as a single hexadecimal number, or as four octets of decimal numbers, as described earlier in this guide. The default is a mask of 0xFF000000 (255.0.0.0) for Class A networks, 0xFFFF0000 (255.255.0.0) for Class B networks, and 0xFFFFFF00 (255.255.255.0) for Class C networks. You only have to specify network masks explicitly when they are wider (that is, have more one-bits) than the default values. One common case is a Class C mask on a Class B network. A Class B network provides you with 256 possible subnets, each one of which can accommodate 254 possible hosts (remember, 0 and 255 are not acceptable host addresses). But you may know that none of your subnets will ever have more than, say, 128 hosts, while you may need more than 256 subnets. In that case, you could decide to use nine bits for the subnet number instead of eight, and seven for the host addresses. The appropriate mask for this would be 0xFFFFFF80, or 255.255.255.128 (2 to the power of 7 is 128, and 128 subtracted from the possible 256 is 128).

Given the above scheme, and a network address of, for instance, 131.60, the address for the first host of the first subnet would be 131.60.0.129.

Changing from a Non-Subnetted to a Subnetted Network

Follow these steps to change from an internetwork that does not use subnets to one that is subnetted.

1. Decide on the new subnet topology, including considerations for subnet routers and locations of hosts on the subnets.
2. Assign all subnet and host addresses.
3. Edit `/etc/hosts` on all hosts to change host address.

Examples of Subnets

The following examples show network installations where subnets are (and are not) in use:

128.32.0.0	Berkeley	Class B network (subnetted)	netmask 255.255.255.0
36.0.0.0	Stanford	Class A network (subnetted)	netmask 255.255.0.0
10.0.0.0	Arpanet	Class A network (non-subnetted)	netmask 255.0.0.0

All of the University of California at Berkeley is assigned the network number 128.32.0.0, so that any external router only needs to know one route to reach Berkeley. Within the campus, a Class C subnet mask is used to give each local network a subnet number, with 254 hosts on each of the 254 possible subnets. (Zero and all ones, that is 255, are reserved.) Stanford University uses a Class A network number with a Class B network mask, for 254 subnets of 65534 hosts each. The Arpanet is a Class A network without subnets; therefore, the default Class A netmask is used.

7 Using Domain Name Service with TCP/IP

An Overview of the Domain Name Service 7-1

The Domain Hierarchy and DNS Administrative Zones 7-1

The Administrator's Role 7-4

- The Domain Administrator 7-5
- The Technical Contact 7-6

DNS Clients and Servers 7-6

- Clients 7-6
- Servers 7-6

Setting Up DNS on a Client 7-8

Creating resolv.conf 7-8

Modifying netconfig 7-9

Setting Up DNS on a Name Server 7-11

Creating Boot and Data Files 7-11

- Setting Up the Boot File 7-13
- Setting Up the Data Files 7-17
- Standard Resource Record Format 7-21
- Modifying the Data Files 7-32

Modifying the Startup Script 7-32

Setting Up a Root Server for a Local Network 7-33

Troubleshooting named 7-34

A Practical Example 7-35

An Overview of the Domain Name Service

Domain Name Service (DNS) is an application layer protocol that is part of the standard TCP/IP protocol suite. Specifically, DNS is a *naming* service; it obtains and provides information about hosts on a network.

Domain Name Service performs naming between hosts *within* your local administrative domain and *across* domain boundaries. It is distributed among a set of servers, commonly known as "name servers," each of which implements DNS by running a daemon called **named**.

The **named** daemon is also called the Berkeley Internet Name Domain service, or BIND, because it was developed at University of California at Berkeley.

On the client's side, DNS is implemented through the "resolver." The resolver is neither a daemon nor a particular program; rather, it is a library compiled into applications that need to know machine names. The resolver's function is to resolve users' queries; to do that, it queries a name server, which then returns either the requested information or a referral to another server.

DNS is dependent on the hierarchical structure of the Internet and adds to that structure the concept of domain "zones." This chapter describes the organization of domains as it relates to DNS on the Internet, then tells you how to set up and maintain DNS on your network machines.

The Domain Hierarchy and DNS Administrative Zones

Domain names used by DNS reflect the hierarchical organization of the public networks. Before you set up DNS for your organization, you should understand the organization of the network, your place in the overall structure of the network, and how domain names reflect that structure.

For information about the structure of the Internet and domain naming conventions, see "Establishing a Domain".

The Domain Name Service introduces the concept of "zones" to the Internet network model. A zone is a hierarchical community of hosts, administered by a single authority and served by a set of name servers. This community can include individual hosts, plus every name server and its clients (a subzone) nested beneath the authoritative set of name servers for the zone. Zones usually represent administrative boundaries, such as your local administrative domain. However, a zone is not limited to just one administrative domain. A zone is a domain, plus all or some of the domains under it.

The next figure shows how some fictional zones might be delegated. The illustration shows four zones: the root zone, served by the Internet root domain name servers, and three zones served by name servers at domain **sun.COM**. The dotted lines point to the areas making up each zone.

Figure 7-1: Administrative Zones

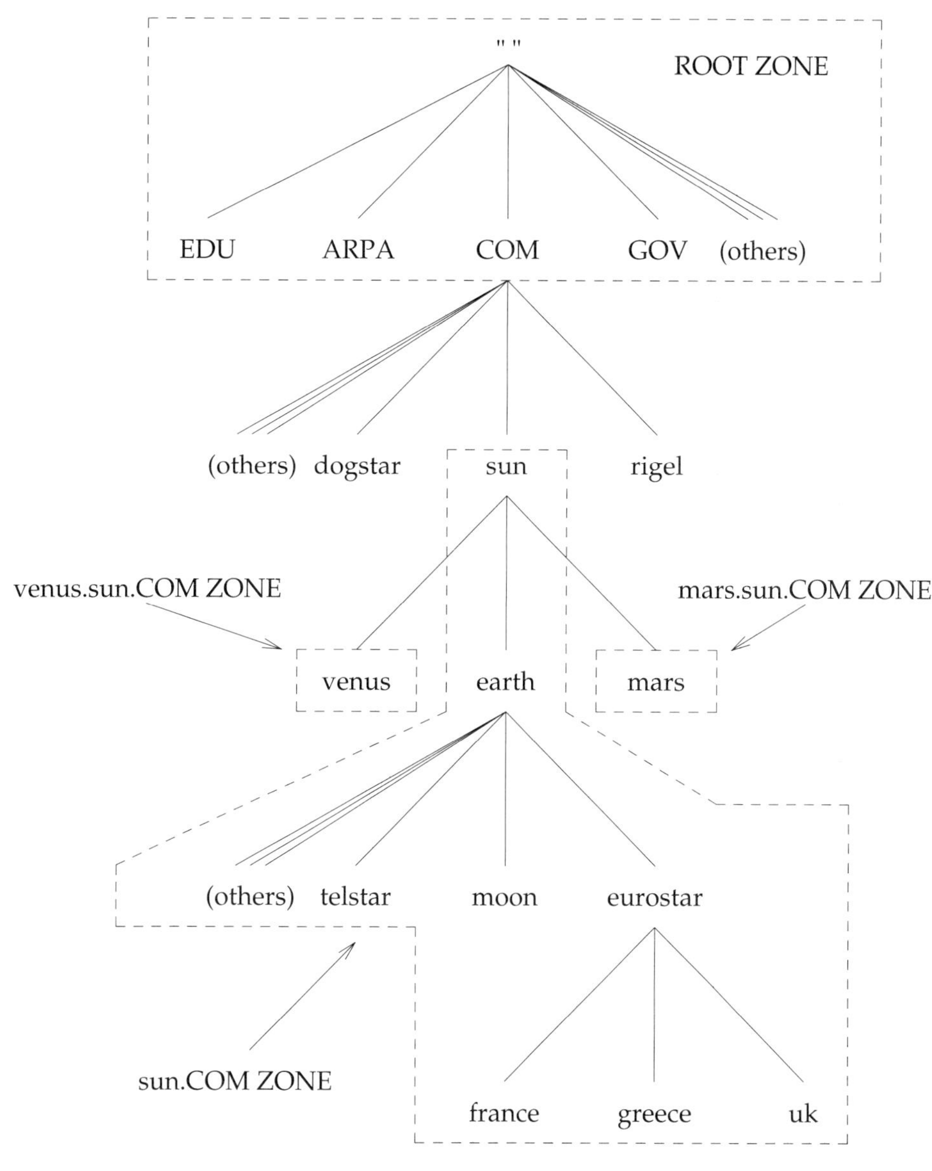

Zones take their names from the label of the domain at the top of the zone hierarchy. In the above figure, the names of the four domains within dotted lines are:

```
sun.COM   venus.sun.COM   mars.sun.COM   . (the root zone)
```

Zone **sun.COM** takes its name from the label of the second level domain **sun.COM**. However, zone **sun.COM** does not have the same administrative authority as the domain of the same name. Zone **sun.COM** consists only of

- domain **sun**
- local administrative domain **earth**
- subdomain **eurostar**.

The zone **sun.COM** does not include domains **venus** and **mars**. They have their own separately administered zones: **venus.sun.COM** and **mars.sun.COM**, respectively. However, **venus** and **mars** are part of the **sun.COM** domain hierarchy.

The domain hierarchy and name space described so far keeps track of information by host name. This enables the **named** daemon to perform name-to-address mapping.

In addition, there is a special domain recognized by DNS called IN-ADDR.ARPA, which facilitates address-to-name mapping. IN-ADDR.ARPA contains essentially the same information as the hosts name space, but it is expressed in terms of IP addresses.

A name in the IN-ADDR.ARPA domain has four labels preceding it, corresponding to the four octets of an IP address. This host address is listed from right to left. For example, a host whose IP address is 128.32.0.4 has the IN-ADDR.ARPA domain name

4.0.32.128.IN-ADDR.ARPA.

Therefore, if **named** knows the IP address of a host, it can find out the host's fully qualified domain name by consulting a file representing the IN-ADDR.ARPA domain. (This file, commonly called **hosts.rev**, is explained in a later section.)

The Administrator's Role

Administering DNS involves not only running the appropriate programs on the servers and clients, but also determining domain names, answering complaints, and filling out registration and other forms, should you join a public network. This section contains overall procedures for setting up DNS, based on the responsibilities you might have as a DNS administrator.

Your administrative responsibilities for DNS depend on your domain's position within the overall network hierarchy. For example, managing one set of name servers in a small administrative domain entails less responsibility than managing the authoritative set for a large zone. Responsibilities depend on whether you are the chief authority for a domain or zone, or an administrator reporting to the chief authority.

The NIC divides administrators on the Internet into domain administrators, who have primary responsibility for a domain, and technical contacts, who work with domain administrators to maintain a zone. Descriptions of each position appear below.

The Domain Administrator

The domain administrator (DA) is a coordinator, manager, and technician for a second-level or lower domain. The DA's responsibilities include:

- Registering the domain.

  If your domain is going to be on a public network, you must register it (if you have not done so already). The domain must have a unique name within its level of the network hierarchy. To register your domain with the Internet, obtain the Domain Registration Form from NIC and complete it according to the instructions in "Guidelines for Completing the Domain Registration Form". To join other public networks, contact the organization in charge of the network and request the appropriate domain registration form.

  To belong to multiple networks such as the Internet, BITNET, CSNET, you need to register with only one network, as domain names are independent of a network's physical topology.

- Naming hosts and verifying that names within the domain are unique.

  At many sites, users name their individual hosts while the administrators name the servers. The administrator should ensure that there are no duplicate names within a zone.

- Understanding the functioning of the name servers and making sure the data is current at all times.

  This includes either setting up the DNS-related files and programs, or delegating this authority to other technically competent people (such as the technical contact). This chapter should provide you with the basic information you need for understanding DNS. However, as the domain administrator, you should gain more specific technical knowledge of your particular network. Contact the public network to which you belong and ask for technical papers regarding it.

The Technical Contact

The primary responsibility of a technical contact is to maintain DNS programs and files for a zone and to keep the zone's name servers running. Technical contacts interact with their Domain Administrators and with DA's of other domains to solve network problems.

DNS Clients and Servers

As mentioned earlier, there are two sides to DNS: name servers running the **named** daemon, and clients running the resolver.

Clients

A name server running **named** can also run the resolver; therefore, there can be two kinds of clients

- client-only
- client/server

A client-only client does not run the **named** daemon; instead, it consults the resolver, which provides a list of possible name serving machines to which queries should be directed.

A client/server is a machine that uses the domain name service provided by **named** in order to resolve a user's queries. However, if the daemon dies or hangs, the client/server might be able to solve queries through its resolver.

Servers

You implement DNS for a zone not on a single server, but on a *set* of servers. This set must include two master servers, and may or may not include other servers.

- Master Servers

  The "master" name servers maintain all the data corresponding to the zone, making them the authority for that zone. These are commonly called "authoritative" name servers. The data corresponding to any given zone must be available on at least *two* authoritative servers. You should designate one name server as the primary master server and at least one as a secondary master server, to act as a backup if the primary is unavailable or overloaded.

The "primary" master server is the name server where you make changes for the zone. This server loads the master copy of its data from disk when it starts up **named**. The primary server may also delegate authority to other servers in its zone, as well as to servers outside of it.

The "secondary" master server is a name server that maintains a copy of the data for the zone. The primary server sends its data and delegates its authority to the secondary server. When the secondary server boots **named**, it requests all the data for the given zone from the primary. The secondary server then periodically checks with the primary to see if it needs to update its data.

A server may function as a master for multiple zones: as a primary for some zones, and as a secondary for others.

A server at the root level of the network is called a "root domain name server." On the Internet, root domain name servers are maintained by the NIC. If a network is not connected to the Internet, primary and secondary name servers must be set up and administered for the root level of the local network.

- Caching and Caching-Only Servers

  All name servers are caching servers. This means that the name server caches received information until the data expires. (The expiration process is regulated by the **time to live** field attached to the data when it is received from another server.)

  Additionally, you can set up a "caching-only server" that is not authoritative for any zone. This server handles queries and asks other name servers who have the authority for the information needed. But the caching-only server does not maintain any authoritative data itself.

Setting Up DNS on a Client

Setting up DNS on a client involves two tasks:

1. creating the file **resolv.conf**
2. modifying the file **netconfig**

If you are setting up DNS on a name server, you need to complete these steps, in addition to setting up boot and data files and editing the startup script. These additional tasks are described in "Setting Up DNS on a Name Server".

Creating resolv.conf

The domain name server uses several files to load its database. At the resolver level, it needs a file (called **/etc/resolv.conf**) listing the addresses of the servers where it can obtain the information needed. Whenever the resolver has to find the address of a host (or the name corresponding to an address) it builds a query package and sends it to the name servers it knows of (from **/etc/resolv.conf**). The servers either answer the query locally or use the services of other servers and return the answer to the resolver.

The **resolv.conf** file is read by the resolver to find out the name of the local domain and the location of name servers. It sets the local domain name and instructs the resolver routines to query the listed names servers for information. Every DNS client-only system on your network must have a **resolv.conf** file in its **/etc** directory.

On a system where a name server is running, an **/etc/resolv.conf** is unnecessary.

The first line of the file lists the domain name in the form

domain *domain_name*

where *domain_name* is the name registered with the NIC. Succeeding lines list the IP addresses that the resolver should consult to resolve queries. IP address entries have the form:

nameserver *IP_address*

A sample **resolv.conf** file is shown in the following figure:

Figure 7-2: Sample /etc/resolv.conf **File**

```
; Sample resolv.conf file
domain Podunk.Edu
; try local name server
nameserver 127.0.0.1
; if local name server down, try these servers
nameserver 128.32.0.4
nameserver 128.32.0.10
```

NOTE: It is not advised that you have an **/etc/resolv.conf** file on a system that is running a name server, as **/etc/resolv.conf** causes the system to be less efficient; however, when the name server is not running, **/etc/resolv.conf** consults other name servers to answer queries. Therefore, if it is important that your system have little or no down-time, create **/etc/resolv.conf** on your system and include the loopback address, followed by the addresses of other name servers.

Modifying netconfig

Once you have created the appropriate **/etc/resolv.conf** file on each machine that is to run the resolver, you need to edit the **netconfig** file. Look at the file and make sure that all transport providers listed in the **/etc/netconfig** file that provide IP connections have the name-to-address resolving routing that uses DNS (**resolv.so**) listed in the name **lookups** field. (See **netconfig**(4) for more information about **netconfig**.)

For example, if your **/etc/netconfig** file lists the following entries:

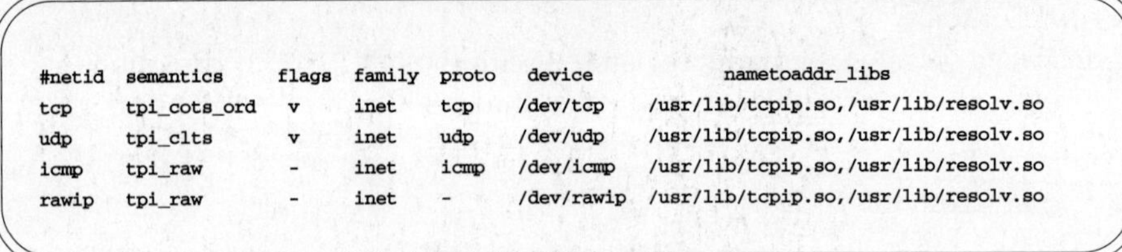

```
#netid  semantics     flags  family  proto  device      nametoaddr_libs
tcp     tpi_cots_ord  v      inet    tcp    /dev/tcp    /usr/lib/tcpip.so,/usr/lib/resolv.so
udp     tpi_clts      v      inet    udp    /dev/udp    /usr/lib/tcpip.so,/usr/lib/resolv.so
icmp    tpi_raw       -      inet    icmp   /dev/icmp   /usr/lib/tcpip.so,/usr/lib/resolv.so
rawip   tpi_raw       -      inet    -      /dev/rawip  /usr/lib/tcpip.so,/usr/lib/resolv.so
```

you will have to modify the **nametoaddr_libs** field so it says:

```
#netid  semantics     flags  family  proto  device      nametoaddr_libs
tcp     tpi_cots_ord  v      inet    tcp    /dev/tcp    /usr/lib/resolv.so,/usr/lib/tcpip.so
udp     tpi_clts      v      inet    udp    /dev/udp    /usr/lib/resolv.so,/usr/lib/tcpip.so
icmp    tpi_raw       -      inet    icmp   /dev/icmp   /usr/lib/resolv.so,/usr/lib/tcpip.so
rawip   tpi_raw       -      inet    -      /dev/rawip  /usr/lib/resolv.so,/usr/lib/tcpip.so
```

NOTE

In single-user mode, **named** is not available, so the **/etc/netconfig** file must include a lookup routine that uses local text files (**tcpip.so** in the example above is the default). You should therefore put the local machines' interface addresses and at least a couple of machine names and addresses in **/etc/hosts**.

Setting Up DNS on a Name Server

Because every name server is a client of other name servers, you must complete the steps involved in setting up DNS on a client when you set up a machine to be a name server. These steps are

1. creating the file `resolv.conf`
2. modifying the file `netconfig`

Instructions for completing these steps appear in "Setting Up DNS on a Client".

Once you complete these steps, you need to do some additional tasks to set up DNS on a machine that is to be a name server. These steps are

1. creating the boot and data files that **named** needs.
2. adding the `/usr/sbin/in.named` line to the server's startup script `/etc/inet/rc.inet` file.

Instructions for completing these steps appear in this section.

If your local network is not on the Internet, you must set up primary and secondary servers in the root-level domain on the local network. Instructions for setting up a root domain name server appear at the end of this section.

Creating Boot and Data Files

In addition to the daemon **named**, DNS on a name server consists of a boot file and local data files. The default location of the boot file is `/etc/named.boot`. Common names for the local data files are `named.ca`, `named.local`, `hosts`, and `hosts.rev`. In the descriptions of these files that follow, these names are used. However, you can name these files whatever you like. In fact, it is suggested that you use names other than the ones used in this guide, to avoid confusion with files with similar names.

- `named.boot`

  The boot file `named.boot` establishes the server as a primary, a secondary, or a caching-only name server. It also specifies the zones over which the server has authority, and which data files it should read to get its initial data.

The boot file is read by **named** when the daemon is started by the server's startup script `/etc/inet/rc.inet`. The boot file directs **named** either to other servers or to local data files for a specified domain.

- **named.ca**

  named.ca establishes the names of root servers and lists their addresses. If you are connected to the Internet, **named.ca** lists the Internet name servers; otherwise, it lists the root domain name servers for your local network.

  named cycles through the list of servers until it contacts one of them. It then obtains from that server the current list of root servers, which it uses to update **named.ca**.

  To avoid confusion with the caching process, with which this has very little to do, you may want to call your file something like **named.root** or **boot.root**.

- **hosts**

  The **hosts** file contains all the data about the machines in the local zone. The name of this file is specified in the boot file. To avoid confusion with `/etc/hosts`, name the file something other than **hosts**. You may want to give the file name the suffix **zone**; in the following illustration, the file is called **A.puzone**.

- **hosts.rev**

  The **hosts.rev** file specifies a zone in the IN-ADDR.ARPA domain (the special domain that allows inverse mapping). The name of this file is specified in the boot file. In the illustration, the file is called **puhosts.rev**.

- **named.local**

  The **named.local** file specifies the address for the local loopback interface, or **localhost**, with the network address 127.0.0.1. The name of this file is specified in the boot file. As with all other files, it can be called something other than the name used in this guide.

The relationship between the boot file and the data files (or, alternatively, other servers) is illustrated in the following figure:

Figure 7-3: Boot File and Data Files

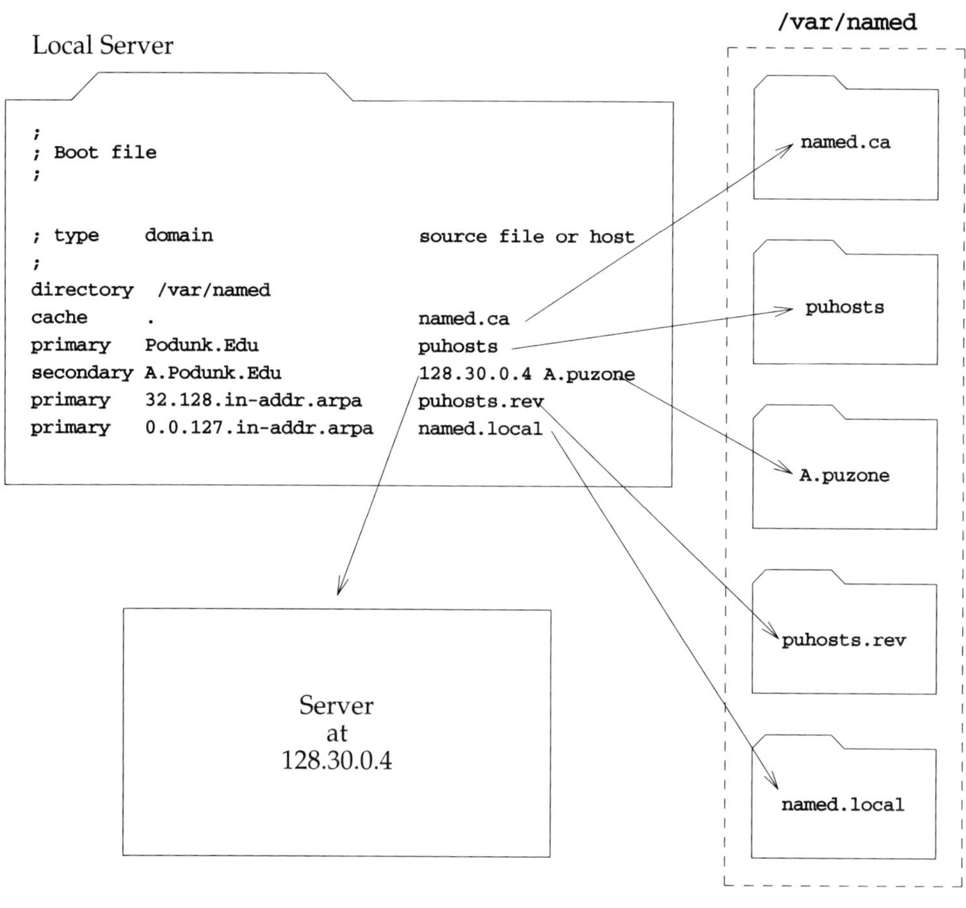

Setting Up the Boot File

The contents of the boot file varies, depending on the type of server. This section describes boot files for primary and secondary master servers and caching-only servers.

Boot File for a Primary Master Server

A sample boot file for a primary server is shown in the following figure:

Figure 7-4: Sample Boot File for a Primary Master Server

```
;
; Sample named.boot file for Primary Master Name Server
;
; type       domain                  source file or host
;
directory /var/named
cache        .                       named.ca
primary      Podunk.Edu              puhosts
primary      32.128.in-addr.arpa     puhosts.rev
primary      0.0.127.in-addr.arpa    named.local
```

The entries in the file are explained below.

directory

The following line in the boot file designates the directory in which you want the name server to run:

```
directory /var/named
```

This allows the use of relative path names for the files mentioned in the boot file or, later, with the **$INCLUDE** directive. It is especially useful if you have many files to be maintained and you want to locate them all in one directory dedicated to that purpose.

If there is no **directory** line in the boot file, all file names listed in it must be full pathnames.

cache

A name server needs to know which servers are the authoritative name servers for the root zone. To do this you have to list the addresses of these higher authorities.

All servers should have the following line in the boot file to find the root name servers:

```
cache   .       named.ca
```

The first field indicates that the server will obtain root servers hints from the indicated file, in this case **named.ca** (located in the directory **/var/named**).

primary To set up a primary server, you need to create a file that contains all the authoritative data for the zone. Then you create a boot file that designates the server as a primary server and tells it where to find the authoritative data.

The following line in the boot file names the server and the data file.

```
primaryPodunk.Edu     puhosts
```

The first field designates the server as primary for the zone stated in the second field. The third field is the name of the file from which authoritative data is read. Note that the domain name in the second field must not end with a "." (dot).

The lines

```
primary    32.128.in-addr.arpa     puhosts.rev
primary    0.0.127.in-addr.arpa    named.local
```

show that the server is also a primary server for the domains **32.128.in-addr.arpa** (that is, the reverse address domain for Podunk.Edu) and **0.0.127.in-addr.arpa** (that is, the local host loopback), and that the data for them is to be found, respectively, in the files **puhosts.rev** and **named.local**.

Boot File for a Secondary Master Server

A sample boot file for a secondary server in the same domain as the above primary server is shown in the following figure:

Figure 7-5: Sample Boot File for a Secondary Master Server

```
;
; Sample named.boot file for Secondary Master Name Server
;
; type        domain                    source file or host
;
directory /var/named
cache         .                         named.ca
secondary     Podunk.Edu                128.32.0.4 128.32.0.10 128.32.136.22 puhosts.zone
secondary     32.128.in-addr.arpa       128.32.0.4 128.32.0.10 128.32.136.22 purev.zone
primary       0.0.127.in-addr.arpa      named.local
```

In appearance, this file is very similar to the boot file for the primary server; the main difference is to be found in the lines

```
secondary    Podunk.Edu               128.32.0.4 128.32.0.10 128.32.136.22 puhosts.zone
secondary    32.128.in-addr.arpa      128.32.0.4 128.32.0.10 128.32.136.22 purev.zone
```

The word **secondary** establishes that this is a secondary server for the zone listed in the second field, and that it is to get its data from the listed servers (usually the primary server followed by one or more secondary ones); attempts are made in the order in which the servers are listed. If there is a filename after the list of servers (as in the example above), data for the zone will be put into that file as a backup. When the server is started, data is loaded from the backup file, if it exists, and then one of the servers is consulted to check whether the data is still up to date.

This ability to specify multiple secondary addresses allows for great flexibility in backing up a zone.

The interpretation of the other "secondary line" is similar to the above. Note also that although this is a secondary server for the domain Podunk.Edu and 32.128.in-addr.arpa, this is a primary server for 0.0.127.in-addr.arpa (the local host).

A server may act as the primary server for one or more zones, and as the secondary server for one or more zones; it is the mixture of entries in the boot file that determines it.

Boot File for Caching-Only Server

A sample boot file for a caching only server is shown in the following figure:

Figure 7-6: Sample Boot File for a Caching Only Server

```
;
; Sample named.boot file for Caching Only Name Server
;

; type   domain                 source file or host
;
cache    .                      named.ca
primary  0.0.127.in-addr.arpa   named.local
```

You do not need a special line to designate a server as a caching only server. What denotes a caching-only server is the absence of authority lines, such as **secondary** or **primary** in the boot file. As explained above, a caching-only server does not maintain any authoritative data; it simply handles queries and asks the hosts listed in the **named** file for the information needed.

Setting Up the Data Files

All the data files used by the DNS daemon **named** are written in Standard Resource Record Format. In Standard Resource Record Format, each line of a file is a record, called a Resource Record (RR). Each DNS data file must contain certain Resource Records. This section describes the DNS data files, and the Resource Records each file should contain. Following this section is a discussion of the Standard Resource Record Format, including an explanation of each Resource Record relevant to the DNS data files.

The hosts File

The **hosts** file contains all the data about all the machines in your zone, including server names, addresses, host information (hardware and operating system information), canonical names and aliases, the services supported by a particular protocol at a specific address, and group and user information related to mail services. This information is represented in the the records NS, A, HINFO, CNAME, WKS, MX, MB, MR, MG. The file also include the SOA record, which indicates the start of a zone and includes the name of the host on which the **hosts** data file resides.

A sample **hosts** file is shown in the following figure:

Figure 7-7: Sample hosts File

```
;       sample hosts file
@                IN  SOA    ourfox.Sample.Edu. kjd.monet.Sample.Edu. (
                            1.1         ; Serial
                            10800       ; Refresh
                            1800        ; Retry
                            3600000     ; Expire
                            86400 )     ; Minimum
                 IN  NS     ourarpa.Sample.Edu.
                 IN  NS     ourfox.Sample.Edu.
ourarpa          IN  A      128.32.0.4
                 IN  A      10.0.0.78
                 IN  HINFO  3B2 UNIX
arpa             IN  CNAME  ourarpa
ernie            IN  A      128.32.0.6
                 IN  HINFO  3B2 UNIX
ourernie         IN  CNAME  ernie
monet            IN  A      128.32.7
                 IN  A      128.32.130.6
                 IN  HINFO  Sun-4/110 UNIX
ourmonet         IN  CNAME  monet
ourfox           IN  A      10.2.0.78
                 IN  A      128.32.0.10
                 IN  HINFO  Sun-4/110 UNIX
                 IN  WKS    128.32.0.10 UDP syslog route timed domain
                 IN  WKS    128.32.0.10 TCP ( echo telnet
                            discard rpc sftp
                            uucp-path systat daytime
                            netstat qotd nntp
                            link chargen ftp
                            auth time whois mtp
                            pop rje finger smtp
                            supdup hostnames
                            domain
                            nameserver )
fox              IN  CNAME  ourfox
toybox           IN  A      128.32.131.119
                 IN  HINFO  3B2 UNIX
toybox           IN  MX     0  monet.Sample.Edu
miriam           IN  MB     vineyd.Neighbor.COM.
postmistress     IN  MR     miriam
bind             IN  MINFO  bind-request kjd. Sample . Edu .
                 IN  MG     ralph . Sample . Edu .
                 IN  MG     zhou . Sample . Edu .
                 IN  MG     painter . Sample . Edu .
                 IN  MG     riggle . Sample . Edu .
                 IN  MG     terry . pa . Xerox . Com .
```

The named.local File

The **named.local** file sets up the local loopback interface for your name server. It needs to contain the host name of the machine, plus a pointer to the host name **localhost**, which represents the loopback mechanism. The server name is indicated in the NS resource record, and the pointer to **localhost** by the PTR record. The file also needs to include an SOA record, which indicates the start of a zone and includes the name of the host on which the **named.local** data file reside.

A sample **named.local** file is shown in the following figure:

Figure 7-8: Sample named.local File

```
;    sample named.local file
@  IN   SOA   ourhost.Podunk.Edu. kjd.monet.Podunk.Edu. (
              1          ; Serial
              3600       ; Refresh
              300        ; Retry
              3600000    ; Expire
              3600 )     ; Minimum
   IN   NS    ourhost.Podunk.Edu.
1  IN   PTR   localhost.
```

The hosts.rev File

hosts.rev is the file that sets up inverse mapping. It needs to contain the names of the primary and master name servers in your local domain, plus pointers to those servers and to other, non-authoritative name servers. The names of the primary and secondary master servers are indicated by NS records, and the pointers by PTR records. The file also needs an SOA record to show the start of a zone and the name of the host on which **hosts.rev** resides.

A sample **hosts.rev** file is shown in the following figure:

Figure 7-9: Sample hosts.rev File

```
;      sample hosts.rev file
@       IN    SOA    ourhost.Podunk.Edu. kjd.monet.Podunk.Edu. (
                     1.1         ; Serial
                     3600        ; Refresh
                     300         ; Retry
                     3600000     ; Expire
                     3600 )      ; Minimum
        IN    NS     ourarpa.Podunk.Edu.
        IN    NS     ourhost.Podunk.Edu.
4.0     IN    PTR    ourarpa.Podunk.Edu.
6.0     IN    PTR    ernie.Podunk.Edu.
7.0     IN    PTR    monet.Podunk.Edu.
10.0    IN    PTR    ourhost.Podunk.Edu.
6.130   IN    PTR    monet.Podunk.Edu.
```

The named.ca File

The `named.ca` file contains the names and addresses of the root servers. Server names are indicated in the record NS and addresses in the record A. You need to add an NS record and an A record for each root server you want to include in the file.

A sample **named.ca** file is shown in the following figure:

Figure 7-10: Sample named.ca File

```
;
;Initial cache data for root domain servers.
;
; list of servers...
.                   99999999    IN      NS    NS.NASA.GOV.
                    99999999    IN      NS    NIC.DDN.MIL.
                    99999999    IN      NS    A.ISI.EDU.
                    99999999    IN      NS    TERP.UMD.EDU.
                    99999999    IN      NS    C.NYSER.NET.
                    99999999    IN      NS    BRL-AOS.ARPA.
                    99999999    IN      NS    GUNTER-ADAM.ARPA.

; ...and their addresses
NIC.DDN.MIL.        99999999    IN      A    10.0.0.51
NIC.DDN.MIL.        99999999    IN      A    26.0.0.73
C.NYSER.NET.        99999999    IN      A    192.33.4.12
BRL-AOS.ARPA.       99999999    IN      A    128.20.1.2
BRL-AOS.ARPA.       99999999    IN      A    192.5.22.82
NS.NASA.GOV.        99999999    IN      A    128.102.16.10
TERP.UMD.EDU.       99999999    IN      A    10.1.0.17
A.ISI.EDU.          99999999    IN      A    26.3.0.103
GUNTER-ADAM.ARPA.   99999999    IN      A    26.1.0.13
```

Standard Resource Record Format

In the Standard Resource Record Format, each line of a data file is a record called a Resource Record (RR), containing the following fields separated by white space:

{name} {ttl} class Record Type Record Specific data

The order of the fields is always the same; however, the first two are optional (as indicated by the braces), and the contents of the last vary according to the **Record Type** field.

name The first field is the name of the domain that applies to the record. If this field is left blank in a given RR, it defaults the name of the previous RR.

A domain name in a zone file can be either a fully qualified name, terminated with a dot, or a relative one, in which case the current domain is appended to it.

`ttl` The second field is an optional time-to-live field. This specifies how long (in seconds) this data will be cached in the database before it is disregarded and new information is requested from a server. By leaving this field blank, the ttl defaults to the minimum time specified in the Start Of Authority resource record discussed below.

If the ttl value is set too low, the server will incur in a lot of repeat requests for data refreshment; if, on the other hand, the ttl value is set too high, changes in the information will not be timely distributed.

Most ttl's should be initially set to between a day (86400) and a week (604800); then, depending on the frequency of actual change of the information, change the appropriate ttl's to reflect that frequency. Also, if you have some ttl's that have very high values because you know they relate to data that rarely changes, and you know that the data is now about to change, reset the ttl to a low value (3600 to 86400) until the change takes place, and then change it back to the original high value.

All RR's with the same name, class and type should have the same ttl.

`class` The third field is the record class. Only one class is currently in use: IN for the TCP/IP Internet protocol family.

`type` The fourth field states the type of the resource record. There are many types of RR's; the most commonly used types are discussed in "Resource Record Types".

RR data The contents of the data field depend on the type of the particular Resource Record.

Although case is preserved in names and data fields when loaded into the name server, all comparisons and lookups in the name server database are case insensitive. However, this situation may change in the future, and you are advised to be consistent in your use of lower and upper case.

Special Characters

The following characters have special meanings:

`.` A free standing dot in the name field refers to the current domain.

@ A free standing @ in the name field denotes the current origin.

..	Two free standing dots represent the null domain name of the root when used in the name field.
\X	Where X is any character other than a digit (0-9), quotes that character so that its special meaning does not apply. For example, you can use \. to place a dot character in a label.
\DDD	Where each D is a digit, this is the octet corresponding to the decimal number described by DDD. The resulting octet is assumed to be text and is not checked for special meaning.
( )	Use parentheses to group data that crosses a line. In effect, line terminations are not recognized within parentheses.
;	Semicolon starts a comment; the remainder of the line is ignored.
*	An asterisk signifies wildcarding.

Most resource records have the current origin appended to names if they are not terminated by a "." This is useful for appending the current domain name to the data, such as machine names, but may cause problems where you do not want this to happen. A good rule of thumb is to use a fully qualified name ending in a period if the name is not in the domain for which you are creating the data file.

Control Entries

The only lines that do not conform to the standard RR format in a data file are control entry lines. There are two kinds of control entries:

`$INCLUDE` An include line begins with **`$INCLUDE`** in column 1, and is followed by a file name. This feature is particularly useful for separating different types of data into multiple files, for example:

```
$INCLUDE /etc/named/data/mailboxes
```

The line is interpreted as a request to load the file **`/etc/named/data/mailboxes`** at that point. The **`$INCLUDE`** command does not cause data to be loaded into a different zone or tree. This is simply a way to allow data for a given zone to be organized in separate files. For example, mailbox data might be kept separately from host data using this mechanism.

`$ORIGIN` The origin command is a way of changing the origin in a data file. The line starts in column 1, and is followed by a domain name. It resets the current origin for relative domain names (that is, not fully qualified names) to the stated name. This is useful for putting more than one domain in a data file.

Resource Record Types

The following table shows some of the most commonly used types of RR's:

Table 7-1: Common Types of Resource Records

Type	Description
SOA	Start of Authority
NS	Name Server
A	Internet Address
CNAME	Canonical Name (nickname)
HINFO	Host Information
WKS	Well Known Services
PTR	Pointer
MX	Mail Exchanger

The following is an example of a hosts file. It is presented here for illustration purposes only. We will shortly analyze it in full.

```
;     sample hosts file
@              IN   SOA     ourfox.Sample.Edu. kjd.monet.Sample.Edu. (
                            1.1        ; Serial
                            10800      ; Refresh
                            1800       ; Retry
                            3600000    ; Expire
                            86400 )    ; Minimum
               IN   NS      ourarpa.Sample.Edu.
               IN   NS      ourfox.Sample.Edu.
ourarpa        IN   A       128.32.0.4
               IN   A       10.0.0.78
               IN   HINFO   3B2 UNIX
arpa           IN   CNAME   ourarpa
ernie          IN   A       128.32.0.6
               IN   HINFO   3B2 UNIX
ourernie       IN   CNAME   ernie
monet          IN   A       128.32.7
               IN   A       128.32.130.6
               IN   HINFO   Sun-4/110 UNIX
ourmonet       IN   CNAME   monet
ourfox         IN   A       10.2.0.78
               IN   A       128.32.0.10
               IN   HINFO   Sun-4/110 UNIX
               IN   WKS     128.32.0.10 UDP syslog route timed domain
               IN   WKS     128.32.0.10 TCP ( echo telnet
                            discard rpc sftp
                            uucp-path systat daytime
                            netstat qotd nntp
                            link chargen ftp
                            auth time whois mtp
                            pop rje finger smtp
                            supdup hostnames
                            domain
                            nameserver )
fox            IN   CNAME   ourfox
toybox         IN   A       128.32.131.119
               IN   HINFO   3B2 UNIX
toybox         IN   MX      0  monet.Sample.Edu
miriam         IN   MB      vineyd.Neighbor.COM.
postmistress   IN   MR      miriam
bind           IN   MINFO   bind-request kjd.Sample.Edu.
               IN   MG      ralph.Sample.Edu.
               IN   MG      zhou.Sample.Edu.
               IN   MG      painter.Sample.Edu.
               IN   MG      riggle.Sample.Edu.
               IN   MG      terry.pa.Xerox.Com.
```

SOA – Start Of Authority

The format of a Start of Authority resource record is shown in the following figure:

Figure 7-11: Format for a Start of Authority Resource Record

```
name   {ttl}   {class}   SOA       origin   person in charge (
                         serial
                         refresh
                         retry
                         expire
                         minimum )
```

The Start of Authority (SOA) record designates the start of a zone. The zone ends at the next SOA record.

`name` indicates the name of the zone. In the example below, `@` indicates the current zone or origin.

`class` is the address class

`SOA` is the type of this Resource Record.

`origin` is the name of the host where this data file resides.

`person in charge`
is the mailing address for the person responsible for the name server.

`serial` is the version number of this data file. You *must* increment this number whenever you make a change to the data: secondary servers use the Serial field to detect whether the data file has been changed since the last time they copied the file from the master server.

Note that the name server cannot handle numbers over 9999 after the decimal point.

`refresh` indicates how often, in seconds, a secondary name server should check with the primary name server to see if an update is needed.

`retry` indicates how long, in seconds, a secondary server is to retry after a failure to check for a refresh.

`expire` is the upper limit, in seconds, that a secondary name server is to use the data before it expires for lack of getting a refresh.

`minimum` is the default number of seconds to be used for the time to live field on resource records that don't have a ttl specified.

There should only be one SOA record per zone. A sample SOA resource record is shown in following figure:

Figure 7-12: Sample SOA Resource Record

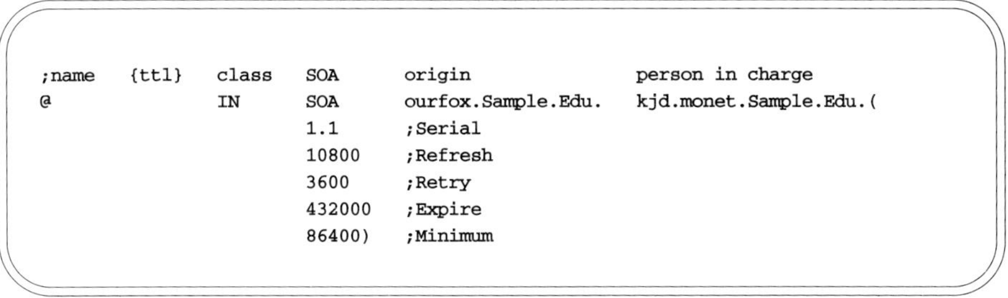

```
;name   {ttl}   class   SOA      origin                 person in charge
@               IN      SOA      ourfox.Sample.Edu.     kjd.monet.Sample.Edu.(
                        1.1      ;Serial
                        10800    ;Refresh
                        3600     ;Retry
                        432000   ;Expire
                        86400)   ;Minimum
```

NS – Name Server

The format of a Name Server (NS) resource record is shown in the following figure:

Figure 7-13: Format for a Name Server Resource Record

```
{name}   {ttl}   class   NS   Name-server name
```

The Name Server record (NS) lists by name a server responsible for a given domain. The name field lists the domain that is serviced by the listed name server. If no name field is listed, then it defaults to the last name listed. One NS record should exist for each primary and secondary master server for the domain. A sample NS resource record is shown in the following figure:

Figure 7-14: Sample NS Resource Record

```
;{name}   {ttl}   class   NS   Name-server name
                  IN      NS   ourarpa.Sample.Edu.
```

A – Address

The format of an Address (A) resource record is shown in the following figure:

Figure 7-15: Format for an Address Resource Record

```
{name}   {ttl}   class   A   address
```

The Address record (A) lists the address for a given machine. The name field is the machine name, and the address is the IP address. One A record should exist for each address of the machine (in other words, gateways should be listed twice, once for each address). A sample Address resource record is shown in the following figure:

Figure 7-16: Sample Address Resource Record

```
;{name}    {ttl}    class   A   address
ourarpa             IN      A   128.32.0.4
                    IN      A   10.0.0.78
```

HINFO – Host Information The format of a HINFO resource record is shown in the following figure:

Figure 7-17: Format for a HINFO Resource Record

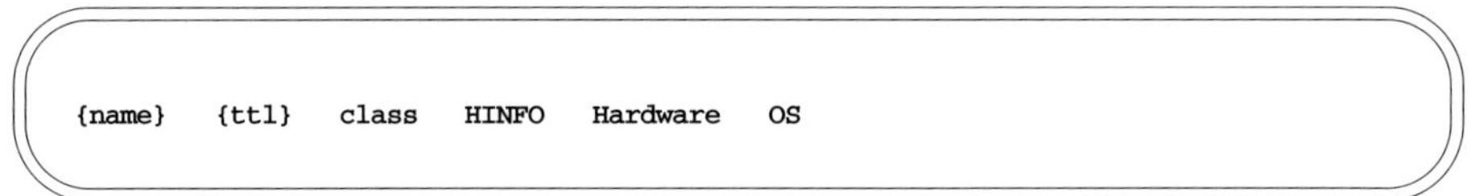

```
{name}   {ttl}   class   HINFO   Hardware   OS
```

The Host Information resource record (HINFO) contains host specific data. It lists the hardware and operating system that are running at the listed host. If you want to include a space in the machine name or in the entry in the `Hardware` field, you must surround the entry with quotes. The name field specifies the name of the host. If no name is specified it defaults to the last named host. One HINFO record should exist for each host. A sample HINFO resource record is shown in the following figure:

Figure 7-18: Sample HINFO Resource Record

```
;{name}   {ttl}   class   HINFO   Hardware    OS
                  IN      HINFO   Sun-3/280   UNIX
```

WKS – Well Known Services

The format of a WKS resource record is shown in the following figure:

Figure 7-19: Format for a WKS Resource Record

```
{name}   {ttl}   class   WKS   address   protocol   list of services
```

The Well Known Services record (WKS) describes the well known services supported by a particular protocol at a specified address. The list of services and port numbers come from the list of services specified in the **services** database. Only one WKS record should exist per protocol per address. A sample WKS resource record is shown in the following figure:

Figure 7-20: Sample WKS Resource Record

```
;{name}   {ttl}   class   WKS   address       protocol   list of services
                  IN      WKS   128.32.0.10   UDP        who route timed domain
                  IN      WKS   128.32.0.10   TCP        (echo telnet
                                                         discard rpc sftp
                                                         uucp-path systat daytime
                                                         netstat qotd nntp
                                                         link chargen ftp
                                                         auth time whots mtp
                                                         pop rje finger smtp
                                                         supdup hostnames
                                                         domain
                                                         nameserver)
```

CNAME – Canonical Name

The format of a CNAME resource record is shown in the following figure:

Figure 7-21: Format for a CNAME Resource Record

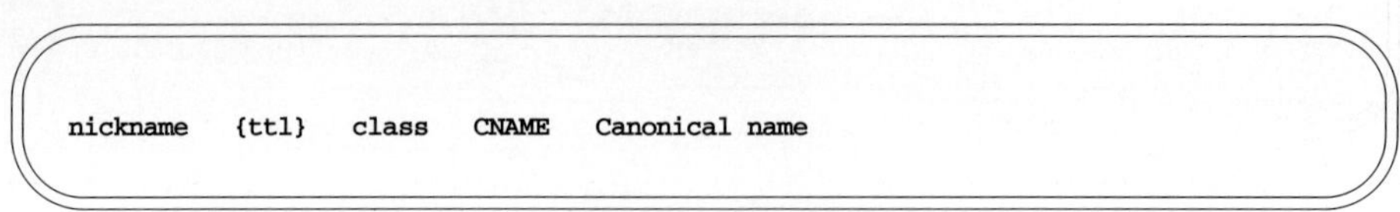

The Canonical Name resource record (CNAME) specifies a nickname for a canonical name. A nickname should be unique. All other resource records should be associated with the canonical name and not with the nickname. Do not create a nickname and then use it in other resource records. Nicknames are particularly useful during a transition period, when a machine's name has changed but you want to permit people using the old name to reach the machine. A sample CNAME resource record is shown in the following figure:

Figure 7-22: Sample CNAME Resource Record

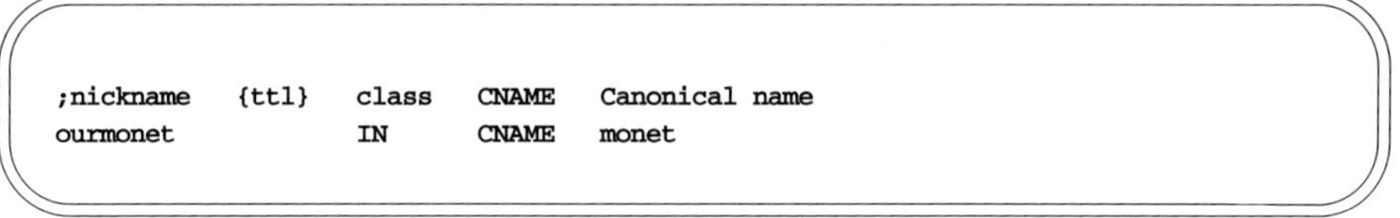

PTR – Domain Name Pointer

The format of a PTR resource record is shown in the following figure:

Figure 7-23: Format for a PTR Resource Record

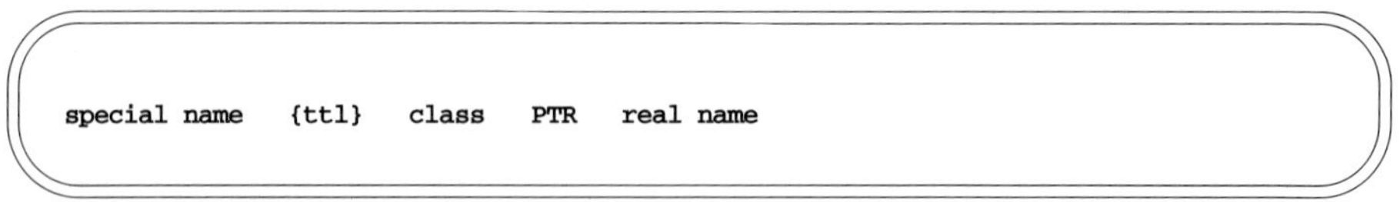

A Pointer record (PTR) allows special names to point to some other location in the domain. PTR's are used mainly in the IN-ADDR.ARPA records for the translation of an address (the special name) to a real name. PTR names should be unique to the zone. The PTR records in the following figure set up reverse pointers for the special IN-ADDR.ARPA domain.

Figure 7-24: Sample PTR Resource Record

```
;special name              {ttl}   class   PTR   real name
7.0                                IN      PTR   monet.Podunk.Edu.
2.2.18.128.in-addr.arpa            IN      PTR   blah.junk.COM.
```

MX – Mail Exchanger

The format of an MX resource record is shown in the following figure:

Figure 7-25: Format for an MX Resource Record

```
name   {ttl}   class   MX   preference value   mailer exchanger
```

The Mail Exchanger (MX) resource records are used to specify a machine that knows how to deliver mail to a domain or machines in a domain. There may be more than one MX resource record for a given name. In the following figure, **Seismo.CSS.GOV**. (note the fully qualified domain name) is a mail gateway that knows how to deliver mail to **Munnari.OZ.AU**. Other machines on the network cannot deliver mail directly to **Munnari**. **Seismo** and **Munnari** may have a private connection or use a different transport medium. The **preference value** field indicates the order a mailer should follow when there is more than one way to deliver mail to a single machine. The value 0 (zero) indicates the highest preference. If there is more than one MX resource record for the same name, they may or may not have the same preference value.

You can use names with the wildcard asterisk (*) for mail routing with MX records. There are likely to be servers on the network that simply state that any mail to a domain is to be routed through a relay. Also in the following figure, all mail to hosts in domain foo.COM is routed through RELAY.CS.NET. You do this by creating a wildcard resource record, which states that the mail exchanger for *.foo.COM is RELAY.CS.NET. Note that the asterisk will match any host or subdomain of foo.COM, but it will not match foo.COM itself.

Figure 7-26: Sample MX Resource Record

```
;name            {ttl}  class  MX   preference value   mailer exchanger
Munnari.OZ.AU.          IN     MX   0                  Seismo.CSS.GOV.
foo.COM.                IN     MX   10                 RELAY.CS.NET.
*.foo.COM.              IN     MX   20                 RELAY.CS.NET.
```

Modifying the Data Files

When you add or delete a host in one of the data files in the master DNS server, or otherwise modify the data files, you must also change the Serial number in the SOA resource record so the secondary servers modify their data accordingly; you should then inform **named** in the master server that it should re-read the data files and update its internal database, as explained below.

When **named** successfully starts up, it writes its process ID to the file **/etc/named.pid**. To have **named** re-read **named.boot** and reload the database, enter

```
# kill -HUP `cat /etc/named.pid`
```

Note that all previously cached data is lost, and the caching process starts over again.

Modifying the Startup Script

Once you create the boot and data files that **named** needs, you have to edit the startup script **/etc/inet/rc.inet**.

Do not attempt to run **named** from **inetd**. This will continuously restart the name server and defeat the purpose of having a cache.

Locate the following line:

```
/usr/sbin/route add default your_nearest_gateway hops_to_gateway
```

in the **etc/inet.rc.inet** file and add **/usr/sbin/in.named** after it.

The above line assumes that your boot file is called **/etc/named.boot**. If you are using a different name, substitute the following lines for the one above and include the name of the boot file. For example, if your boot file is called **/etc/named.init**, this is what should appear in the **/etc/inet/rc.inet** startup script:

```
if [ -f -a /etc/named.init]; then
  /usr/sbin/in.named [options] -b /etc/named.init & echo \c ' named'  >/dev/console
fi
```

Setting Up a Root Server for a Local Network

If you are not connecting your local network to the Internet, you must set up primary and secondary name servers in the root-level domain on the local network. This is so all domains in the network have a consistent authoritative server to which to refer; otherwise, machines may not be able to resolve queries.

Since a single machine can be the primary domain name server for more than one machine, the easiest way to create a root domain name server is to have a server be the name server for all the domains that make up its own domain name. For example, if a server is named **x.sub.dom.**, then it should be designated the primary name server for ".", **dom.**, and **sub.dom**.

Since the root name server provides an authoritative name server at the root level of the network, all top-level domains should have their name server records (IN NS) defined in the root domain.

It is strongly recommended that the root domain server name be the primary name server for all top-level domains in the network.

Troubleshooting named

From time to time, you may need to debug **named**. You can do this by sending it signals through the **kill** [see **kill**(1)] command. Depending on the signal received **named** will change its behavior.

To get a good idea of what **named** thinks the database is, enter

```
kill -INT `cat /etc/named.pid`
```

Upon receiving this signal, **named** dumps the current data base and cache to **/var/tmp/named_dump.db**. This should give you an indication of whether the database was loaded correctly.

When **named** is running incorrectly, you can also look in **/var/adm/messages** and check for any messages logged by **syslog**. For instance, if there is a data file that lists a hostname as a nickname and also has other data under that name instead of the machine's canonical name, you may see a message similar to:

> **May 4 02:35:26** *hostname* **named[4804]:** *hazy.widget.junk.COM*
> **has CNAME and other data (illegal)**

Or, if there is a problem with the database, you may see

> **May 1 11:02:33** *hostname* **named[17808]:** */etc/named/junk.zone:*
> *line 759:* **database format error ()**

To turn on debugging, you can start **named** with the **-d** option, or you can enter, if **named** is already running,

```
kill -USR1 `cat /etc/named.pid`
```

Each following USR1 increments the debug level. The output goes to **/var/tmp/named.run**.

To turn off debugging completely, enter

```
kill -USR2 `cat /etc/named.pid`
```

A Practical Example

We can now start building up the files that an *imaginary* network would need. Let's assume that our network is composed of three networks, all with access to the Internet. Each network has a Class C Network Number:

```
name    number
junk    223.100.100
widget  223.100.101
zap     223.100.102
```

The names of the zones are also the names of the hosts that we are designating as the master servers.

Our imaginary network can therefore be represented in the following figure:

Figure 7-27: An Imaginary Network

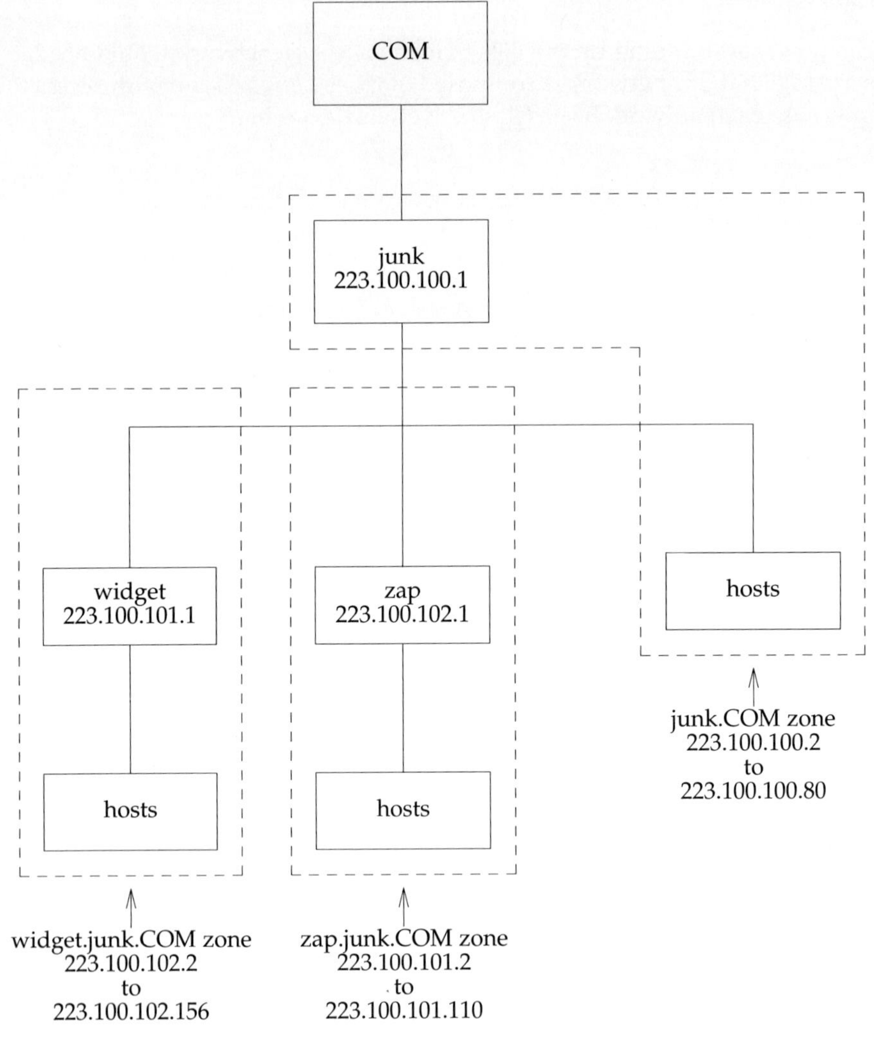

Let's further assume that after careful consideration we decide that we want to set up the Domain Name Service in our network so that each master server is the primary server for its zone and a secondary server for the other zones. All this can be summed up by the following tables:

junk zone

hostname	function	address
junk	primary	223.100.100.1
widget	secondary	223.100.101.1
zap	secondary	223.100.102.1
	hosts	223.100.100.2-80

widget zone

hostname	function	address
widget	primary	223.100.101.1
junk	secondary	223.100.100.1
zap	secondary	223.100.102.1
	hosts	223.100.101.2-110

zap zone

hostname	function	address
zap	primary	223.100.102.1
junk	secondary	223.100.100.1
widget	secondary	223.100.101.1
	hosts	223.100.102.2-156

The following are the boot files for the three servers in the network:

```
;
;         Boot file for server junk
directory   /var/named
cache       .                          named.root
primary     junk.COM                   junk.zone
primary     100.100.223.in-addr.arpa   junk.revzone
primary     0.0.127.in-addr.arpa       named.local

secondary   widget.junk.COM            223.100.101.1 223.100.102.1 widget.zone
secondary   zap.junk.COM               223.100.101.1 223.100.102.1 zap.zone
secondary   101.100.223.in-addr.arpa   223.100.101.1 widget.rev
secondary   102.100.223.in-addr.arpa   223.100.102.1 zap.rev
```

```
;
;         Boot file for server widget
directory   /var/named
cache       .                           named.root
primary     widget.junk.COM             widget.zone
primary     101.100.223.in-addr.arpa    widget.revzone
primary     0.0.127.in-addr.arpa        named.local

secondary   junk.COM                    223.100.100.1 223.100.102.1 junk.zone
secondary   zap.junk.COM                223.100.100.1 223.100.102.1 zap.zone
secondary   100.100.223.in-addr.arpa    223.100.100.1 junk.rev
secondary   102.100.223.in-addr.arpa    223.100.102.1 zap.rev
```

```
;
;         Boot file for server zap
directory   var/named
cache       .                           named.root
primary     zap.junk.COM                zap.zone
primary     102.100.223.in-addr.arpa    zap.revzone
primary     0.0.127.in-addr.arpa        named.local

secondary   junk.COM                    223.100.100.1 223.100.102.1 junk.zone
secondary   widget.junk.COM             223.100.100.1 223.100.101.1 widget.zone
secondary   100.100.223.in-addr.arpa    223.100.100.1 junk.rev
secondary   101.100.223.in-addr.arpa    223.100.101.1 widget.rev
```

Note that the domain names in the boot files must not end with a "." (dot).

The following are some sample **resolv.conf** files. Note that if the host in question is not running **named** the local host address should not be used as a nameserver.

```
;
; resolv.conf file for server junk
;
domain          junk.COM
nameserver      127.0.0.1
nameserver      223.100.101.1
nameserver      223.100.102.1
```

```
;
; resolv.conf file for a host in zone junk not running named
;
domain          junk.COM
nameserver      223.100.100.1
nameserver      223.100.101.1
nameserver      223.100.102.1
```

```
;
; resolv.conf file for a host in zone widget.junk not running named
;
domain          widget.junk.COM
nameserver      223.100.100.1
nameserver      223.100.101.1
nameserver      223.100.102.1
```

```
;
; resolv.conf file for a host in zone zap.junk not running named
;
domain          zap.junk.COM
nameserver      223.100.100.1
nameserver      223.100.101.1
nameserver      223.100.102.1
```

The following are sample **named.local** files:

```
;
; named.local for server junk
;
@      IN    SOA        junk.COM.    ralph.sysad.zap.junk.COM. (
             1.1        ;Serial'
             10800      ;Refresh
             3600       ;Retry
             432000     ;Expire
             86400)     ;Minimum

       IN    NS         junk.COM.
1      IN    PTR        localhost.
```

```
;
; named.local for server widget
;
@     IN    SOA       widget.junk.COM.    ralph.sysad.zap.junk.COM. (
            1.1       ;Serial'
            10800     ;Refresh
            3600      ;Retry
            432000    ;Expire
            86400)    ;Minimum

      IN    NS        widget.junk.COM.
1     IN    PTR       localhost.
```

```
;
; named.local for server zap
;
@    IN    SOA       zap.junk.COM.    ralph.sysad.zap.junk.COM. (
           1.1       ;Serial
           10800     ;Refresh
           3600      ;Retry
           432000    ;Expire
           86400)    ;Minimum

     IN    NS        zap.junk.COM.
1    IN    PTR       localhost.
```

The following is the **hosts** file for server **junk**, followed by its **$INCLUDE**'d file:

```
;
; junk zone hosts file for server junk
;
@                   IN   SOA      junk.COM.          ralph.sysad.zap.junk.COM. (
                         1.1       ;Serial
                         10800     ;Refresh
                         3600      ;Retry
                         432000    ;Expire
                         86400)    ;Minimum

                    IN   NS       junk.COM.
                    IN   NS       widget.junk.COM.
                    IN   NS       zap.junk.COM.
widget.junk.COM.    IN   NS       widget.junk.COM.
                    IN   NS       junk.COM.
                    IN   NS       zap.junk.COM.
zap.junk.COM.       IN   NS       zap.junk.COM.
                    IN   NS       junk.COM.
                    IN   NS       widget.junk.COM.
junk.COM.           IN   MX       10 junk.COM.
*.junk.COM.         IN   MX       10 junk.COM.

; junk.COM hosts
$INCLUDE /var/named/hosts/junk
```

```
; hosts in junk zone as listed in /var/named/hosts/junk

junk      A       223.100.100.1
          A       10.1.0.56
          MX      10 junk.COM.
widget    A       223.100.101.1
          HINFO   "Sun 3/180"     Unix
          MX      10 junk.COM.
          WKS     223.100.101.1   UDP syslog timed domain
          WKS     223.100.101.1   TCP (echo telnet
                                  discard rpc sftp
                                  uucp-path systat daytime netstat
                                  qotd nntp link chargen ftp auth
                                  time whots mtp pop rje finger
                                  smtp supdup hostnames
                                  domain nameserver)
zap       A       223.100.102.1
          HINFO   Sun-4/110       Unix
          MX      10 junk.COM.
          WKS     223.100.102.1   UDP syslog timed domain
          WKS     223.100.102.1   TCP (echo telnet
                                  discard sftp
                                  uucp-path systat daytime netstat
                                  qotd nntp link chargen ftp auth
                                  time whots mtp pop rje finger
                                  smtp supdup hostnames
                                  domain nameserver)
lazy      A       223.100.100.2
          HINFO   Sun 3/50"       Unix
          MX      10 junk.COM.
crazy     A       223.100.100.3
          HINFO   3B2             Unix
          MX      10 junk.COM.
hazy      A       223.100.100.4
          HINFO   3B2             Unix
          MX      10 junk.COM.

; all other hosts follow, up to 223.100.100.80
```

The following is the **hosts** file for server **widget**, followed by its **$INCLUDE**'d file:

```
;
; widget zone hosts file for server widget
;
@    IN    SOA     widget.junk.COM.    ralph.sysad.zap.junk.COM. (
           1.1       ;Serial
           10800     ;Refresh
           3600      ;Retry
           432000    ;Expire
           86400)    ;Minimum

     IN    NS      widget.junk.COM.
     IN    NS      junk.COM.
     IN    NS      zap.junk.COM.

; junk.COM hosts
$INCLUDE /var/named/hosts/widget
```

```
; hosts in widget zone as listed in /var/named/hosts/widget

widget     A       223.100.101.1
           HINFO   "Sun 3/180"       Unix
           MX      10 junk.COM.
whatsit    CNAME   widget.junk.COM
smelly     A       223.100.101.2
           HINFO   3B2               Unix
           MX      10 junk.COM.
stinky     A       223.100.101.3
           HINFO   3B2               Unix
           MX      10 junk.COM.
dinky      A       223.100.101.4
           HINFO   Sun 3/160"        Unix
           WKS     223.100.101.4     UDP who route
           WKS     223.100.101.4     TCP (echo telnet
                                     discard sftp
                                     uucp-path systat daytime netstat
                                     ftp finger domain nameserver)
           MX      10 junk.COM.

; all other hosts follow, up to 223.100.101.110
```

The following is the sample file of reverse addresses for hosts in the zone `junk`. Note that the name of the domain is fully qualified, so that the addresses of the hosts (without the network address) is sufficient in this case:

```
; reverse address file for server junk, in /var/named/junk.revzone

100.100.223.in-addr.arpa.  IN   SOA     junk.COM.    ralph.sysad.zap.junk.COM. (
                                1.1i    ;Serial'
                                10800   ;Refresh
                                3600    ;Retry
                                432000  ;Expire
                                86400)  ;Minimum

                           IN   NS      junk.COM.
1                               PTR     junk.COM.
2                               PTR     lazy.junk.COM.
3                               PTR     crazy.junk.COM.
4                               PTR     hazy.junk.COM.

; all other hosts follow, up to 223.100.100.80
```

The reverse address files for servers **widget** and **zap** should be written in a manner similar to the above.

8 Troubleshooting TCP/IP

Troubleshooting Commands 8-1
The ping Command 8-1
The ifconfig Command 8-2
The netstat Command 8-3
- Displaying Per Protocol Statistics 8-4
- Displaying Communications Controller Status 8-5
- Displaying Routing Table Status 8-6
- Displaying Routing Statistics 8-6

The netinfo Command 8-7
- Adding a Device Entry to the netdrivers File 8-7
- Adding a device-to-protocol Mapping Entry to the netdrivers File 8-7
- Listing Entries in the netdrivers File 8-8
- Removing Entries in the netdrivers File 8-8

Verifying the Contents of the Protocol-specific interface File 8-9

Running Software Checks 8-10

Restarting TCP/IP 8-12

Improving System Performance 8-13

Logging Network Problems 8-14

Troubleshooting Commands

TCP/IP includes several commands that help you troubleshoot, should you have problems with the network. These commands are:

```
ping
ifconfig
netstat
```

This chapter describes these commands and gives suggestions for using them.

The ping Command

The **ping** command offers the simplest way to find out if a host on your network is up or down. The basic syntax of **ping** is:

/usr/sbin/ping *host* [*timeout*]

where *host* is the hostname of the machine in question. The optional *timeout* argument indicates the time in seconds for **ping** to keep trying to reach the machine—20 seconds by default. See **ping**(1M) for further information on the **ping** command.

When you run **ping**, the ICMP protocol sends a datagram to the host you specify, asking for a response. (Recall that ICMP is the protocol responsible for error handling on a TCP/IP network.)

Suppose you typed:

```
ping elvis
```

If host **elvis** is up, you receive the following message:

```
elvis is alive
```

indicating that **elvis** responded to the ICMP request. However, if host **elvis** is down or cannot receive the ICMP packets, you receive the following response from **ping**:

```
no answer from elvis
```

If you suspect that a machine may be loosing packets even though it is up, you can use the **-s** option of **ping** to try and detect the problem. For example, suppose you type:

```
ping -s elvis
```

ping then continually sends packets to host **elvis** until you press the BREAK key or a timeout occurs. Sample output from **ping -s elvis** is shown in Figure 8-1:

Figure 8-1: Sample Output from ping -s elvis

```
PING elvis: 56 data bytes
64 bytes from elvis 129.144.50.21: icmp_seq=0. time=80. ms
64 bytes from elvis 129.144.50.21: icmp_seq=1. time=0. ms
64 bytes from elvis 129.144.50.21: icmp_seq=2. time=0. ms
64 bytes from elvis 129.144.50.21: icmp_seq=3. time=0. ms
    .
    .
    .
----elvis PING Statistics----
4 packets transmitted, 4 packets received, 0% packet loss
round-trip (ms)  min/avg/max = 0/20/80
```

The statistical message appears after you type the BREAK key, or a timeout is reached. The packet loss statistic indicates whether the host has dropped packets.

If **ping** fails, check the status of the network reported by **ifconfig**, and **netstat** (described in the following sections).

The ifconfig Command

The **ifconfig**(1M) command displays information about the configuration of an interface that you specify.

The **ifconfig** command has the following syntax:

/usr/sbin/ifconfig {-a|*interface***}** [*af* [*address* [*dest_addr*]]
[up] [down] [**netmask** *mask*]] [**metric n**] [**trailers|-trailers**]

If you want to find out the configuration for all of the network devices that are currently installed, enter:

```
ifconfig -a
```

you may receive the following output:

Figure 8-2: Sample Output from `ifconfig -a`

```
lo0: flags=49<UP,LOOPBACK,RUNNING>
        inet 127.0.0.1 netmask ff000000
imx5860: flags=23<UP,BROADCAST,NOTRAILERS>
        inet 174.2.110.56 netmask ffff0000 broadcast 174.2.255.255
```

This example shows the output for **ifconfig** when used on an Ethernet interface. When using **ifconfig** on a different type of interface, the characteristics of that interface are displayed, and therefore different output is seen.

This tells you several things about the Ethernet interface. First, the flags section shows that the interface is up, broadcasting to the network, not using "trailer" link level encapsulation, and that the interface is running with no problems. Information included on the second line are the internet address of the host you are using, the netmask being currently used, and the address of the network that broadcasts are sent over.

If you get output that indicates an interface is not running, it might mean a problem with that interface. In this case, refer to the **ifconfig**(1M) manual page.

The netstat Command

The **netstat** [see **netstat**(1M)] command generates displays that show network status. You can run **netstat** to display the status of network traffic in table format, including routing table information (available routes and their status), and interface information.

netstat can display, according to the command line options chosen, one of the various network data structures available. These displays are the most useful for system administration. The syntax for this form is:

netstat [-Aainrs] [-f *address_family*] [-I *interface*] [system] [core]**

or

netstat [-I *interface*] *interval* **[system] [core]**

The options you might use most frequently to determine network status are **-I**, **-s**, **-r**, **-i**, and **-rs**. The **-I** option displays the number of packets sent and received on a given interface every *interval* seconds. This example would show the activity on the **imx586_0** driver every 5 seconds.

```
netstat -I imx586_0 5
```

Displaying Per Protocol Statistics

The **-s** option displays per-protocol statistics for the UDP, TCP, ICMP, and IP protocols. When you run **netstat -s**, the result is a display resembling the following:

Figure 8-3: Sample Output from `netstat -s`

```
ip:
        227201 total packets received
        0 bad header checksums
        0 with size smaller than minimum
        0 with data size < data length
        0 with header length < data size
        0 with data length < header length
        12 fragments received
        0 fragments dropped (dup or out of space)
        0 fragments dropped after timeout
        3086 packets forwarded
        0 packets not forwardable
        0 redirects sent
icmp:
        0 calls to icmp_error
        0 errors not generated 'cuz old message was icmp
        Output histogram:
                address mask reply: 3
        .
        .
        .
        Input histogram:
                address mask request: 3
        3 message responses generated
tcp:
        connections initiated: 7
        connections accepted: 59
        connections established: 66
        connections dropped: 5
        embryonic connections dropped: 9
                   .
        .
        .
        packets rcvd after "close": 1
        rcvd window probe packets: 0
```

(continued on next page)

Figure 8-3: Sample Output from `netstat -s` (continued)

```
            rcvd duplicate acks: 90
            rcvd acks for unsent data: 0
            rcvd ack packets: 11230
            bytes acked by rcvd acks: 901832
            rcvd window update packets: 95
    udp:
            0 incomplete headers
            0 bad data length fields
            0 bad checksums
```

The statistical information can show areas where a protocol is having problems. For example, statistical information from ICMP can indicate where this protocol has found errors.

Displaying Communications Controller Status

The **`-i`** option of **`netstat`** shows the state of the communications controllers that are configured with the machine where you ran the command. Here is a sample display produced by **`netstat -i`**.

Figure 8-4: Sample Output from `netstat -i`

```
Name    Mtu   Network    Address     Ipkts   Ierrs Opkts  Oerrs Collis
imx586  1500  174.2      hulk        107800  5859  31549  0     6
lo0     8256  loopback   localhost   16      0     16     0     0
```

Using this display, you can find out how many packets a machine thinks it is transmitting and receiving on each network. For example, the input packet count (Ipkts) displayed for a server may increase each time a client tries to boot, while the output packet count (Opkts) remains steady. This suggests that the server is seeing the boot request packets from the client, but does not realize it is supposed to respond to them. This might be caused by an incorrect address in the **`hosts`** or **`ethers`** database.

On the other hand, if the input packet count is steady over time, it means that the machine does not see the packets at all. This suggests a different type of failure, possibly a hardware problem.

Displaying Routing Table Status

The **-r** option of **netstat** displays the IP routing table. Here is a sample display produced by **netstat -r** run on machine **ballet**.

Figure 8-5: Sample Output from netstat -r

```
Routing tables
Destination      Gateway     Flags  Refcnt Use     Interface
temp8milptp      elvis       UGH     0        0       xxn
irmcpeb1-ptp0    elvis       UGH     0        0       xxn
route93-ptp0     speed       UGH     0        0       xxn
mtvb9-ptp0       speed       UGH     0        0       xxn
                   .
                   .
                   .
mtnside          speed       UG      1      567       xxn
ray-net          speed       UG      0        0       xxn
mtnside-eng      speed       UG      0       36       xxn
mtnside-eng      speed       UG      0      558       xxn
mtnside-eng      ballet      U      33   190248       xxn
```

The first column shows the destination network, the second the router through which packets are forwarded. The **U** flag indicates that the route is up; the **G** flag indicates that the route is to a gateway. The **H** flag indicates that the destination is a fully qualified host address, rather than a network.

The **Refcnt** column shows the number of active uses per route, and the Use column shows the number of packets sent per route. Finally, the Interface column shows the network interface that the route uses.

Displaying Routing Statistics

Combining the options **-rs** with **netstat** produces routing statistics. You can use the resulting display to determine if your network is having routing problems. Here is sample output from **netstat -rs**:

Figure 8-6: Sample Output from `netstat -rs`

```
routing:
        0 bad routing redirects
        0 dynamically created routes
        0 new gateways due to redirects
        2 destinations found unreachable
        2330 uses of a wildcard route
```

If the output indicates that bad routing redirects occurred or that a number of destinations were found unreachable, this is indicative of problems on your network.

The netinfo Command

The **netinfo** command [see **netinfo**(1M)] allows you to add, list, or remove entries from the **/etc/confnet.d/netdrivers** file [see **netdrivers**(4)]. The syntax of the **netinfo** command is:

> **netinfo** [**-l dev**] [**-l proto**] [**-d** *device*] [**-p** *protocol*]
> **netinfo** [**-u -l dev**] [**-u -l proto**]
> **netinfo** [**-a -d** *device*] [**-a -d** *device* **-p** *protocol*]
> **netinfo** [**-r -d** *device*] [**-r -p** *protocol*] [**-r -d** *device* **-p** *protocol*]

Adding a Device Entry to the netdrivers File

To add an entry for a network card (device) to the **netdrivers** file, enter:

> **netinfo -a -d** *device*

where *device* is the name of the transport provider as it appears in the **/dev** directory.

Adding a device-to-protocol Mapping Entry to the netdrivers File

To add a device-to-protocol mapping in the **netdrivers** file, enter:

> **netinfo -a -d** *device* **-p** *protocol*

where *device* is the name of the transport provider as it appears in the **/dev** directory and *protocol* is the name of a protocol that has been installed on the machine (for example, **inet**).

Listing Entries in the netdrivers File

There are a few ways that information in the **netdrivers** file can be displayed.

To list all of the devices that are installed in your machine, enter:

```
netinfo -l dev
```

To list all of the protocols that are installed in your machine, enter:

```
netinfo -l proto
```

To list all of the devices that are not mapped to any protocol(s), enter:

```
netinfo -u -l dev
```

To list all of the protocols that are not mapped to any device(s), enter:

```
netinfo -u -l proto
```

To show what protocol is mapped to a specific device, enter:

netinfo -d *device*

where *device* is the name of the transport provider as it appears in the **/dev** directory.

To show what devices are mapped to a specific protocol, enter:

netinfo -p *protocol*

where *protocol* is the name of a protocol that has been installed on the machine (for example, **inet**).

Removing Entries in the netdrivers File

There are three ways to properly remove information from the **netdrivers** file.

To remove a *device* from the **netdrivers** file, enter:

netinfo -r -d *device*

where *device* is the name of the transport provider as it appears in the **/dev** directory.

To remove all device-to-protocol mapping for a specific protocol, enter:

netinfo -r -p *protocol*

where *protocol* is the name of a protocol that has been installed on the machine (for example, **inet**).

To remove a specific device-to-protocol mapping, enter:

netinfo -r -d *device* **-p** *protocol*

where *device* is the name of the transport provider as it appears in the **/dev** directory and *protocol* is the name of a protocol that has been installed on the machine (for example, **inet**).

Verifying the Contents of the Protocol-specific interface File

Since **inet** is the only networking protocol supported under UNIX SVR4.2, the only **interface** file that would need verification is located in **/etc/confnet.d/inet/interface**.

For more information on **/etc/confnet.d/inet/interface**, see INET-specific **interface**(4).

Running Software Checks

If there is trouble on the network, here are some actions you can take to diagnose and fix software-related problems.

1. Use the **netstat** command to determine network status as described previously.
2. Check the **/etc/hosts** file to make sure that the entries are correct and up-to-date.
3. If you are running RARP, check to see if RARP is running by entering:

   ```
   ps -ef | grep rarp
   ```

   or check the **/etc/inet/rc.inet** file to see if there is an entry similar to the following:

   ```
   /usr/sbin/in.rarpd
   ```

   Also, check the Ethernet addresses in the **/etc/ethers** database to make sure that the entries are correct and up to date.
4. Check the accuracy of the line(s) in the **/etc/confnet.d/inet/interface** file. See INET-specific **interface**(4) for the format of an entry in the **interface** file.
5. Try to **rlogin** to yourself by entering one of the following commands:

   a. **rlogin \`uname -n\`**

   b. **rlogin localhost**

   If "a" is successful, then you are able to send TCP packets and process them on the **\`uname -n\`** machine. The **\`uname -n\`** system name is usually associated with first network device installed in the machine. If "a" is successful, and other machines cannot **rlogin** into the machine being troubleshooted (in "a"), then check the hardware and cables associated with the first network device.

   If "b" is successful and "a" is not, verify the **localhost** entry in the **/etc/confnet.d/inet/interface** file. Some configuration files are **date** dependent. If you have restored some old files or updated a number of files manually, enter:

   ```
   touch /etc/confnet.d/inet/interface
   ```

and reboot the machine so that the INET-specific files will be updated. See **interface**(4) for information about the **/etc/confnet.d/inet/interface** file.

If you do not have an entry for yourself in your *$HOME*/**.rhosts** file, you will be prompted for your password.

6. Make sure the network daemon **inetd** is running. Log in and type the following:

   ps -ef | grep inetd

   The resulting display should resemble the following if the **inetd** daemon is running.

Figure 8-7: Sample Output from `ps -ef | grep inetd`

```
root     57      1  0    Apr 04 ?        3:19 /usr/sbin/inetd
root   4218   4198  0 17:57:23 pts/3     0:00 grep inetd
```

If **inetd** is not running, it may be restarted by entering:

   sacadm -s -p inetd

or by rebooting the machine.

Restarting TCP/IP

If you are a privileged user and need to stop and restart TCP/IP, use the following procedure.

The following should only be done if you are willing to loose all current network connections. You should only stop TCP when debugging **interface** or other boot sensitive files. Make sure that any remotely mounted or shared resources are not in use when you do the following procedure.

1. To stop TCP/IP, do the following:
   a. If you are running RFS, stop RFS by issuing the **rfstop** command.
   b. If you are running NFS, stop NFS by entering:

      ```
      sh -x /etc/init.d/nfs stop
      ```

   c. Stop other processes using TCP/IP.
   d. Kill **inetd** and the TCP/IP listener by entering the commands

      ```
      sacadm -k -p inetd
      sacadm -k -p tcp
      ```

   e. Shut down and unlink STREAMS by entering:

      ```
      sh -x /etc/init.d/inetinit stop
      ```

2. To restart TCP/IP, do the following:
   a. Start and link the STREAMS by entering:

      ```
      sh -x /etc/init.d/inetinit start
      ```

   b. Restart **inetd** and the listener by entering the commands

      ```
      sacadm -s -p inetd
      sacadm -s -p tcp
      ```

   c. If you use RFS on your system, restart RFS by entering **rfstart**.
   d. If you use NFS on your system, restart NFS by entering:

      ```
      sh -x /etc/init.d/nfs start
      ```

Improving System Performance

If you are having performance problems, you may be running the daemons **routed** and **rwhod**. The **rwho** daemon (**rwhod**) is not run by default because it has a severe impact on performance. You are strongly advised not to run it.

The routing daemon **routed** is run by default. If your machine has limited memory and there are no routers on your network, then you do not need to run **routed**. You can disable **routed** by commenting out (inserting the "#" character) the line

```
/usr/sbin/in.routed -q
```

in the startup script **/etc/inet/rc.inet**.

If your machine has limited memory *and* only one router in your network, then you can run **routed** only on the router, and disable it on all other machines.

For more information about configuring a router, see "Expanding Your TCP/IP Network".

Logging Network Problems

If you suspect a routing daemon malfunction, you may log its actions—and even all the packet transfers. To create a log file of routing daemon actions, just supply a file name when you start up the **routed** daemon (in **/etc/inet/rc.inet**), for example:

```
/usr/sbin/in.routed -q /var/routerlog
```

(Refer to the **routed**(1M) manual page for more information about **routed**.)

CAUTION On a busy network this generates almost constant output.

Whenever a route is added, deleted, or modified, a log of the action and a history of the previous packets sent and received will be printed in the log file. To force full packet tracing, specify the **-t** option when the daemon is started up.

9 Guidelines for Completing the IP Number Registration Form

Guidelines for Completing the IP Number Registration Form 9-1

Guidelines for Completing the IP Number Registration Form

The following questions appear on the IP Number Registration Form provided by the Hostmaster at SRI-NIC. You can request the form via electronic mail from **HOSTMASTER@SRI-NIC.ARPA**, or, if electronic mail is not available to you, write to:

DDN Network Information Center
SRI International
Room EJ217
333 Ravenswood Avenue
Menlo Park, CA 94025

Answer the questions according to the guidelines presented here, and return the form to the same address.

If the network will not be connected to either the DARPA Internet or the DDN Internet, then you do not need to provide this information.

1. If the network will be connected to the DARPA Internet or the DDN Internet, you must provide the name of the sponsoring organization, and the name, title, mailing address, phone number, net mailbox, and NIC Handle (if any) of the contact person (POC) at that organization who has authorized the network connection. This person will serve as the POC for administrative and policy questions about authorization to be a part of the DARPA Internet or the DDN Internet. Examples of such sponsoring organizations are: Defense Communications Agency (DCA), Defense Advanced Research Projects Agency (DARPA), the National Science Foundation (NSF), or similar military or government sponsors.

Example:

Sponsor

Organization	DARPA
Name	Lastname, Firstname
Title	Program Manager
Mail Address	DARPA/ISTO Office 1400 Wilson Boulevard Arlington, VA 22209
Phone Number	(XXX) XXX-XXX
Net Mailbox	progmgr@VAX.DARPA.MIL
NIC Handle	AA12

2. Provide the name, title, mailing address, phone number, and organization of the administrative POC for the network requesting the number. This is the POC for administrative and policy questions about the network itself. If the network is associated with a research project this POC should be the Principal Investigator of the project. The online mailbox and NIC Handle (if any) of this person should also be included.

Example:

Administrator

Organization	SRI International Network Information Center
Name	Lastname, Firstname
Title	Principal Investigator
Mail Address	SRI International 333 Ravenswood Avenue Menlo Park, CA 94025
Phone Number	(XXX) XXX-XXXX
Net Mailbox	pi@SRI-NIC.ARPA
NIC Handle	BB34

3. Provide the name, title, mailing address, phone number, and organization of the technical POC. The online mailbox and NIC Handle (if any) of the technical POC should also be included. This is the POC for resolving technical problems associated with the network and for updating information about the network. The technical POC may also be responsible for hosts attached to this network.

Example:

Technical POC

Organization	SRI International Network Information Center
Name	Lastname, Firstname
Title	Computer Scientist
Mail Address	SRI International 333 Ravenswood Avenue Menlo Park, CA 94025
Phone Number	(XXX)XXX-XXXX
Net Mailbox	cs@SRI-NIC.ARPA
NIC Handle	CC56

4. Supply the short mnemonic name for the network (up to 12 characters). This is the name that will be used as an identifier in internet name and address tables.

   Example:

   ALPHA-BETA

5. Supply the descriptive name of the network (up to 20 characters). This name might be used to clarify the ownership, location, or purpose of the network.

   Example:

   Greek Alphabet Net

6. Identify the network geographic location.

   Example:

   SRI International
   Network Information Center
   333 Ravenswood Avenue
   Menlo Park, CA 94025

7. Provide a citation to a document that describes the technical aspects of the network. If the document is online, give a pathname suitable for online retrieval.

   Example:

   "The Ethernet, a Local Area Network: Data Link Layer and Physical Layer Specification," X3T51/80-50 Xerox, Stamford Connecticut, October 1980.

NOTE For networks connected to the DARPA Internet or the DDN Internet the gateway must be either a core gateway supplied and operated by BBN, or a gateway of another Autonomous System. If this gateway is not a core gateway, then an identifiable gateway in this gateway's Autonomous System must exchange routing information with a known core gateway via EGP.

8. Gateway information required:

   If the network is to be connected to the DARPA Internet or the DDN Internet, answer questions 8a and 8b.

   a. Describe the Gateway that connects the new network to the DARPA Internet or the DDN Internet, and the date it will be operational. The gateway must be either a core gateway supplied and operated by BBN, or a gateway of another Autonomous System. If this gateway is not a core gateway, then an identifiable gateway in this gateway's Autonomous System must exchange routing information with a known core gateway via EGP.

      A good way to answer this question is to say "Our gateway is supplied by person or company X and does whatever their standard issue gateway does."

      Example:

      Our gateway is the standard issue supplied and operated by BBN, and will be installed and made operational on 1-April-83.

   b. Describe the gateway machine, including:

      (a) Hardware (LSI-11/23, VAX-11/750, and so on, interfaces)
      (b) Addresses (what host on what net for each connected net)
      (c) Software (operating system and programming language)

      Example:

      (a) Hardware

         PDP-11/40, ARPANET Interface by ACC, Ethernet Interfaces by 3COM.

      (b) Address

         10.9.0.193 on ARPANET

      (c) Software

         Berkeley UNIX 4.2 BSD and C

9. Estimate the number of hosts that will be on the network:

   (a) Initially,
   (b) Within one year,
   (c) Within two years
   (d) Within five years.

   Example:

   (a) initially = 5
   (b) one year = 25
   (c) two years = 50
   (d) five years = 200

10. Unless a strong and convincing reason is presented, the network (if it qualifies at all) will be assigned a class C network number. If a class C network number is not acceptable for your purposes state why. (Note: If there are plans for more than a few local networks, and more than 100 hosts, you are strongly urged to consider subnetting. See RFC 950.)

    Example:

    Class C is fine.

11. Networks are characterized as being either Research, Defense, Government - Non Defense, or Commercial, and the network address space is shared between these three areas. Which type is this network?

    Example:

    Research

12. What is the purpose of the network?

    Example:

    To economically connect computers used in DARPA sponsored research project FROB-BRAF to the DARPA Internet or the DDN Internet to provide communication capability with other similar projects at UNIV-X and CORP-Y.

For further information contact the DDN/ARPANET Network Information Center (NIC):

Via electronic mail:	`HOSTMASTER@SRI-NIC.ARPA`
Via telephone:	(800) 235-3155
Via postal mail:	SRI International DDN Network Information Center 333 Ravenswood Avenue EJ217 Menlo Park, CA 94025

10 Guidelines for Completing the Domain Registration Form

Guidelines for Completing the Domain Registration Form 10-1

Guidelines for Completing the Domain Registration Form

To establish a domain, the following information must be sent to the NIC Domain Registrar (**HOSTMASTER@SRI-NIC.ARPA**). Questions may be addressed to the NIC Hostmaster by electronic mail at the above address, or by phone at (415) 859-3695 or (800) 235-3155.

The key people must have electronic mailboxes and NIC "handles," unique NIC database identifiers. If you have access to "WHOIS," please check to see if you are registered and if so, make sure the information is current. Include only your handle and any changes (if any) that need to be made in your entry. If you do not have access to WHOIS, please provide all the information indicated and a NIC handle will be assigned.

1. The name of the top-level domain to join.

   Example:

   COM

2. The NIC handle of the administrative head of the organization. Alternately, the person's name, title, mailing address, phone number, organization, and network mailbox. This is the contact point for administrative and policy questions about the domain. In the case of a research project, this should be the principal investigator.

   Example:

   Administrator

Organization	The NetWorthy Corporation
Name	Penelope Q. Sassafrass
Title	President
Mail Address	The NetWorthy Corporation 4676 Andrews Way, Suite 100 Santa Clara, CA 94302-1212
Phone Number	(XXX) XXX-XXXX
Net Mailbox	Sassafrass@ECHO.TNC.COM
NIC Handle	PQS

3. The NIC handle of the technical contact for the domain. Alternately, the person's name, title, mailing address, phone number, organization, and network mailbox. This is the contact point for problems concerning the domain or zone, as well as for updating information about the domain or zone.

   Example:

   Technical and Zone Contact

Organization	The NetWorthy Corporation
Name	Ansel A. Aardvark
Title	Executive Director
Mail Address	The NetWorthy Corporation 4676 Andrews Way, Suite 100 Santa Clara, CA. 94302-1212
Phone Number	(XXX) XXX-XXXX
Net Mailbox	Aardvark@ECHO.TNC.COM
NIC Handle	AAA2

4. The name of the domain (up to 12 characters). This is the name that will be used in tables and lists associating the domain with the domain server addresses. [While, from a technical standpoint, domain names can be quite long (programmers beware), shorter names are easier for people to cope with.]

   Example:

   TNC

5. A description of the servers that provide the domain service for translating names to addresses for hosts in this domain, and the date they will be operational.

   Example:

   Our server is a copy of the one operated by the NIC; it will be installed and made operational on 1 November 1987.

6. Domains must provide at least two independent servers for the domain. Establishing the servers in physically separate locations and on different PSNs is strongly recommended. A description of the primary and secondary server machines, including

- Host domain name and network addresses
- Any domain-style nicknames (please limit your domain-style nickname request, if any, to one)
- Hardware and software, using keywords from the Assigned Numbers RFC.

The preferred format for this information is:

Primary Server: *HOST-DOMAIN-NAME, NETADDRESS, HARDWARE, SOFTWARE*

Secondary Server: *HOST-DOMAIN-NAME, NETADDRESS, HARDWARE, SOFTWARE*

Example:

Primary Server: `BAR.FOO.COM, 10.9.0.13, VAX-11/750, UNIX`

Secondary Server: `XYZ.ABC.COM, 128.4.2.1, IBM-PC, MS-DOS`

7. Planned mapping of names of any other network hosts (including any ARPANET or MILNET hosts), other than the server machines, into the new domain's naming space.

   Example:

```
BAR-FOO2.ARPA (10.8.0.193) -> FOO2.BAR.COM
BAR-FOO3.ARPA (10.7.0.193) -> FOO3.BAR.COM
BAR-FOO4.ARPA (10.6.0.193) -> FOO4.BAR.COM
```

8. An estimate of the number of hosts that will be in the domain.

   (a) Initially
   (b) Within one year
   (c) Two years
   (d) Five years.

   Example:

   (a) Initially = 50
   (b) One year = 100
   (c) Two years = 200
   (d) Five years = 500

Registration of a domain does not imply an automatic name change to previously registered ARPANET or MILNET hosts that will be included in the domain. Please list below the official host names and network addresses of any ARPANET or MILNET hosts that now appear in **HOSTS.TXT** whose names will change as a result of this domain registration. (Also be sure to answer question # 7, above.)

9. The date you expect the fully qualified domain name to become the official host name in **HOSTS.TXT**, if applicable.

10. Please describe your organization briefly.

    Example:

    The NetWorthy Corporation is a consulting organization of people working with the UNIX system and the C language in an electronic networking environment. It sponsors two technical conferences annually and distributes a bimonthly newsletter.

Setting Up DFS

11 Introduction to Distributed File System (DFS) Administration

About DFS Administration 11-1
Organization 11-1

System V File Sharing 11-3

RFS vs. NFS 11-5

An Overview of DFS Administration 11-9
DFS Commands and Files 11-9

About DFS Administration

UNIX System V provides you with two distributed file system packages, both of which have been implemented as file system types—Remote File Sharing (RFS) and Network File System (NFS). Both packages allow you to access resources residing on remote machines, and to make resources on your machine available to remote machines. You may choose to run one or the other package, depending on the specific needs of your users, or you may want to run both packages, so that you can take advantage of the different services each package provides. See ''RFS vs. NFS'' for a comparison of RFS and NFS.

The DFS Administration chapters, ''Introduction to Distributed File System (DFS) Administration'', ''Setting Up DFS Administration'', ''Using DFS Commands and Files'' and ''DFS sysadm Interface'', describe the tasks you can perform using Distributed File System Administration—a set of commands and files that allows you to administer RFS and NFS (as well as other distributed file system types that may be available in the future) in a consistent way. The files and commands that support common administration of RFS and NFS are provided in the Distributed File System (DFS) Administration Utilities package.

These chapters discuss administration that is common to distributed file systems in UNIX System V; it is not intended to be a complete reference for administering either RFS or NFS. Although there are a number of tasks common to the administration of both packages, there are many differences as well. Therefore, you must see the chapters ''RFS Introduction'', ''RFS sysadm Interface'', and ''RFS Command Interface'' for a complete discussion of RFS administration, and the chapters ''NFS Introduction'', ''Setting Up NFS'', ''Sharing and Mounting NFS Resources Explicitly'', ''Obtaining NFS Information'', ''Handling NFS Problems'', ''Setting Up Secure NFS'', ''Using the NFS Automounter'', ''The NFS Network Lock Manager'', and ''Using the NFS sysadm Interface'' for a discussion of NFS administration.

Organization

The DFS Administration chapters are organized by the tasks that can be performed using DFS Administration commands and files.

In addition to the command line interface, a menu interface is provided through which you can enter DFS commands. The menus are included with System Administration Menus (**sysadm**), a menu-based administration interface that is standard with System V. Once you access a **sysadm** menu, help screens provide you with all the information you need to complete a task. Therefore, the ''DFS sysadm Interface'', chapter does not lead you step-by-step through the menu-based procedures. Instead, it documents DFS commands as you would enter them at the command line. This chapter describes the DFS menus and directs you to ''Using the sysadm Interface'' (Appendix B) of *Basic System Administration* for instruction in using the menu interface.

The organization of the DFS Administration chapters are as follows:

- ''Introduction to Distributed File System (DFS) Administration'' presents an overview of DFS Administration, and describes all the commands and files that the Distributed File System Administration Utilities package either installs or utilizes.
- ''Setting Up DFS Administration'' describes the software that must be installed before you can use DFS Administration and directs you to installation instructions.
- ''Using DFS Commands and Files'' tells you how to share and unshare RFS and NFS resources using DFS commands and files; how to mount and unmount remote resources; and how to display information about resources that are shared and mounted on your local system and on network clients.
- ''DFS sysadm Interface'', describes the System Administration Menu (**sysadm**) interface to DFS Administration.

System V File Sharing

File sharing employs a *client/server* model. A computer that wishes to share file systems with other computers on a network acts as a *server*. Files are physically owned and managed by the server machine. A computer that wants to access file systems shared by the server acts as a *client* of the server machine. Acting on behalf of its applications, the client makes requests to a server to access data in a file or to perform file manipulations. A single machine may be both a client and a server, making it possible to share its local file systems and to access remote file systems.

A server may offer any directory tree for access over the network. Once shared, an authorized client may mount the remote file system on any of its local directories. The mount procedure behaves in a manner similar to mounting local file systems.

Transparency is the key to the usefulness of file sharing. Once mounted, remote file systems look like local file systems from a user or application perspective. Applications, in most cases, run unchanged.

Since remote file systems may be mounted anywhere in the local tree, existing programs can run on several different computers while still having the same files and directory structure available to them. Creating the file environment is now mainly an administrative task, not one requiring program changes.

Servers do not need to make all their files accessible to network clients. In the following illustration, the server is sharing `/public/tkit`. The client mounts `/public/tkit` on its local directory `/usr/tools`. The remote directory tree now appears to be a directory tree under `/usr/tools`, and files in that tree may be accessed as though they were local. Note that the client cannot access `/public/tkit2`.

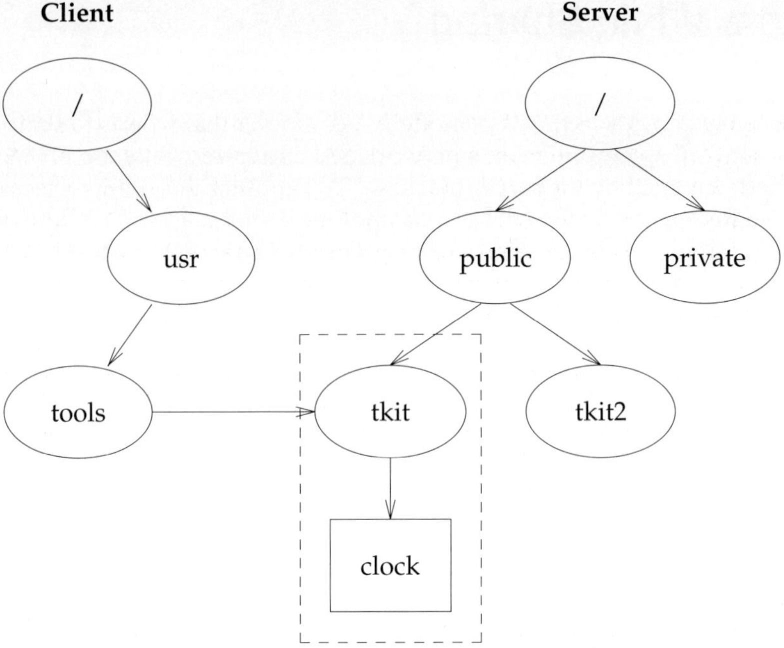

In a file sharing environment, a large number of users can access a program as though it were on their local machines, when actually the program resides on a single file server. This is a great benefit to small workstations, where disk space is at a premium. A user can have access to a much larger program repertoire than could fit on a private disk.

By having a resource reside physically on a single server, then distributed throughout the network, you can greatly simplify administration. First, you reduce the number of copies of various programs that need to be maintained on the network. Second, you reduce the problems involved in performing backups for a number of machines dispersed over a wide geographical area. By keeping files in a single location, this task becomes comparable to backing up a single machine.

Centralizing files on a few file servers not only simplifies administration, it helps maintain consistency of shared data files. When changes are made to a shared file, they become available to all users immediately.

As an alternative to centralizing files on a few file servers, files may be shared in a peer manner. When a single computer runs out of capacity, more computers can be added to a configuration. Files can be moved to the new computers, while a consistent view of the file system from the user's perspective is maintained.

RFS vs. NFS

In UNIX System V Release 4, RFS and NFS had been integrated as file system types under the Virtual File System mechanism. This means that the benefits of both RFS and NFS can be realized on the same computer. RFS and NFS will operate on the same machine and over the same network. Since the same directory trees may be mounted simultaneously over RFS and NFS, applications that require one or the other can co-exist. However, RFS and NFS protocols are different, and do not inter-operate.

NOTE Because RFS and NFS are implemented as file system types under the Virtual File System (VFS) mechanism, applications see a normal file system interface. The same open, read, write, and close operations as used for local files work for remote files. The distributed file system uses the VFS interface to take care of translations between the UNIX file system interface and internal protocols. For more information about Virtual File System, see *Basic System Administration*.

In Release 4, the syntax of administrative commands for RFS and NFS had been standardized to provide a uniform interface to distributed file systems. File system-dependent options allow differences to be accommodated, while integrating common features. Older forms of commands are still available to provide compatibility with previous systems.

Both RFS and NFS provide a comparable file sharing capability but have some differences, resulting from their different goals.

The goal of NFS is to provide file sharing in a heterogeneous environment potentially containing many different operating systems. The NFS internal protocol has been designed to be implementable on non-UNIX operating systems in order to provide an open file sharing capability. NFS clients and servers have been implemented on many operating systems including MS-DOS and VMS. A secondary goal of NFS is to provide good recovery characteristics when file servers fail; this has resulted in a design where the NFS servers do not keep any state information about clients accessing them. Thus, servers are not sensitive to client crashes, which results in a robust environment.

The major goal of RFS is to provide file sharing in a UNIX System V environment as transparently as possible. A file system shared using RFS closely supports UNIX file system semantics. This makes it relatively easy to migrate programs written to use the local file system.

The following sections highlight some of the similarities and differences between RFS and NFS.

- **Shared Objects**

  An RFS server can share any local directory, and all local files and directories under the shared directory are made accessible to remote users. RFS clients can access all file types transparently, including ordinary files, directories, named pipes, and special devices. Because computers running RFS can access remote devices, expensive peripherals, such as tape drives, can be used for backups by smaller computers that could not justify the cost of a dedicated drive; media incompatibilities (such as diskette formats) can be overcome by using devices supporting required formats on remote computers; and the reliability of the environment can be increased by making remote devices such as printers available if the locally attached device breaks down.

  An NFS server can share a file system or any part of a file system, including a single file. All files and directories below the root of the shared resource are made available to clients. A machine cannot share a file hierarchy that overlaps with one that is already shared. For example, it is invalid to share both `/public` and `/public/tkit`.

- **Transparency and Consistency**

  The same system calls and command syntax used to access local files are used to access RFS and NFS resources. Remote data is cached on both RFS and NFS clients. Cache consistency is guaranteed on RFS clients, but not on NFS clients.

- **Location Independence**

  RFS provides a name server with which to register resource names; the administrator of the client does not need to know where a resource resides. If resources (such as on-line manual pages or line printers) are moved, the client does not need to know about the move or modify its actions to access the resources at their new locations.

  The administrator of an NFS client machine must specify the name of the server machine when mounting an NFS file system. If a resource moves, all clients must be aware of the new location when mounting the resource.

- **Heterogeneity**

  RFS can operate over a network of computers running UNIX System V Release 3.0 and later System V releases, regardless of the underlying computer architecture.

NFS can operate on a variety of operating systems implemented on a variety of computer architectures.

- **Network Protocol Independence**

  RFS can run over any network protocol that conforms to the System V Transport Provider Interface and provides virtual circuit service. In UNIX SVR4.2, if multiple network protocols exist on the machine, RFS may run over all of them simultaneously.

  NFS is built on top of the Remote Procedure Call (RPC) facility, which requires the User Datagram Protocol (UDP), a member of the TCP/IP protocol family.

- **Full Semantics**

  RFS supports full UNIX system semantics, including file and record locking, open with append mode, access to remote devices and pipes, and so on.

  NFS uses of a network locking facility called the Lock Manager. The Lock Manager supports the UNIX System V style of advisory and mandatory file and record locking.

- **Application Compatibility**

  Since full file system semantics are supported, RFS allows all applications to run without recompilation.

  Because NFS provides transparent access, within limits, NFS allows existing applications that do not attempt to use unsupported features to run without recompilation.

- **Security**

  RFS allows file access based on machine passwords and user and group IDs. It also provides an administrator with the ability to specify read-only access to resources; to share directories selectively; to restrict which machines can access resources; to unshare a resource to prevent further client mounts; and to force a client to unmount a resource.

  NFS assumes global UID/GID space, and provides an administrator with the ability to restrict which machines can access resources; to specify read-only access to shared directories; and to unshare a directory, causing client access to that directory to fail. NFS also provides an option called Secure NFS, which supports encrypted machine and user identification along with ID mapping.

- **State**

  RFS servers maintain the state of local resources. The server knows which clients hold references to each of its files at any given time.

  NFS servers do not maintain the state of local resources. The server does not know which client has its files open at any given time.

- **Recovery**

  With RFS, if a client crashes, the server removes the client's locks and performs other clean-up actions. If the server crashes, the client acts as if that portion of the file tree has been removed (reads fail, and so on).

  With NFS, if the client crashes, the server is oblivious to it. If the server crashes, clients can either block until the server comes up or return an error after a timeout.

An Overview of DFS Administration

Some tasks involved in the administration of a distributed file system package are the same, whether you are using RFS or NFS. The Virtual File System architecture of UNIX SVR4 provides a mechanism for administering file system types in a general, or generic, way. Administrators of RFS and NFS are provided with a common set of commands which can be used to administer both RFS and NFS (as well as any distributed file system type that may be supported in System V in the future).

For example, to share a resource on your computer with remote systems, you must make the resource available and communicate its availability. To make a resource available using earlier versions of RFS, you would "advertise" it, using the **adv** command. To make a local resource available running earlier versions of NFS, you would "export" it, using the **exportfs** command. If you were to run both distributed file system packages, keeping the corresponding package-specific commands straight might be difficult. Multiply this by the number of corresponding package-specific commands in both packages, and the job becomes even more difficult.

DFS Administration provides generic commands that call package-specific commands, freeing you of the need to learn two sets of corresponding commands. For example, DFS Administration provides you with the **share** command, which lets you both advertise a resource over RFS and export a resource over NFS.

DFS Commands and Files

The DFS Administration Utilities package installs seven commands: **share**, **unshare**, **shareall**, **unshareall**, **dfshares**, **dfmounts**, and **lidload**. In addition to these commands, DFS Administration utilizes a number of files and commands installed by the other packages.

All the files and commands relevant to DFS administration are described in this section. Files and commands that operate on all file system types are described in this section only as they relate to administering distributed file systems.

The DFS Administration files are:

- **/etc/dfs/fstypes**, which is used to register the distributed file system packages you have installed on your system and establishes the default package (the first line in this file is the default package). The **fstypes** file is created by the distributed file system package you install first.

- **/etc/dfs/dfstab**, which allows you to share a resource or a set of resources automatically when you enter system state 3.
- **/etc/vfstab**, which allows you to mount resources automatically when you enter system state 3.
- **/etc/dfs/sharetab**, which logs the resources currently shared on your system. The **sharetab** file is created by the **share** command and does not require handling by an administrator.
- **/etc/mnttab**, which logs the file systems currently mounted by your system, including remote file systems and directories. The **mnttab** file is created by the **mount** command and does not require handling by an administrator.

DFS Administration commands are:

- **share**(1M), which allows you to make a resource available for mounting by clients, or to display a list of the resources on your system that are currently shared.
- **unshare**(1M), which allows you to make a previously available resource unavailable for mounting by clients.
- **shareall**(1M), which executes a script that shares a pre-determined set of resources, listed in **/etc/dfs/dfstab**.
- **unshareall** [see **shareall**(1M)], which executes a script that unshares all currently shared resources, listed in **/etc/dfs/dfstab**.
- **mount**(1M), which allows you to mount a remote resource on your system, or to display a list of resources, both local and remote, that are currently mounted on your system.
- **umount** [see **mount**(1M)], which allows you to remove a remote resource you previously mounted.
- **mountall**(1M), which executes a script that mounts a pre-determined set of resources.
- **umountall** [see **mountall**(1M)], which executes a script that unmounts all currently mounted resources.
- **dfshares**(1M), which displays a list of remote resources that are available to you, as well as a list of local resources that are currently shared.
- **dfmounts**(1M), which shows you which local resources are mounted by which clients.

12 Setting Up DFS Administration

DFS Administration Setup 12-1

Installing the Software 12-2

Changing the File Sharing Package Default 12-3

Starting Distributed File System Operation 12-4

DFS Administration Setup

This chapter describes the tasks you must complete before you execute DFS Administration commands. These tasks are installing the software, possibly editing a file to establish a default file sharing package, and starting distributed file system operation.

Installing the Software

If you installed all the software when you received UNIX SVR4.2, DFS Administration is already installed on your system. If you did not install all the add-on utilities, you'll need to install DFS Administration Utilities, as well as RFS and NFS Utilities and all the hardware and software required to run RFS and NFS.

Installation instructions for all UNIX SVR4.2 software—including DFS Administration Utilities, RFS Utilities, and NFS Utilities—appear in the *Release Notes*. Hardware and software prerequisites for RFS and NFS appear in chapters ''RFS Introduction'' and ''Setting Up NFS'', respectively.

Once all your network hardware and software are installed, you must set up your file sharing packages before you can enter DFS commands. The setup procedures for RFS and NFS differ; for RFS setup procedures, see ''RFS sysadm Interface''; for NFS setup procedures, see ''Setting Up NFS''.

Changing the File Sharing Package Default

So that the system can distinguish between local and remote file system types, the distributed file system packages you have installed must be "registered." When you install either RFS or NFS, the installation script creates the **fstypes** file and populates it. If the file already exists when you install either package, the installation script adds a line to the file. RFS package adds:

rfs Remote File Sharing Utilities: Version *number*

and NFS package adds:

nfs Network File System Utilities: Version *number*

where *number* indicates the version number of the package installed.

The package indicated in the first line of the file becomes your default file sharing package. If you enter DFS Administration commands without specifying a package (or file system type), the system assumes the first entry in the **/etc/dfs/fstypes** file. Therefore, if you know that you will administer one package more frequently than the other, make that the first entry in the file. This saves you from specifying the package every time you enter a DFS command.

To change the default package, edit the file using any supported text editor.

Starting Distributed File System Operation

Both RFS and NFS normally become operational automatically whenever you take your system to init state 3; however, both can be started in other run levels by entering commands at the command prompt.

You use different procedures and commands to start and stop RFS and NFS operations manually. For information, see the RFS administration chapters, "RFS Introduction", "RFS sysadm Interface" and "RFS Command Interface", and the NFS administration chapters, "NFS Introduction", "Setting Up NFS", "Sharing and Mounting NFS Resources Explicitly", "Obtaining NFS Information", "Handling NFS Problems", "Setting Up Secure NFS", "Using the NFS Automounter", "The NFS Network Lock Manager", and "Using the NFS sysadm Interface".

To start RFS and NFS automatically, use the **init** command to take your system to init state 3. If you choose, you can have your system enter init state 3 automatically when you boot by changing the **initdefault** line in the **/etc/inittab** file to read:

```
is:3:initdefault:
```

As explained earlier, DFS Administration allows you to share and mount resources *explicitly*, by entering commands at the command line, and *automatically*, by editing files that share and mount resources when you take the system to init state 3. Commands can be entered explicitly in any init state once you start distributed file system operation. Automatic sharing and mounting is done *only* when your system enters init state 3. When you exit init state 3, any resource you shared is automatically unshared, and any remote resource you mounted is automatically unmounted.

13 Using DFS Commands and Files

Sharing and Unsharing Resources 13-1
Sharing a Resource Explicitly—the share Command 13-1
Sharing a Resource Automatically—the /etc/dfs/dfstab File 13-2
Unsharing a Resource—the unshare Command 13-3
Sharing a Set of Resources—the shareall Command 13-4
Unsharing a Set of Resources—the unshareall Command 13-5

Mounting and Unmounting Remote Resources 13-6
Mounting a Remote Resource Explicitly—the mount Command 13-6
Mounting a Remote Resource Automatically—the /etc/vfstab File 13-7
Unmounting a Remote Resource—the umount Command 13-8
Mounting a Set of Resources—the mountall Command 13-9
Unmounting a Set of Resources—the umountall Command 13-10

Displaying Information 13-11
Displaying Shared Local Resources—the share Command 13-11
Displaying Mounted Resources—the mount Command 13-11
Browsing Shared Remote Resources—the dfshares Command 13-12
Monitoring the Use of Local Resources by Remote Systems—the dfmounts Command 13-13

Sharing and Unsharing Resources

This section tells you how to share and unshare RFS and NFS resources in a consistent way, using a common commands and files. The commands and files described in this chapter are the **share**, **unshare**, **shareall**, and **unshareall** commands; and the **/etc/dfs/dfstab** file.

Before you unshare a resource, using either the **unshare** or **unshareall** command, be sure you understand the effect of unsharing on existing mounts. When you unshare an RFS resource, existing mounts are unaffected; clients with the resource mounted can continue to use the resource, but no new mounts are permitted. When you unshare an NFS resource, access to existing mounts is inhibited; for more information, see "Sharing and Mounting NFS Resources Explicitly".

Sharing a Resource Explicitly—the share Command

To make a resource on your computer available to clients, you use the **share** command, which has the following syntax:

share [**-F** *fstype*] [**-o** *fs_options*] [**-d** *description*]
[*pathname* [*resourcename*]]

See the **share**(1M) manual page for an explanation of the options accepted by the **share** command.

For an explanation of the options available for sharing a resource over RFS or NFS, see the RFS-specific **share**(1M) or NFS-specific **share**(1M) manual pages. For more information about NFS-specific options, see "Sharing and Mounting NFS Resources Explicitly".

If no argument is specified when the **share** command is entered, then the command displays all resources on your system that are currently shared. If only a file system type is specified, then the **share** command displays all resources of the specified type that are currently shared. The **share** command can be used in this capacity by users as well as administrators.

Example 1

You want to share a directory called **mtgnotes** over RFS, which is a sub-directory to your **/usr/reports** directory. RFS is your default file sharing package. You want to share the directory by the name FORUM. You want to share the directory read-only to all clients. At the command line, type the following:

```
share -o ro -d "oct 9 materials" /usr/reports/mtgnotes FORUM
```

Example 2

You want to share a partial file system on your computer. The root directory of the branch of the file system is **graphics**, which is a subdirectory to your **/export** directory. The directory is an NFS resource. You want to share the directory read-only to all clients except a client named "art.dept," with which you want to share the directory read/write. At the command line, type the following:

```
share -F nfs -o ro,rw=art.dept /export/graphics
```

Sharing a Resource Automatically—the /etc/dfs/dfstab File

The **/etc/dfs/dfstab** file allows you to share a set of resources automatically whenever your system enters init state 3. For example, if you want a directory to be available to clients on a regular basis, and you can anticipate few occasions when you would need to make it unavailable, you can enter a **share** command for that directory into the **dfstab** file. Then, whenever you take the system to init state 3, the directory becomes available to clients automatically.

Each line of the file consists of the **share** command line needed to **share** a particular resource; the **share** command you enter in the file has the same syntax as the **share** command you enter at the command line. (See the description of the **share** command in the preceding section.)

If you want to add or delete a resource from a list of sharable resources, or to modify the way the sharing is done, edit the file with your text editor. The next time you enter init state 3 from another init state, the changes you made to the file will take effect.

Example

You want the directory **editors** to be available to all clients at all times. The directory is an NFS resource, located in your **/export** directory. Use your text editor to add the **share** command to the **/etc/dfs/dfstab** file. The file entry should look like this:

```
share -F nfs /export/editors
```

Unsharing a Resource—the unshare Command

If you want to reclassify a resource you have shared so that it is no longer available for mounting by remote systems, you "unshare" it. To unshare a resource, you use the **unshare** command.

The **unshare** command can be used to unshare any resource—whether the resource was shared explicitly with the **share** command or automatically through the **dfstab** file. If you use the **unshare** command to unshare a resource that you shared through the **dfstab** file, remember that it will be shared again when you exit and re-enter init state 3. The syntax for the **unshare** command is:

unshare [**-F** *fstype*] [**-o** *fs_options*] {*pathname* | *resourcename*}

See **unshare**(1M) for an explanation of the options accepted by the **unshare** command.

When unsharing an RFS resource, you supply either a pathname or a resource name, not both. When unsharing an NFS resource, you specify a pathname only.

NOTE

The **unshare** command supports file system type specific options so that file system types developed in the future can offer package specific functionality. At this time, RFS and NFS do not supply specific options to the **unshare** command.

Example 1

You want to unshare a directory called **invdata.88**. The directory is an RFS resource, which you shared by the name **OLDSTATS**. RFS is your default file sharing package. Type the following:

```
unshare OLDSTATS
```

Example 2

Although the directory **/export/templates** on your machine is shared continually through the **dfstab** file, you need to unshare the directory temporarily. The directory is an NFS resource. Type the following:

```
unshare -F nfs /export/templates
```

Now you can share the directory immediately using the **share** command, or the directory will be shared again automatically when you exit and re-enter init state 3.

Sharing a Set of Resources—the shareall Command

DFS Administration lets you share a set of resources, including a combination of RFS and NFS resources, by entering a single command—the **shareall** command. To use the command, you first create a file that lists the resources you want to share. The syntax of the entries in your file is the same syntax as the **share** command and the entries in the **dfstab** file, as follows:

```
share [-F fstype] [-o fs_options] [-d description]
        [pathname [resourcename]]
```

Once you create the file, you specify it as the input file when you enter the **shareall** command.

If you do not specify an input file, the **/etc/dfs/dfstab** file is used by default. If you enter a dash (-) in place of the name of an input file, the system accepts standard input, which means you can enter a number of **share** commands in succession, then execute the commands all at once by pressing CTRL-d. This saves you from entering one **share** command, waiting for the system to execute the command and return your prompt, entering another command, and so on.

The syntax of the **shareall** command is as follows:

```
shareall [-F fsys[,fsys . . . ]] [- | file]
```

See the **shareall**(1M) manual page for an explanation of the options accepted by the **shareall** command.

Example 1

You create an input file called **misc** that contains commands to share three separate resources. The file looks like this:

```
#cat misc
share -F rfs -o ro /usr/reports/mtg.notes FORUM
share -F nfs -o ro,rw=art.dept /export/graphics
share -F nfs /usr/man
```

To share all the resources listed in the file you created, type the following:

```
shareall misc
```

To share only the NFS resources listed in the **misc** file, type the following:

```
shareall -F nfs misc
```

Example 2

You want to share three separate resources. Because you will not be sharing the same resources as a set on a regular basis, you do not want to create an input file. Type the following:

```
shareall -
```

Your cursor moves to a new line. Enter the following commands, pressing RETURN after you enter each command.

```
share -F rfs -o ro /usr/reports/mtg.notes FORUM
share -F nfs -o ro,rw=art.dept /export/graphics
share -F nfs /usr/man
```

To execute the commands once they are entered, press CTRL-d.

Unsharing a Set of Resources—the unshareall Command

DFS Administration provides you with the **unshareall** command, which lets you unshare all the shared resources on your system, or all the shared resources of a specified file system type. The syntax of the **unshareall** command is

unshareall [-F *fsys* **[,***fsys* . . . **]]**

When you specify a file system type, the command unshares all local resources of the distributed file system type you specified. If no **-F** option is specified, then the command unshares all local resources currently shared.

For **unshareall**, see the **shareall**(1M) manual page for an explanation of the options accepted by the **unshareall** command.

Example 1

You want to unshare all the currently shared RFS resources on your computer. Type the following:

```
unshareall -F rfs
```

Example 2

You want to unshare all currently shared local resources, regardless of file system type. Type the following:

```
unshareall
```

Mounting and Unmounting Remote Resources

This section tells you how to mount and unmount remote resources explicitly, using the generic **mount**, **umount**, **mountall**, and **umountall** commands. It also tells you how to mount remote resources automatically, using the **/etc/vfstab** file. The command and files described in this section are described only as they relate to the administration of remote resources.

Mounting a Remote Resource Explicitly—the mount Command

The **mount** command allows you to mount both local and remote file systems. To mount a remote resource using the **mount** command, you must be able to reach, via a network, the server that is sharing the resource you want to mount.

The syntax of the **mount** command as it relates to mounting distributed file systems is:

mount [**-F** *FSType*] [**-V**] [*current_options*] [**-o** *specific_options*]
{*special* | *mount_point*}

mount [**-F** *FSType*] [**-V**] [*current_options*] [**-o** *specific_options*]
special mount_point

See the **mount**(1M) manual page for an explanation of the options accepted by the **mount** command.

For information about NFS-specific options, see "Sharing and Mounting NFS Resources Explicitly".

Resources mounted explicitly with the **mount** command stay mounted unless you unmount them, using **umount**, or if you exit init state 3. If you exit init state 3 and re-enter it, the resource is no longer mounted (unless you edited the **/etc/vfstab** file to include the mount automatically).

Example 1

You want to mount an RFS resource called **BLUEPRINTS**. You have created a mount point called **/usr/old.blues**. To mount the remote directory, type the following:

```
mount -F rfs BLUEPRINTS /usr/old.blues
```

Because no access rights are specified, the directory is mounted read/write.

Example 2

You want to mount an NFS resource residing on a server called "tools.srv." The resource is a directory called **graphics** in the server's **/usr** directory. You created a mount point called **graphics** in your **/usr/tools** directory. You want to mount the resource read/write, and you want set-uid bits to be ignored. Type the following:

```
mount -F nfs -o nosuid tools.srv:/usr/graphics\
  /usr/tools/graphics
```

Because no access rights are specified, the directory is mounted read/write.

Example 3

You want to hard mount a directory containing manual pages that resides on a server called "docgroup." You want the directory mounted read-only, with interrupt enabled. The directory is an NFS resource named **/usr/man**. You want to mount the directory to a mount point of the same name on your machine. Type the following:

```
mount -F nfs -o ro,intr docgroup:/usr/man /usr/man
```

Mounting a Remote Resource Automatically—the /etc/vfstab File

The **/etc/vfstab** file allows you to mount a local file system automatically when you boot the system. If you edit the file to include a remote file system or directory, the remote resource is mounted automatically when you take the system to init state 3.

To mount a remote resource automatically, create a mount point for the resource using the **mkdir** command, then edit the **vfstab** file. Entries in the **vfstab** file require the following syntax:

special fsckdev mountp fstype fsckpass automnt mntopts

See the **vfstab**(4) manual page for a description of the fields in the **/etc/vfstab** file.

Once you create the mount point and edit the **/etc/vfstab** file, the file system or directory will be mounted automatically when you enter init state 3. It will be mounted automatically every time you enter init state 3 until you modify the **vfstab** file (unless, of course, the server sharing the directory unshares it). The contents of **/etc/vfstab** remain the same until you edit the file.

Example

Assume you want to mount the resource **/usr/share** from a server named "frontoffice." You want the resource to be mounted automatically every time you take your system to init state 3. The directory is an NFS resource. You want to mount the directory on the mount point **/usr/local/tmp** with read-only access. First create the mount point by typing the following:

```
mkdir /usr/local/tmp
```

Make sure the mode and permissions of the new mount point match those of the resource you want to mount on it. Then edit the **/etc/vfstab** file, using any supported text editor. The file entry should look like this:

```
frontoffice:/usr/share - /usr/local/tmp nfs - yes ro
```

Unmounting a Remote Resource—the umount Command

The **umount** command allows you to unmount both local and remote file systems. You can unmount a resource with **umount** whether is was mounted explicitly using the **mount** command or automatically through the **vfstab** file.

The syntax of the **umount** command, as it relates to unmounting distributed file systems, is:

umount [-V] [**-o** *specific_options*] {*resource* | *mount_point*}

For **umount**, see the **mount**(1M) manual page for an explanation of the options accepted by the **umount** command.

Example 1

You want to unmount a remote resource called **BLUEPRINTS**, which you mounted on a mount point called **old.blues** in your **/etc** directory. The resource is an RFS resource. Type the following command:

```
umount /etc/old.blues
```

Example 2

You want to unmount a remote NFS resource by specifying the server sharing the resource and the pathname of the resource on the server. Type the following command:

```
umount docgroup:/usr/man
```

Mounting a Set of Resources—the mountall Command

DFS Administration lets you mount a set of resources, including a combination of remote RFS and NFS resources, by entering a single command—the **mountall** command. To use the command, you first create a file that lists the resources you want to mount. The syntax of the entries in your file is the same syntax as the entries in the **/etc/vfstab** file, as follows:

special fsckdev mountp fstype fsckpass automnt mntopts

See the **vfstab**(4) manual page for a description of the fields in the **/etc/vfstab** file.

Once you create a file, you specify it as the input file for the **mountall** command.

If you do not specify an input file, the **/etc/vfstab** file is used by default. If you enter a dash (-) in place of the name of an input file, the system accepts standard input, which means you can enter a number of **mount** commands in succession, then execute the commands all at once by pressing CTRL-d. This saves you from entering one **mount** command, waiting for the system to execute the command and return your prompt, entering another command, and so on.

The syntax of the **mountall** command is as follows:

mountall [-F *FSType*] **[-l | -r]** [*file_system_table*]

See the **mountall**(1M) manual page for an explanation of the options accepted by the **mountall** command.

If the **mountall** command is entered without arguments, it mounts all local file systems and remote resources in the **vfstab** file that have the *automnt* field set to "yes."

Example 1

You want to mount a set of remote resources. You create an input file called **mntlist** that lists three remote resources. The file looks like this:

```
#cat mntlist
docgroup:/usr/man - /usr/man nfs - yes ro
BLUEPRINTS - /usr/old.blues rfs - yes rw
frontoffice:/usr/share - /usr/local/tmp nfs - yes rw
```

To mount all the resources listed in the file you created, type

```
mountall mntlist
```

To mount only the NFS resources listed in the **mntlist** file, type

```
mountall -F nfs mntlist
```

Example 2

Your system mounts resources automatically when you entered init state 3, using the **/etc/vfstab** file. While resources are still mounted, you add entries to the **vfstab** file. Now you want to mount the resources you added to the file, without exiting init state 3 and unmounting currently mounted resources. Type the following command:

```
mountall -r
```

The system uses the updated **vfstab** file as the input file. It mounts all remote resources in the file that are not currently mounted and displays error messages for those resources that are mounted already.

Unmounting a Set of Resources—the umountall Command

DFS Administration utilizes the **umountall** command, which lets you unmount mounted resources on your system or all the mounted resources of a specified file system type. The syntax of the **umountall** command is the following:

umountall [-F *FSType***] [-k] [-l | -r]**

For **umountall**, see the **mountall**(1M) manual page for an explanation of the options accepted by the **umountall** command.

Example 1

You want to unmount all the remote RFS resources currently mounted on your system. Type the following:

```
umountall -F rfs
```

Example 2

You want to unmount all remote file systems currently mounted on your system. You want to kill all processes that have open files. Type the following:

```
umountall -k -r
```

Displaying Information

This section tells you how to determine what resources are available to you from network servers, what resources are shared and mounted on your system, and what resources shared on your system have been mounted by network clients. The commands described in this chapter are the **share**, **mount**, **dfshares**, and **dfmounts** commands.

Displaying Shared Local Resources—the share Command

You use the **share** command to share resources on your system with network clients; however, you can also use the command to display information about shared resources on your system. The command's syntax when used in this capacity is:

    share [-F fstype]

If you enter the command without arguments, it displays all RFS and NFS resources on your system that are currently shared. If you specify a file system type and no other options, the command displays all resources of the specified type that are currently shared.

Displaying Mounted Resources—the mount Command

Generally, you use the **mount** command to mount local and remote resources on your system. However, if you enter the command without arguments, it displays a list of local and remote resources that are currently mounted on your system.

NOTE You cannot limit the display to remote resources or to resources of a specific file system type by entering arguments. If you enter **mount -F rfs**, for example, the system displays an error message.

Browsing Shared Remote Resources—the dfshares Command

To "browse" shared resources means to determine what resources are available from remote systems. For browsing, DFS Administration gives you the **dfshares** command, which displays information about the RFS and NFS resources that are available from network servers. The syntax of the **dfshares** command is:

`dfshares [-F` *fstype*`] [-h] [-o` *fs_options*`]` [*server* . . .]

See **dfshares**(1M) for an explanation of the options accepted by the **dfshares** command.

The syntax of the *server* option depends on the server's file system type. If you are browsing for shared RFS resources, the *server* field can be any name that is supported by the RFS command **nsquery**. You can use a *system* name, which specifies a system in the domain of the local system, a *domain* name, which specifies *all* the systems in the domain, or you can enter both the domain and the system, in the form *domain.system*, to display resources on a specific remote system in a remote domain.

To display resources on an NFS server, you can enter a *system* name for the server option, which specifies a system on the network.

When you enter the command, your system displays output consisting of the fields:

resource server access transport description

where *resource* is the shared resource name; *server* is the system from which the resource is available; *access* refers to the access granted client systems—either read/write or read-only; *transport* is the transport provider over which communication is carried, such as tcp; and *description* is a description of the resource provided by an administrator when the resource was shared.

For NFS resources, the command cannot determine the access rights granted to client systems or the transport provider; therefore, the access and transport fields are filled with hyphens (–) when **dfshares** displays a list of NFS resources. The description field does not appear at all in a display of NFS resources.

If you enter the **dfshares** command without arguments, the system displays all resources (both RFS and NFS) currently shared on your system, along with remote resources that are currently available for mounting.

Example 1

You want to browse the RFS resources available from a server named "lib" in a domain named "sales." You want the display to include a header. Type the following:

dfshares -F rfs sales.lib

The system displays output similar to the following:

```
RESOURCE       SERVER    ACCESS  TRANSPORT  DESCRIPTION
sales.CONV89   lib       ro      tcp        "material from 1989 sales convention"
sales.PROJ1    lib       ro      tcp        "1990 sales projections by product"
sales.PROJ2    lib       ro      tcp        "1990 sales projections by territory"
sales.TRAIN    lib       ro      tcp        "sales force training materials"
```

Example 2

You want to browse NFS resources on a server called "main." You do not want the display to include a header. Type the following:

dfshares -F nfs -h main

The system displays the following output:

```
main:/export        main     -    -
main:/usr/man       main     -    -
main:/usr/share     main     -    -
```

Monitoring the Use of Local Resources by Remote Systems—the dfmounts Command

The **dfmounts** command shows you which local resources are mounted by clients. The command accepts the following syntax:

dfmounts [**-F** *fstypes*] [**-h**] [**-o** *fs_options*] [*restriction*]

See **dfmounts**(1M) for an explanation of the options accepted by the **dfmounts** command.

If you enter **dfmounts** without arguments, the system displays all local resources (both RFS and NFS) currently mounted by remote systems.

The **dfmounts** command displays a header, which is optional, followed by lines consisting of the fields

resource server pathname clients . . .

where *resource* is the shared resource name; *server* is the system from which the resource is available; *pathname* is the pathname of the shared resource as it was given to the **share** command; and *clients* is a list (separated by commas) of clients that have mounted the resource.

Example 1

Your machine is called "lib"; it resides in domain "sales." You want to display the RFS resources on your system that are currently mounted by clients. RFS is the only file sharing package installed on your system. You want the display to include a header. Type the following:

```
dfmounts
```

The system displays the following output:

```
RESOURCE     SERVER       PATH                 CLIENTS
CONV89       lib          /usr/share/conv89    sales.dept120
PROJ1        lib          /usr/share/proj1     sales.dept122
PROJ2        lib          /usr/share/proj2     sales.dept122
TRAIN        lib          /usr/share/train
```

Example 2

You want to see which clients are mounting the NFS resources on the system called "main." You do not want a header to be displayed. Type the following:

```
dfmounts -F nfs -h main
```

The system displays the following output:

```
-      main     /export         dancer, runner
-      main     /usr/man        jogger
-      main     /usr/share      dancer, runner
```

14 DFS sysadm Interface

Introduction 14-1

The DFS Management Menu Tree 14-2

DFS Menu Options 14-3

Introduction

UNIX SVR4.2 provides a menu interface to system administration called System Administration Menus (or *sis-adam*, because it is accessed through the **sysadm** command). When you install DFS Administration Utilities, menus are added to the interface for administering distributed file systems. These menus are known collectively as the Distributed File System Management menus. This section describes the DFS Management menus and the options the menus provide.

A complete description of the menu interface, including a tutorial, appears in *Basic System Administration*.

The DFS Management Menu Tree

All DFS Administration commands can be accessed through the Distributed File System Management menus in the System Administration Menus.

To display the DFS Management menus, do the following:

1. Type **sysadm network_services**.

   The Network Services Management menu is displayed.

2. From the Network Services Management menu, select the option **remote_files**.

   The Distributed File System Management menu is displayed.

From the Distributed File System Management menu, you can access submenus that provide you with commands that correspond to the commands described in this guide.

Here is an illustration of **sysadm** menus that relate to distributed file system administration:

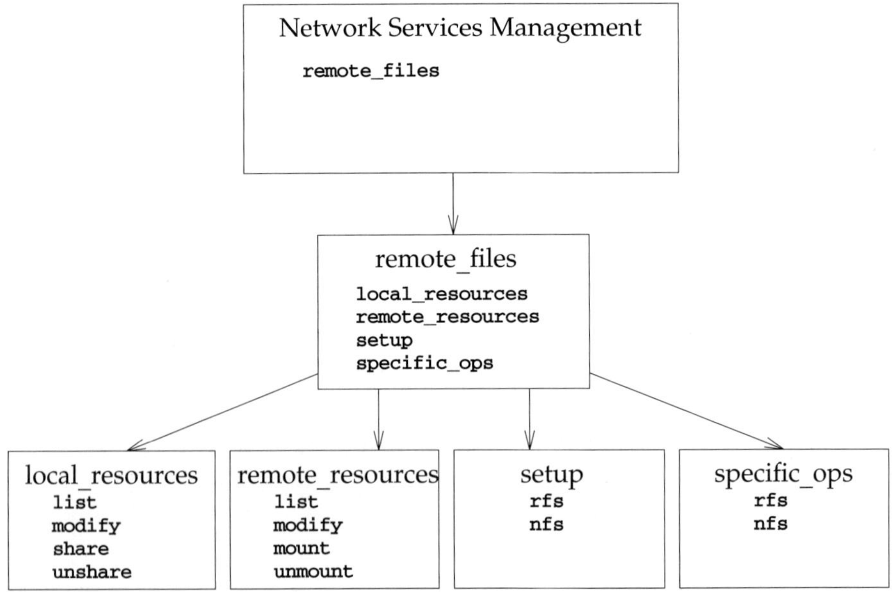

DFS Menu Options

The commands that correspond to the commands described in this chapter are the commands for administering local and remote resources, which are accessed through the **local_resources** and the **remote_resources** submenus. The **setup** submenu gives you package-specific commands for setting up RFS and NFS. The **specific_ops** submenu gives you package-specific commands for administering RFS and NFS.

Menu options on the **local_resources** and the **remote_resources** submenus allow you to share, unshare, mount, and unmount resources *immediately*, or to specify resources to be shared and mounted *automatically* whenever your system enters system state 3.

The **local_resources** submenu provides you with the following menu options.

- **list**, which allows you to list the resources on your system currently available to network clients, or that are shared automatically whenever distributed file system operation begins.
- **modify**, which allows you to change the options with which resources on your system are currently shared, as well as the options with which resources are shared when they are shared automatically.
- **share**, which allows you to share selected resources on your system with network clients. The menu option lets you share resources immediately or specify resources to be shared automatically.
- **unshare**, which allows you to unshare resources on your system that are currently shared with network clients. The menu option also lets you cancel the automatic sharing of local resources.

The **remote_resources** submenu provides you with the following menu options:

- **list**, which allows you to list the remote resources that are currently mounted on your system and the remote resources that are mounted automatically.
- **modify**, which allows you to change the options with which remote resources are currently mounted on your system, as well as the options with which remote resources are mounted when they are mounted automatically.
- **mount**, which allows you to mount remote resources on your system and make them available to your users. The menu option lets you mount resources immediately, and specify resources to be mounted automatically every time distributed file system operation begins.

- `unmount`, which allows you to unmount currently mounted remote resources. The menu option also lets you cancel the automatic mounting of remote resources.

Once you select a menu option from either submenu, screen messages and prompts lead you through the task you want to perform. If a message or a prompt is unclear to you, you can display a help screen, which gives you additional information for completing the task.

Setting Up RFS

15 RFS Introduction

About RFS Administration 15-1

Organization 15-1

Introduction to RFS 15-2

Resource Sharing 15-2

Domains 15-4

- Name Service 15-4

Transport Provider 15-5

- Network Listener 15-6
- Network Specification 15-6
- Network Addresses 15-6

Security 15-6

- Verify Computers 15-7
- Restrict Resources 15-7
- Map IDs 15-8

RFS Features 15-9

About RFS Administration

The Remote File Sharing (RFS) administration chapters tell you how to administer RFS. As a distributed file system package, RFS allows you to share resources on your computer with remote computers across a network of systems running UNIX System V.

Remote File Sharing is administered from the System Administration Menus (**sysadm**). Once you access a **sysadm** menu, help screens provide you with all the information you need to complete a task. Therefore, the "RFS sysadm Interface" chapter does not lead you step-by-step through the menu-based procedures. Instead, it provides background information and reference material you will need to administer and fine tune your RFS network.

Organization

The RFS Administration chapters are organized as follows:

- "RFS Introduction", presents a general model of an RFS network, introduces some basic terminology, and describes the services that RFS provides.
- "RFS sysadm Interface", explains how to set up and maintain RFS Utilities on your computer, using the **sysadm** interface.
- "RFS Command Interface", shows you how to administer RFS through shell level commands and give you tips on troubleshooting problems. As you become a more experienced administrator, use this information as reference material to fine tune your RFS network.

Introduction to RFS

The primary function of RFS is to allow computers running UNIX SVR4.2 to selectively share resources (directories containing files, subdirectories, devices, and/or named pipes) across a network. As an administrator of a computer on an RFS network, you can choose directories on your system you want to share and add them to a list of available resources on the network. From this same list, you can choose resources on remote computers that you would like to use on your computer.

Resource Sharing

An RFS network generally consists of sub-groups of computers called domains. An RFS network may contain many domains. Sharing resources is a fundamental RFS operation that can be done between computers in the same domain, as well as between computers in different domains. It involves the notion of a server (a computer in the RFS network that offers a resource to others) and a client (a computer in the RFS network that uses a server's resource).

Sharing a resource on a Remote File Sharing system begins by identifying the pathname to a UNIX system directory you want to share. After identifying the directory you want to share, you then assign it a resource identifier (a name that other computers will use to reference that directory) and "share" it to other machines, using the **share** command. Computers that pass the security checks you have set up can then mount resources that you have made available as they would mount a file system locally. The **mount** command with the **-F rfs** option is used for mounting remote resources.

Figure 15-1 shows how two computers can share resources. In this example, the administrator of a computer named **fie** on a Remote File Sharing system wants to share all files and directories under **/fs1** on its file system tree. The administrator shares **/fs1** as a resource called FSLOGS.

Figure 15-1: Example — Sharing Resources

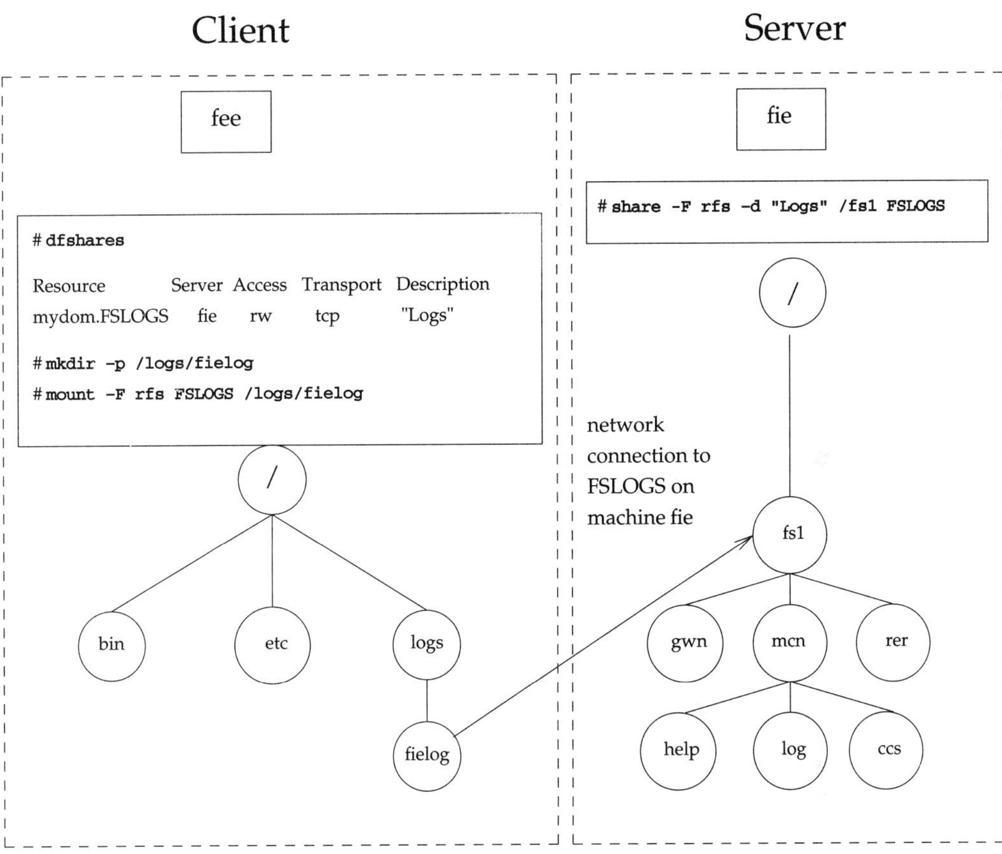

Another machine in **fie**'s domain is called **fee**. The administrator from **fee** uses the **dfshares** command to see that FSLOGS is available on **fie**. The administrator then creates a directory called **/logs/fielog** on **fee** (**mkdir** command) and **mount**s FSLOGS on **/logs/fielog**.

Files or subdirectories from **/fs1** are now accessible to users on **fee**. Users can **cd** to the remote directory, list the contents, and run a remote program locally. If the resource contained the **/dev** directory, users could direct output to a remote device as though the device were on the local machine.

Domains

Each machine on a Remote File Sharing network must be assigned to a domain. The main reasons for domains are to simplify name service and provide a focal point for security of a group of machines.

Domain names act like telephone area codes. You can address all computers (nodes) and resources in your domain directly. For outside domains, you simply attach the domain name to the node name or resource identifier. This becomes increasingly valuable as RFS networks expand.

Name Service

Each domain must be assigned a primary and zero or more secondary domain name servers. These machines can share resources, like any other computer in the domain, but they have some special responsibilities.

Primary

The main duty of the primary domain name server is to keep track of all computers and resources within the domain it serves. It ensures that all resource identifiers and machine node names are unique within the domain.

One task of the primary domain name server is to add each computer to the domain member list and assign each computer an RFS password.

A list of resources is stored on the primary, so any computer can see what resources are available for the domain. Also, when a computer shares a resource, it registers its network address with the primary.

This way when a computer tries to mount another machine's resource the primary can tell the computer where the resource can be found on the network.

An optional function of the primary is to store lists of each computer's users (**/etc/passwd**) and groups (**/etc/group**). Each computer in the domain can then use these lists to specifically define the permissions each machine's users will have to its resources.

A primary can also have names and network addresses of other domains' name servers. Once the primary knows another domain name server's address, machines in its domain have the potential to access resources from machines in the other domain.

Secondaries If the primary crashes or gets shutdown, domain name service functions are automatically assumed by the first secondary domain name server defined in the **rfmaster** file. The secondary is intended to take over temporarily, until the primary comes back up.

While the secondary will have information needed to run the domain name server, domain information (for example, RFS passwords) should not be modified on the secondary. When the primary comes back up, the secondary should be instructed to pass name server responsibility back to the primary (**rfadmin -p** command). Afterwards, standard administrative changes can be made on the primary server.

Transport Provider

The transport provider provides the pathway used by Remote File Sharing to communicate with other machines. The term transport provider is used to refer to the physical network that connects the machines and the software needed to send messages across the network.

Remote File Sharing can communicate using any transport provider that is compatible with the Transport Interface Specification. TCP/IP is one transport provider that can be used with RFS.

Although the transport provider is not considered part of the RFS package, RFS will not work if the transport provider is not functioning properly. Also, some information needed to configure RFS varies from one transport provider to another. For example, network addresses of the primary and secondaries and the network specification to identify the transport provider to RFS are dependent on the particular transport provider used.

Most of the scenarios in this guide show RFS running over a single transport provider; however, RFS can run over multiple transport providers at the same time. This optional feature is discussed in the "Multiple Transport Providers (Optional)" section.

The following sections describe transport provider information that relates to RFS administration: "Network Listener", "Network Specification", and "Network Addresses".

Network Listener

The network listener is part of the Networking Support Utilities package. Essentially, the listener's function is to wait for requests from the network. A call coming in from the network will request a particular service code. The service code will tell the listener to direct the call to a particular process.

Service code `105` is used to request RFS services. If all software installation was done correctly, the RFS service code will be automatically configured for the listener of every transport provider you installed. Otherwise you will need to use the **pmadm** command to manually configure the listener. (See "Setting Up RFS".)

Network Specification

Since you could have several transport providers on one computer, you must tell RFS which transport provider will handle RFS on your machine. The network specification is the name you will use when you initially configure RFS to indicate its transport provider. TCP/IP, for example, uses **tcp** as its network specification. This tells RFS that **/dev/tcp** is the device representing the transport provider to use.

Network Addresses

When Remote File Sharing is started on a machine, the machine tries to contact its domain's primary name server. In order to do that, the machine must know the primary's network address.

The form of the network address varies according to the transport provider used. The **nlsadmin** command is used to obtain your machine address, regardless of the network used. See **nlsadmin**(1M) for more information on **nlsadmin**.

Security

RFS provides several mechanisms for ensuring the security of your resources. Some of these mechanisms, however, require diligence to set up and maintain. This is especially true if the machines, resources, and users are constantly changing on the network.

As a system administrator you can maintain strict control of your resources. No files, directories, or devices in an unshared file system can be accessed by other computers. Standard UNIX system file security measures can be used in combination with special RFS facilities to protect your resources.

Direct access to your computer is controlled because local users still have to log in as they always have. As for remote accessibility, you can set up security to allow only certain remote computers to access your resources.

The major mechanisms in RFS for protecting your resources are described in the sections "Verify Computers," "Restrict Resources," and "Map IDs."

Verify Computers

When a remote computer tries to mount a resource from your computer, and no other resources are mounted, it tries to set up a connection (virtual circuit) across the network to your machine. Once this virtual circuit is set up, the remote machine can mount any resource you have made available to it. This virtual circuit is closed when the last resource is unmounted.

Before this virtual circuit is created, you can verify that the computer is the one it claims to be by checking its RFS password. The following text describes what happens when verification is and is not used.

- No verify: any computer can connect

  If the computer is listed in the **/etc/rfs/auth.info/***domain***/passwd** file, your machine will check its password. Otherwise, your computer will accept it as the machine it claims to be.

- Verify: some computers can connect

  If you use the RFS verification feature, you can make sure that only specific machines can use any of your resources. Those machines must be listed in the proper **/etc/rfs/auth.info/***domain***/passwd** file and must match the password you have for them. (*domain* is the domain name of the requesting machine.) You can tailor this file if you only want a subset of machines to be allowed to connect. (A description of how to use this feature is contained in "Setting Up RFS".)

Restrict Resources

Once a remote computer has established a connection to your computer, the resources it can mount from your machine depend on how you shared each resource. These are your choices:

- any machine can mount

  You may have shared the resource so that any machine that can connect to your machine can mount it.

- some machines can mount

  You restricted access to the resource to certain machines. The remote computer trying to mount it must be one of those machines.

You also may have shared the resource as read-only. In that case, the remote computer must mount the resource read-only instead of read/write (default).

Map IDs

Remote users' permissions can be defined to provide another layer of security for a mounted resource. Remote users and groups can be mapped into your local computer's user and group list to set permissions of your resources.

You can set these mapping rules on a global or per-machine basis. The global rules set user and group permissions for all remote machines that do not have explicit mapping rules.

Here are the ways you can map remote machines' user-ids into your machine. These rules apply to both global and per-machine mapping.

- no mapping

  If you don't set any special mapping for any remote computer, all users are mapped into your machine as a "special guest" user ID/group ID. This is the easiest approach because you don't need to keep any records for the remote machine, create rules files or run the **`idload`** command.

- default mapping

  You can set default mapping so that all remote users are mapped into one of these permissions:

  - the local user ID number that matches each remote user's ID (**`default transparent`**)
  - a single local ID number
  - a single local ID name
  - the local user name that matches each remote user's name (**`map all`**)

  Group permissions can be mapped in the same way. Users and groups are mapped independently. If there are exceptions to the default mapping, you can **`exclude`** certain users and groups so they only have special guest permissions (for example, **`exclude 0`**).

- specific mapping

  You can map any user or group from any remote machine into a specific user or group on your machine. This can be done by user name or numeric ID.

Using these mapping techniques and standard methods for setting file permissions, you can keep strict controls over your resources, even after they are remotely mounted. (See "Mapping Remote Users" for more details.)

RFS Features

Here are some RFS feature design considerations.

Compatibility
: Once you mount a remote resource on your system it will look to your users as though it is part of the local system. You will be able to use most standard UNIX system features on the resource. Standard commands and system calls, as well as features like File and Record Locking, work the same on remote resources as they do locally. Applications should be able to work on remote resources without modification.

Flexibility
: Since you can mount a remote resource on any directory on your system, you have a lot of freedom to set up your computer's view of the world. You do not have to open up all your files to every machine on the network. Likewise, you do not have to make all files on the network available to your computer's users.

Performance (Client Caching)
: The client caching feature of RFS provides substantial performance improvements over non-caching systems by reducing the number of times data must be read across the network. Client refers to the computer that is using a remote resource, while caching refers to the client's ability to store data in local buffer pools.

The first time a client process reads a block of data from a remote resource, it is placed in local buffer pools. Subsequent client processes reading a server file can avoid network access by finding the data already present in local buffers. This generally causes a large reduction in network messages, resulting in improved performance.

In order for client caching to work simply and reliably, the following features were built into it:

- Cache consistency. Checking mechanisms are used to ensure that the cache buffers accurately reflect the contents of the remote file the user is accessing.

- Transparency. The only difference users should see between caching and non-caching systems is improved response time. RFS-based applications do not have to be changed to run on a Remote File Sharing system that caches remote data.
- Administration. By default, client caching is on. However, options are available to turn off caching for an entire system or for a particular resource. (You would probably only do this if you have an application that does its own network buffering.) There are also some tunable parameters available to fine tune your system according to the way you use RFS. (See ''Monitoring'' and ''Parameter Tuning'' in ''RFS Command Interface'' for more information.)

16 RFS sysadm Interface

Overview of RFS sysadm 16-1

Procedure 1: Set Up Remote File Sharing 16-3
Prerequisites 16-3

Procedure 2: Start/Stop Remote File Sharing 16-5

Procedure 3: Local Resource Sharing 16-6

Procedure 4: Remote Resource Mounting 16-7

Procedure 5: Change RFS Configuration 16-8
RFS Configuration/Domain Management 16-8
Transport Providers 16-9
RFS ID Mapping 16-9

Overview of RFS sysadm

System Administration Menus (**sysadm**) is a menu interface through which you can perform most of the tasks involved in setting up and maintaining your RFS network. Before you begin any of the menu procedures described in this chapter, it is assumed that you've completed software installation. Installation instructions appear in the UNIX System V *Release Notes*. Once you've installed your software you can do all the basic RFS setup and administration from the **sysadm** menus. Here are the RFS procedures you can complete using **sysadm.**

Procedure 1: Set Up Remote File Sharing

To set up all basic information needed to run Remote File Sharing.

Procedure 2: Start/Stop Remote File Sharing

To start and stop Remote File Sharing, check if it is currently running, and set up RFS to start automatically at system boot time.

Procedure 3: Local Resource Sharing

To manage the local resources you make available to other machines.

Procedure 4: Remote Resource Mounting

To manage remote resources made available to your machine.

Procedure 5: Change RFS Configuration

To change your ID mapping, show your current RFS configuration, or update the domain member list.

The **sysadm** interface not only lets you add all basic RFS configuration information, but it also acts as a tutorial by introducing and explaining key RFS concepts. Once you access a **sysadm** menu, help screens provide you with background information and explanations regarding menu selections. Access the help screens by using the "HELP" function key; use the "CANCEL" function key to exit the help mode. Continue making menu selections until you complete the particular task.

These procedures are designed to help you set up and maintain Remote File Sharing (RFS) Utilities on your computer. Should you need more information as you are setting up RFS, you should consult the glossary of terms provided in the back of this chapter, or you should consult the corresponding section names for each procedure.

The **sysadm** interface lets you do everything necessary to set up and run RFS in a basic configuration. There are several optional features that are not available through the **sysadm** interface, however.

The optional features not available using the **sysadm** interface are described at the end of the "Setting Up RFS" section. The word "Optional" is placed in the heading of each optional feature. The features include the following:

Remote Computer Verification.
: By default, when a machine requests the use of one of your resources, your machine will process the request without verifying the remote machine's password. This procedure describes how to restrict access of all your resources to a limited group of remote machines whose names and passwords match those in lists you set up.

Complex user ID/group ID mapping.
: ID mapping defines the permissions remote users will have to your resources. The choices of ID mapping schemes are limited when you use the **sysadm** interface to set up mapping. This procedure gives you more flexibility in setting up permissions for remote users.

Multiple Domain Resource Sharing.
: The **sysadm** interface assumes that you are only sharing resources within one domain. However, it is possible to have more than one domain on a network. This procedure describes how to share resources among multiple domains on the same network.

Multiple Domain Name Service.
: When you define the primary and secondary name servers using **sysadm**, you are defining them to serve a single domain. You can, however, define the same set of machines to be the name server for several domains using this procedure.

More experienced RFS administrators will also be interested in "Monitoring" and "Parameter Tuning" in "RFS Command Interface". Information in these sections will help you fine tune your system so RFS can make the most efficient use of your system's resources.

Procedure 1: Set Up Remote File Sharing

This procedure is used to set up Remote File Sharing on your machine. When the procedure is done, you will have completed everything needed to run RFS on your system.

Prerequisites

In addition to the prerequisite steps you followed in the section, "Before You Begin", you should do the following before you begin setting up RFS:

- Choose one or more computers on the network to act as domain name servers. Exactly one primary is required. All domain administration is done from the primary. You can choose zero or more secondary domain name servers. These are defined simply to keep the name server running temporarily, should the primary fail. (You can configure RFS on your machine before the primary is configured and running RFS. However, you cannot start RFS until the primary begins running RFS.)
- Log in.

After you have accomplished the prerequisites, begin to set up RFS by typing **`sysadm network_services`** and selecting **`remote_files`**. Continue by selecting **`setup`** and then **`rfs`** to bring you to the following screen:

```
                    Initial Remote File Sharing Setup

set_networks          - Sets Up Network Support for RFS
set_domain            - Sets the Current Domain for RFS
add_nameserver        - Adds Domain Name Servers
add_host              - Adds Systems to the Domain Password File
set_uid_mappings      - Sets Up UID Mappings
set_gid_mappings      - Sets Up GID Mappings
start                 - Starts Remote File Sharing
share                 - Shares Local Resources via Remote File Sharing
mount                 - Mounts Remote Resources via Remote File Sharing
```

You should execute each of the tasks in the order listed. Continue making interactive menu selections until the job is done. Remember, the ''HELP'' function key will provide you with help messages along the way. After completing this procedure, you can check if RFS is running by returning to the shell and typing **rfadmin -q**, or, you can use the **check_status** menu function described in the next procedure. The chapter section ''Setting Up RFS'' will provide you with detailed background information in this area.

The **sysadm** interface assumes that the name server is running UNIX SVR4.0 or later. If this is not the case, the command interface should be used. See "rfmaster File for Pre-UNIX SVR4.0 Systems" in "RFS Command Interface" for more information.

Procedure 2: Start/Stop Remote File Sharing

This procedure is used to start and stop RFS. It's also used to determine if RFS is running. As a prerequisite, you should have already set up RFS.

Begin by typing **sysadm network_services** and selecting **remote_files**. Continue by selecting **specific_ops**, **rfs**, and **control**. You are now at the following screen:

```
                    Remote File Sharing Control

check_status         - Checks Whether Remote File Sharing Is Running
pass_control         - Passes Name Server Responsibility back to the Primary
start                - Starts Remote File Sharing
stop                 - Stop Remote File Sharing
```

Select **start** to start RFS. If RFS does not start, see the "Starting/Stopping RFS" in "RFS Command Interface" for a list of possible problems. Selecting **stop** will stop RFS and selecting **check_status** will report if RFS is running. Remember, the "HELP" function key will provide you with help messages along the way.

Procedure 3: Local Resource Sharing

This procedure allows you to selectively make your resources available or unavailable (share/unshare) to remote systems. You can arrange this to happen automatically when RFS is started, to happen immediately, or both. You can also modify the options by which your local resources are currently or automatically shared, via RFS. Finally, this procedure enables you to list your local resources currently available to be shared by remote systems, via RFS.

As a prerequisite, RFS should be set up and running. Begin by typing **`sysadm network_services`** and selecting **`remote_files`**. Continue by selecting **`local_resources`**. You are now at the following screen:

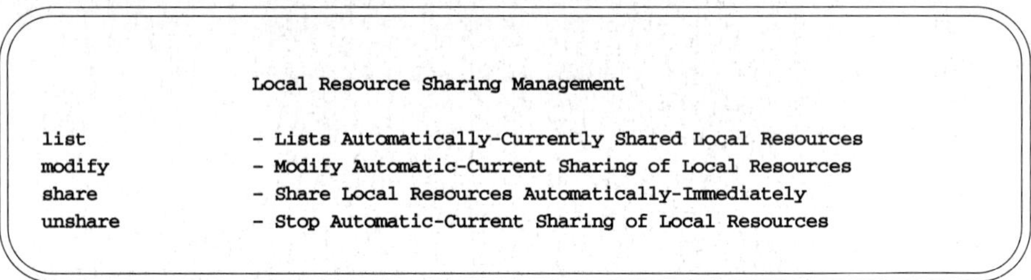

Select **`list`** then **`rfs`**. This gives you access to menu selections allowing you to list the local resources currently shared by RFS. Select **`modify`** then **`rfs`** to modify sharing permissions of local resources via RFS. Select **`share`** then **`rfs`** to share local resources via RFS. Select **`unshare`** then **`rfs`** to unshare local resources currently shared via RFS. Remember, the "HELP" function key will provide you with help messages along the way. Consult "Sharing RFS Resources" in "RFS Command Interface" for further details on these tasks.

Procedure 4: Remote Resource Mounting

This procedure enables you to selectively make remote resources available or unavailable (mount/unmount) to your local computer. You can arrange to have this happen automatically, immediately, or both. You can also modify the options by which remote resources are currently or automatically mounted on your local computer. Finally, this procedure enables you to list the resources of remote systems that are currently available to users on your local computer system, via RFS.

As a prerequisite, RFS should be set up and running. Begin by typing **sysadm network_services** and selecting **remote_files**. Continue by selecting **remote_resources**. You are now at the following screen:

```
                    Remote Resource Access Management

list            - Lists Automatically-Currently Mounted Remote Resources
modify          - Modifies Automatic-Current Mounting of Remote Resources
mount           - Mounts Remote Resources Automatically-Immediately
unmount         - Terminates Automatic-Current Mounting of Remote Resources
```

Select **list** then **rfs**. This gives you access to menu selections allowing you to list the remote resources currently mounted via RFS. Select **modify** then **rfs** to modify mount permissions of remote resources. Select **mount** then **rfs** to mount remote resources. Select **unmount** then **rfs** to terminate mounting of remote resources currently or automatically shared via RFS. Remember, the "HELP" function key will provide you with help messages along the way. Consult "Remote Resource Mounting" for further details on these tasks.

Procedure 5: Change RFS Configuration

This procedure covers how to examine your RFS network configuration, how to update domain member lists, and how to change ID mapping. As prerequisites, RFS should be set up and running.

RFS Configuration/Domain Management

The task of examining your current RFS network configuration and effectively changing it can be accomplished using the **sysadm** menu **Cooperating Systems Management**. When you type **sysadm network_services** and select **remote_files**, **specific_ops**, **rfs**, and **systems**, the following menu will appear on your screen:

```
                    Cooperating Systems Management

add_host               - Adds Systems to the Domain Password File
add_nameserver         - Adds Domain Name Servers
display_domain         - Displays the RFS Domain of the Local System
list_active_nsvr       - Lists the Active RFS Domain Name Servers
list_hosts             - Lists Systems in the Domain Password File
list_nameservers       - Lists RFS Name Servers
remove_host            - Removes Systems from the Domain Password File
remove_namesvr         - Removes Domain Name Servers
set_domain             - Sets the RFS Domain of the Local System
```

The **list_***name* selections, and **display_domain**, will show you how your RFS network is currently configured (set up). The other menu selections will allow you to configure the various domain parameters of your network. Here again, the "HELP" messages are extensive in their explanation of each menu selection. In addition, the "RFS Domain Name Servers" section in "RFS Command Interface" will provide more detailed information.

The **sysadm** interface assumes that the name server is running UNIX SVR4.0 or later. If this is not the case, the command interface should be used. See "rfmaster File for Pre-UNIX SVR4.0 Systems" in "RFS Command Interface" for more information.

Transport Providers

The software path over which your RFS network applications can communicate is important. The **Supporting Networks Management** menu will allow you to display and set the transport provider for your RFS network. You can access this menu by typing **sysadm network_services** and selecting **remote_files**, **specific_ops**, **rfs**, and **networks**. The following menu will appear on your screen:

```
                     Supporting Networks Management

display          - Displays Networks Supporting Remote File Sharing
set              - Sets Network Support for Remote File Sharing
```

RFS ID Mapping

ID mapping, or, defining remote users' permissions to your files, is the final ingredient to configuring your RFS network. The **sysadm** menu **User and Group ID Mapping Management** allows you to display and set up some simple user and group ID mappings. (See the "Mapping Remote Users" section for more sophisticated mapping schemes.) You can access this menu by typing **sysadm network_services** and selecting **remote_files**, **specific_ops**, **rfs**, and **id_mappings**. The following menu will appear on your screen:

```
                 User and Group ID Mapping Management

display                - Displays Current User and Group ID Mappings
set uid mapping        - Sets Up Standard UID Mappings
set gid mapping        - Sets Up Standard GID Mappings
```

17 RFS Command Interface

Setting Up RFS 17-1
Set Node Name 17-1
Set Up Network Listener 17-1
Set the Domain Name 17-2
Set the Transport Provider 17-3
Create rfmaster File 17-3
- rfmaster File for Pre-UNIX SVR4.0 Systems 17-5
Add/Delete Password for Domain Members 17-6
Remote Computer Verification (Optional) 17-6
Resource Sharing with Other Domains (Optional) 17-8
Multiple Domain Name Service (Optional) 17-9
Complex User ID/Group ID Mapping (Optional) 17-10
- When Not to Map 17-11
- When to Map 17-11
- Mapping Tools and Files 17-12
- Step 1: Create uid.rules File 17-15
- Step 2: Create gid.rules File 17-18
- Step 3: Add passwd and group Files 17-18
- Step 4: Run idload 17-19
Multiple Transport Providers (Optional) 17-20
- Compatibility 17-20
- File Location Changes 17-21
- Command-Line Argument Changes 17-21
- Command Output Changes 17-21
- Administrative Tips 17-22

Starting/Stopping RFS 17-25
Is RFS Running? 17-25
Initial RFS Start 17-25
- RFS Password 17-26
Automatic RFS Startup (init 3) 17-28
- Entering System State 3 17-28

- init 3 Processing 17-29
- Changing init 3 Processing 17-30
- Adding RFS Mode Scripts 17-30

Stopping RFS 17-31

Sharing RFS Resources 17-32

Local Resource Sharing 17-32
- Automatic Sharing 17-32
- Resource Security 17-33
- Local Share Table 17-33
- Domain Share Table 17-34
- Shared Resources in Use 17-34
- Unshare 17-35
- Forced Unmount 17-36

Remote Resource Mounting 17-37
- Automatic Remote Mounts 17-37
- Mounting Guidelines 17-37
- Mounting Rules 17-38
- Local Mount Table 17-39
- Remote Resource Disconnected 17-40
- Unmounting 17-42

Sharing Printers 17-42

Mapping Remote Users 17-43

How Mapping Works 17-43

Multiple Groups 17-44

Mapping Components 17-45
- Rules Files 17-45
- idload Command 17-48
- Remote Computer passwd and group Files 17-48

Example Rules Files 17-49
- No Mapping 17-49
- Mapping Remote IDs 17-49
- Mapping Remote Names 17-50
- List Current Mapping 17-52

RFS Domain Name Servers 17-54
Primary Name Server 17-54
Secondary Name Server 17-55
Recovery 17-55
- Primary Goes Down 17-56
- Primary and Secondaries Go Down 17-56
- Server Goes Down 17-57

Monitoring 17-58
Remote System Calls (sar –Dc) 17-58
RFS Operations (sar –x) 17-60
CPU Time (sar –Du) 17-61
Client Caching (sar –Db and sar –C) 17-63
- Caching Buffer Usage 17-63
- Cache Consistency Overhead 17-65

Server Processes (sar –S) 17-66
- Too Few Servers 17-67
- Too Many Servers 17-67

Resource Usage (fusage) 17-67
Remote Disk Space (df) 17-69

Parameter Tuning 17-70
RFS Parameters 17-70

Setting Up RFS

In most cases, you will not need the set of tasks described in this section because the basic Remote File Sharing (RFS) configuration and reconfiguration can be handled using the **sysadm** interface, as described in Procedure 1. These tasks are for those who want to go deeper into the workings of RFS or are having problems with particular components.

These tasks are run from the shell. They should be run initially in the order described.

Once these tasks are completed, go to the "Starting/Stopping RFS" section for information on starting RFS.

Set Node Name

Changing the node name of your computer requires careful coordination with all machines that communicate with yours using RFS or other communications packages that rely on node name.

Check to see if your computer's node name is set to the name you want (`uname -n`). If it's not, set it by typing:

```
uname -S nodename
```

A node name that is valid for RFS can consist of up to 8 characters of letters (upper and lower case), digits, hyphens (–), and underscores (_). RFS only requires that every node name in a domain be different.

Set Up Network Listener

If you have installed the Networking Support Utilities, TCP/IP, and RFS Utilities in the order described in the *Release Notes*, The listener will already be installed and set up to run automatically, and RFS will be listed as an available service.

If you are using another transport provider, or suspect that your TCP/IP listener is improperly set up, see "Setting Up the Listener" in "Setting Up TCP/IP" for the steps on how to manually set up the listener.

With the RFS service over TCP/IP, a debugging option (`-L`) can be used with **rfsetup** for distinguishing RFS network problems from general network problems. The debugging information is stored in **/var/adm/net/servers/rfs/rfs.log**. To add the RFS service (**rfsetup**), with logging activated, to the list of services available, type the following:

```
pmadm -a -p tcp -s 105 -i root -v `nlsadmin -V` \
      -m "`nlsadmin -c \"/usr/net/servers/rfs/rfsetup -L\"`" \
      -y "RFS Server"
```

Use the following command line to report the status of the **tcp** listener process installed on this machine (ENABLED or NOTRUNNING):

```
sacadm -l -p tcp
```

To start the listener, type:

```
sacadm -s -p tcp
```

Normally, it will be started automatically when your machine enters multi-user state (**init 2**).

Set the Domain Name

Set the domain name by typing:

dname -D *domain*

where *domain* is replaced by the domain your machine will be a member of. The domain name must:

- contain no more than 14 characters
- consist of any combination of letters (upper or lower case), digits, hyphens, and underscores
- be different from the name of any other domain used on the network

You can check the current domain name by simply typing:

```
dname
```

Set the Transport Provider

To identify the network, you must tell RFS the network (transport provider) it should use. (In our example, this is **tcp** for TCP/IP.)

```
dname -N tcp
```

This command indicates the device, relative to the **/dev** directory, that is used for the transport provider. If RFS is going to be run over multiple transport providers, then the transport providers must be specified as a comma-separated list.

```
dname -N tcp,starlan
```

Create rfmaster File

The primary and secondary name server assignments for a domain are stored in the **/etc/rfs/***transport***/rfmaster** file. The primary keeps the definitive copy of this file and distributes it automatically to each computer in the domain when each starts RFS. This file also contains the network address of other name servers.

The **rfmaster** file should only be created manually on the primary. If your machine is not the primary, you should skip this task; the **rfmaster** file for your domain will automatically be placed on your machine the first time you start RFS (**rfstart -p** *primary_addr*).

If you are on the primary, you can create an **rfmaster** file in the **/etc/rfs/***transport* directory using any standard file editor. The contents of this file will define:

- the primary name server for your domain
- secondary name servers for your domain
- network addresses for each of these machines

If you specified multiple transport providers (**dname** command), you must have an **rfmaster** file in each **/etc/rfs/***transport* directory. (See the section on "Multiple Domain Name Service (Optional)" in this chapter for a description of other information you may want to put into the **rfmaster** file.)

Here is an example of an **rfmaster** file for a domain, called **peanuts**, whose primary is **charlie** and whose secondary name servers' node names are **linus** and **lucy**. Adding each machine's domain name (**peanuts**) to its node name, separated by a period, forms its full RFS machine name. Each line of the example translates as follows.

- For domain **peanuts**, the primary is **peanuts.charlie**.
- For domain **peanuts**, the first secondary is **peanuts.linus**.
- For domain **peanuts**, another secondary is **peanuts.lucy**.
- For computer **peanuts.charlie**, the network address is **\x00020ACE***Internet*0000000000000000.
- For computer **peanuts.linus**, the network address is **\x00020ACE***Internet*0000000000000000.
- For computer **peanuts.lucy**, the network address is **\x00020ACE***Internet*0000000000000000.

where *Internet* is the 8-digit, hexadecimal host IP address. Each machine must have a unique host IP address. See "Converting Your IP Address to Hexadecimal Notation" in "Setting Up TCP/IP" for the steps to convert a decimal IP address to the hexadecimal format.

```
#Name            Type        Rdata

peanuts          p           peanuts.charlie
peanuts          s           peanuts.linus
peanuts          s           peanuts.lucy
peanuts.charlie  a           charlie_network_address
peanuts.linus    a           linus_network_address
peanuts.lucy     a           lucy_network_address
```

where *machinename_network_address* is the complete unique network address for the respective machine. The format of the *machinename_network_address* is dependent upon the transport provider that is used.

Each line in the example is an entry. The second field is the *Type* field, which indicates whether the entry defines a primary name server (**p**), secondary name server (**s**), or the network address (**a**) for one of these name servers. The following list shows the valid entries, and a description of each entry, for the second field in the **rfmaster** file.

p Primary entry. *Name* is the domain name. *Rdata* is the full RFS machine name of the domain's primary name server (*domain***.***nodename*).

s Secondary entry. *Name* is the domain name. *Rdata* is the full RFS machine name of the domain's secondary name server (*domain***.***nodename*).

a Address entry. *Name* is the full RFS machine name (*domain*.*nodename*) of a name server computer. *Rdata* is the network address of the computer. The manuals that come with your network should describe how to find a computer's network address.

See **rfmaster**(4) for more information on **rfmaster**.

Here are some special considerations when creating the file.

- Fields in each entry must be separated by whitespace.
- The address must be in ASCII text or hexadecimal notation. For hexadecimal, the field must begin with **\x** and contain an even number of digits. If the address contains tabs or spaces, the field must be surrounded by double quotes (" ").
- An entry can extend beyond one line if you enter a backslash (\), then press RETURN to continue to the second line.
- This file should be write protected from all but the privileged user, but all read permissions should be enabled (644 permissions).
- If you start a line with the # character in column 1, the entire line will be treated as a comment.
- There can be multiple **rfmaster** files when operating RFS over multiple transport providers. Each transport provider has its own directory, and there is only one **rfmaster** file per transport provider.

rfmaster File for Pre-UNIX SVR4.0 Systems

When using RFS over TCP/IP with machines that are pre-UNIX SVR4.0, there are changes that need to be made to the **rfmaster** file.

In UNIX SVR4.0 and later versions, entries in the **rfmaster** file have a reserved field that is padded with 16 zeros.

Machines that are running pre-UNIX SVR4.0 don't know how to handle the reserved field.

In order for a pre-UNIX SVR4.0 machine to "talk" to a UNIX SVR4.0 (or later) machine, the 16 zeros in the reserved field need to be removed from the UNIX SVR4.0 machine.

Another difference in the **rfmaster** file is that in a UNIX SVR4.0 (and later) machine, the port number 0ACE is used. The port number 0401 is used in a pre-UNIX SVR4.0 machine, and the entry for a pre-UNIX SVR4.0 machine must be updated to reflect this change.

Add/Delete Password for Domain Members

If your computer is the current primary name server for the domain, you must add each computer to the list of the computers that make up an RFS domain (domain member list). If a secondary has temporarily taken over, the secondary must pass name server responsibility back to the primary using the **rfadmin -p** command. To add members, use the following command:

```
# rfadmin -a domain.nodename
Enter password for nodename:
Re-enter password for nodename:
```

where *nodename* is replaced by the node name of the computer you want to add to your *domain*. (The two names must be connected by a period.)

You will be prompted for an initial password, which will be stored in the **/etc/rfs/auth.info/***domain***/passwd** file for your *domain*. When the computer you added starts RFS, the computer's administrator must enter this password. You can simply type a <CR> for a null password. Otherwise, the password must conform to the same criteria used with the **passwd** command. Repeat this command for each computer you want to add to the domain.

Adding a primary and secondary to the **rfmaster** file does not automatically add them to the domain. You must do this procedure for each of those machines.

You can also use the **rfadmin** command to delete members from the domain member list, as follows:

```
rfadmin -r domain.nodename
```

Remote Computer Verification (Optional)

This procedure assumes you are starting RFS from the shell using **rfstart -v**, executing **init 3** manually, or automatically at boot time to start RFS.

When you start RFS, you can indicate that all remote machine passwords be verified when they try to use your computer's resources. The **rfstart** command is run automatically when you go into RFS state (**init 3**).

If you use **rfstart** with the **-v** option, any machine that tries to mount your resources must match a name and password you have in the **passwd** file in the **/etc/rfs/auth.info/***domain* directory on your machine, where *domain* is replaced by the name of the remote computer's domain. If the remote computer is not listed in this **passwd** file, if it is listed and the password doesn't match, or if no **passwd** file exists, the remote mount will fail. (This file is automatically on the primary, but it must be added to other machines, as described in this procedure, to use verification.)

If you don't use the **-v** option, the following validation occurs: If a **passwd** exists for the remote computer's domain on your computer and the remote computer is listed, but the password doesn't match, a mount request will fail. If the computer is not listed in the file or if the **passwd** file doesn't exist, the computer will be allowed to mount your resources without validation. (Of course, a remote mount could still fail if the resource was shared to a limited subset of machines or was shared read-only and the machine tried to mount it read/write.)

The following steps describe how verification is set up.

Step 1: Obtain the **passwd** file from the **/etc/rfs/auth.info/***domain* directory on the primary. (*domain* is replaced by the domain name.) The file will have the name and encrypted password for each machine in the domain.

You must make the **/etc/rfs/auth.info/***domain***/passwd** file, plus the **passwd** file for any outside domains containing machines you want to verify, accessible to your machine in one of the following ways:

Step 1A: Place a copy of this file(s) in the same directory on your machine. The **passwd** file for each domain must be in the appropriate *domain* subdirectory.

or

Step 1B: Have the primary for each domain share the **/etc/rfs/auth.info** directory; then have it automatically mounted in the same location on your computer. This way you can automatically pick up any changes in machines or passwords. (See the description of **/etc/vfstab** in the "Automatic Remote Mounts" section of this chapter for information on setting up automatic mounts.)

Step 2: **rfstart -v**. You must edit the **/etc/rc3.d/S21rfs** file to automatically run **rfstart** with the **-v** option. You will add the **-v** after the **rfstart** command, as shown in the following example.

```
'rfstart')
   trap 'rm -f /var/tmp/rfs$$;exit' 0 1 2 3 15
   stat=1
   retries=0
   while [ ${stat} -eq 1 ]
   do
     /usr/sbin/rfstart -v </dev/console >/dev/console 2>/var/tmp/rfs$$
     stat=$?
     case ${stat} in
```

Step 3: If you want to verify only a limited subset of these computers, you must use manually edited versions of the **passwd** files, removing any computers you want to prevent from using your resources. (You cannot edit this file if you are a primary or secondary name server or if you have mounted the file from the primary.)

Resource Sharing with Other Domains (Optional)

For computers in your domain to share resources with computers in other domains on your network, you must do the following.

Step 1: Find out:

- □ the primary name server for each domain
- □ the secondary name server(s) for each domain
- □ the network address for each of the above name servers

Step 2: You must see that the information in Step 1 is added to your domain's **/etc/rfs/***transport***/rfmaster** file on the primary. For a format description of the **rfmaster** file, see "Create rfmaster File". The following example shows the information added to contact a domain called **docs**.

docs	**p**	**docs.big**
docs	**s**	**docs.little**
docs.big	**a**	*network_address*
docs.little	**a**	*network_address*

where *network_address* is the complete network address for the respective machine. The format of the *network_address* is dependent upon the transport provider.

Step 3: Stop RFS on the primary (**rfstop**, **init 2**, or use the **sysadm** menus as described in "RFS sysadm Interface".

Step 4: Restart RFS on the primary (**rfstart**, **init 3**, or use the **sysadm** menus as described in "RFS sysadm Interface". Make sure start up has completed before going to the next step.

Step 5: If a secondary machine took over name service when the primary was stopped, pass name service responsibilities back to the primary by typing the following from the secondary:

```
rfadmin -p
```

Step 6: Mount resources from an outside domain. Once the name server machines have picked up the new domain names, you can mount a resource from a remote domain on your own machine. You would use the same method of mounting a resource from an outside domain as you would to mount a resource from your domain, with one exception. When you specify the resource to be mounted, you must prepend the domain name to the resource identifier. For example, the command:

```
mount -F rfs docs.INFO /usr/info
```

could be used to mount resource **INFO**, shared in domain **docs**, with read/write permissions, onto directory **/usr/info**.

Multiple Domain Name Service (Optional)

Once you have defined a set of primary and secondary name servers to serve a domain, that set of machines may also be name servers for another domain on the same network. The following procedure describes how this can be configured:

Step 1: Edit **rfmaster** file. You must add the information on the new domain's name servers to the **rfmaster** file on the primary. The following is an example of two sets of name servers that serve domains called **docs** and **peanuts**.

```
docs            p    docs.big
docs            s    docs.little
docs.big        a    network_address
docs.little     a    network_address

peanuts         p    peanuts.charlie
peanuts         s    peanuts.linus
peanuts.charlie a    network_address
peanuts.linus   a    network_address
```

where *network_address* is the complete network address for the respective machine. The format of the *network_address* is dependent upon the transport provider.

Step 2: Stop and restart RFS. You must stop all machines served by the primary (**rfstop**, **init 2**, or use the **sysadm** menus as described in "RFS sysadm Interface".

Step 3: You must then restart the primary (**rfstart**, **init 3**, or use the **sysadm** menus as described in "RFS sysadm Interface".

Step 4: Then start each machine on the system, starting machines that previously had other machines as domain name servers with the **rfstart -p** *address*, where *address* is replaced by the network address of the new primary domain name server. This will ensure that the new information is picked up by each machine.

Complex User ID/Group ID Mapping (Optional)

ID mapping lets you control the access remote users will have to files and directories that make up your shared resources. This feature lets you assign each remote user the permissions of one of your local users (listed in **/etc/passwd**) or the permissions of a special "guest ID," with respect to your shared resources. The guest ID will never overlap with any of your local users. The same mechanism can be used to define group permissions (listed in **/etc/group**).

Use this procedure as a tutorial for ID mapping and as a procedure for setting up mapping. If you have questions about particular mapping components, refer to "Mapping Remote Users".

When Not to Map

In most cases, ID mapping is not necessary. If you never set up mapping using this or the **sysadm** procedures, all users will be mapped into a single special guest ID. This special guest ID is represented by an ID number that is one higher than the maximum allowed for your system. By default, the maximum number of users and groups on a system is 60000, so the special guest is ID number 60001 (**nobody**).

No mapping, or the default mapping, provides the maximum security for your shared resources. When a remote user lists the permissions of your files (**ls -l**), all files will be owned by **nobody** (UID 60001) or **noaccess** (UID 60002). A file owned by **nobody** means the file was created by a remote user and, therefore, is owned by every remote user that can access your resource. A file owned by **noaccess** means the file was created by one of your local users and, therefore, remote users can only access the file if the "other" permissions are set [see **chmod**(1)].

When to Map

Using mapping increases the power and flexibility of RFS. The following are some reasons you may want to use mapping:

Special permissions.
: You may want to map some or all remote users into particular local users' permissions. For example, if you are the administrator of several machines, you may want to map administrative logins together across the machines. That way you would be able to modify any remote resources mounted on any machine you are working from.

Transparent mapping.
: If you set up a group of computers to have the exact same **/etc/passwd** and **/etc/group** files, mapping transparently can be a very powerful technique. When a user creates a file, the user will maintain sole ownership to the file, whether or not the file resides on a remote resource.

: With transparent mapping, you could share many resources that require a consistent view of user ownership. For example, you could share your **/var/mail** directory, mount it on **/var/mail** on other computers, and have one mail directory for the entire set of machines. The basic concept is that you can avoid duplication of many files and directories while maintaining consistent user permissions.

Mapping by machine.

You may want to map users from one machine differently than users from another machine. For example, you may want to map all users from one machine into user ID 600, from another machine into 700, and from a third into 800. In that way you could monitor which remote machine's users were creating files within your resources.

> **NOTE** The default mapping and transparent mapping can be set up using the **sysadm** interface described in "RFS sysadm Interface". For other mapping techniques, see "Mapping Tools and Files".

Mapping Tools and Files

The result of this procedure is "mapping translation tables." These tables will be used by your system to process requests from remote users for access to your resources that are mounted on their computers.

The command used to create the translation tables is **idload**. When **idload** is run with no options, it does the following:

- reads the rules files (See Figure 17-2) to determine how you want to set up the mapping
- reads the **/etc/passwd** and **/etc/group** files on your computer, and copies them from other computers, if needed
- creates translation tables

There are two options to **idload** you also may want to use when setting up translation tables.

idload -n Before you run **idload** with no options, the **-n** option lets you do a trial run without actually changing the mapping tables. The result is a listing at your terminal of the tables you would create if you ran **idload** with no options.

idload -k After you run **idload** with no options, the **-k** option lets you read the mapping that is currently in effect on your computer.

The components described in the previous paragraphs are illustrated in Figure 17-1.

Figure 17-1: ID Mapping Components

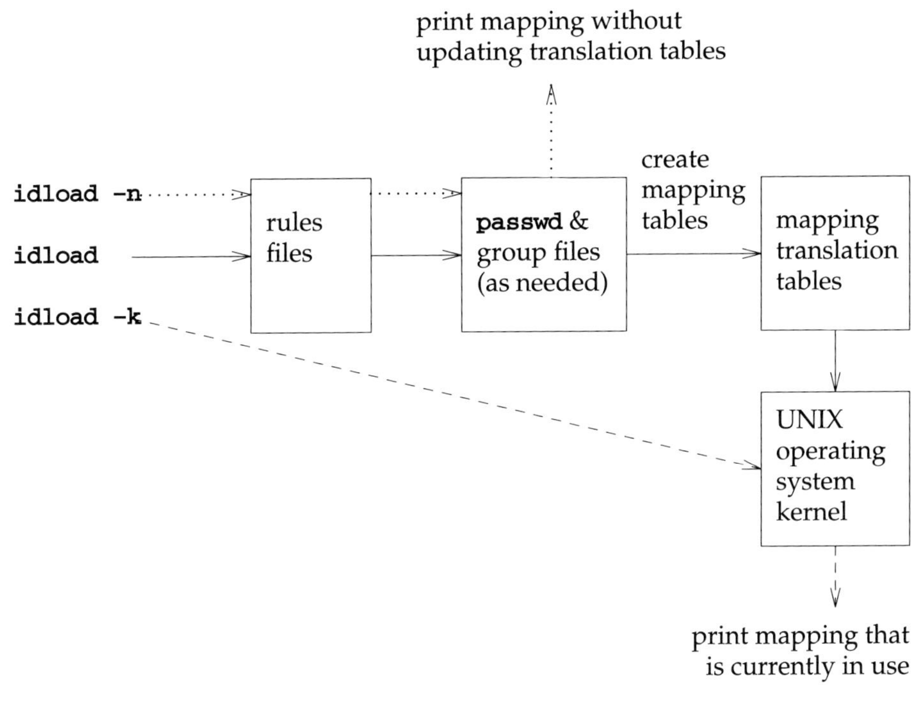

The files that are involved in setting up ID mapping are illustrated in Figure 17-2.

Figure 17-2: ID Mapping Files

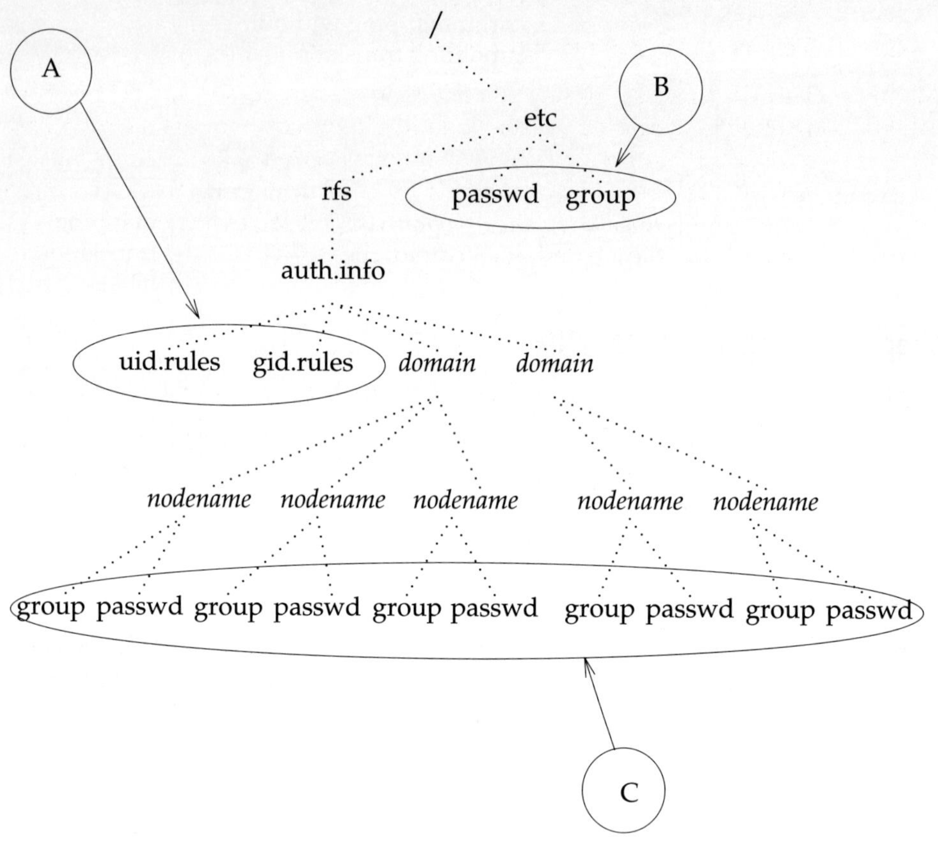

The files used for ID mapping are divided into the following three groups, as shown in Figure 17-2.

A. Rules Files

   The **uid.rules** and **gid.rules** files are located in the **/etc/rfs/auth.info** directory. The information you add to these files tells the **idload** command how to create the mapping tables.

B. Local **/etc/passwd** and **/etc/group** Files

   The **/etc/passwd** and **/etc/group** files contain lists of the local users on your system. Though you don't modify these files to do ID mapping, you will be interested in the information that is in these files. The first field in each line of your **/etc/passwd** and **/etc/group** files contain local user and group names, respectively. The third field contains the related ID number. If you map by local name in the rules files, these files are read to translate the names into numbers.

C. Remote **/etc/passwd** and **/etc/group** Files

Because mapping translation tables are sets of numbers, if you want to map a remote user by name you must have a copy of the **/etc/passwd** and/or **/etc/group** files for the remote user's machine. These files should be placed in the **/etc/rfs/auth.info/***domain***/***nodename* directories, where *domain* and *nodename* are replaced by the remote computer's domain and node names, respectively.

Step 1: Create uid.rules File

The following steps describe how to create the rules used to map remote users.

Using any standard file editor (**ed** or **vi**, for example), create or edit the **uid.rules** file in the **/etc/rfs/auth.info** directory. Steps 1A-1D will help you set up a **global** block of mapping information; steps 1E-1H are for **host** blocks of mapping information. The **global** block defines the permissions that will apply to the users on all computers that do not have specific mapping. Note that all lines within a **global** block are optional.

Step 1A: Add the **global** line. (Only add this line if you want to define a block of global information.) The global block of information must begin with the following keyword on a line by itself:

```
global
```

Step 1B: Add a **default** line. (Only add this line if you want to define default information for a global block.) Following the **global** line, you can choose the default permissions that will apply to users from all machines that are not specifically mapped. If this line is not used, the system assumes **default 60001**. (In most cases, **default 60001** is fine.) The two types of default lines are illustrated below.

The line **default transparent** means that each user will have the permissions of the user with the same ID number on your system. (This strategy is most valuable when the **/etc/passwd** files are identical on the two machines.) In the line **default** *local*, the word *local* can be replaced by a local ID number or ID name. This means that any users that are not specifically mapped will have the permissions of a particular user on your system. (Use only one **default** line in a **global** block.)

```
default transparent
```

or

default *local*

Step 1C: Add **exclude** line(s). (Only add this line(s) if you want to exclude certain users.) The **exclude** lines let you exclude certain users from having the permissions defined in the default line. For example, if you used **default transparent**, you may want to use **exclude 0** to make sure that the **root** user doesn't have permission to modify the restricted files owned by **root** in your resources. The two types of exclude lines are illustrated below.

In **exclude** *remoteid*, *remoteid* is replaced by a remote user ID number. The remote user would then have the permissions of the guest user (UID 60001 — **nobody**) to your resources. The **exclude** *remoteid-remoteid* line lets you specify a range of remote IDs to exclude. For example, **exclude 0-100** could be used to exclude all administrative logins from your default mapping.

exclude *remoteid*

or

exclude *remoteid-remoteid*

Step 1D: Add **map** line(s). (Only add this line if you want to map specific users from global machines.) **map** lines let you take specific remote user IDs and map them into the permissions of one of your local users. The two types of map lines are illustrated below.

In **map** *remoteid*:*local*, *remoteid* is replaced by a remote user ID number and *local* is replaced by a local user's name or ID number. For example, the line **map 20:root** would map the remote user with ID number 20 into your machine's **root** permissions (UID 0). The line **map** *remoteid* says give the remote user the permissions of the user with the same ID number on the local system. For example, **map 0** would give **root** from a remote machine the same permissions as **root** on your machine.

map *remoteid*:*local*

or

map *remoteid*

Once **global** mapping is done, you may want to add **host** mapping information to the **uid.rules** file. A **host** block defines the permissions that will apply to the users on particular remote machines. You can have one **host** block for each remote machine you want to map specifically. Note that all lines within a **`host`** block are optional.

Step 1E: Add a **`host`** line. (Only add this line if you want to define a block of host information.) The host block of information must begin with the following keyword on a line by itself:

`host` *domain*`.`*nodename*

where *domain* is replaced by the remote machine's domain name and *nodename* is replaced by the machine's node name.

Step 1F: Add a **`default`** line. Add the line only if you want to define default information for a host block. Following the **`host`** line, you can choose the default permissions that will apply to all users on the remote machine that are not specifically mapped or excluded. If this line is not used, the system assumes **`default 60001`**. (In most cases, **`default 60001`** is fine.) Two types of default lines are illustrated in Step 1B.

Step 1G: Add **`exclude`** line(s). Add the line(s) only if you want to exclude certain users from default permissions. To add the line(s), repeat the instructions in Step 1C.

Step 1H: Add **`map`** line(s). Add the line(s) only if you want to map particular users. To map user names into the permissions of the users with the same names on your system, add the line

`map all`

Two additional types of map lines are illustrated in Step 1H.

Repeat steps 1E-1H for each specific computer whose users you want to map.

THE **`uid.rules`** FILE IS NOW COMPLETE!

An example of what your rules file may look like is shown in Figure 17-3.

Figure 17-3: Example `uid.rules` File

```
global
default 1000
exclude 0

host peanuts.snoopy
default transparent
exclude 0

host peanuts.linus
default 60001
map 0:100
```

Step 2: Create gid.rules File

The following steps describe how to create the rules used to map remote groups.

Create **`gid.rules`** file. Using any standard file editor (**`ed`** or **`vi`** for example), edit the **`gid.rules`** file in the **`/etc/rfs/auth.info`** directory. The **`gid.rules`** file follows the same format as the **`uid.rules`** file. Therefore, you can use Steps 1A through 1H to set up the **`gid.rules`** file, replacing any references to users with references to groups.

If you create a **`uid.rules`** file you should also create a **`gid.rules`** file. Though **`idload`** will still work without the **`gid.rules`** file (**`idload`** will use defaults for mapping groups) a warning message will be produced.

Step 3: Add passwd and group Files

If, when you edited the **`uid.rules`** and **`gid.rules`** files, you referenced any remote users by name, you must have copies of the **`passwd`** file from the remote users' computers in the **`/etc/rfs/auth.info/`***`domain`***`/`***`nodename`* directories on your machine. The same is true of the **`group`** file for groups referenced by name. (Note that **`map all`** maps by name.)

The best way to obtain these files is as follows:

Step 3A: Obtain files. Have each machine whose users you want to map by name send you its **`/etc/passwd`** and **`/etc/group`** files using any standard file transfer method (such as **`uucp`**).

Step 3B: Create directories. You must create a separate directory on your machine for each computer whose users and groups you map by name. Each directory must be created using the path **/etc/rfs/auth.info/***domain***/***nodename*, where *domain* is replaced by the remote machine's domain name and *nodename* is replaced by the remote machine's node name. For example, you must create the following directory for a machine called **linus** in domain **peanuts**:

```
/etc/rfs/auth.info/peanuts/linus
```

Step 3C: Place the remote machines' **passwd** and **group** files in the directory you created in the previous step.

Step 4: Run idload

Step 4A: Run **idload -n**. This command will print a listing of the mapping rules you set up, without creating translation tables. The output from **idload -n** using the **uid.rules** file shown after Step 1H and a **gid.rules** file with simply **default 60001** in the global block is shown in Figure 17-4.

Figure 17-4: Sample Output from `idload -n`

```
TYPE  MACHINE          REM_ID    REM_NAME    LOC_ID        LOC_NAME

USR   GLOBAL           DEFAULT   n/a         1000          n/a
USR   GLOBAL           0         n/a         60001         guest_id
USR   peanuts.snoopy   DEFAULT   n/a         transparent   n/a
USR   peanuts.snoopy   0         n/a         60001         guest_id
USR   peanuts.linus    DEFAULT   n/a         60001         n/a
USR   peanuts.linus    0         n/a         100           n/a

GRP   GLOBAL           DEFAULT   n/a         60001         n/a
```

Step 4B: Run **idload**. If the output from **idload -n** was acceptable, type the **idload** command with no options to create the translation tables. The **global** and **host** rules for any computer that currently has your resources mounted will immediately take effect. Rules for any other computer that you mapped will take effect as soon as that computer mounts one of your resources.

Step 4C: Run **`idload -k`**. This will print the mapping that is currently in use on your computer. (Remember that rules for any other computer that you mapped will not be in effect until that computer mounts one of your resources.)

ID MAPPING IS NOW COMPLETE!

Once mapping is set up, it can be changed. You can edit rules files and run **`idload`** again at any time. It doesn't matter if resources are mounted or if RFS is running.

Multiple Transport Providers (Optional)

This section describes how to run RFS over several transport providers simultaneously. You will find this capability useful in some of the following cases.

- Sharing resources between machines, regardless of the networks they are using. A server machine using multiple transport providers can make its resources available to client machines on different networks (similar to a gateway).
- Establishing a backup network. If your main network goes down, you will still be able to use RFS.
- Better matching network speed to bandwidth. Machines with high traffic between them can use a faster (often more expensive) network, while machines with little traffic between them can use slower (often less expensive) networks.
- Migrating to new networks by initially adding the new network to the server machines, while introducing client machines to the new network as time permits.
- Spreading your networking load over multiple networks.

Compatibility

UNIX SVR4.0 (and later) RFS can run simultaneously over multiple transport providers. Because of this added functionality, you will notice minor differences from pre-UNIX SVR4.0 RFS. These differences are described in the following sections.

File Location Changes

Prior to UNIX SVR4, versions of RFS allowed using one transport provider and **rfmaster** file at a time. In the UNIX SVR4 version (and later) of RFS, multiple transport providers, with their associated **rfmaster** file, can be used simultaneously.

rfmaster files are now in directory **/etc/rfs/***transport* and contain only entries for their associated transport provider. In addition, each transport provider now has an associated **loc.passwd** file in directory **/etc/rfs/***transport*. For more information, see **rfmaster**(4).

Finally, **/usr/nserve/rfmaster** and **/usr/nserve/loc.passwd** files are not used in the UNIX SVR4.0 (and later) version of RFS.

Command-Line Argument Changes

Several commands now have new or modified options allowing transport providers to be specified.

The **rfadmin** command now has a **-t** *transport,transport . . .* option that specifies the transport provider(s) to use. Without the **-t** option, all the transport providers are used. See **rfadmin**(1M).

The **-N** option of the **dname** command now accepts a comma-separated list of transport providers. See **dname**(1M).

The **-p** option of the **rfstart** command now has an additional format for when multiple transport providers are used. **-p** *address* is the format when a single transport provider is used. **-p** *transport1:address1,transport2:address2 . . .* is the format when multiple transport providers are used. Using the **-p** *address* format to specify multiple transport providers produces an error message. See **rfstart**(1M).

Command Output Changes

The **nsquery** SERVER field now contains just the machine name. The ACCESS field now contains mnemonics, like "rw," instead of "read/write." In addition, the **nsquery** command now displays a TRANSPORT field listing transport providers that resources are available on. With multiple transport providers, a resource can be available on more than one transport provider. When this is true, that resource is listed twice in the TRANSPORT field. For example, if resource XYZ is advertised and two transport providers are used, **nsquery** will list two lines for resource XYZ; one for each transport provider. See **nsquery**(1M).

For each transport provider, the **rfadmin** command now prints one line containing the name of the transport provider. See **rfadmin**(1M).

Upon initial invocation, the **rfstart** command now prompts for an RFS password for each transport provider, with the particular transport provider specified in the message prompt.

There is now one global name server process (called "nserve") and separate transport provider-specific name server processes (called "TPnserve"). These additional processes are displayed by the **ps** command.

When appropriate, RFS error messages now contain the name of the transport provider associated with that particular error message. This makes debugging problems much easier in a multi-transport provider environment.

Local programs that depend on the output of any of the above commands may need to be modified.

Administrative Tips

Administering RFS with multiple transport providers is very similar to administering RFS with a single transport provider, but there are some items that need special attention when running RFS with multiple transport providers.

Error Messages — Most RFS messages that deal with transport providers list the transport provider(s) causing the problem; some messages do not. For example, the message, **warning: no secondary name servers active** does not specify which transport provider(s) have no secondary name servers. For instances like this, it may help to debug the problem by stopping RFS, setting up RFS to use a single transport provider (using the **dname -N transport** command), and then restarting RFS. Doing this for all the transport providers will usually show which transport provider is causing the problem.

Passwords — It is easiest to make all the RFS passwords for a given machine the same. Having different passwords for each transport provider could lead to problems.

Suppose you have two machines, MACH1 and MACH2, with two transport providers (hypothetical transports TP1 and TP2) running on each machine. Since there is only one **/etc/rfs/auth.info/domain/passwd** file, each machine can only have one password for each machine in the domain. Let's assume the RFS passwords on machine MACH1 were

PASSWD1 and PASSWD2 for transport providers TP1 and TP2 respectively. If MACH2's **/etc/rfs/auth.info/domain/passwd** file contained PASSWD1, then any time you tried to mount one of MACH2s resources on MACH1 using TP2, it would fail.

Specify Transport Provider

Currently there is no way to specify the transport provider to use to mount a resource for entries in the **/etc/vfstab** file. If you want certain resources to use specific transport providers, you must mount those resources manually. It will help to put the necessary **mount** commands in a shell script and execute that shell script when you need the resources. Also note that by default, the **mount** command uses the order of the transport providers in the **/etc/rfs/netspec** file (which is the same as the output from **dname -n**) to determine which transport provider to use. If a resource cannot be mounted with the first transport provider, then the second one is used, and so on. Be sure you list them in the order you want them used. In most cases this means listing the fastest or most reliable networks first.

`rfmaster`

To avoid receiving confusing messages, be sure the primary and secondary name servers listed in the **rfmaster** files are correct for each transport provider. A special case arises when your RFS network contains both UNIX SVR4 and UNIX SVR3 machines.

Here's an example of what could happen when you incorrectly set up the **rfmaster** files. Suppose you have two machines in separate domains. One machine is running Release 4 RFS over both the TP1 and TP2 and is in domain D4. The other machine is running Release 3 RFS over only the TP1 in domain D3, but the machine also has TP2 running (that is, there are two listener processes; one for TP1 and one for TP2). The Release 4 machine is the primary name server for domain D4, while the Release 3 machine is the primary name server for domain D3. On the Release 4 machine, the **/etc/rfs/***tp1***/rfmaster** file correctly contains an entry for the Release 3 machine. Let's also assume the Release 4 machine incorrectly contains an entry in the **/etc/rfs/***tp2***/rfmaster** file for the Release 3 machine. (This is incorrect because the Release 3 machine is not running RFS on TP2, hence cannot be the primary name server for TP2 in its domain.) The output of **nsquery D3.** on the Release 4 machine will incorrectly show that the Release 3 machine's resources are available over both the TP1 and TP2. Trying to mount one of those resources using TP2 will fail, which could lead to much confusion. Removing the incorrect entry from the **/etc/rfs/***tp2***/rfmaster** file on the Release 4 machine and re-starting RFS will resolve the problem. While this example may seem far-fetched, it's easy to incorrectly set up the **rfmaster** files; especially if you copy one transport provider's file to edit for use with another transport provider. You must delete the unneeded lines.

Name Servers

Since each transport provider has its own **rfmaster** file, it's now possible to have different name servers within one domain. For example, MACH1 could be the TP1 primary name server, while MACH2 could be the TP2 primary name server. Although this is allowed, it is usually easier to have the same primary and secondary name servers for all transport providers. For example, if MACH1 is the primary name server for TP1, it would also be the primary name server for TP2. Doing this makes it easier to administer the RFS network and makes it easier to remember what machine(s) are name servers.

Starting/Stopping RFS

Before a non-primary machine can start RFS, RFS must be configured on the machine and the primary must be up and running RFS.

Is RFS Running?

If you're not sure if RFS is running, type **rfadmin -q** or use **sysadm** as described in "RFS sysadm Interface". These will tell you if RFS is or is not running.

Another way is to check if processes related to RFS are active. To do this, enter **ps -ef**. These processes should be active:

```
rf_daemon
nserve
rfudaemon
rf_recovery
rf_server
TPnserve
rf_tmo
```

There may be multiple processes, with these names, running. For example, the number of **rf_server** processes depend on the **MINSERVE** parameter. Also, there is a **TPnserve** process for each netspec in **/etc/rfs/netspec**.

Initial RFS Start

The first time you start RFS on a non-primary machine, if you are not using the **sysadm** interface, you should use the **rfstart** command. (A primary can start RFS initially by using **init 3**.)

rfstart -p *primary_ns_address*

rfstart: Please enter machine password for *transport***:**

The *primary_ns_address* is replaced by the network address of the primary name server for your domain. The format of the *primary_ns_address* is dependent upon the transport provider. If you are running multiple transport providers and reside on a non-primary machine, use the following **rfstart** command:

```
rfstart -p transport1:primary_ns_address,transport2:primary_ns_address

rfstart: Please enter machine password for transport1:
rfstart: Please enter machine password for transport2:
```

primary_ns_address is replaced by the network address of the primary name server for each transport provider.

RFS Password

You will be prompted for a password the first time you start RFS. The password must match the password entered when your machine was added to the domain member list in the primary name server (the **rfadmin -a** command). If password verification succeeds, your computer will save this password automatically in **/etc/rfs/***transport***/loc.passwd**. You do not have to enter it again.

When operating RFS over multiple transport providers, there can be multiple **loc.passwd** files. This means that there can be multiple prompts for passwords (one for each **loc.passwd** file).

Likewise, your machine will save the network address of the primary name server. Therefore, the next time you start up RFS, you will be able to do it via **init 3**.

RFS Password Mismatches

Any time you start RFS and your password doesn't match the one on the current domain name server, you will receive a warning, but **rfstart** will NOT fail.

Though RFS will be active, you may have a problem if the *domain*/**passwd** file from the primary domain name server is shared with other machines to use for verification. In that case, your remote **mount** requests will fail if the passwords don't match. For this reason, it is recommended that RFS passwords always be kept up to date on each computer and the primary name server. If passwords aren't important to you, you can simply press RETURN for the passwords on each computer and the primary.

If you do get warnings that your password is out of sync with the current domain name server and you want to fix it, you should handle it differently if the primary is the current domain name server than if the secondary has temporarily taken over.

First find out which machine is the current name server, and whether it is the primary or the secondary, by using the following **rfadmin** and **cat** commands:

```
$ rfadmin
the acting name server for domain domain on transport is domain.nodename
$ cat /etc/rfs/transport/rfmaster
domain   P  domain.nodename
domain   S  domain.nodename
domain.nodename A network_address
domain.nodename A network_address
```

where *network_address* is the complete network address for the respective machine. The format of the *network_address* is dependent upon the transport provider.

When operating RFS over multiple transport providers, there will be one line for each transport provider from the **rfadmin** command.

Then, depending on which machine is the current name server, do one of the following:

- secondary is the current name server

  If the primary went down and a secondary took over as domain name server, the secondary may not have a *domain*/**passwd** file or may have one that is out of date. In this case, do not try to correct your password until the primary takes over as domain name server again.

- primary is the current name server

  Try to correct your password by reentering it with the **rfpasswd** command. If that doesn't work, follow the sequence shown below, replacing *domain.nodename* with your computer's RFS machine name.

  From the primary name server:

  ```
  rfadmin -r domain.nodename
  rfadmin -a domain.nodename

  Enter password for nodename:
  Re-enter password for nodename:
  ```

  From your computer:

  ```
  rfstop
  rm /etc/rfs/transport/loc.passwd
  rfstart

  rfstart: Please enter machine password for transport:
  ```

You should then make sure that any computer that verifies your computer's password copies the new *domain*/**passwd** file from the primary.

Changing RFS Password

If you want to change your RFS password later, you must use the **rfpasswd** command. This will change your RFS password, both on your computer and on the primary domain name server.

Since changing passwords requires communication with the primary domain name server, RFS must be running on both your computer and the primary domain name server. You cannot change your RFS password if the primary is down and a secondary is the current domain name server.

When you change your password, computers that are authenticating your computer may not automatically receive the change. If you are unable to mount a resource from a remote machine after you change your password, check that the remote machine has copied the latest version of your domain's **passwd** file from your primary domain name server.

Automatic RFS Startup (init 3)

There are several steps involved in starting up RFS and sharing resources. To simplify this procedure, a special RFS system state has been defined: system state 3.

When you enter system state 3 using the **init 3** command, RFS is automatically started via **/etc/rc3** from a shell procedure in your computer's **/etc/rc3.d** directory. This script starts RFS, shares local resources, and mounts remote resources. When you leave system state 3 (using **shutdown** or **init 2**, for example), RFS processes will be stopped.

You can add your own shell scripts to those that start system state 3. You can also tailor the system state 3 shell scripts to suit the way you use RFS.

Entering System State 3

You can go into **init** state 3 in one of three ways:

1. From single-user state (system state **s**)

   RFS mode is also a multi-user state. Therefore, when you type **init 3** from single user state, all multi-user processes (**ttymons**, **cron**, and so on) will be started, followed by RFS mode processes.

2. From multi-user state (system state 2)

   When `init 3` is run from system state 2, init checks that all multi-user processes are running, then starts the RFS mode processes. (`init 3` will not spawn another process for a state 2 script that is already running.)

3. At boot time

   By default, your system will enter system state 2 at boot time. You can change that to have system state 3 start automatically at boot time by changing the value for **initdefault** in the **/etc/inittab** file so it reads as follows:

```
is:3:initdefault:
```

The entry for **initdefault** should also be changed in the **/etc/conf/init.d/kernel**, so that if the kernel is rebuilt, this change will not be overwritten. See **init**(4) and **idmkinit**(1M) for further information.

init 3 Processing

When `init 3` is run, all entries in the **inittab** file that indicate state 3 are started, including **/etc/rc3**. **/etc/rc3** executes all shell procedures in **/etc/rc3.d** that begin with **S**.

The RFS file in **/etc/rc3.d** is **S21rfs**. This file is linked to the **rfs** file in **/etc/init.d**, the **K50rfs** file in **/etc/rc2.d**, and the **K65rfs** file in **/etc/rc0.d** and **/etc/rc1.d**.

The **S21rfs** shell procedure does the following:

- Validates that the domain name has been defined for your machine.
- Validates that the **rfmaster** file has been created. (This may have been created automatically the first time you ran `rfstart -p` if your machine is not the primary. The latest copy is then sent to your machine from the primary domain name server.)
- Executes the **rfstart** command continuously, with 60 second sleep intervals, until it succeeds or returns a fatal error.
- Executes **/etc/init.d/adv** to share all system resources you set up in the **/etc/dfs/dfstab** file. (The **/etc/dfs/dfstab** file contains an entire **share** command line for each shared resource.)
- Executes **/usr/sbin/rmountall** to mount all remote resources you listed in your **/etc/vfstab** file. (See "Automatic Remote Mounts" for the format of **/etc/vfstab**.) Any remote mount that does not succeed will be tried every 15 minutes via **rmnttry**. The time interval can be changed by modifying the **/etc/rfs/rmnttry** entry in the **crontab** file.

When you leave system state 3, **/etc/init.d/rfs** is executed with the **stop** option. This will kill the **rfstart** and **rfudaemon** daemons.

NOTE

If for some reason RFS fails to terminate **rfudaemon**, RFS may continue to run in the lower system state. You can always bring down RFS by running **fumount** and **unshare** for each shared resource or **rumountall** to unmount all resources, and **rfstop**.

Changing init 3 Processing

Going to **init 3** makes some assumptions about how you use your RFS system. Here is a description of how to change some of the processing that takes place.

- retry **rfstart**

  By default, **init 3** will keep trying to execute **rfstart** until it succeeds. If you want it to try a limited number of times, you must edit the **/etc/rc3.d/S21rfs** file. Find the line retries=0 and change the number **0** (try forever) to the number of times you want it to retry.

- retry mounts

  When you enter **init 3**, the system tries separately, every 15 minutes, to mount each resource listed in **/etc/vfstab** until it succeeds or you leave state 3. To change this behavior, execute **crontab -e** and change the time interval **rmnttry** is running at.

Adding RFS Mode Scripts

All RFS files in **/etc/rc3.d** and other **/etc/*.d** directories are shell procedures, so you can read them to see what they do. You can modify the existing files, though it is preferable to add your own since the delivered scripts may change in future releases. To create your own scripts you should follow these rules:

- Place the file in **/etc/init.d**.
- Link the file to files in appropriate system state directories using the naming convention described below.
- Have the file accept the **start** and/or **stop** options.

You should name the files using the following conventions:

  S*00name*

or

  K*00name*

The file names can be split into three parts:

S or **K** — The first letter of each file name defines whether the process should be started (**S**) or killed (**K**) upon entering the new system state.

00 — The next two characters represent a number from 00 to 99. These numbers indicate the order in which the files will be started (S00, S01, S02, etc.) or stopped (K00, K01, K02, etc.).

name — The rest of the file name is the **/etc/init.d** file this file is linked to.

Stopping RFS

If you started RFS using **init 3**, you can stop it by going to a lower system state (**init 2**, **init S**, or **shutdown**). If you started RFS using **rfstart**, you can stop it by typing **rfstop** while in system state **init 2** or **init 3**.

Before you can use **rfstop**, you must:

- unshare all your resources (**unshare**, **unshareall**)
- unmount everything you have mounted from remote machines (**rumountall**)
- make sure all your shared resources are unmounted from remote machines (can be forced by using **fumount**)

You can use the **dfmounts** command to determine if any of your shared resources are being used.

These steps will happen automatically when you leave **init** state 3.

If you are the primary name server, you should not stop RFS unless a secondary is up and ready to take over. If the primary goes down and no secondary is available to take over, computers in the domain that are not the primary or a secondary will not be able to start RFS. Computers that are already running RFS will continue to run RFS; however, they will not be able to mount or share new resources.

Sharing RFS Resources

This section describes how to share your local resources with other computers (sharing) on a RFS system and how to use the resources other machines have made available (mounting).

Local Resource Sharing

The **share** command is used to make a local directory (one that physically resides on your machine) accessible to other machines. When you share a directory you must assign it a resource name. This resource must have a unique name within your domain.

When **share** is executed, the resource is registered with your domain name server. Any computer that has access to your domain can find a listing of your resource from your domain's share table (**dfshares** command). A remote computer will not know the exact location of the resource on your machine. All the remote computer will know is its resource name, the short description you assign, that it resides on your computer, the access permissions, and the transport provider over which it is available.

Below are two examples of **share** command lines:

```
share -F rfs -d "Department news" -o ro=peanuts. /var/news DNEWS
share -F rfs -d "My devices" -o ro=lucy:linus:doc.comp1 /dev MDEV
```

The first example shares your **/var/news** directory with read-only permissions under the resource name **DNEWS** to all computers in the **peanuts** domain. The second shares your **/dev** directory as **MDEV** to computers **lucy** and **linus** in your domain and **comp1** in the **doc** domain. See **share**(1M) for more details.

Automatic Sharing

You can set up all your **share** commands to start automatically when the system enters the RFS state (**init 3**). This is done by placing full **share** command lines in the **/etc/dfs/dfstab** file. As soon as **init 3** successfully starts RFS, all **share** commands in **/etc/dfs/dfstab** will be run.

The following is an example of an **/etc/dfs/dfstab** file to automatically share the two resources shown previously:

```
$ cat /etc/dfs/dfstab
```

```
share -F rfs -d "Department news" -o ro=peanuts. /var/news DNEWS
share -F rfs -d "My devices" -o ro=lucy:linus:doc.comp1 /dev MDEV
```

Resource Security

These are the levels of security that protect your resource once you have shared it:

Verify computers	Only those remote computers that pass your security checks can connect to your machine. You may have indicated that only those machines you have a record of can connect (see **rfstart -v**).
Restrict Resource	You may have shared your resource so only selected remote computers can mount it [see the *client* option of **share**(1M)].
Map IDs	The permissions remote users will have access to your resources are set on a computer-by-computer basis. In other words, the user and group mappings you set up for a remote computer will apply to any of your resources that computer mounts.
UNIX System Security	Normal UNIX system access security, governing read, write, and execute/search permissions will apply to any shared resource.

Local Share Table

All shared resources for your computer are contained in your computer's local share table. Any user can use the **share** command with no options to display the local share table. The output will be a listing like the one that follows:

```
# share -F rfs
CUSTOMER  /usr/bin/cust  ro=lucy:linus:doc.tick  "Atlanta customers"
SCCS      /sccs          rw                      "Project Y source"
CALENDAR  /usr/bin/cal   ro=peanuts.compgrp      "UNIX System calendar"
```

The information will match what you entered using the **share** command, with appropriate options, for each resource. Some of the information shown was implied when the resource was shared. Unless you restrict/specify clients when a resource is shared, the resource becomes available to all clients in all domains on your network. The *clients* listed in the access field can be:

- computer names in your domain (**lucy**)
- computer names in other domains (**doc.comp1**)
- domain names (**peanuts.**)
- unrestricted if the resource is not restricted to certain machines (default)

Domain Share Table

All shared resources for your domain are listed in the domain share table on your domain name server. The **dfshares** command is available to all users to list any or all of the shared resources in a domain.

When invoked with no options, **dfshares** will print a list of all shared resources in your domain. Here is an example of output from a **dfshares** command:

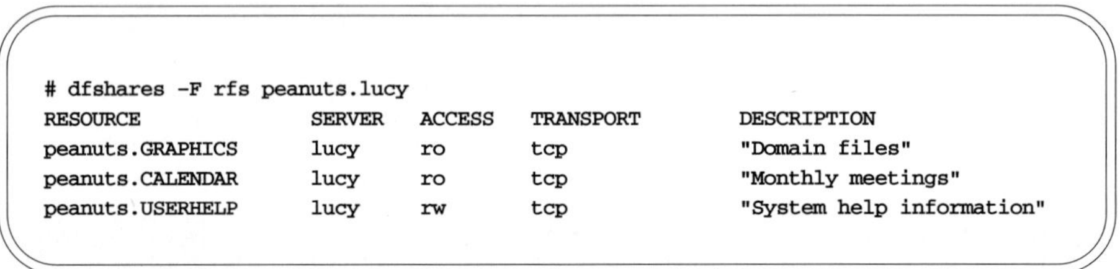

```
# dfshares -F rfs peanuts.lucy
RESOURCE            SERVER   ACCESS   TRANSPORT        DESCRIPTION
peanuts.GRAPHICS    lucy     ro       tcp              "Domain files"
peanuts.CALENDAR    lucy     ro       tcp              "Monthly meetings"
peanuts.USERHELP    lucy     rw       tcp              "System help information"
```

For each available resource, **dfshares** will list the resource name (RESOURCE), the computer that owns the resource (SERVER), access permissions of the resource (ACCESS), the transport provider (TRANSPORT), and the description of the resource (DESCRIPTION).

The output from **dfshares** does not indicate whether you have permission to mount the resource.

Shared Resources in Use

You can use the **dfmounts** command to find out what remote computers have mounted your shared resources. This command can print output for all your resources or the one you choose. Here is an example of the output from the **dfmounts** command:

```
# dfmounts -F rfs
RESOURCE      SERVER   PATH        CLIENTS
DNEWS         lucy     /var/news   peanuts.linus peanuts.lucy
MDEV          lucy     /dev        peanuts.linus
SPECIAL       lucy     unknown     peanuts.charlie
```

The output shows the resource name given when the resource was mounted, the system from which the resource was mounted, the pathname given when the resource was shared, the resource access permissions given to the clients, and a list of systems (clients) that mounted the resource.

If **unknown** appears in the pathname field, it means you have unshared the resource, but it is still mounted on the listed remote machines.

Unshare

You can unshare any of your computer's shared resources using the **unshare** command. It will remove the resource from the share tables on your computer and the domain name server.

The domain administrator can use **unshare** to unshare any resource within the domain.

Unsharing does not remove a currently-mounted resource from a remote computer [see the **umount**(1M)]. It does, however, prevent additional machines from mounting the resource. There are two reasons you may want to use **unshare**.

1. Before you can unmount (**umount** or **fumount**) one of your file systems containing a shared directory, it must be unshared.
2. If you want to restrict a previously shared directory to only local access, you will want to unshare it.

Because share commands can be set up to run automatically in **init 3**, you may have to remove them if you want them permanently unshared. (See "Sharing RFS Resources" for information on how to modify the **/etc/dfs/dfstab** file.). See **unshare**(1M) for further information.

Forced Unmount

You cannot unmount a local file system using the **umount** command if any part of that file system is mounted remotely. Normally, you should tell each administrator whose machine has mounted such a resource to unmount it. In this way, a resource can be removed in an orderly fashion.

When you have to unmount a local file system immediately, however, you can use the **fumount** command. This command will remove a remotely-mounted resource from all machines that have mounted it. You should only do this in cases where it is urgent that the resource be removed, because you may be cutting off remote processes that are accessing the resource.

When you execute **fumount**, this is what happens:

1. The resource is unshared.
2. If the **fumount** command is executed with a grace period of several seconds, the following shell script is run on all client machines currently using the resource.

   /etc/rfs/rfuadmin fuwarn *resource sec*

   By default, this shell script will write to all terminals on all client machines:

   resource **will be disconnected from the system in** *sec* **seconds.**

   (You can edit **/etc/rfs/rfuadmin** to tailor the action taken in response to **fumount**.)
3. After the grace period of *sec* seconds, the resource is removed from all remote machines it is mounted on. The following message is then sent to all terminals:

   resource **has been disconnected from the system.**
4. On each client machine, **rfuadmin** then executes **rmount** to queue the resource for mounting. The **rmnttry** command will try to remount the resource every 15 minutes until it succeeds.

See **rfuadmin**(1M) and **rmount**(1M) for further information on the processing of these commands.

Remote Resource Mounting

You can attach another computer's shared resource to your system using the `mount` command. You simply choose an existing directory, preferably empty, or create a directory to use as a mount point and `mount` the resource.

When you try to `mount` a remote resource, a request is sent to the computer that shared the resource. If you have permission to mount the resource, the resource will be added to your mount table and connected to the mount point you specified. When used with no options, `mount` lists the remote resources, as well as local file systems, mounted on your computer. See `mount`(1M) for further details.

You can mount the resource explicitly, by entering the `mount` command, or you can mount the resource automatically by every time you start RFS by adding an entry to the `/etc/vfstab` file. Automatic mounts are described in the following section.

Automatic Remote Mounts

You can set up your `mount` commands to run automatically when your computer enters the `init 3` state. You do this by adding mount information to the `/etc/vfstab` file. See `vfstab`(4) for the format of remote mounts.

Mounting Guidelines

Below are some guidelines that apply to resources.

- Once you have shared a resource from your computer, you can:
  - Mount a local file system on a subdirectory of the shared resource. The new file system will become part of the shared resource. (You cannot mount directly on the shared mount point, however.)
  - Mount a remote resource on subdirectories of your shared resource. The remote resource you mount will not become part of the resource, however. Only your local users will be able to access it. (Remote users will be able to see this mount point directory, but will get a ''multihop'' error message if they try to access the directory in any way.)

NOTE You cannot mount a remote resource directly on a shared directory.

- If a resource was shared with read-only permissions, you must mount it read-only. If it was shared read/write, you have a choice of mounting it read-only or read/write.

If RFS is running over multiple transport providers, you can set the NETPATH environment variable to define the order of the transport providers `mount` will use to attempt a connection to a server machine. If the NETPATH variable is not set, `mount` will try each transport provider in turn, as they were specified with the `dname -N` command.

Mounting Rules

There are some rules you must follow to avoid unexpected results when mounting remote resources.

Rule #1 Mounting over basic directories

A directory containing files that define your local machine should not be used as a mount point for a remote resource. This will result in essential local files being inaccessible to your system.

For example, you shouldn't mount a remote **/dev** on your machine's **/dev** directory or you will make your machine's console inaccessible (**/dev/console**). As another example, if you mounted an **/etc** directory on your **/etc** directory, you would cover your local **inittab**, **passwd**, and **mnttab** files, to name a few.

Some other directories that fall into this category are: **/**, **/usr**, **/usr/bin**, **/etc/rfs**, **/usr/net**, and **/usr/lib**.

Rule #2 Mounting spool and work directories

Like Rule #1, Rule #2 has to do with mounting a directory from one computer on the same directory on another. In this case the problem is spool files and workspace directories. Applications such as **uucp** and **lp** can run into problems when multiple machines are trying to create spool files or lock files in the same directory. For example, if you share the **/var/spool/locks** directory, by using a tty device for **uucp** on one machine, you would prevent use of a device of the same name on another machine. Also, mounting **/tmp** can cause collisions among temporary files.

Rule #3 File systems on remote devices

When a remote machine shares a directory containing a device and that device contains a file system, you would not be able to mount the file system by simply mounting the resource containing the device. To access the file system on the remote device, the remote machine would have to mount the device locally, then share that mount point. (You can access the remote as a raw device, however, by simply mounting the resource containing the device.)

Rule #4 Using remote sticky bit programs

Mounting remote resources that contain executable files with the sticky bit on can improve performance of those files. When executed on your machine, the text portion of the sticky bit program will remain in main memory on your machine, thereby reducing the network overhead on future executions. From your perspective as a client, you should be careful not to mount too many sticky bit programs or you could unknowingly gobble up a lot of memory.

If your machine is a server sharing sticky bit files, you should be aware that they are treated differently from strictly local sticky bit files. Before removing sticky bit programs from a shared resource, you must unmount the resource from all client machines (**`fumount`**), remove the program, then reshare the resource. You should do this to prevent out-of-date text for recompiled or deleted files from remaining in memory on client machines. (See the "Monitoring Performance" in *Advanced System Administration* and "Basic Security" in *Basic System Administration* for more discussion of sticky bit usage.)

Local Mount Table

You can list the remote resources that are mounted on your computer as you would list local file systems: the **`mount`** command with no options. Remote resource output from this command will appear in the form:

directory **`on`** *resource permission* **`on`** *date*

where *directory* is the name of the directory where the remote *resource* is mounted, the *permission* is **`read only/remote`** or **`read/write/remote`**, and *date* is the time and date the resource was mounted.

The following is an example of output from the mount command, with no options. The last two entries in this example are remote resource mounts.

```
# mount
/ on /dev/root read/write/setuid on Thu Aug 31 11:30:14 1989
/proc on /proc read/write on Thu Aug 31 11:30:16 1989
/dev/fd on /dev/fd read/write on Thu Aug 31 11:30:18 1989
/stand on /dev/dsk/c1d0s3 read/write on Thu Aug 31 11:30:19 1989
/var on /dev/dsk/c1d0s8 read/write/setuid on Thu Aug 31 11:30:22 1989
/home on /dev/dsk/c1d0s9 read/write/setuid on Thu Aug 31 11:34:25 1989
/usr on /dev/dsk/c1d0s2 read/write/setuid on Thu Aug 31 11:34:27 1989
/s/codes on LCODE read/write/remote on Thu Aug 31 15:20:09 1989
/s/timing on TEMPO read only/remote on Thu Aug 31 15:20:15 1989
#
```

Remote Resource Disconnected

When a machine that shares its resources with you goes down or the network connection is broken, resources that you have mounted from that server will be disconnected.

An RFS daemon process (**/usr/lib/rfs/rfudaemon**) runs an administrative shell script (**rfuadmin**) that kills all processes using a particular resource and then unmounts that resource. It then queues the remote resource to be mounted by **rmnttry**.

rfudaemon

The **rfudaemon** process is run automatically when RFS is started and continues to run until it is stopped. The **rfudaemon** process listens for one of the following events to occur, then passes that information to the **rfuadmin** administrative shell script.

RFUD_DISCONN — When a link is cut to a remote resource, **rfudaemon** sends a disconnect message and the resource name to the **rfuadmin** shell script.

RFUD_FUMOUNT — When a resource is unmounted by **fumount** on the server, **rfudaemon** sends a fumount message and the resource name to the **rfuadmin** shell script.

RFUD_GETUMSG — When a server sends a message that a resource is about to be unmounted with (**fumount**), **rfudaemon** sends a **fuwarn** message, the resource name, and the number of seconds before the resource will be unmounted to the **rfuadmin** shell script.

RFUD_LASTUMSG The local machine wants to stop rfudaemon (**rfstop**). This causes **rfudaemon** to exit.

rfuadmin

When links to resources are disconnected, the response to the disconnect is handled at the user level by the **/etc/rfs/rfuadmin** shell script. By editing this shell script, you can tailor the response your system makes when the connection to a remote resource is lost. The **rfudaemon** process starts **rfuadmin** with one of the following arguments.

disconnect *resource*

When **rfuadmin** is started by **rfudaemon** with these arguments, **rfuadmin** sends this message to all terminals using the **wall** command:

resource **has been disconnected from the system.**

Then it executes **fuser** to kill all processes using the resource, unmounts the resource (**umount**) to notify the kernel, and starts **rmount** to queue the resource for mounting. The assumption is that the link was either broken by mistake or that as soon as the server makes the resource available again, the client will want to mount it.

fumount *resource*

When **rfuadmin** is started by **rfudaemon** with these arguments, a forced unmount has occurred. The processing is similar to a disconnect.

fuwarn *resource seconds*

When **rfuadmin** is started by **rfudaemon** with these arguments, **rfuadmin** sends this message to all terminals:

resource **is being removed from the system in** # *seconds.*

There are many reasons you may want to change the **rfuadmin** shell script. If access to a resource is lost, you may want to respond by trying to mount another resource. You may want to send different messages when a resource is lost.

When a resource is disconnected, **rfuadmin** queues the resource using **/usr/sbin/rmount**. The **rmnttry** command tries to remount the resource every 15 minutes. To change this behavior, you must edit **/etc/rfs/rfuadmin** so it no longer does an **rmount**.

Unmounting

You can unmount any remote resource you have mounted with the **umount** command. Before you run **umount**, you should make sure none of your users are using the resource with the **fuser** command. When the **fuser** command is run, it lists the processes on your computer that are accessing a mounted remote resource. It can then be used to kill all processes relating to a resource. See **fuser**(1M) and **mount**(1M) (for **umount**) for further information.

Sharing Printers

If you have access to other systems via the Remote File Sharing Utilities (RFS), you may want to share printers with those systems by running the print service over RFS. You can do so by following these instructions.

On the server machine:

1. Set up the LP print service on the server machine as you would on any machine. (The server is the computer that does all the spooling.) Make sure that the printer works and that you are able to print text on it.

2. Share **/var/spool/lp**, **/etc/lp**, and **/var/lp** with all the *client(s)* that will be using this printer.

3. In **/etc/rfs/auth.info/uid.rules**, map the user ID (UID) of **lp** to itself, so the entry in **uid.rules** appears as follows:

```
map lp
```

On the client machines:

1. Do not run the scheduler on the client machines. On the client machines you need only **lp**, **lpstat**, and other LP print service commands.

2. Mount the resource that was shared by the server on the client's **/var/spool/lp**, **/etc/lp**, and **/var/lp**.

On client machines, the **-c** option of **lp** should be used for any user file not in a shared resource. This will force a copy of the file to be sent to the server machine. The LP print service cannot access local files that are not in a shared resource.

Mapping Remote Users

The "Complex User ID/Group ID Mapping (Optional)" procedure is designed to act as a tutorial for setting up ID mapping. This section provides further reference information to support that section.

Your computer has a set of users, defined in the **/etc/passwd** file. These users can also be members of groups that are defined in the **/etc/group** file. The user and group ID assignments are used by the system to evaluate requests by the user for access to local files, directories, and devices.

When you share your directories with other computers using RFS, you have the ability to define the permissions each remote user will have to your resources. You do this by mapping remote users and groups into the permissions of existing users and groups on your computer. You also have the option of mapping remote users and groups into a special "guest ID" that doesn't map into permissions of any existing users and groups on your system.

If you don't want to map remote users, you don't have to. The default treats all remote users as the special guest ID, which has the ID number of MAXUID plus one. MAXUID is the maximum ID number defined for the system, so MAXUID+1 is always guaranteed not to overlap with any current or future users (by default, MAXUID+1 is 60001).

When a remote user checks the ownership of one of your resources, the user might see another special ID: MAXUID+2 (or 60002). No files will ever be owned by 60002 (**noaccess**) on the system where a file resides. MAXUID+2 is simply a way of telling remote users that a file or directory is not owned by them or any other users from their system. For example, if all users on a remote system were mapped to 60001 (**nobody**) any files created by one of your local users would appear to be owned by user ID 60002 (**noaccess**).

How Mapping Works

When you set up your remote user and group mapping for a remote computer, you define how requests from users and groups will be handled. This mapping has an impact on the remote users' access to files and directories on your resources, as well as each remote user's view of ownership.

For example, say you map user ID 101 from machine abc into user ID 115 on your machine. When 101 from abc tries to create a file in a directory of one of your shared resources, your machine will translate the request from abc's 101 into a request from 115. If local ID 115 has permissions to create a file in that directory, then the file will be created.

If you tried to stat the file on your machine (ls -l, for example) you would see that user ID 115 was the owner. However, if a stat comes from machine abc, your machine would do inverse mapping. Therefore, the user from abc would see the file as being owned by user ID 101.

Inverse mapping from the machine that owns the resource (the server) provides the most consistent file system view to a remote user. It could potentially cause confusion, though. Continuing with the example, say that instead of just mapping 101 into 115, you also mapped 102 from abc into 115 on your machine. A file created by 102 would correctly create the file as owned by 115 on your machine. However, when a user from abc stats the file, it would always show ownership by the smaller numeric value: 101 user ID.

This same result would occur if you gave several local user names the same numeric user ID.

If users are confused when files they create do not seem to belong to them, the situation described above could be the reason. This does not cause any problems with each user's ability to access the resource. However, it could break some programs that are dependent on local IDs. The most consistent way to map, however, is one-to-one remote to local IDs.

Multiple Groups

Another feature that can be used to extend your user privileges on the remote machine (server) is multiple groups. This feature allows your single user process to have the combined privileges of all group user processes to which it is a member of, up to a local system maximum.

An instance of note occurs when a client machine has a larger maximum group setting than a server machine. When this occurs, you, the user on the client machine accessing a file on the server machine, will have your multiple groups privileges limited by the server's lower value of the maximum number of groups to which you can belong. That is, you may be able to access a file on the client side, however, because you are a member of that file's group, you may be denied access to that file on the server side. This is because your user process already belongs to the maximum number of group processes you can belong to, as set by that server machine. If you should recognize this behavior occurring, simply use the **newgrp** command to change your group id to match the group id of the file in question.

The multiple group feature uses the **/etc/rfs/auth.info/gid.rules** file (see "Mapping Components" later in this chapter).

The RFS multiple groups feature is only available when UNIX SVR4.0 systems, or later versions, are used.

Mapping Components

You must use the **idload** command to do the user and group mappings. This command reads the user and group mapping rules you create, reads your computer's **/etc/passwd** and **/etc/group** files, if needed, and maps the remote users into your users' permissions. If you are using remote user and group names to map into your computer, you must have access to user and group lists from the remote computers, so **idload** can read the files and translate those names into the appropriate numeric ID numbers.

Rules Files

The rules files you create will tell **idload** how to map remote users. Both files are in **/etc/rfs/auth.info** under the names **uid.rules** and **gid.rules**

A sample of how the user rules file can be structured is shown in Figure 17-5. The format of the group rules files is exactly the same. All lines in each file are optional.

Figure 17-5: Format of `uid.rules` and `gid.rules` Files

```
global
default local_id | transparent
exclude [remote_id-remote_id . . . ] | [remote_id]
map [remote_id:local . . . ]

host domain.nodename . . .
default local | transparent
exclude [remote_id-remote_id . . . ] | [remote_id . . . ] | [remote_name . . . ]
map [remote:local . . . ] | remote | all
```

The following notation is used in the previous figure:

> *local_name* = a local user name
> *local_id* = a local user ID number
> *remote_id* = a remote user ID number
> *remote_name* = a remote user name
> *local* = a local name or ID number
> *remote* = a remote name or ID number

A rules file is divided into blocks of information. Each block is either a **`global`** or **`host`** block. There is only one **`global`** block per file, but there can be one **`host`** block for each computer mapped.

`global` This line starts the block of global information. Each line of definitions after **`global`** and before the first **`host`** line will be applied to all computers that are not explicitly defined in **`host`** blocks. You can use **`default`**, **`exclude`**, and **`map`** inside **`global`** blocks.

You cannot map or exclude names in **`global`** blocks. You must use ID numbers.

`host` *domain.nodename . . .*

This line starts a block of information for a particular computer. Each line of definitions following this line and before the next **`host`** line will be applied to the *domain.nodename* specified. You can use **`default`**, **`exclude`**, and **`map`** inside **`host`** blocks.

If you want to map more than one computer from a single set of **`passwd`** and **`group`** files, you can put several computer names on one line. In this case, **`idload`** will read the **`passwd`** and **`group`** files for the first computer referenced (if you map by name) and use the information in those files for all computers that are referenced. A computer can only be mapped once in each rules file.

Each of the following lines of information can appear in either a **host** block or a **global** block. A name or an ID should only be mapped once in each block. If one is mapped more than once, the first reference is in effect and the others will produce warning messages from **idload**.

1. **default** *local* | **transparent**

   One **default** line can be put in each block to indicate how to handle remote users and groups that aren't explicitly mapped or excluded.

   transparent means use the same numeric ID on your machine that the user had on the remote machine for undefined users. So if a request comes from remote uid **101**, that request will have the permissions of local uid **101**.

   local is replaced by a local user name or ID number. By default, all remote users will be mapped into the permissions of the local user indicated by name or ID. If a default line does not appear in a block, MAXUID+1 permission will be assigned.

2. **exclude** [*remote_id-remote_id*] | [*remote_id*] | [*remote_name*] . . .

   Optional **exclude** lines can go into a block to exclude certain users from the default mapping. Zero or more ranges of ID numbers (*remote_id-remote_id*), single *remote_names*, or single *remote_id* numbers can be excluded. (*remote_name* is not available in the global block.)

   A user who is excluded will still have access to your resources but will only have permissions of the MAXUID+1 user. All **exclude** lines must go before any **map** lines in a block.

3. **map** [*remote:local*] | *remote* | **all**

   You can use **map** lines in each block to assign local permissions to particular remote users. There are several ways to use the **map** command. You can set any remote user's permissions to any local user's permissions by either local user *id#* or *name*, separated by a colon (:). By entering a single *remote_id* or *remote_name*, the remote user who matches will have the permissions of the local user of the same ID or name. For example:

   ```
   map mcn
   ```

   would give the remote user **mcn** the same permissions of the local user **mcn**.

   The literal entry **all** maps all users by user name into the permissions of users with the same name on your computer.

Multiple **map** lines are valid. You cannot map by remote name in **global** blocks.

map all and mapping by name are not allowed in a global block. **map all** will usually produce warning messages, since multiple administrative logins will have uid 0, and **idload** will try to map each 0 to 0. There is no harm in this.

idload Command

Once the rules files are created, use the **idload** command to read your rules files and create mapping translation tables. When you run **idload**, the rules in **global** blocks and any **host** blocks that have resources currently mounted immediately take effect. All other **host** block rules will take effect when the remote machine mounts one of your resources.

You must then run **idload** for the rules to go into effect. See **idload**(1M) for further details.

Remote Computer passwd and group Files

If you are mapping remote users by name, you will need lists of these users from each remote computer. These lists should be copies of the **/etc/passwd** and **/etc/group** files from each computer.

If **idload** finds a request for a remote user name in a **host** information block, it will check the directory for that computer for **passwd** and **group** files. The path-name to the remote computer's directory will be **/etc/rfs/auth.info/***domain***/***nodename* on your system, where *domain* and *nodename* are replaced by the remote computer's domain and the remote computer's nodename, respectively (unless you overrule this using the **-g** and **-u** options).

Mapping by name can be a very useful feature. However, if you map only by ID number or local name, and avoid mapping by remote names, you will avoid the need to coordinate distributing and updating remote **passwd** and **group** files and rerunning **idload**.

Example Rules Files

This section describes some strategies you can use to map users. It describes the easiest way to deal with remote user permissions and progresses to more complicated methods. Read through each example to decide what strategy is best for your computer.

No Mapping

If you don't run **idload** to map users, all remote users will have the permissions of the user ID number MAXUID +1. Because there are no users on your system with that user ID number, remote users will only have access to files created by your users that are open to all users.

Mapping Remote IDs

If you map remote users using remote ID numbers and local ID numbers and names, you do not need to get any **passwd** and **group** files from remote computers. The following displays contain some simple examples of mapping that only involve remote ID numbers.

In Figure 17-6, all remote user IDs will be mapped into the same user ID permissions on your computer, except for **root** (ID number 0), which would only have special guest permissions. This would apply to all remote computers.

The **exclude 0** line is strongly recommended to prevent possible security breaches from **root** users on other systems.

Figure 17-6: uid.rules File: Setting Global Defaults

```
global
default transparent
exclude 0
```

In Figure 17-7, users have the same permissions as in the previous example, except remote user IDs 0 through 100 will have MAXUID +1 permissions, and any user ID 732 would have the same permission as local user ID 106.

Figure 17-7: `uid.rules` File: Global Mapping by Remote ID

```
global
default transparent
exclude 0-100
map 732:106
```

In Figure 17-8, the users from computer **`lucy`** in domain **`peanuts`** will not be mapped by the global rules. Instead, all users will have the permissions of local user **`mpg`** except that user IDs 0 through 50 will have MAXUID +1 permissions.

Figure 17-8: `uid.rules` File: Host Mapping by Remote ID

```
global
default transparent
exclude 0-100
map 732:106

host peanuts.lucy
default mpg
exclude 0-50
```

Mapping Remote Names

If you want to use specific remote user names to map into your local users' permissions you will need to have access to **`passwd`** and **`group`** files from those computers on your system. Below are some examples of ways you can map remote user names.

map all

If you have the same set of user names on different machines, but the user IDs differ, you may want to use **`map all`** as shown in Figure 17-9.

Figure 17-9: `uid.rules` File: Mapping by Name with map all

```
global
default transparent
exclude 0

host peanuts.lucy
exclude mary 0 uucp
map all
```

In the above example, each user name from computer **`lucy`** in domain **`peanuts`** will have the same permissions as the same user name on your computer. The only exceptions will be users **`mary`**, **`root`**, and **`uucp`**, who will have MAXUID +1 permissions.

map name:name

You can also map particular remote user names into local user names or user IDs on your computer. A sample uid.rules file is shown in Figure 17-10.

Figure 17-10: `uid.rules` File: Mapping Specific Users by Name

```
global
default transparent
exclude 0

host peanuts.lucy
default transparent
exclude 0
map mcn:jcb ral gwn:103
```

Here all users from the computers will be mapped into their same user ID with the following exceptions. Remote user **`mcn`** will have the permission of local user **`jcb`**, remote user **`ral`** will have permissions of local user **`ral`**, remote user **`gwn`** will have permissions of local user ID **`103`**, and **`root`** will have MAXUID+1 permissions.

List Current Mapping

There are two ways to list the mapping you have set up: **idload -n** and **idload -k**. The **-n** option inspects the rules files and prints a listing of what would be in effect were you to load them. The **-k** option prints the mapping that is currently in effect in the kernel.

The result of **idload -n** used for the example shown previously is in Figure 17-11. (The **gid.rules** file simply has the global block set at **default transparent**.) The **-n** option says to print the mapping that is set up in the rules file. You should do this before you run **idload** without options so you can see the mapping that will take effect.

Figure 17-11: Sample Output from `idload -n`

```
# idload -n
TYPE  MACHINE       REM_ID    REM_NAME   LOC_ID       LOC_NAME

USR   GLOBAL        DEFAULT   n/a        transparent  n/a
USR   GLOBAL        0         n/a        60001        guest_id
USR   peanuts.lucy  DEFAULT   n/a        transparent  n/a
USR   peanuts.lucy  0         n/a        60001        guest_id
USR   peanuts.lucy  100       mcn        105          jcb
USR   peanuts.lucy  102       gwn        103          n/a
USR   peanuts.lucy  191       ral        101          ral

GRP   GLOBAL        DEFAULT   n/a        transparent  n/a
```

If you were to then run **idload**, the mapping shown above would take effect. If you were then to run **idload -k**, and the machine called **peanuts.lucy** did not have a resource mounted, you would see the output in Figure 17-12 printed.

Figure 17-12: Sample Output from `idload -k`

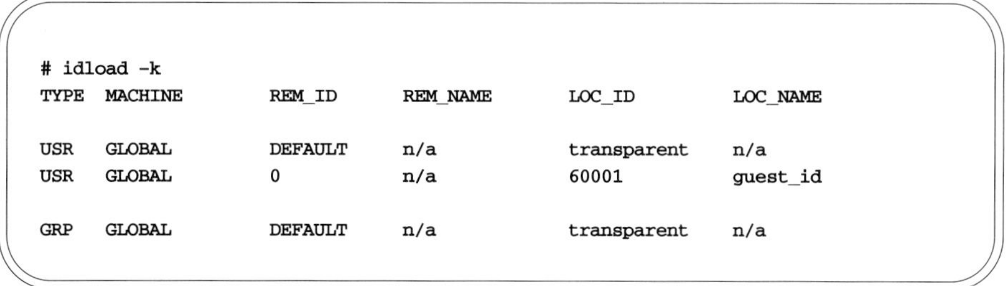

```
# idload -k
TYPE  MACHINE     REM_ID     REM_NAME    LOC_ID       LOC_NAME

USR   GLOBAL      DEFAULT    n/a         transparent  n/a
USR   GLOBAL      0          n/a         60001        guest_id

GRP   GLOBAL      DEFAULT    n/a         transparent  n/a
```

All mapping to **`peanuts.lucy`** would be active as soon as one of your resources is mounted there.

NOTE

The output from `idload` with the `n` and `k` options could be different if you have changed the rules files, but not yet run `idload` without options.

RFS Domain Name Servers

One machine in each RFS domain must be chosen to be the primary name server and zero or more can be secondary name servers. The duties of these machines are described briefly in "Name Service" under "RFS Introduction". This section describes the "how-to" of being a name server.

Before you run any of the Domain Name Server tasks, you will want to know which machines are assigned as name servers and which machine is the current name server. To find out the current name server, type:

```
rfadmin
```

To find out the name server assignments, type:

cat /etc/rfs/*transport***/rfmaster**

The line in the **rfmaster** file that has a **P** in the second field designates the primary name server. If an **S** is in the second field, the entry designates a secondary name server. (Lines with **A** in the second field designate the network address of a primary or secondary.)

Primary Name Server

If your machine is the primary domain name server, you are responsible for maintaining domain information. The "Setting Up RFS" section of this chapter describes primary name server responsibilities as you set up your machine and domain. You may want to refer to the following paragraphs in that section if you want to change your RFS configuration after initial configuration.

- Create **rfmaster** File
- Add/Delete Domain Members (Optional)
- Resource Sharing with Other Domains
- Multiple Domain Name Service

NOTE

If you want to change the primary and secondary designations in the **rfmaster** file for a domain that is currently running, you must follow this procedure to make sure those changes are properly put in place.

1) Stop RFS on all primary and secondary domain name servers for the domain (**rfstop** or **init 2**). 2) Change the **rfmaster** file on the old primary and the new primary. 3) Start the primary designated in the new **rfmaster** file (**rfstart** or **init 3**). 4) Start the secondaries designated in the new **rfmaster** file (**rfstart** or **init 3**).

Once changed on the name servers, each individual computer will pick up the change the next time it starts RFS.

Secondary Name Server

Because a secondary is only intended to take over domain name service temporarily, its main responsibility is to pass name server responsibility back to the primary as soon as possible. It does not happen automatically! Most domain maintenance cannot be done while the secondary is acting domain name server. The secondary simply maintains name server information that machines need to mount and share resources.

To pass name server responsibility back to the primary once it is again running RFS, type the following from the secondary:

```
rfadmin -p
```

The **rfadmin -p** command will pass the domain name server information to the primary, or one of the other computers listed in the domain's **rfmaster** file if it can't contact the primary. (Note that name service will automatically be passed off when the current name server goes down.)

Recovery

As a domain name server, computers in your domain, and other domains, rely on your machine for information on domain resources and domain member machines. RFS is designed to recover quickly when communication is cut between machines and the name server. The following sections describe RFS events that can occur and the recovery mechanisms designed to handle them.

Primary Goes Down

All essential domain records are maintained on the primary domain name server. The primary regularly distributes the most critical of these records to secondary domain name servers. (These records do not include files and directories under **/etc/rfs/auth.info**.)

If the primary goes down, domain name server responsibilities are passed to the first secondary name server listed in the **rfmaster** file. The secondary is only intended to take over temporarily. The reason is that a secondary has limited name service capabilities. This is done to maintain the definitive domain records on the primary. Changing the name server does not affect any currently mounted resources.

While a secondary is acting domain name server, these functions cannot be done:

- maintaining domain member lists

  Computers cannot be added or deleted from domain member lists while a secondary is acting domain name server.

- changing RFS passwords

  Neither the secondary nor another computer can change RFS authentication passwords while a secondary is acting domain name server.

The secondary will maintain lists of shared resources for the domain and continue basic name server functions so activities can continue. In most cases, the computers in the domain won't be aware the primary is down. When the primary comes back up, the secondary should pass name server responsibilities back to the primary.

Primary and Secondaries Go Down

If all primary and secondary name servers go down at once, all information on shared resources will be lost. Active mounts and links, however, are not disturbed. The problem is that when the primary comes back up, each computer will still think its resources are shared but the primary will have no record of these shared resources.

As soon as the primary is running, each computer can make sure its shared resources are in sync, with those listed on the primary, by restarting RFS. To restart RFS, you can bring down RFS, bring it back up, and then reshare your resources. This can be done automatically by going from **init 3** to **init 2** to **init 3**.

Server Goes Down

When a server that is neither a primary nor a secondary name server crashes, the domain name server (primary or secondary) will still have its resources listed as being shared. Attempts to mount those resources will fail until the server that crashed comes back up and reshares those resources. (See "Automatic Sharing" for information on how to share resources automatically.) In the meantime, the domain name server can **`unshare`** resources to clean up.

Monitoring

This section describes the commands used to monitor RFS activity, the reports they produce, and possible action you can take to make sure that your system is operating at peak efficiency. In general, these reports can help you decide if you want to:

- change parameter settings to match the way your system is used
- move resources from machines with heavy RFS traffic to machines with lighter traffic

  (See "Mounting Guidelines" for special rules relating to sharing sticky bit programs.)

A description of all RFS tunable parameters and suggested initial settings appear at the end of this section.

The **-D** option of **sar** is used to produce RFS-specific information along with standard **sar** reports (**c**, **u**, and **b** options).

NOTE

The **sar** command, along with other performance analysis tools, are in the System Performance Analysis Utilities. You must install these utilities before you can use the performance analysis tools.

Remote System Calls (sar –Dc)

Your computer collects data each time a system call sends a message across an RFS network to access a remote file. You can print this information using **sar -Dc** (see Figure 17-13).

The report produced by **sar -Dc** contains the average system calls per second and the average read and write system calls per second (this includes the average characters read and written per second). In UNIX SVR4.2, RFS does not count the average incoming (in) and outgoing (out) **execs** per second; they are always zero.

Information is divided into three categories: incoming requests (another computer's request for your resources), outgoing requests (your computer's request for a remote resource), or strictly local system calls.

Figure 17-13: Sample Output from `sar -Dc`

```
$ sar -Dc

UNIX_System_V hulk 4.2 1 i386   05/01/92

00:00:04    scall/s  sread/s  swrit/s  fork/s  exec/s  rchar/s  wchar/s
01:00:04
   in             4        1        2            0.00      350      220
   out            3        2        1            0.00      240      300
   local        133       30       12    0.73    1.33    11202     3813
02:00:04
   in             4        1        2            0.00      350      220
   out            3        2        1            0.00      240      300
   local        133       30       12    0.73    1.33    11202     3813
03:00:02
   in             4        1        2            0.00      350      220
   out            3        2        1            0.00      240      300
   local        133       30       12    0.73    1.33    11202     3813
04:00:02
   in             4        1        2            0.00      350      220
   out            3        2        1            0.00      240      300
   local        133       30       12    0.73    1.33    11202     3813

Average
   in             4        1        2            0.00      350      220
   out            3        2        1            0.00      240      300
   local        133       30       12    0.73    1.33    11202     3813
$
```

NOTE

Some statistics will not reflect the actual number of messages sent across the network, since the client caching feature allows some remote read requests to be satisfied from data in local buffers. Outgoing scall/s, sread/s, and rchar/s fields include statistics for these read "hits" of remote data in the client cache. Though these reads do not result in actual messages to the remote machine, they are still categorized as outgoing, since they access remote data.

The following paragraphs describe how information from the **sar -Dc** report can be useful to you. If performance is poor, you can see how efficiently system read and write calls to and from your computer are using the RFS network. For in and out system calls, divide the characters read or written by the reads and writes, respectively.

You may want to consider moving resources to machines where they are most in demand. (Use the **fusage**(1M) command to determine what resources are being used most heavily.)

RFS Operations (sar –x)

RFS is a file system type that performs file system operations. These operations are reported by the **sar -x** command, as shown below:

Figure 17-14: Sample Output from sar -x

```
$ sar -x

UNIX_System_V prism 4.2 1 i386    05/01/92

18:03:38 open/s create/s lookup/s readdir/s getpage/s putpage/s other/s
18:04:38
  in       0.67      0.20      5.48      0.27      0.05      0.00     18.50
  out      0.32      0.07      3.08      0.10      0.12      0.00      1.13
18:05:38
  in       0.57      0.20      5.72      0.27      0.08      0.00     11.61
  out      0.77      0.27      4.99      0.23      0.00      0.00      4.12
18:06:38
  in       0.23      0.00      1.00      0.34      0.00      0.00      7.23
  out      0.58      0.13      5.56      0.53      0.00      0.00      4.18

Average
  in       0.49      0.13      4.06      0.29      0.04      0.00     12.44
  out      0.56      0.16      4.54      0.29      0.04      0.00      3.14
```

The report gives the average number of I/O operations per second. The reported operations are:

open/s The number of file open operations per second.

create/s The number of file create operations per second.

lookup/s The number of lookup operations per second. The number of out lookups can be compared to the number of name/s given by **sar -a** to see if a large percentage of the lookups are due to servicing remote requests.

readdir/s The number of readdir operations per second.

getpage/s The number of getpage operations per second. These are the page fault operations the server sees from the client.

putpage/s The number of putpage operations per second. A putpage operation flushes pages to file systems on the server.

other/s The number of other operations per second. This count does not include the above operations or the close, read and write operations. **sar -Dc** reports the read and write operations as read and write system calls.

High outgoing (out) values indicate that your machine is accessing files on server machines frequently. If they are especially high, you may want to determine if there are files you are using remotely that should be copied to your local machine.

High incoming (in) values indicate that your machine is spending a large amount of its resources servicing clients. If your computer is a server machine, this is to be expected. However, if your computer is not primarily a server machine, the local users could be experiencing degraded response time. **sar -S** and **sar -Du** can verify whether a machine is spending too much of its resources servicing clients. To reduce the time spent servicing remote requests, you may want to move resources that are in demand to another computer (see **fusage**(1M) for details).

CPU Time (sar –Du)

You can list the percent of total central processing unit (CPU) time spent on system calls from remote computers (%sys remote) with the **sar -Du** command (see Figure 17-15).

Figure 17-15: Sample Output from `sar -Du`

```
$ sar -Du

UNIX_System_V hulk 4.2 1 i386   05/01/92

00:00:04    %usr    %sys    %sys    %wio   %idle
                   local  remote
01:00:04       7      21      10      28      44
02:00:04      11       9      10       4      76
03:00:02       8      18      10      17      57
04:00:02       2       4      10       1      93
05:00:03       1       4      10       1      93
06:00:02       2       5      10       2      91
07:00:02       1       4      10       1      94
08:00:02       2       5      10       2      91
08:20:02      26      16      10      11      48
08:40:02      18      11      10       9      62
09:00:17      25      21      10      13      41
09:20:18      23      21      10      11      45
09:40:20      21      24      10      15      39
10:00:09      21      29      10      17      33
10:20:14      29      28      10      13      31
10:40:18      19      20      10       7      54

Average        9      12      10       8      71
$
```

If the percent of CPU time spent servicing remote system calls is high, your local users may be suffering. (However, if the computer is a server machine, you would expect %sys remote to be high.)

To reduce the time spent servicing remote requests, you may want to place the resource(s) in demand on another computer (see **fusage**(1M) for details) or limit resource access by changing some of the tunable parameters. (See ''Parameter Tuning''). You may also want to make sure clients are doing I/O in an efficient way (see **sar -Dc**).

Client Caching (sar –Db and sar –C)

The client caching feature of RFS improves RFS performance by reducing the number of times data is retrieved across the network. With client caching, the first read of data will bring the data into local buffers. Once data is in the local buffer, it will remain there so subsequent reads can get the data locally.

Client caching is assigned by default on a system-wide basis (**`RCACHETIME`** parameter) and when you mount a remote resource. You will almost always want to take advantage of the improved performance of client caching. There are only two very rare occasions when you may not want to use client caching.

- If buffer space is limited on your system, you may choose to turn off client caching for some resources or the entire system.
- If you are using programs that do their own private network buffering, you may not want to use client caching.

You can produce two **`sar`** reports to monitor caching activities.

Caching Buffer Usage

The **`-b`** option of **`sar`** reports the buffer pool usage for local (disk) reads and writes. The **`sar -Db`** option reports the same information, plus information on buffer pool usage of locally mounted remote resources (see Figure 17-16).

Figure 17-16: Sample Output from `sar -Db`

```
$ sar -Db

UNIX_System_V charlie 4.2 1 i386   05/01/92

14:37:15 bread/s lread/s %rcache bwrit/s lwrit/s %wcache pread/s pwrit/s
14:37:18
   local     2      40      93       1       3      64       0       0
   remote    1      11      92       1       1       0
14:37:21
   local     2      39      92       1       3      63       0       0
   remote    0      10      94       1       1       0
14:37:24
   local     2      40      93       1       3      64       0       0
   remote    1      12      93       1       1       0

Average
   local     2      40      93       1       3      64       0       0
   remote    1      11      93       1       1       0
```

The fields on this report are as follows:

`bread/s` The number of read buffer misses per second. (Each miss results in a read message to the server.)

`lread/s` The number of read cache accesses per second.

`%rcache` Read cache hit ratio (100 – ((breads)/(lreads) * 100)).

`bwrit/s` Number of write buffer misses per second. All writes are sent to the server. Cache buffers affected by the writes are updated (write-through policy). This field indicates the numbers of lwrits that did not require a write-through. If data did not require a write-through it means that no data affected by the lwrit were present in the cache. (The information in this field has no performance implications when comparing using caching versus not using caching.)

`lwrit/s` The total write cache accesses per second.

`%wcache` Write cache hit ratio (100 – ((bwrits)/(lwrits) * 100)).

`pread/s` Not reported for remote use.

`pwrit/s` Not reported for remote use.

Cache Consistency Overhead

Information on the overhead related to maintaining cache consistency is listed with **sar -C** (see Figure 17-17).

Figure 17-17: Sample Output from `sar -C`

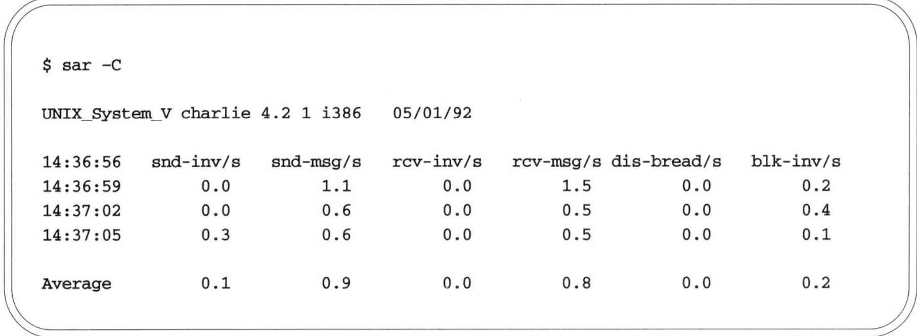

```
$ sar -C

UNIX_System_V charlie 4.2 1 i386    05/01/92

14:36:56    snd-inv/s    snd-msg/s    rcv-inv/s    rcv-msg/s dis-bread/s    blk-inv/s
14:36:59          0.0          1.1          0.0          1.5         0.0          0.2
14:37:02          0.0          0.6          0.0          0.5         0.0          0.4
14:37:05          0.3          0.6          0.0          0.5         0.0          0.1

Average           0.1          0.9          0.0          0.8         0.0          0.2
```

The fields on this report are as follows:

snd-inv/s The number of invalidation messages sent by the server per second to inform client machines about changes to server files.

snd-msg/s The total number of outgoing RFS messages sent per second.

rcv-inv/s The number of invalidation messages received by the client from the server. Each message informs the client that the contents of one or more of its cache buffers may have been modified by a write on the server. The client machine reacts by invalidating data in the affected buffers, so the buffers can be used for other purposes.

rcv-msg/s The total number of incoming RFS messages received per second.

dis-bread/s When an invalidation message is received, caching is turned off until the writing process closes or until a time interval has elapsed (set by the tunable parameter **RCACHETIME**). This counter tracks the number of buffer reads that normally would be eligible for caching in a resource with caching turned on, but that are not added to the buffer pool because caching for this resource is temporarily turned off. It indicates the penalty of running uncached and provides a basis for tuning the **RCACHETIME** parameter.

blk-inv/s The number of buffers removed from the client cache as a result of receiving an invalidation message while a remote file is open or re-opening a remote file that has been modified since the last close on the client.

If the overhead for maintaining cache consistency becomes to high, the administrator may want to turn caching off by changing the **RCACHETIME** parameter. See "Parameter Tuning" for more information on **RCACHETIME**. For such file usage patterns (where the overhead for cache consistency is high), better performance might be obtained by making the clients always go to the server for file data.

Server Processes (sar –S)

Every request from a remote computer to access your resources is handled by a server process. When there are too many requests for the servers to handle, they are delayed and placed on the request queue. Requests leave the request queue when servers are available. Information on server availability and requests awaiting service are listed with **sar -S** (see Figure 17-18).

Figure 17-18: Sample Output from sar -S

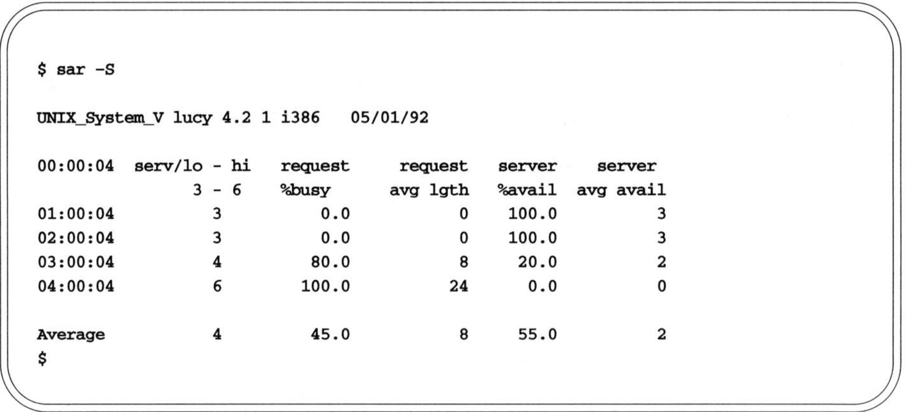

```
$ sar -S

UNIX_System_V lucy 4.2 1 i386    05/01/92

00:00:04  serv/lo - hi   request      request   server    server
                3 - 6    %busy       avg lgth   %avail  avg avail
01:00:04          3         0.0            0     100.0          3
02:00:04          3         0.0            0     100.0          3
03:00:04          4        80.0            8      20.0          2
04:00:04          6       100.0           24       0.0          0

Average           4        45.0            8      55.0          2
$
```

As an administrator you can set the number of server processes available to service remote system calls (see "Parameter Tuning"). There are two server variables you can set: **MINSERVE** and **MAXSERVE**. **MINSERVE** is the number of servers that are initially running to service remote requests.

MAXSERVE is the maximum number of servers that may ever exist. If demand goes beyond what the **MINSERVE** servers can handle, extra servers can be dynamically allocated so the total number of servers can be as high as the value of **MAXSERVE**. These processes disappear when they are no longer needed.

Information from **sar -S** can be used to tune your server parameters as shown below.

Too Few Servers

If the receive queue is almost always busy (request %busy), you may want to raise the number of servers. Here is how to decide the parameter to raise:

- Raise the **MAXSERVE** if the total average servers is high.
- Raise the **MINSERVE** if the total average servers is low.

Too Many Servers

If servers are available nearly 100% of the time (server %avail), you may have allocated too many servers. To decide the parameter to lower:

- Check the number of total servers. If this number is near the **MINSERVE** value, you can lower **MINSERVE**. Try reducing it by 50% or by the number of idle servers.
- Check the total servers that are idle. If this number is near the **MAXSERVE** value, you can lower **MAXSERVE**. Try reducing it by 50%.

Resource Usage (fusage)

You can find out how extensively remote computers are using your resources with the **fusage** command. It reports how many kilobytes were read and written from your resources, as categorized by remote computers that mounted the resources. The form for **fusage** for reporting on a resource you have shared is:

fusage *advertised-resource*

where *advertised-resource* is the resource you have shared. **fusage** with no options produces a full report of data usage for all disks and shared directories on your system, as shown in Figure 17-19.

Figure 17-19: Sample Output from `fusage`

```
# fusage

FILE USAGE REPORT FOR charlie


                /dev/root          /dev/root

                                   /
                                           charlie          292 KB

                /proc              /proc

                                   /proc
                                           charlie            0 KB

                /dev/fd            /dev/fd

                                   /dev/fd
                                           charlie            0 KB

                /dev/dsk/c1d0s3    /dev/dsk/c1d0s3

                                   /stand
                                           charlie         1039 KB

                /dev/dsk/c1d0s8    /dev/dsk/c1d0s8

                                   /var
                                           charlie            0 KB

                /dev/dsk/c1d0s2    /dev/dsk/c1d0s2

                       CHUCKUSR      /usr
                                     peanuts.linus          649 KB
                                     peanuts.lucy            51 KB
                                         Sub Total          700 KB

                                   /usr
                                           charlie          988 KB

                /dev/dsk/c1d0s9    /dev/dsk/c1d0s9

                                   /home
                                           charlie            0 KB
```

If a remote computer's requests for your resources are high, it may be causing performance problems on your computer. With the output from **`fusage`**, you can see what resources are being particularly hard hit. You may want to move or copy a resource to a computer that is constantly accessing it.

Remote Disk Space (df)

You can use the standard **df** command with a remote resource name to see the space left on the disk on which the remote resource resides. The form of the command to report on a remote resource is:

df *resource*

where *resource* is the name of a remote resource mounted on your machine. (**df** with no options will produce information for all mounted remote resources, plus all locally mounted devices.) An example of the **df** command using resource names as options is shown in Figure 17-20.

Figure 17-20: Sample Output from `df`

```
# df DOC NEWS LIB

/doc            (DOC          ):   30415 blocks   45391 files
/usr/news       (NEWS         ):   26832 blocks   25177 files
/usr/lib        (LIB          ):   26832 blocks   25177 files
```

If you have write permission to a resource, you have as much access to file system space as a user on the system who owns a resource. This command will tell you the potential disk space available for you to write in. If the server has shared more than one directory from a single file system, the client's df output will show that same values for the corresponding resources. Free space is always tracked on a file system basis. In Figure 17-20, **/usr/news** and **/usr/lib** are part of the same file system on the server, and the **df** command reports the same values.

Parameter Tuning

There are several parameters you can tune to best suit the way you use RFS. RFS parameters control the amount of resources you devote to Remote File Sharing service. Each network transport provider may also have some tunable parameters that may affect performance characteristics of that particular network. See the network documentation for your network for more details.

All parameters have set default values that should work well for an average system (see the table at the end of this section). The following paragraphs describe these parameters and cases where you may want to change them.

RFS Parameters

RFS parameters define the extent remote computers can use your resources, but they also control your own remote access to remote resources. If the values are too small, you may not be providing enough resources to handle your RFS load properly. Requests for mounts, shares, or even a file could fail if either of those values reach the maximum number allowed for your machine. If these parameters are too large, you could be allocating more system resources than you need to use.

The parameters described below are in **`/etc/conf/mtune.d/rfs`**. Read these files for default values. If you change any of these values, see "Setting Up the Work Environment" in *Basic System Administration* for information on how to make the updated parameters take effect.

NRCVD (maximum number of receive descriptors)

> Your system creates one receive descriptor for each file or directory being referenced by remote users and one for each process on your machine awaiting response to a remote request. If you limit the number of receive descriptors, you limit the number of local files and directories that can be accessed at a time by remote users. The result of exceeding the limit would be error messages for remote user commands.

NSNDD (maximum number of send descriptors)

> For each remote resource (file or directory) your users reference, your system creates a send descriptor. A send descriptor is also allocated for each server process and each message waiting on the receive queue. You can change this value to limit how many remote files and directories your machine can access at a time. This would, in effect, limit the amount of RFS activities your users can perform. The result of exceeding the limit would be error messages for user commands.

NSRMOUNT (server mount table entries)

Each time a remote machine mounts one of your resources, an entry is added to your server mount table. This number limits the total number of your resources that can be mounted at a time by remote machines.

MAXGDP (virtual circuits)

There are up to two connections (virtual circuits) set up on the network between you and each machine with which you are currently sharing resources. There is one for each computer whose resources you mount and one for each computer that mounts your resources. A virtual circuit is created when a computer first mounts a resource from another, and it is taken down when the last resource is unmounted.

This parameter limits the number of RFS virtual circuits your computer can have open on the network at a time. It limits how many remote computers you can share resources with at a time. Note that a given network may have a limited number of circuits on any one computer, so this parameter influences the maximum percentage of those that might be used for RFS.

MINSERVE (minimum server processes)

Your system uses server processes to handle remote requests for your resources. This parameter sets how many server processes are always active on your computer. (See the **sar -S** command for information on monitoring server processes.)

MAXSERVE (maximum server processes)

When there are more remote requests for your resources than can be handled by the minimum servers, your computer can temporarily create more. This parameter sets the maximum total server processes your system can have (**MINSERVE** plus the number it can dynamically create).

NRDUSER

This value specifies the number of receive descriptor **user** entries to allocate. Each entry represents a client machine's use of one of your files or directories. While there is one receive descriptor allocated for each file or directory being accessed remotely (**NRCVD**), there can be multiple receive descriptor **user** entries for each client using the file or directory (**NRDUSER**). These entries are used during recovery when the network or a client goes down. This value should be about one and one half times the value of **NRCVD**.

RCACHETIME (caching time off)

This parameter can be used in two ways:

1. to turn off caching for your entire machine;
2. to define the number of seconds that network caching is turned off when a file is modified.

To turn off caching for your entire machine, the parameter must be set to `-1`.

The second use of **RCACHETIME** requires some explanation. When a write to a server file occurs, the server machine sends invalidation messages to all client machines that have the file open. The client machines remove data affected by the write from their caches. Caching of that file's data is not resumed until the writing processes close the file or until the seconds in this parameter have elapsed.

The assumption is that write traffic is "bursty" and that the first write may be closely followed by other writes. Turning off caching avoids the overhead of sending invalidation messages for subsequent writes.

RF_MAXKMEM (limit persistent use of kernel memory)
The default value for this parameter is 0, which means there is no limit. It cannot be applied to allocations that are otherwise limited (**NRCVD**, **NSNDD**, **NRDUSER**, **MAXGDP**, **NSRMOUNT**), to stream messages that are not persistent, or to certain allocations that are directly controlled by an administrator (for example, the number of resource advertisements allowed). A suggested value for a moderately used RFS server machine would be 10000. This means that 10000 bytes of kernel memory could be devoted to persistent use by RFS.

RFTMO_TIME (control the RFS circuit timeout mechanism)
This parameter determines the maximum number of seconds that can elapse between messages received over a virtual circuit before that circuit is shut down and marked for recovery. Many transport providers have their own timeout mechanisms. If they are acceptable, the RFS mechanism can be disabled by setting **RFTMO_TIME** to `-1`.

A sample table of the RFS tunable parameter values are shown in Figure 17-21.

Figure 17-21: RFS Tunable Parameter Settings

RFS Tunable Parameter Settings
(file `/etc/conf/mtune.d/rfs`)

Parameter	Default	Minimum	Maximum
`NSRMOUNT`	20	1	50
`NRCVD`	150	40	500
`NSNDD`	150	100	350
`MAXGDP`	24	10	32
`MINSERVE`	3	3	3
`MAXSERVE`	6	3	6
`NRDUSER`	250	1	700
`RCACHETIME`	10	–1	10
`RFTMO_TIME`	60	30	120
`RF_MAXKMEM`	0	0	50

Setting Up NFS

18 NFS Introduction

About NFS Administration 18-1
Organization 18-1

Introduction to NFS 18-3
NFS Resources 18-3
NFS Servers and Clients 18-4

An Overview of NFS Administration 18-6

About NFS Administration

UNIX System V allows you to share files, file hierarchies, and entire file systems across a network using the Network File System (NFS).

The NFS administration chapters explain how to administer the SVR4.2 implementation of the Network File System. They explain how NFS works, and provide the procedures for sharing resources on the network, and for accessing resources shared by other machines.

Organization

The NFS administration chapters assume you are setting up your machine both to share local resources on the network, and to mount remote resources shared by other systems. If you are administering a machine that will mount but not share resources, you can limit your reading to the NFS overview in this chapter, and to the chapters that explain how to mount resources, set up network security, and diagnose problems on an NFS client.

The NFS chapters are organized as follows:

- "NFS Introduction", which describes this guide and provides an introduction to NFS.
- "Setting Up NFS", which directs you to installation instructions and tells you how to start NFS operation and set up automatic sharing and mounting.
- "Sharing and Mounting NFS Resources Explicitly", which tells you how to share and mount resources on an "as needed" basis, using the command line.
- "Obtaining NFS Information", which tells you how to get information about resources that have been shared and mounted across the network.
- "Handling NFS Problems", which provides solutions to problems you may encounter when using NFS.
- "Setting Up Secure NFS", which introduces options to NFS that provide for encryption and other security measures.
- "Using the NFS Automounter", which tells you how to use the automatic mounting facility of NFS.

- "The NFS Network Lock Manager", which discusses how to prevent multiple processes from modifying the same file at the same time.
- "Using the NFS sysadm Interface", which tells you how to set up and administer NFS through a series of **sysadm**(1M) menus.

Introduction to NFS

NFS is a service that enables machines of different architectures running different operating systems to share resources across a network. NFS makes it possible for a machine to share local files and directories, and permits remote users to access those files and directories as though they were local to the user's machine.

NFS provides file sharing in a heterogeneous environment, potentially containing many different operating systems; it has been implemented on operating systems including MS-DOS® and VMS®.

NFS can be implemented on different operating systems because it defines an abstract model of a file system. On each operating system, the NFS model is mapped into the local file system semantics. As a result, normal file system operations, such as read/write, operate in the same way that they operate on a local file system.

The benefits of NFS are significant. NFS allows multiple machines to use the same files, so the same data can be accessible to everyone on the network. Storage costs can be kept down by having machines share applications.

NFS Resources

The objects that can be shared through NFS include any whole or partial directory tree or file hierarchy—including a single file. However, a machine cannot share a file hierarchy that overlaps one that is already shared, and peripheral devices such as modems and printers cannot be shared.

In most UNIX system environments, a file hierarchy that can be shared corresponds to a file system or to a portion of a file system; however, NFS works across operating systems, and the concept of a file system may be meaningless in other, non-UNIX system environments. Therefore, the term *resource* is used throughout the NFS chapters to refer to a file or file hierarchy that can be shared and mounted over NFS.

When you mount a remote file system on a local mount point, you mount the entire file system, starting at its root. When you mount a remote resource through NFS, you are not restricted to mounting the entire file system. You can mount any directory or file in the file system tree, and gain access only to that directory or file and anything beneath it. For example, in the illustration, Machine A is sharing its entire `/usr` file system. If Machine B wants access only to the files and subdirectories in `/usr/man` on Machine A, it can mount `/usr/man`, rather than `/usr`; then, nothing above `usr/man` on Machine A appears in Machine B's directory tree.

Figure 18-1: Mounting a Remote Resource

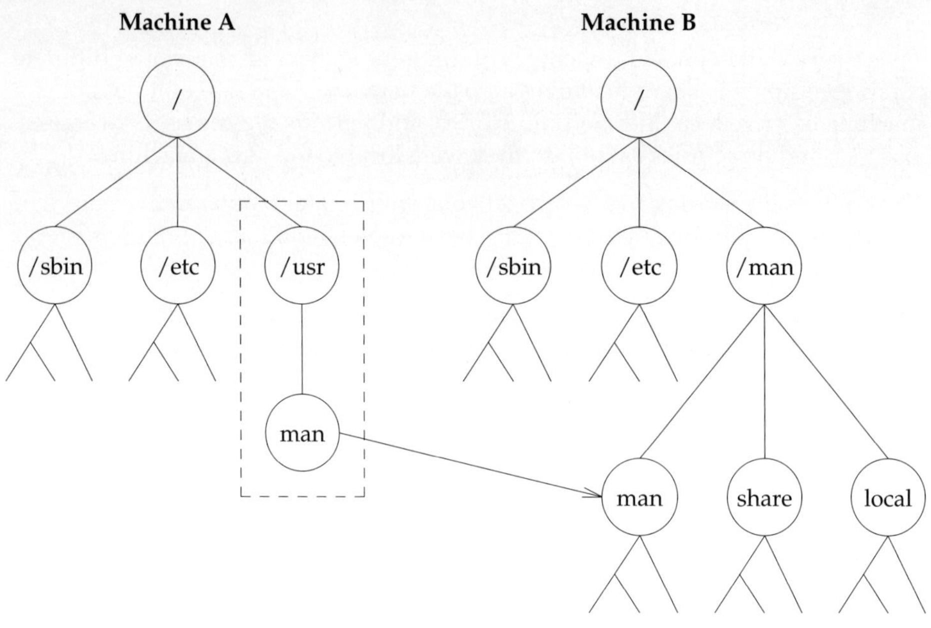

It would be invalid for Machine A to share both **/usr** and **/usr/man** if both resources reside on the same disk partition. In this case, you would have to share **/usr** and leave it to network machines to decide whether to mount **/usr** or **/usr/man**.

If you want to mount a single file, you must mount the file on a directory. Once it is mounted, you cannot remove it (using **rm**) or move it to another directory (using **mv**); you can only unmount it.

NFS Servers and Clients

A machine that makes its' local resource available for mounting by remote machines is called a *server*. A machine that mounts a resource shared by a remote machine is a *client* of that machine. Any machine with a disk can be a server, a client, or both at the same time.

A server can support a *diskless* client, a machine that has no local disk. A diskless client relies completely on the server for all its file storage. A diskless client can act only as a client—never as a server.

Clients access files on the server by mounting the server's shared resources. When a client mounts a remote resource, it does not make a copy of the resource; rather, the mounting process uses a series of remote procedure calls that enable the client to access the resource transparently on the server's disk. The mount looks like a local mount, and users enter commands just as if the resources were local.

An Overview of NFS Administration

Your responsibilities as an NFS administrator depend on your site's requirements and the role of your machine on the network. You may be responsible for all the machines on your local network, in which case you may be responsible for installing the software on every machine, determining which machines, if any, should be dedicated servers, which should act as both servers and clients, and which should be clients only.

If your site has a network administrator, and you are the administrator of a client-only machine, you may be responsible only for mounting and unmounting remote resources on that machine.

Maintaining a machine once it has been set up involves the following tasks:

- Starting and stopping NFS operation.
- Sharing and unsharing resources.
- Mounting and unmounting resources.
- Modifying administrative files to update the lists of resources your machine shares and/or mounts automatically.
- Checking the status of the network.
- Diagnosing and fixing NFS-related problems as they arise.
- Maintaining security.
- Setting up maps to use the optional automatic mounting facility called the Automounter.

19 Setting Up NFS

Introduction 19-1

Starting and Stopping NFS Operation 19-2

Setting Up Automatic Sharing 19-3

Setting Up Automatic Mounting 19-5

Introduction

Setting up NFS involves the following tasks:

- Installing NFS software on your servers and clients (for information on installing the NFS software, see the UNIX SVR4.2 *Installation Guide*.)
- Setting up automatic sharing on servers
- Setting up automatic mounting on clients
- Starting NFS operation

Remember, a machine can be both a server and a client—both sharing local resources with remote machines and mounting remote resources. Throughout the NFS chapters, it is assumed you are setting up your machine as both a server and a client. If you are setting up machines that are to be dedicated servers or clients, follow the instructions for sharing and mounting as appropriate.

Starting and Stopping NFS Operation

If NFS is installed on your system, your system will come up in init state 3, and NFS will be started automatically.

If your system is not in init state 3, you can take your system to init state 3 by entering `init 3`, or you can set up your system to enter init state 3 immediately on rebooting (for information, see *Basic System Administration*.)

NFS allows you to share and mount resources *explicitly*, by entering commands at the command line. You can also set up the system to share and mount resources *automatically*, by editing a few of administration files. If you set up automatic sharing and mounting, a pre-determined set of resources is shared and/or mounted whenever you start NFS operation.

To start NFS using the command line, type the following command:

```
sh /etc/init.d/nfs start
```

To stop NFS using the command line, type the following command:

```
sh /etc/init.d/nfs stop
```

When NFS is stopped, the resources you shared and mounted are automatically unshared and unmounted.

If your system does not automatically enter init state 3 upon startup or reboot, edit the **/etc/inittab** file and change the line

```
is:2:initdefault:
```

to the following:

```
is:3:initdefault:
```

See **inittab**(4) for more information on the **/etc/inittab** file.

Setting Up Automatic Sharing

If you want to set up your system so that certain files and directories are shared automatically whenever you start NFS operation, you need to edit an administrative file. It is recommended that you set up automatic sharing when you first set up NFS if you need to share the same set of resources on a regular basis. For example, if your machine is a server that supports diskless clients, you need to make your clients' root directories available at all times.

The file you need to edit to set up automatic sharing is **dfstab**, located in **/etc/dfs**. **dfstab** is installed by the Distributed File System Administration Utilities.

The **dfstab** file lists all the resources that your server shares with its clients and controls which clients may mount a resource. If you want to modify **dfstab** to add or delete a resource, or to modify the way sharing is done, simply edit the file with your text editor. The next time the machine enters init state 3, the system reads the updated **dfstab** to determine which resources should be shared automatically.

Each line in the file consists of a **share** command—the same command you enter at the command line to share a resource explicitly. The **share** command is located in **/usr/sbin**. When it is used to share a resource over NFS, it has the following syntax:

share [-F nfs] [-o *specific-options*] **[-d** *description*] *pathname*

See the **NFS-specific share**(1M) manual page for the options supported by the **share** command.

You can omit the **-F** option if

```
nfs     Network File System Utilities: Version x.x
```

is the first line in **/etc/dfs/fstypes** or if it is the only Distributed File System (DFS) package installed. If NFS is the only DFS package installed, it becomes the default for the **-F** option.

If you enter the **-d** option, the description is stored in your **sharetab** file. However, clients will not see the description displayed when they use the **dfshares** command to list the resources shared on your system.

Under NFS, a server shares resources it owns so clients can mount them. However, a user who becomes the superuser on a client may be denied superuser access to mounted remote resources, unless the appropriate option is used when the resource is shared. Otherwise, when a user logged in as **root** on one host requests access to a remote file shared through NFS, the user's ID is changed from 0 to the user ID of the username **nobody**. The access rights of user *nobody* are the same as those given to the public for a particular file. For example, if the public only has execute permission for a file, then user **nobody** can only execute that file.

When you share a resource, you can permit **root** on a particular machine to have root access to that resource by editing **/etc/dfs/dfstab** on the server, or by specifying the appropriate options on the command line. For example, suppose you want the machine "samba" (but no others) to have superuser access to the shared directory **/usr/src**. You enter the following command in **/etc/dfs/dfstab**, or on the command line.

```
share -F nfs -o root=samba /usr/src
```

If you want more than one client to have root access, you can specify a list, as follows:

```
share -F nfs -o root=samba:raks:jazz /usr/src
```

If you want all client processes with uid 0 to have superuser access to **/usr/src**, you enter

```
share -F nfs -o anon=0 /usr/src
```

anon is short for "anonymous." Anonymous requests, by default, get their user ID changed from its previous value (whatever it may be) to the user ID of username **nobody**. NFS servers label as anonymous any request from a root user (someone whose current effective user ID is 0) who is not in the list following the **root=** option in the **share** command. The command above tells the kernel to use the value 0 for anonymous requests. The result is that all root users retain their user ID of 0.

Setting Up Automatic Mounting

Once a resource has been shared on a server through NFS, it can be accessed from a client. Mounting can be done automatically when NFS operation begins on the client (when the client enters init state 3), or explicitly, by executing the NFS startup script (**/etc/init.d/nfs**) on the command line. If you need to mount certain remote resources on a regular basis, it is recommended that you set up automatic mounting when you first set up NFS operation. Automatic mounting is handled through the **/etc/vfstab** file.

A server can be a client of another server on a local network, in which case, the server's **vfstab** may need to include both local and remote mounts. For information about adding local mounts to the **vfstab** file, see "/etc/vfstab" in *Basic System Administration*.

Entries in the **/etc/vfstab** file have the following syntax:

special fsckdev mountp fstype fsckpass automnt mntopts

See the **vfstab**(4) manual page for an explanation of the fields in the **/etc/vfstab** file.

The contents of **/etc/vfstab** remain the same until you change them.

Example

To specify that the directory **/usr/local** of the server **dancer** should be mounted automatically on the client's directory **/usr/local/tmp** with read/only permission, you add the following line to the client's **vfstab.**

```
dancer:/usr/local  -  /usr/local/tmp nfs - yes ro
```

20 Sharing and Mounting NFS Resources Explicitly

Sharing and Unsharing Resources 20-1
Sharing Resources with the share Command 20-1
Sharing a Set of Resources with the shareall Command 20-2
- shareall Example 20-2
Unsharing Resources with the unshare Command 20-3
Unsharing Resources with the unshareall Command 20-3

Mounting and Unmounting NFS Resources 20-4
Mounting Resources with the mount Command 20-4
Unmounting Resources with the umount Command 20-5

Sharing and Unsharing Resources

In addition to sharing and unsharing resources automatically, you can share and unshare *explicitly* by entering commands on the command line. To share resources explicitly, use the **share** and **shareall** commands; to unshare explicitly, use the **unshare** and **unshareall** commands.

Sharing Resources with the share Command

The **share** command lets you share resources as needed. You should use **share** at the command line prompt when you want to share a resource for a brief period of time, or on an irregular basis.

The **share** command is located in **/usr/sbin** and has the following syntax:

share [-F nfs] [-o *specific-options***] [-d** *description***]** *pathname*

See NFS-specific **share**(1M) for the options supported by the **share** command.

If you enter the **-d** option, the description is stored in your **sharetab** file. However, clients will not see the description displayed when they use the **dfshares** command to list the resources shared on your system.

Examples

1. To share the directory **/usr** with all the server's clients, enter the following command:

   ```
   share -F nfs /usr
   ```

   The resource is shared with read/write permissions by default.

2. If you want to make sure that client **dancer** can access **/usr** with read-only permission, enter the following command:

   ```
   share -F nfs -o rw,ro=dancer /usr
   ```

3. If you want to see a listing of the local resources currently available through NFS, enter the following command:

   ```
   share -F nfs
   ```

   If you have more than one distributed file system package installed, the **share** command without arguments displays a list of all the resources shared on your system through the default file sharing package, with the default being the first file system type listed in **/etc/dfs/fstypes**.

4. If you want to permit root access on **/usr** by any user or process whose user ID is 0, enter the following command:

```
share -F nfs -o anon=0 /usr
```

You would share a resource this way only if you are in a trusting environment.

Sharing a Set of Resources with the shareall Command

The **shareall** command allows you to share a set of resources. To use the command, you first create a file that lists the resources you want to share. The syntax of the entries in your file is the same syntax as the NFS-specific **share** command and the entries in the **dfstab** file, as follows:

share [-F nfs] [-o *specific_options*] **[-d** *description*] [*pathname*]

Once you create the file, you specify it as the input file when you enter the **shareall** command.

If you do not specify an input file, the **/etc/dfs/dfstab** file is used by default. If you enter a dash (-) in place of the name of an input file, the system accepts standard input, which means you can enter a number of **share** commands in succession, then execute the commands all at once by pressing CTRL-d. This saves you from entering one **share** command, waiting for the system to execute the command and return your prompt, then entering another command, and so on.

The syntax of the **shareall** command is as follows:

shareall [-F nfs] [- | *file*]

See **shareall**(1M) for the options supported by the **shareall** command.

shareall Example

You need to share the same set of resources on a fairly regular basis, but you do not want the resources shared automatically. You create an input file called **misc** that looks like this:

```
#cat misc
share -F nfs -o ro,rw=artdept /export/graphics
share -F nfs /usr/man
share -F nfs -o rw,ro=dancer,root=jogger:jumper /local
```

To share the resources listed in the **misc** file, type

```
shareall misc
```

This example assumes that NFS is the only package installed; the **-F** option is omitted from the **shareall** command and from the **share** commands in the input file.

Unsharing Resources with the unshare Command

Resources that are shared either explicitly or automatically (through the **/etc/dfs/dfstab** file) can be unshared at any time by using the command **unshare**.

unshare is located in **/usr/sbin**, and has the following syntax:

unshare [-F nfs] *pathname*

where **-F nfs** indicates the kind of share, and *pathname* is the full name of the shared resource, beginning with root (/). For information on the **unshare** command, see NFS-specific **unshare**(1M).

Example

If you want to unshare the directory **/usr**, enter this command:

```
unshare -F nfs /usr
```

Unsharing Resources with the unshareall Command

When you want to unshare all the resources that are currently shared on your system through NFS, use the **unshareall** command, located in **/usr/sbin**. If NFS is the only distributed file system installed, or it is the default file sharing package on your system, simply enter the following command:

```
unshareall
```

If you have more than one distributed file system installed and NFS is not the default, include the **-F** option, as follows:

```
unshareall -F nfs
```

For information on the **unshareall** command, see **shareall**(1M).

Mounting and Unmounting NFS Resources

Once a resource has been shared on a server through NFS, you can explicitly mount and unmount the resource, using the **mount** and **umount** commands.

Mounting Resources with the mount Command

You can use the **mount** command any time during client operations to mount a remote resource, provided the resource is shared and you can reach the server over the network. However, you must be a privileged user to use **mount**.

NFS supports two types of mounts—hard mounts and soft mounts. If a mount is a hard mount, an NFS request affecting any part of the mounted resource is issued repeatedly until the request is satisfied (for example, the server crashes and comes back up at a later time). When a mount is a soft mount, an NFS request returns an error if it cannot be satisfied (for example, the server is down), then quits.

Before you issue the **mount** command, use the **mkdir** command to create a mount point for the remote resource. As with a local mount, if you mount a remote resource on an existing directory that contains files and sub-directories, the contents of the directory are obscured.

The syntax of the **mount** command, as it relates to an NFS mount, is:

mount [-F *fstype*] [-o *specific_options*] {*special* | *mount_point*}

mount [-F *fstype*] [-o *specific_options*] *special mount_point*

See NFS-specific **mount**(1M) for the options supported by the **mount** command.

Resources accessed through the **mount** command stay mounted, unless you unmount them with the **umount** command or exit init state 3. Also, if you exit and re-enter init state 3, the resource will no longer be mounted (unless you edited the **vfstab** file to mount the resource automatically.)

When you mount an NFS resource, it is suggested that you do the following:

- Use the **hard** option with any resource you mount read-write. Then, if a user is writing to a file when the server goes down, the write will continue when the server comes up again, and nothing will be lost.

- Use the **nosuid** option with any resource you mount read-write, unless you have good reasons to do otherwise.

NFS mount Examples

1. You want to soft mount on-line manual pages from remote machine **dancer** on the local directory **/usr/man**. You want the pages mounted read-only. Type the following command:

   ```
   mount -F nfs -o ro,soft dancer:/usr/man /usr/man
   ```

2. You want to hard mount the resource **/usr/local** from the remote machine **dancer** on the mount-point **/usr/local/dancer**. You want the resource mounted read-write, with the set-uid bits ignored and the keyboard interrupt enabled. Enter the following, all on one line:

   ```
   mount -F nfs -o hard,nosuid,intr \
        dancer:/usr/local /usr/local/dancer
   ```

Unmounting Resources with the umount Command

The `umount` command allows you to unmount a remote resource, whether the resource was mounted automatically or explicitly. However, you must be a privileged user to use `umount`.

The syntax of `umount`, as it relates to NFS, is:

umount [-V] {*server*:*path* | *mount-point*}

See `mount`(1M) for the options supported by the `umount` command.

21 Obtaining NFS Information

Obtaining Information About NFS Resources 21-1

Browsing Available Resources with the dfshares Command 21-2

Displaying Shared Local Resources with the share Command 21-3

Monitoring Shared Local Resources with the dfmounts Command 21-4

Obtaining Information About NFS Resources

System administrators have at their disposal a variety of tools to obtain information about the status of the networked file system services.

This chapter tells you how to determine what resources are available to you from remote servers, what resources you have shared and mounted on your machine, and what shared resources have been mounted by remote clients.

Browsing Available Resources with the dfshares Command

The command **dfshares** allows you to "browse" remote servers to find out the names of remote resources available to your client machine. The syntax of the command is:

dfshares [-F nfs] [-h] [*server* **...]**

See **NFS-specific dfshares**(1M) for the options supported by the **dfshares** command.

If NFS is the only file sharing package you have installed, you can omit the **-F** option.

Unless it is suppressed with the **-h** option, the output from the **dfshares** command is preceded by the header:

resource server access transport

where *resource* is of the form *server*:*pathname*, and *server* is the name of the server sharing the resource.

At this time, NFS does not populate the *access* and *transport* fields; a hyphen appears in place of access and transport information.

Displaying Shared Local Resources with the share Command

You can obtain a list of all the NFS resources currently shared on your machine by entering the following command:

```
share
```

If you have more than one distributed file system package installed, the **share** command without arguments displays *all* the resources shared on your system, including the resources shared through NFS.

You do not have to be a privileged user to use the **share** command in this capacity. See NFS-specific **share**(1M) for the options supported by the **share** command.

Monitoring Shared Local Resources with the dfmounts Command

The command **`dfmounts`** lets you display a list of shared resources by server that tells you which resources are currently mounted over NFS, and by which clients. The syntax of the command is shown below:

`dfmounts [-F nfs] [-h]` `[`*server*` ...]`

See **`NFS-specific dfmounts`**(1M) for the options supported by the **`dfmounts`** command.

If NFS is the only file sharing package you have installed, you can omit the **`-F`** option.

Unless it is suppressed with the **`-h`** option, the output from the **`dfmounts`** command is preceded by the header:

resource   server   pathname   clients

where *resource* is of the form *server:pathname*; *server* is the name of the server from which the resource was mounted; *pathname* is the pathname of the shared resource as it appears in the second part of *resource*; and *clients* is a comma-separated list of clients that have mounted the resource.

The *server* can be any system on the network. If a *server* is not specified, **`dfmounts`** displays the resources of the local system that have been mounted by remote clients.

22 Handling NFS Problems

NFS Troubleshooting 22-1

An Overview of the Mount Process 22-2

Determining Where NFS Service Has Failed 22-4

Clearing Startup Problems 22-5

Clearing Server Problems 22-5

Clearing Remote Mounting Problems 22-7

Fixing Hung Programs 22-9

NFS Troubleshooting

This chapter describes problems that may occur on machines using NFS services. It covers the following topics:

- A summary of NFS sequence of events
- Strategies for tracking NFS problems
- NFS-related error messages.

Before trying to clear NFS problems, you need some understanding of the issues involved. The information in this chapter contains enough technical details to give experienced network administrators a thorough picture of what is happening with their machines. If you do not yet have this level of expertise, note that it is not important to understand fully all the daemons, system calls, and files. However, you should be able to at least recognize their names and functions. Before you read this chapter, familiarize yourself with the following man pages:

> `NFS-specific mount`(1M)
> `NFS-specific share`(1M)
> `mountd`(1M)
> `nfsd`(1M)
> `biod`(1M)

An Overview of the Mount Process

This section describes the remote mount process. It is not critical that you understand in depth how the daemons mentioned here work; however, you need to know that they exist, because you may need to restart them should they stop for any reason.

Here is the sequence of events when you first enter init state 3. (The **/etc/rc3.d/S22nfs** script contains other commands not related to the mounting process, and they are not shown in the following list.)

1. The **S22nfs** file in **/etc/rc3.d** starts several **nfsd** daemons (the default is four). The **nfsd** daemons are used in server operations.
2. The same file starts several (the default is four) **biod** daemons. The **biod** daemons are used in client operations.
3. **S22nfs** then starts **mountd**. This is used to process mount requests.
4. It then starts **lockd**, which is used to process lock requests, and **statd**, which interacts with **lockd** to provide crash and recovery functions for the locking services.
5. The same file executes the **shareall** program, which reads the server's **/etc/dfs/dfstab** file, then tells the kernel which resources the server can share and what access restrictions—if any—are on these files.
6. The same file starts the **mountall** program, which reads the client's **vfstab** file and mounts all NFS-type files mentioned there in a manner similar to an explicit mount (described below).

Here is the sequence of events when an administrator mounts a resource during a work session, using the command line:

1. The administrator enters a command, such as

   ```
   mount -F nfs -o ro,soft dancer:/usr/src /usr/src/dancer.src
   ```

2. The **mount** command verifies that the mount point is a full pathname and that there is a file **/usr/lib/fs/nfs/mount**. **/sbin/mount** then passes all the relevant arguments and options to **/usr/lib/fs/nfs/mount**, which takes control of the process (when we say **mount** from now on in this section, we will be referring to this last file.)

3. **mount** then opens **/etc/mnttab** and checks that the mount was not previously done.

4. **mount** parses the argument **dancer:/usr/src** (*server*:*path*)into host **dancer** and remote directory **/usr/src**.

5. **mount** calls **dancer's rpcbind** to get the port number of **dancer**'s **mountd**.

6. **mount** calls dancer's **mountd** daemon and passes it **/usr/src**, requesting it to send a file handle (**fhandle**) for the directory.

7. The server's **mountd** daemon handles the client's mount requests. If the directory **/usr/src** is available to the client (or to the public), the **mountd** daemon does a **NFS_GETFH** system call on **/usr/src** to get the **fhandle**, and it sends it to the client's mount process.

8. **mount** checks if **/usr/src/dancer.src** is a directory.

9. **mount** does a **mount**(2) system call with the **fhandle** and **/usr/src/dancer.src**.

10. The client kernel looks up the directory **/usr/src/dancer.src** and, if everything is in order, ties the file handle to the hierarchy in a mount record.

11. The client kernel looks up the directory **/usr/src** on **dancer**.

12. The client kernel does a **statvfs**(2) call to **dancer**'s NFS server **nfsd**.

13. Mount's **mount**(2) system call returns.

14. **mount** opens **/etc/mnttab** and adds an appropriate entry to the end, reflecting the new addition to the list of mounted files.

15. When the client kernel does a file operation, once the resource is mounted, it sends the NFS RPC information to the server, where it is read by one of the **nfsd** daemons to process the file request.

16. The **nfsd** daemons know how a resource is shared from the information sent to the server's kernel by **share**. These daemons allow the client to access the resource according to its permissions.

Determining Where NFS Service Has Failed

When tracking down an NFS problem, keep in mind that there are three main points of possible failure: the server, the client, or the network itself. The strategy outlined in this section tries to isolate each individual component to find the one that is not working.

For NFS to operate properly, the NFS daemons shown below must be running. To check the status of the NFS daemons, use **nfsping**. The syntax of the **nfsping** is:

```
nfsping [-a|-s|-c|-o name]
```

For more information about **nfsping**, see **nfsping**(1M).

The **mountd** daemon must be running on the server for a remote mount to succeed. Make sure **mountd** will be available for an RPC call by checking that **/etc/init.d/nfs** has lines similar to the following:

```
if [ -x /usr/lib/nfs/mountd ]
then
        echo > /etc/rmtab
        $TFADMIN /usr/lib/nfs/mountd > /dev/console 2>&1
fi
```

Remote mounts also need a number of **nfsd** daemons to execute on NFS servers (the default is four). Check the server's file **/etc/init.d/nfs** for the following (or similar) lines:

```
if [ -x /usr/lib/nfs/nfsd ]
then
      $TFADMIN /usr/lib/nfs/nfsd -a 4 > /dev/console 2>&1
fi
```

To enable these daemons without rebooting, log in as the network administrator (or as a privileged user) and type:

```
/usr/lib/nfs/nfsd -a 4
```

The client's **biod** daemons are not necessary for NFS to work, but they improve performance. Make sure the following (or similar) lines are present in the client's file **/etc/init.d/nfs**:

```
if [ -x /usr/lib/nfs/biod ]
then
      $TFADMIN /usr/lib/nfs/biod 4 > /dev/console 2>&1
fi
```

To enable these daemons without rebooting, log in as the network administrator and type:

```
/usr/lib/nfs/biod 4
```

Clearing Startup Problems

A potential problem can occur if the name of the machine is changed with the **uname** command.

When the system hostname is changed with the **uname** command, the hostname entries in the **/etc/net/*/hosts** files are not updated. This causes the NFS daemons and/or the **rpcbind** daemon to fail. To check if the NFS daemons and the **rpcbind** daemon are running, use **nfsping -a**. For more information on **nfsping**, see **nfsping**(1M). Next, check to see if the system hostname (**uname -n**) matches the first entry in the **/etc/net/*/hosts** files. For example, if the machine's hostname was **hulk** (use **uname -n**), the first entry in each of the **/etc/net/*/hosts** files should look like:

```
hulk   hulk
```

If the first entry in each of the **/etc/net/*/hosts** files do not match the machine's hostname, you must stop NFS, update the first entry in the **/etc/net/*/hosts** files, and restart NFS. For information on starting and stopping NFS, see "Starting and Stopping NFS Operation". You must also restart the **rpcbind** daemon, to do this, enter:

```
/usr/sbin/rpcbind
```

Clearing Server Problems

When the network or server has problems, programs that access hard mounted remote files will fail differently than those that access soft mounted remote files. Hard mounted remote resources cause the client's kernel to retry the requests until the server responds again. Soft mounted remote resources cause the client's system calls to return an error after trying for a while. **mount** is like any other program: if the server for a remote resource fails to respond, and the **hard** option has been used, the kernel retries the mount until it succeeds. When you use **mount** with the **bg** option, it retries the mount in the background if the first mount attempt fails.

When a resource is hard mounted, a program that tries to access it hangs if the server fails to respond. In this case, NFS displays the message

NFS server *hostname* **not responding, still trying**

on the console. When the server finally responds, the message

NFS server *hostname* **ok**

appears on the console.

Any program accessing a soft mounted resource whose server is not responding may or may not check the return conditions. If it does, it prints an error message in the form

...*hostname* **server not responding: RPC: Timed out**

If a client is having NFS trouble, check first to make sure the server is up and running. From the client, type

/usr/bin/rpcinfo *server_name*

to see if the server is up. If it is up and running, it prints a list of program, version, protocol, and port numbers, similar to the following:

```
program  version  netid      address          service    owner
 100000     3      icmp      0.0.0.0.0.111    rpcbind    superuser
 100000     2      icmp      0.0.0.0.0.111    rpcbind    superuser
 100000     3       udp      0.0.0.0.0.111    rpcbind    superuser
 100000     2       udp      0.0.0.0.0.111    rpcbind    superuser
 100000     3       tcp      0.0.0.0.0.111    rpcbind    superuser
 100000     2       tcp      0.0.0.0.0.111    rpcbind    superuser
 100000     3     ticotsord  hulk.rpc         rpcbind    superuser
 100000     3     ticots     hulk.rpc         rpcbind    superuser
 100000     3     ticlts     hulk.rpc         rpcbind    superuser
   .        .        .           .               .           .
   .        .        .           .               .           .
   .        .        .           .               .           .
```

If the server fails to print a list, try to log in at the server's console. If you can log in, check to make sure the server is running **rpcbind**.

If the server is up but your machine cannot communicate with it, check the network connections between your machine and the server.

Clearing Remote Mounting Problems

This section deals with problems related to mounting. Any step in the remote mounting process can fail—some of them in more than one way. Below are the error messages you may see and detailed descriptions of the failures associated with each error message.

`mount` can get its parameters explicitly from the command line or from `/etc/vfstab`. The examples below assume command line arguments, but the same debugging techniques work if mounting is done automatically through `/etc/vfstab`.

- **`mount:... server not responding: RPC:Program not registered`**

  Either the server sharing the resource you are trying to mount is down, at the wrong init state, or its `rpcbind` is dead or hung, or `mount` got through to `rpcbind`, but the NFS mount daemon `mountd` is not registered. You can check the server's init state by entering (at the server) the following command:

  ```
  who -r
  ```

  If the server is at init state 3, try going to another init state and back, or try rebooting the server to restart `rpcbind`. Try to log in to the server from your machine, using the `rlogin` command. If you can't log in, but the server is up, try to log in to another remote machine to check your network connection. If that connection is working, check the server's network connection. See **who**(1) for more information on the **who** command. If `mountd` is not running, try restarting NFS. See "Starting and Stopping NFS Operation" in "Setting Up NFS" for information on restarting NFS.

- **`mount:... : No such file or directory`**

  Either the remote directory or the local directory does not exist. Check the spelling of the directory names. Use `ls` on both directories.

- **`mount: not in share list for...`**

  Your machine name is not in the list of clients allowed access to the resource you want to mount. From the client, you can display the server's share list by entering the following command:

  `dfshares -F nfs` *server*

  If the resource you want is not in the list, log in to the server and run the `share` command without options.

- **mount: ... : Permission denied**

  This message indicates that the user does not have the appropriate permissions or that some authentication failed on the server. It may be that you are not in the share list (see the preceding error message and explanation), or that the server could not verify that you are who you say you are. Check the server's **/etc/dfs/sharetab** file.

- **mount: ... : Not a directory**

  The local path is not a directory. Check the spelling in your command, and try to run **ls** on both directories.

- **mount: mount-point does not exist.**

  The local directory where the resource in being mounted (mount-point) does not exist.

- **nfs mount: access denied for** *host***:***path*

  This is similar to the **mount: ... : Permission denied** error message.

- **nfs mount: nfs file system; use** *host***:***path*

  The command used to mount a resource is missing information.

The **mount** command hangs indefinitely if there are no **nfsd** daemons running on the NFS server. This happens when there is no **/etc/dfs/dfstab** file on the server when it enters init state 3. To clear the problem, restart the **nfsd** daemons by executing the following command:

```
/usr/lib/nfs/nfsd 4
```

If you are mounting resources from a fast server, it is advised that you use the NFS-specific **mount** options **rsize** and **wsize**. These options should be set to **rsize=1024** and **wsize=1024** because fast servers cause data overruns on the ethernet driver on slow client machines. One symptom of this problem has the following message being written to the console of the client machines:

```
RPC: Timed out.
```

Another symptom of this problem may be that the client machine appears to be hung, with the following message being written to the console of the client machine:

NFS server *hostname* **not responding, still trying**

Fixing Hung Programs

If programs hang while doing file-related work, your NFS server may be dead. You may see the following message on your console:

NFS server *hostname* **not responding, still trying**

This message indicates that NFS server *hostname* is down, or that there is a problem with the server or with the network.

If your machine hangs completely, check the server(s) from which you mounted the resource. If one or more are down, do not be concerned. When the server comes back up, programs resume automatically. No files are destroyed if the resource was **hard** mounted.

If you soft mount a resource and the server dies, other work should not be affected. Programs that time out trying to access soft mounted remote files will fail with **errno ETIMEDOUT**, but you should still be able to access other resources.

If all servers are running, ask someone else using these same servers if they are having trouble. If more than one machine is having problems getting service, there is a problem with the server. Log in to the server. Use **nfsping -o nfsd** to see if **nfsd** is running. Enter **ps -ef | grep nfsd** a few times to see if **nfsd** is accumulating CPU time (let some time pass between each call). If it is not accumulating CPU time, you may be able to kill and then restart **nfsd**. If this does not work, you have to reboot the server. If **nfsd** is not running, it may be that the server has been taken to a init state that does not support file sharing. Use **who -r** to obtain the server's current init state.

If other systems seem to be up and running, check your network connection and the connection of the server.

If programs on the client are hung but the server is up, NFS requests to the server other than reads and writes are succeeding, and messages of the form

xdr_opaque: encode FAILED

are appearing on either the client or the server console, you may be requesting more data than the underlying transport provider can provide. Try remounting the file system using the **-o rsize=***nnn***,wsize=***nnn* options to **mount**(1M) to restrict the request sizes the client will generate. The maximum **rsize** and **wsize**, which is also the default, is 8K.

Fixing a Machine That Hangs Part Way through Boot

If your machine boots normally, then hangs when it tries to mount resources automatically, most likely one or more servers are down. Use **init** to go to single user mode or to a init state that does not mount remote resources automatically. Then start the appropriate daemons in the background and use the **mount** command to mount each resource usually mounted automatically through the **/etc/vfstab** file. By mounting resources one at a time, you can determine which server is down. To restart a server that is down or hung, see the preceding section.

If you cannot mount any of your resources, most likely your network connection is bad.

Improving Access Time

If access to remote files seems unusually slow, enter the following command:

```
ps -ef
```

on the server and look for abnormal (high) execution times for NFS daemon processes to check that the access time is not being affected adversely by a runaway daemon. If there is nothing unusual (processes with excessive CPU time) in the display, and other clients are getting good response, make sure your **biod** daemons are running. At the client, type the following command:

```
ps -ef | grep biod
```

Look for **biod** daemons in the display, then enter the command again. If the **biod**s do not accumulate excessive CPU time, they are probably hung. If they are dead or hung, follow these steps:

1. Kill the daemon processes by determining their process ID (*pid*) numbers:

   ```
   ps -ef | grep biod
   ```

   The second field contains the *pid* number. Then enter the following command:

   kill -9 *pid1 pid2 pid3 pid4*

   where *pidx* is the process ID of the appropriate **biod** daemon.

2. Restart the **biod** daemons by typing:

   ```
   /usr/lib/nfs/biod 4
   ```

If the **biod**s are running, check your network connection. The **netstat -i** command can help you determine if you are dropping packets; for more information, see **netstat**(1M).

23 Setting Up Secure NFS

Introduction to Secure NFS 23-1

An Overview of Secure RPC 23-2
DES Authentication 23-3
A Secure RPC Client/Server Session 23-3

Administering Secure NFS 23-7

Important Considerations 23-9

Introduction to Secure NFS

NFS is a powerful and convenient way to share resources on a network of different machine architectures and operating systems. However, the same features that make sharing resources through NFS convenient also pose some security problems. An NFS server authenticates a file request by authenticating the machine making the request, but not the user.

Systems should take advantage of an authentication mechanism provided with NFS. The authentication system exists at the level of Remote Procedure Call (RPC)—the mechanism on which NFS is built. The system, known as Secure RPC, greatly improves the security of network environments and provides additional security to NFS. The security features that Secure RPC provides to NFS are known collectively as Secure NFS.

Because Secure RPC is at the core of Secure NFS, it is necessary to understand how authentication works in RPC to understand Secure NFS. This chapter first presents an overview of Secure RPC, then tells you how to set up Secure NFS. Following the set up procedure are a few important points you should be aware of if you plan to use Secure NFS.

An Overview of Secure RPC

The goal of Secure RPC is to build a system at least as secure as a normal time-sharing system. The way a user is authenticated in a time-sharing system is through a login password. With Data Encryption Standard (DES) authentication, the same is true. Users can log in on any remote machine, just as they can on a local terminal, and their login passwords are used for authentication on the remote machines. For time-sharing systems, the trusted person is the system administrator, who has an ethical obligation not to change a password in order to impersonate someone. In secure RPC, the network administrator is trusted not to alter entries in a database that stores "public keys."

You need to be familiar with two terms to understand an RPC authentication system: *credentials* and *verifiers*. Using ID badges as an example, the credential is what identifies a person: a name, address, birth date, and so on. The verifier is the photo attached to the badge: you can be sure the badge has not been stolen by checking the photo on the badge against the person carrying it. In RPC, the client process sends both credentials and a verifier to the server with each RPC request. The server sends back only a verifier, since the client already knows the server's credentials. If the server doesn't recognize the client's credentials, the server sends back an error message stating that the client sent invalid credentials.

RPC's authentication is open-ended, which means that a variety of authentication systems may be plugged into it. Currently, there are two such systems: the UNIX system, and the Data Encryption Standard (DES) system.

When the UNIX system authentication is used by a network service, the credentials contain the client's machine-name, UID, `gid`, and group-access-list, but the verifier contains nothing. This presents a problem. Because there is no verifier, users could deduce appropriate credentials. Another problem with UNIX system authentication is that it assumes all machines on a network are UNIX system machines. UNIX system authentication breaks down when applied to other operating systems in a heterogeneous network.

To overcome the problems of UNIX system authentication, Secure RPC uses DES authentication—a scheme that employs verifiers, yet allows Secure RPC to be general enough to be used by most operating systems.

thousand trials, however, there is a good chance that the random window/timestamp pair will pass the authentication system. The window verifier makes guessing the right credential much more difficult.

Step 5 When the server receives the transmission from the client

1. the Keyserver local to the server looks up the client's public key in the public database.
2. the Keyserver uses the client's public key and the server's secret key to deduce the common key—the same common key computed by the client. (No one but the server and the client can calculate the common key, since doing so requires knowing one secret key or the other.)
3. the kernel uses the common key to decrypt the conversation key.
4. the kernel calls the Keyserver to decrypt the client's timestamp with the decrypted conversation key.

Step 6 After the server decrypts the client's timestamp, it stores four things in a credential table:

- the client's machine name.
- the conversation key.
- the window.
- the client's timestamp.

The server stores the first three things for future use. It stores the timestamp to protect against replays. The server will only accept timestamps that are chronologically greater than the last one seen, so any replayed transactions are guaranteed to be rejected.

Step 7 The server returns a verifier to the client, which includes

- the index ID, which the server records in its credential table.
- the client's timestamp minus one, encrypted by conversation key.

The reason for subtracting one from the timestamp is to insure that it is invalid and cannot be reused as a client verifier.

Step 8 The client receives the verifier and authenticates the server. The client knows that only the server could have sent the verifier, since only the server knows what timestamp the client sent.

Step 9 The client returns the index ID to the server in its second transaction and sends another encrypted timestamp.

Step 10 The server sends back the client's timestamp minus 1, encrypted by the conversation key.

With every transaction after the first, the client sends its index ID and another encrypted timestamp, and the server returns the timestamp minus 1.

Implicit in these procedures is the name of caller, who must be authenticated in some manner. The Keyserver cannot use DES authentication to do this, since it would create a deadlock. The Keyserver solves this problem by storing the secret keys by UID, and only granting requests to local root processes. The client process then executes a set-UID process, owned by root, which makes the request on the part of the client, telling the Keyserver the real UID of the client.

Administering Secure NFS

To use Secure NFS, all the machines for which you are responsible must have a domain name. A *domain* is an administrative entity, typically consisting of several machines, that joins a larger network. If you are running the Network Information Service (NIS), you should also establish the NIS name service for the domain. See "Network Information Service" for information on setting up NIS.

With UNIX system authentication, the name of a domain is the UID. UIDs are assigned per domain. A problem with this scheme is that UIDs clash when domains are linked across the network. Another problem with UNIX system authentication has to do with superusers; with UNIX system authentication, the superuser ID (uid 0) is assigned one per machine, not one per domain, which means that a domain can have multiple superusers—all with the same uid.

DES authentication corrects these problems by using netnames. A *netname* is simply a string of printable characters created by concatenating the name of the operating system, a user ID, and a domain name. For example, a UNIX system user with a user ID of 508 in the domain **eng.acme.COM** would be assigned the following netname: **unix.508@eng.acme.COM**. Because user IDs are unique within a domain, and because domain names are unique on a network, this scheme produces a unique netname for every user.

To overcome the problem of multiple super-users per domain, netnames are assigned to machines as well as to users. A machine's netname is formed much like a users—by concatenating the name of the operating system and the machine name with the domain name. A UNIX system machine named **hal** in the domain **eng.acme.COM** would have the netname **unix.hal@eng.acme.COM**.

1. Assign your domain a domain name by following the instructions in "Setting Up TCP/IP", and make the domain name known to each machine in the NIS/RPC domain by using **domainname** on each machine. See "The SRPC_DOMAIN Variable" for further information on **domainname**.

2. Either establish public keys and secret keys for your clients' users using the **newkey** command, or have each user establish their own public and secret keys using the **chkey** command.

   When public and secret keys have been generated, the public keys are stored in the **publickey** database, and users' secret keys are stored in **/etc/keystore**. Secret keys for root users are stored in **/etc/.rootkey**.

For information about these commands, see **newkey**(1M) and the **chkey**(1).

3. If you choose, put the **keylogin** program in **/etc/profile** so that it runs automatically whenever a user logs in. Otherwise, make sure users know to run **keylogin** when they log in.
4. If you are running NIS, verify that the **ypbind** daemon is running and that there is a **ypserv** running in the domain.
5. Verify that the **keyserv** daemon (the Keyserver) is running by typing

   ```
   ps -ef | grep keyserv
   ```

   If it isn't running, start the Keyserver by typing

   ```
   /usr/sbin/keyserv
   ```

6. Edit the **/etc/dfs/dfstab** file and add the **secure** option to the appropriate entries (those that indicate resources you want clients to mount using DES authentication).
7. On each client machine, edit **/etc/vfstab** to include **secure** as a mount option in the appropriate entries (those that indicate resources that should be mounted using DES authentication).

If a client does not mount as **secure** a resource that is shared as secure, everything works, but users have access as user **nobody**, rather than as themselves.

If you are not running NIS, all users must keep their secret keys synchronized with their login passwords by invoking **chkey** if they change their entries in the password database.

When you reinstall, move, or upgrade a machine, remember to save **/etc/keystore** and **/etc/.rootkey**.

Important Considerations

The following are points you should be aware of if you plan to use Secure RPC:

- If a server crashes when no one is around (after a power failure for example), all of the secret keys that are stored on the system are wiped out. Now no process is able to access secure network services, or mount an NFS file system. The important processes at this time are usually root processes, so things would work if root's secret key were stored away, but nobody is around to type the password that decrypts it. If the machine has a local disk, the solution to the problem is to store root's decrypted secret key in a file, which the Keyserver can read.
- Some systems boot in single-user mode, with a `root` login shell on the console and no password prompt. Physical security is imperative in such cases.
- A problem with diskless clients is that diskless machine booting is not totally secure. It is possible for somebody to impersonate the boot-server, and boot a devious kernel that, for example, makes a record of your secret key on a remote machine. Secure NFS provides protection only after the kernel and the Keyserver are running. Before that, there is no way to authenticate the replies given by the boot server. This is not considered a serious problem, because it is highly unlikely that somebody would be able to write this compromised kernel without source code. Also, the crime is not without evidence. If you polled the network for boot-servers, you would discover the devious boot-server's location.
- Most set-UID programs are owned by root; since root's secret key is always stored at boot time, these programs will behave as they always have. If a set-UID program is owned by a user, however, it may not always work. For example, if a set-UID program is owned by **dave**, and **dave** has not logged into the machine since it booted, then the program would not be able to access secure network services.
- If you log in to a remote machine (using **login**, **rlogin**, or **telnet**) and use **keylogin** to gain access, you give away access to your account. This is because your secret key gets passed to that machine's Keyserver, which then stores it. This is only a concern if you don't trust the remote machine. If you have doubts, however, don't log in to a remote machine if it requires a password. Instead, use NFS to mount resources shared by the remote machine. As an alternative, you can use **keylogout**(1) to delete the Keyserver.

- Using secure NFS can result in some degrading of performance. However, that is the impact on network performance. Not all file operations go over the network, so the impact on total system performance is actually lower. Secure NFS is an optional feature; environments that require higher performance at the expense of security can turn it off.

24 Using the NFS Automounter

The NFS Automounter 24-1

How the Automounter Works 24-2

Preparing the Automounter Maps 24-3

Conventions 24-3
Writing a Master Map 24-4
Writing a Direct Map 24-5
Writing an Indirect Map 24-6
- Example of an Indirect Map 24-6

Specifying Multiple Mounts 24-7
Specifying Multiple Locations 24-9
Specifying Subdirectories 24-9
Using Substitutions 24-11
Using Environment Variables 24-12

Invoking the Automounter 24-14

Updating the Mount Table 24-16

Modifying the Maps 24-17

Troubleshooting the Automounter 24-18

The NFS Automounter

Resources shared through NFS can be mounted using a method called "automounting." The **automount** program (located in **/usr/lib/nfs/automount**) mounts and unmounts remote directories on an as-needed basis. Whenever a user on a client running the automounter invokes a command that needs to access a remote file, the shared resource to which that file belongs is mounted automatically. When a certain amount of time has elapsed without the resource being accessed, it is automatically unmounted. For additional information on **automount**, see **automount**(1M).

Once the automounter is invoked, an administrator does not have to set up automatic mounting with the **vfstab** file, or use the **mount** and **umount** commands at the command line. All mounting is done automatically and transparently.

Mounting some resources with `automount` does not exclude the possibility of mounting others with `mount`; in fact, in a diskless machine you must mount root (`/`) and `/usr` with `mount`.

This chapter explains how the automounter works and provides instructions for setting it up.

How the Automounter Works

Unlike **mount**, **automount** does not consult the file **/etc/vfstab** for a list of resources to mount automatically. Rather, it consults a series of maps.

The automounter mounts everything under the directory **/tmp_mnt**, and provides a symbolic link from the requested mount point to the actual mount point under **/tmp_mnt**. For instance, if a user wants to mount a remote directory **src** under **/usr/src**, the actual mount point will be **/tmp_mnt/usr/src**, and **/usr/src** will be a symbolic link to that location.

When **automount** is called, it forks a daemon (**automountd**) to serve each mount point in the maps and makes the kernel believe that the mount has taken place. The daemon sleeps until a request is made to access the corresponding resource. In the mount state, the daemon intercepts the request, mounts the remote resource, creates a symbolic link between the requested mount point and the actual mount point under **/tmp_mnt**, passes the symbolic link to the kernel, and steps aside.

When a predetermined amount of time has passed with the link not being touched (generally five minutes), the daemon unmounts the resource and resumes its previous position.

Preparing the Automounter Maps

A server never knows, nor cares, whether the files it shares are accessed through `mount` or `automount`. Nothing, therefore, needs to be done to a server to run the automounter.

A client, however, needs special files for the automounter. As mentioned earlier, `automount` does not consult `/etc/vfstab`; command line.

There are three basic kinds of automounter maps:

- a master map
- a direct map
- an indirect map

The master map is a general map that uses other maps that contain more specific information. When you enter a command to invoke the automounter and you specify the master map, the master map is used to reference direct and indirect maps and get the information it needs to give to the `automount` command.

A direct map contains all the information `automount` needs to do the mount. It can be called directly by the automounter, or through a master map.

An indirect map allows you to specify alternate servers for a set of resources. It also allows you to specify resources to be mounted as a hierarchy under the same mount point. The indirect map is called only through a master map, which specifies the mount point on which all resources listed in the indirect map should be mounted.

You should create all your automounter maps in your `/etc` directory, using any supported text editor.

Conventions

When creating any of the automounter maps, follow these conventions:

- Use a backslash before characters that may confuse the automounter's parser. For example, suppose you want to mount a directory whose name includes a colon, such as `rc0:dk1`. This resource name might result in the map entry

```
/junk    -ro    vmsserver:rc0:dk1
```

The automounter will be confused by the second colon in this entry. To avoid a problem, the entry should look like this:

```
/junk -ro vmsserver:rc0\:dk1
```

- Use double quotes around a resource name to hide white space.
- If you enter a comment into a map, make sure that it is preceded by #.
- If you include a long entry in a map, use backslashes to split the line into two or more shorter lines. For example, the entry

```
/usr/frame -ro,soft redwood:/usr/frame1.3 balsa:/export/frame
```

could be written as

```
/usr/frame -ro,soft  redwood:/usr/frame1.3 \
                     balsa:/export/frame
```

Writing a Master Map

Each line in a master map has the syntax:

mount-point map [*mount–options*]

where *mount-point* is the full pathname of a directory on which resources should be mounted; *map* is the name of the map that lists the resources to be mounted and their locations; and *mount-options* is a comma-separated list of options that regulates the mounting of the entries mentioned in the *map* (unless the *map* entries list other options).

The options that can be specified for *mount-options* are the same options that can be specified with the **mount** command, except for **fg** and **bg**. See the NFS-specific **mount**(1M) manual page for information.

The *mount-point* can be any mount point you have created for a remote mount. Here is a sample entry in a master map:

```
/usr/man  /etc/libmap  -ro
```

This entry tells the automounter to look in the indirect map **/etc/libmap** and to mount everything listed there on **/usr/man** on the local system. This entry also tells the automounter to mount resources on **/usr/man** read-only; however, if **libmap** indicates that a resource should be mounted read-write, it will be mounted read-write.

If the master map calls a direct map, *mount-point* should be **/-**. This tells the automounter to mount the entries in a direct map on the mount point(s) specified in that map (the *location* field in a direct map contains a full pathname).

Below is a sample master map:

```
#Mount-point   Map                Mount-options
/usr/reports   /etc/reportmap     -rw,intr,secure
/usr/man       /etc/libmap        -ro
/-             /etc/direct.map    -ro,intr
```

Writing a Direct Map

All entries in a direct map have the syntax

key [*mount-options*] *location*

where *key* is the full pathname of the mount point; *mount-options* is a comma-separated list of options that regulates the mounting of the resource specified in the entry; and *location* is the location of the resource, specified as *server*:*pathname*.

The *mount-options* can be any of the options that can be specified with the **mount** command, except for the options **fg** and **bg**. For a list of valid options, see the NFS-specific **mount**(1M) manual page.

The following is a sample entry in a direct map:

```
/usr/fun -ro,soft peach:/usr/games
```

This entry means that the remote resource **/usr/games** on the server named **peach** should be soft mounted read-only on the local mount point **/usr/fun**. Whenever a user tries to access a file or directory that is part of the **/usr/games** directory tree, the automounter reads the direct map, mounts the resource from server **peach** onto the mount point **/tmp_mnt/usr/fun** on the local system, then creates a symbolic link between **/tmp_mnt/usr/fun** and **/usr/fun**. The user is unaware that the mount operation is taking place, and the resource appears to the user to be at **/usr/fun**.

The following is a typical direct map:

```
/usr/local \
                    /bin     -ro,soft   ivy:/export/local/sun3 \
                    /share   -ro,soft   ivy:/export/local/share \
                    /src     -ro,soft   ivy:/export/local/src
/usr/man                     -ro,soft   oak:/usr/man \
                                        rose:/usr/man \
                                        willow:/usr/man
/usr/games                   -ro,soft   peach:/usr/games
/var/spool/news              -ro,soft   pine:/var/spool/news
/usr/frame                   -ro,soft   redwood:/usr/frame1.3 \
                                        balsa:/export/frame
```

Note that, in the first entry, more than one mount point is specified, and more than one location is specified. Specifying multiple mounts and locations is discussed later in this chapter.

Writing an Indirect Map

Entries in an indirect map have the syntax

key [*mount-options*] *location*

where *key* is the name (not the full pathname) of the directory that will be used as the mount point; *mount-options* is a comma-separated list of options that regulates the mount; and *location* is the location of the resource, specified as *server*:*pathname*.

Once the key is obtained by the automounter, it is suffixed to the mount point associated with it either on the command line or in the master map.

For example, suppose one of the entries in the master map reads:

```
/usr/reports /etc/reportmap -rw,intr,secure
```

Here **/etc/reportmap** is the name of the indirect map that lists the remote resources to be mounted under **/usr/reports**.

Example of an Indirect Map

Assume that the following map is the master map on our system.

```
/home          /etc/indirect.map
/-             /etc/direct.map
```

The indirect map has been specified as being mounted on **/home**, and the indirect map has the following entries:

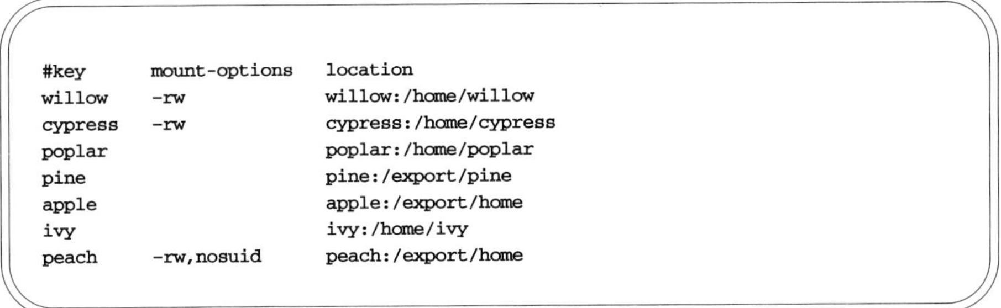

```
#key      mount-options    location
willow    -rw              willow:/home/willow
cypress   -rw              cypress:/home/cypress
poplar                     poplar:/home/poplar
pine                       pine:/export/pine
apple                      apple:/export/home
ivy                        ivy:/home/ivy
peach     -rw,nosuid       peach:/export/home
```

Assume that this map resides on host **oak**. If the login **laura** exists on the machine **oak**, and her home directory is specified as **/home/willow/laura**, every time user **laura** logs into the system **oak**, the automounter will mount the resource specified in the indirect map (**willow:/home/willow**). If the directory **laura** exists on the remote system under **/home/willow**, user **laura** will be in her home directory. Thus, when she logs off (and if no one else is using this resource), the resource will be unmounted automatically, after the specified timeout interval (the default is 5 minutes).

Any option in the indirect map overrides all options specified in the master map or on the command line.

Specifying Multiple Mounts

An entry in a direct or indirect map can describe multiple mounts, where the mounts can be from different locations and with different mount options. In the sample map shown below, the first entry (which is actually one long entry whose readability has been improved by splitting it into three lines) mounts **/usr/local/bin**, **/usr/local/share** and **/usr/local/src** from the server **ivy**, with the options "read-only" and "soft." The entry could also read:

```
/usr/local \
                /bin      -ro,soft     ivy:/export/local/sun3 \
                /share    -rw,secure   willow:/usr/local/share \
                /src      -ro,intr     oak:/home/jones/src
```

where the options are different and more than one server is used.

Multiple mounts can be hierarchical. When resources are mounted hierarchically, each resource is mounted on a subdirectory within another resource. When the root of the hierarchy is referenced, the automounter mounts the entire hierarchy. The concept of *root* here is very important. In the case of a single mount, there is no need to specify the root of the mount point, because it is assumed that the location of the mount point is at the mount root or `/`. When mounting a hierarchy, however, the automounter must have a mount point for each mount within the hierarchy. The following illustration shows a true hierarchical mounting.

```
/usr/local \
                /         -rw,intr     peach:/export/local \
                /bin      -ro,soft     ivy:/export/local/sun3 \
                /share    -rw,secure   willow:/usr/local/share \
                /src      -ro,intr     oak:/home/jones/src
```

The mount points used here for the hierarchy are `/`, **`/bin`**, **`/share`**, and **`/src`**. Note that these mount point paths are relative to the *mount* root, not the host's *file system* root. The first entry in the example above has `/` as its mount point. It is mounted at the mount root. There is no requirement that the first mount of a hierarchy be at the mount root. The automounter will issue **`mkdir`** commands to build a path to the first mount point if it is not at the mount root.

A true hierarchical mount can be a problem if the server for the root of the hierarchy goes down; any attempt to unmount the lower branches will fail, since the unmounting has to proceed through the mount root, which also cannot be unmounted while its server is down.

Specifying Multiple Locations

A mount entry in a direct or indirect map can include more than one location in its *location* field. This means that the mounting can be done from any of the locations specified.

Specifying multiple locations makes sense when you are mounting a resource read-only, since you generally want to have control over the locations of files you write or modify. An example of a read-only resource you might mount from a variety of locations is on-line documentation. In a large network, the current set of on-line manual pages may be available from more than one server. It doesn't matter which server you mount them from, as long as the server is up and running and sharing its files. If manual pages reside in a directory **/usr/man** on three different hosts, called **oak**, **rose**, and **willow**, you can mount from any location by specifying the following in the direct map:

```
/usr/man   -ro,soft oak:/usr/man rose:/usr/man \
        willow:/usr/man
```

This could also be expressed as a comma-separated list of servers, followed by a colon and the pathname (as long as the pathname is the same on all servers):

```
/usr/man -ro,soft oak,rose,willow:/usr/man
```

From the list of servers, the automounter first selects those that are on the local network and queries or "pings" them. The first server to respond is selected, and an attempt is made to mount from it.

If the server goes down while the mount is in effect, the resource becomes unavailable. A choice here is to wait five minutes until the auto-unmount takes place and try again; next time around, the automounter will choose one of the available servers. (Another choice is to use the **umount** command, inform the automounter of the change in the mount table, and retry the mount; see "Updating the Mount Table" later in this chapter for more information.)

Specifying Subdirectories

Until now we have used the form *server*:*pathname* to specify a location in a map entry; you can also specify a subdirectory in the *location* field, using the syntax *server*:*pathname*:*directory*.

Assume you have a master map on host **oak** that contains the following entry:

```
/home    /etc/auto.home    -rw, intr, secure
```

Here **/etc/auto.home** is the name of an indirect map that contains the entries to be mounted under **/home**.

Below is the **auto.home** map:

```
#key        mount-options    location

cypress                      cypress:/home/cypress
poplar                       poplar:/home/poplar
pine                         pine:/export/pine
apple                        apple:/export/home
ivy                          ivy:/home/ivy
peach       -rw,nosuid       peach:/export/home
john                         willow:/home/willow:john
mary                         willow:/home/willow:mary
joe                          willow:/home/willow:joe
```

Look at the first entry in the map, and assume user Adam has his home directory on host **cypress**. If Adam has an entry in host **oak**'s password database specifying his home directory as **/home/cypress/adam**, then he can log in to **oak** and the automounter will mount (as **/tmp_mnt/home/cypress**) the directory **/home/cypress** residing on **cypress**. If one of the directories is **adam**, then Adam will be in his home directory. Because of the options specified in **oak**'s master map, Adam's home directory is mounted read/write, interruptible, and secure.

Now look at the last three entries in the indirect map. Note that these entries refer to the same resource on the same host (**/home/willow**). They also specify subdirectories in the *location* field (**john**, **mary**, and **joe**).

Now when a user logs in to host **oak** and requests access to the home directory **john** on host **willow**, the automounter mounts **willow:/home/willow**. It then places a symbolic link between **/tmp_mnt/home/willow/john** and **/home/john**.

If user Mary then tries to access her home directory from host **oak**, the automounter sees that **willow:/home/willow** is already mounted, so all it has to do is return the link between **/tmp_mnt/home/willow/mary** and **/home/mary**.

In general, it's a good idea to provide a *subdirectory* entry in the *location* field when different map entries refer to the same resource shared by the same server.

Using Substitutions

If you have a map with a lot of subdirectories specified, as in the following indirect map

```
#key      mount-options   location

john                      willow:/home/willow:john
mary                      willow:/home/willow:mary
joe                       willow:/home/willow:joe
able                      pine:/export/home:able
baker                     peach:/export/home:baker
          [. . .]
```

you should consider using string substitutions. The ampersand character (&) can be used to substitute the key wherever it appears. Using the ampersand, the above map would look like this:

```
#key      mount-options   location

john                      willow:/home/willow:&
mary                      willow:/home/willow:&
joe                       willow:/home/willow:&
able                      pine:/export/home:&
baker                     peach:/export/home:&
          [. . .]
```

If the name of the server is the same as the key itself, for instance:

```
#key      mount-options   location

willow                    willow:/home/willow
peach                     peach:/home/peach
pine                      pine:/home/pine
oak                       oak:/home/oak
poplar                    poplar:/home/poplar
          [. . .]
```

the use of the ampersand would result in:

```
#key        mount-options   location

willow                      &:/home/&
peach                       &:/home/&
pine                        &:/home/&
oak                         &:/home/&
poplar                      &:/home/&
           [. . .]
```

If all entries in a map have the same format, you can use the catch-all substitute character, the asterisk (*), as in the following example:

```
#key        mount-options   location

oak                         &:/export/&
poplar                      &:/export/&
*                           &:/home/&
```

The catch-all key (*) matches on everything that reaches this point in the map. Once the automounter reads the catch-all key, it does not continue to read the map.

Using Environment Variables

You can use the value of an environmental variable by prefixing a dollar sign (**$**) to its name. Braces can also be used to delimit the name of the variable from appended characters.

The environmental variables can be inherited from the environment or can be defined explicitly with the **-D** option on the command line. For example, if you want each client to mount client-specific files in the network in a replicated format, you could create a specific map for each client according to its name, so that the relevant line for host **oak** would be:

```
/mystuff    cypress,ivy,balsa:/export/hostfiles/oak
```

and for **willow**:

```
/mystuff    cypress,ivy,balsa:/export/hostfiles/willow
```

This scheme is viable within a small network, but maintaining this kind of host-specific map across a large network usually isn't feasible. The solution in this case would be to invoke the automounter with a command line similar to the following:

```
automount -D HOST=`uname -n` . . .
```

and have the entry in the direct map read:

```
/mystuff    cypress,ivy,balsa:/export/hostfiles/$HOST
```

Now each host would find its own files in the **mystuff** directory, and the task of centrally administering and distributing the maps becomes easier.

Invoking the Automounter

Once the maps are written, you should make sure that there are no equivalent entries in **/etc/vfstab**, and that all the entries in the maps refer to NFS shared resources.

The syntax to invoke the automounter is:

automount [-mnTv] [-D *name=value*] **[-M** *mount-directory*] **[-f** *master-file*] \
 [-t *sub-options*] [*directory map* [*–mount-options*]] . . .

See **automount**(1M) for a complete description of options. The sub-options are the same as those for NFS **mount**, with the exception of **bg** (background) and **fg** (foreground), which do not apply.

The default mount point for all mounts is **/tmp_mnt**. Like the other names, this is an arbitrary name. It can be changed when you enter the automount command with the **-M** option. For example,

```
automount -M /auto . . .
```

causes all mounts to happen under the directory **/auto**, which the automounter creates if it doesn't already exist.

The automounter can be invoked in one of the following ways:

1. You can specify all arguments to the automounter without reference to the master map:

   automount /net /home /etc/*indirect_map* \
   -rw,intr,secure /- /etc/*direct_map* **-ro,intr**

   /net is the directory/mount-point, **/home** is the mount point for the indirect map, **/etc/***indirect_map* is the location for the *indirect_map* that is to be used, **-rw,intr,secure** are the mount options for the *indirect_map*, **/-** means use a *direct_map*, **/etc/***direct_map* is the location for the *direct_map* that is to be used, and **-ro,intr** are the mount options for the *direct_map*.

2. You can specify all arguments in the master map and instruct the automounter to look in it for instructions:

   automount -f /etc/*master_map*

3. You can specify more mount points and maps in addition to those mentioned in the master map:

   automount -f /etc/*master_map* **/src /etc/auto.src -ro,soft**

4. You can nullify one of the entries in the master map (particularly useful if you are using a map that you cannot modify but does not meet the needs of your machine):

   automount -f /usr/lib/*master_map* /home –null

5. You can override an entry in the master map by specifying a different indirect map on the command line, as follows:

   ```
   automount -f /usr/lib/master_map /home \
           /myown/indirect_map -rw,intr
   ```

   This command tells the automounter to mount **/home** according to instructions in **/myown/***indirect_map*, not according to instructions in the indirect map specified in the master map.

Updating the Mount Table

If you use **umount** to unmount explicitly one of the automounted resources, have the automounter re-read the **/etc/mnttab** file to update the internal database used by the automounter. This can be accomplished by sending signal 1 to the automount daemon. First, find out the **automount**'s *pid* number by entering:

```
ps -ef | grep automount
```

The second field contains the *pid* number. Then enter the following command:

kill -1 *pid*

where *pid* is the automount process ID.

Modifying the Maps

You can modify the automounter maps at any time; however, the automounter looks at the master and indirect maps only when it is invoked. To make changes take effect, stop NFS operation and start it again (for example, you can exit and re-enter init state 3).

You do not have to exit and re-enter init state 3 to make changes to a direct map take effect. Changes to a direct map take effect the next time the automounter has to mount the modified entry.

Troubleshooting the Automounter

The following are error messages you may see if the automounter fails.

- *mapname*: **Not found**

  The required map cannot be located. This message is produced only when the **-v** (verbose) option is given. Check the spelling and pathname of the map name.

- **dir** *mountpoint* **must start with '/'**

  The automounter mount point must be given as full pathname. Check the spelling and pathname of the mount point.

- *mountpoint*: **Not a directory**

  The *mountpoint* exists but it is not a directory. Check the spelling and pathname of the mount point.

- **hierarchical mountpoint:** *mountpoint*

  The automounter will not allow itself to be mounted within an automounted directory. You will have to think of another strategy.

- **WARNING:** *mountpoint* **not empty!**

  The mount point is not an empty directory. This message is produced only when the **-v** (verbose) option is given, and it is only a warning. All it means is that the previous contents of *mountpoint* will not be accessible.

- **Can't mount** *mountpoint*: *reason*

  The automounter cannot mount itself at *mountpoint*. The *reason* should be self-explanatory.

- *hostname*:*filesystem* **already mounted on** *mountpoint*

  The automounter is attempting to mount a resource on a mount point, but the resource is already mounted on that mount point. This happens if an entry in **/etc/vfstab** is duplicated in an automounter map (either by accident or because the output of **mount -p** was redirected to **vfstab**). Delete one of the redundant entries.

- **WARNING:** *hostname*:*filesystem* **already mounted on** *mountpoint*

  The automounter is mounting itself on top of an existing mount point.

- **couldn't create** *directory*: *reason*

  The system could not create a directory. The *reason* should be self-explanatory.

- **bad entry in map** *mapname* "*map entry*"

  The *map entry* in map *mapname* is incorrect.

- **map** *mapname*, **key** *map key*: **bad**

  The map entry is malformed, and the automounter cannot interpret it. Recheck the entry; perhaps there are characters in it that need escaping.

- *hostname*: **exports:** *rpc_err*

  There is an error when the automounter tries to get a share list from *hostname*. This indicates a server or network problem.

- **host** *hostname* **not responding**

  A resource was trying to be mounted from host *hostname* while the host was down.

- *hostname*:*filesystem* **server not responding**

  A resource that is currently mounted from host *hostname* (that is down) has been accessed.

- **Mount of** *hostname*:*filesystem* **on** *mountpoint*: *reason*

  You will see these error messages after the automounter attempts to mount from *hostname* but gets no response or fails. This may indicate a server or network problem.

- *mountpoint* - *pathname* **from** *hostname*: **absolute symbolic link**

  When mounting a resource, the automounter has detected that *mountpoint* is an absolute symbolic link (beginning with `/`). The content of the link is *pathname*. This may have undesired consequences on the client; for example, the content of the link may be **/usr**.

- **Cannot create socket for broadcast rpc:** *rpc_err*
- **Many_cast select problem:** *rpc_err*
- **Cannot send broadcast packet:** *rpc_err*

- **`Cannot receive reply to many_cast:`** *rpc_err*

  All these error messages indicate problems attempting to "ping" servers for a replicated file system. This may indicate a network problem.

- **`trymany: servers not responding:`** *reason*

  No server in a replicated list is responding. This may indicate a network problem.

- **`Remount`** *hostname*`:`*filesystem* **`on`** *mountpoint*`:` **`server not responding`**

  An attempted remount after an unmount failed. This indicates a server problem.

- **`NFS server (pid`***n*`@`*mountpoint*`)` **`not responding still trying`**

  An NFS request made to the automount daemon with PID *n* serving *mountpoint* has timed out. The automounter may be overloaded temporarily, or dead. Wait a few minutes; if the condition persists, the easiest solution is to reboot the client. If you don't want to reboot, exit all processes that make use of automounted resources (or change to a non-automounted resource, in the case of a shell), kill the current automount process, and restart it again from the command line. If this fails, you must reboot.

25 The NFS Network Lock Manager

An Overview of the Network Lock Manager 25-1
The Locking Protocol 25-4
The Network Status Monitor 25-5

An Overview of the Network Lock Manager

NFS takes advantage of a network locking facility, accomplished via a user-level daemon called the Network Lock Manager. The Lock Manager supports the UNIX System V style of advisory and mandatory file and record locking—provided via `lockf()` and `fcntl()`.

Locking prevents multiple processes from modifying the same file at the same time, and allows cooperating processes to synchronize access to shared files. The user interfaces with the network locking service by way of the standard `fcntl()` system-call interface, and rarely requires any detailed knowledge of how it works. The kernel maps user calls to the `fcntl()` system call or the `lockf()` library call into RPC-based messages to the local lock manager. The fact that the file system may be spread across multiple machines is really not a complication—until a crash occurs.

All computers crash from time to time, and in an NFS environment, where multiple machines can have access to the same file at the same time, the process of recovering from a crash is necessarily more complex than in a non-network environment. First of all, locking is inherently stateful (it requires information about locks to be maintained on the server). If a server crashes, clients with locked files must be able to recover their locks. If a client crashes, its servers must release the locks held by processes running on the client. Second, to preserve NFS's overall transparency, the recovery of lost locks must not require the intervention of the applications themselves. This is accomplished as follows:

- Basic file access operations, such as read and write, use a stateless protocol (the NFS protocol). All interactions between NFS servers and clients are atomic—the server doesn't remember anything about its clients from one interaction to the next. In the case of a server crash, client applications will simply sleep until the server comes back up and their NFS operations can complete.
- Stateful services (those that require the server to maintain client information from one transaction to the next), such as the locking service, are not part of the NFS per se. They are separate services that use the status monitor to ensure that their implicit network state information remains consistent with the real state of the network. There are two specific state-related problems involved in providing the locking in a network context:

1. If the client has crashed, the lock can be held forever by the server.
2. If the server has crashed, it loses its state (including all its lock information) when it recovers.

The Network Lock Manager solves both of these problems by cooperating with the Network Status Monitor to ensure that it is notified of relevant machine crashes. Its own protocol then allows it to recover the lock information it needs when crashed machines recover.

The lock manager [**lockd**(1M)] and the status monitor [**statd**(1M)] are both network-service daemons—they run at user level, but they are essential to the kernel's ability to provide fundamental network services, and they are therefore run on all network machines. Like other network-service daemons—which provide, for example, remote-login services (**rlogind**)—they are best seen as extensions to the kernel, which, for reasons of space, efficiency, and organization, are implemented as daemons. Application programs that need a network service can either call the appropriate daemon directly with RPC/XDR, or use a system call to call the kernel. In this later case, the kernel will use RPC to call the daemon. The network daemons communicate among themselves with RPC. (See "The Locking Protocol" later in this section for some details about the lock manager protocol.)

It should be noted that the daemon-based approach to network services allows for tailoring by users who need customized services. It is possible, for example, for users to alter the lock manager to provide locking in a different style.

The following figure depicts the overall architecture of the locking service.

Figure 25-1: Architecture of the Locking Service Over NFS

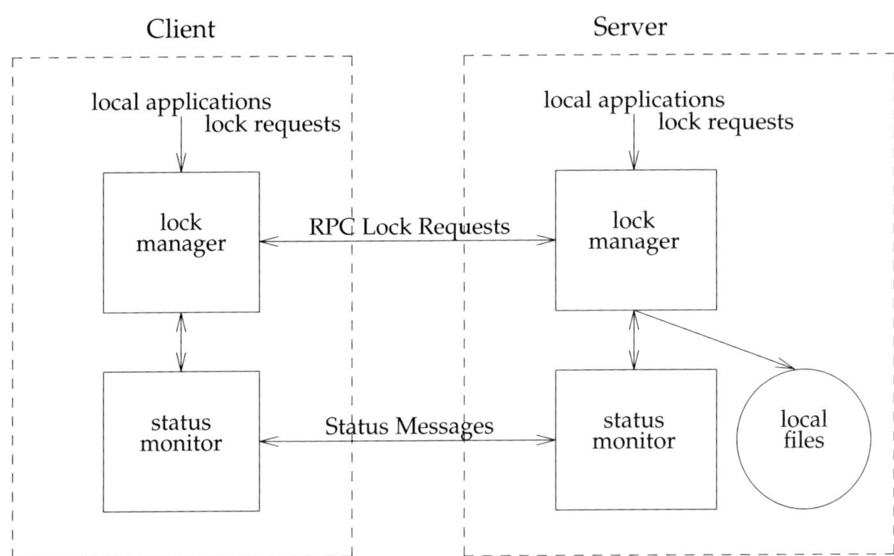

At each server site, a lock manager process accepts lock requests, made on behalf of client processes by a remote lock manager, or on behalf of local processes by the kernel. The client and server lock managers communicate with RPC calls. Upon receiving a remote lock request for a machine that it doesn't already hold a lock on, the lock manager registers its interest in that machine with the local status monitor, and waits for that monitor to notify it that the machine is up. The monitor continues to watch the status of registered machines, and notifies the lock manager if one of them is rebooted (after a crash). If the lock request is for a local file, the lock manager tries to satisfy it, and communicates back to the application along with the appropriate RPC path.

The crash recovery procedure is very simple. If the failure of a client is detected, the server releases the failed client's locks, on the assumption that the client application will request locks again as needed. If the recovery (and, by implication, the crash) of a server is detected, the client lock manger retransmits all the lock requests previously granted by the recovered server. This retransmitted information is used by the server to reconstruct its locking state.

The locking service, then, is essentially stateless. Or to be more precise, its state information is carefully circumscribed within a pair of system daemons that are set up for automatic, application-transparent crash recovery. If a server crashes, and thus loses its state, it expects that its clients will be notified of the crash and that they will send it the information it needs to reconstruct its state. The key in this approach is the status monitor, which the lock manager uses to detect both client and server failures.

For more information about the lock manager daemon, see the **lockd**(1M) manual page.

The Locking Protocol

There are four basic kernel-to-Lock Manager requests:

KLM_LOCK	Lock the specified record.
KLM_UNLOCK	Unlock the specified record.
KLM_TEST	Test if the specified record is locked.
KLM_CANCEL	Cancel an outstanding lock request.

Despite the fact that the network lock manager adheres to the `lockf()` and `fcntl()` semantics, there are a few subtle points about its behavior that deserve mention. These arise directly from the nature of the network:

- The first and most important point to be made about the lock manager's behavior has to do with crashes. When an NFS client goes down, the lock managers on all of its servers are notified by their status monitors, and they simply release their locks, on the assumption that the client will request them again when it wants them. When a server crashes, however, matters are different. Clients will wait for the server to come back up. When it does, the server's lock manager will give the client lock managers a grace period to submit lock reclaim requests; during this period, the server will accept only reclaim requests. The client status monitors will notify their respective lock managers when the server recovers. The default grace period is 45 seconds.
- It is possible that, after a server crash, a client will not be able to recover a lock that it had on a file on that server. This can happen for the simple reason that another process may have beaten the recovering application process to the lock. In this case the **SIGLOST** signal will be sent to the process (the default action for this signal is to kill the application).
- The local lock manager does not reply to the kernel lock request until the server lock manager has gotten back to it. Further, if the lock request is on a server new to the local lock manager, the lock manager registers its interest in that server with the local status monitor and waits for its reply. Thus, if either the status monitor or the server's lock manager are unavailable, the reply to a lock request for remote data is delayed until it becomes available.

For more information about UNIX System V locking, see the **fcntl**(2) and **lockf**(3C) manual pages.

The Network Status Monitor

The lock manager relies heavily on a service called the Network Status Monitor to maintain the inherently stateful locking service within the stateless NFS environment. However, the status monitor, implemented as **statd**(1M), is very general and can also be used to support other kinds of stateful network services and applications. Normally, crash recovery is one of the most difficult aspects of network application development, and requires a major design and installation effort. The status monitor simplifies crash recovery.

The status monitor works by providing a general framework for collecting network status information. Implemented as a daemon that runs on all network machines, it provides a simple protocol that allows applications to monitor easily the status of other machines. Its use improves overall robustness, and avoids situations in which applications running on different machines (or even on the same machine) come to disagree about the status of a site—a potentially dangerous situation that can lead to inconsistencies in many applications.

Applications using the status monitor do so by registering with it the machines that they are interested in. The monitor then tracks the status of those machines, and when one of them crashes (actually, when one of them recovers from a crash), it notifies the interested applications to that effect. Then they take whatever actions are necessary to reestablish a consistent state.

This approach provides the following advantages:

- Only applications that use stateful services must pay the overhead—in time and in code—of dealing with the status monitor.
- The implementation of stateful network applications is eased, since the status monitor shields application developers from the complexity of the network.

For more information about the status monitor, see the **statd**(1M) manual page.

26 Using the NFS sysadm Interface

NFS sysadm Interface 26-1

Procedure 1: Set Up Network File System 26-2

Procedure 2: Start/Stop Network File System 26-3

Procedure 3: Local Resource Sharing 26-4

Procedure 4: Remote Resource Mounting 26-5

NFS sysadm Interface

UNIX SVR4.2 provides you with an interface, called **sysadm**, that lets you set up and administer NFS through a series of menus. The **sysadm** interface not only lets you enter basic NFS configuration information, but it also acts as a tutorial by introducing and explaining key NFS concepts. Once you access a **sysadm** menu, help screens provide you with background information and explanations regarding menu selections. Access the help screens by using the HELP function key; use the CANCEL function key to exit the help mode. Continue making menu selections until you complete the particular task.

NOTE For instruction on moving through the interface, selecting menu options, and so on, see the tutorial in "Using the sysadm Interface" in *Basic System Administration*.

Here are the NFS procedures you can perform through the **sysadm** menu interface.

Procedure 1	Set Up Network File System To perform initial NFS setup.
Procedure 2	Start/Stop Network File System To start and stop NFS and check if it is currently running.
Procedure 3	Local Resource Sharing To manage the local resources you make available to other machines.
Procedure 4	Remote Resource Mounting To manage remote resources made available to your machine.

Procedure 1: Set Up Network File System

This procedure is used to set up NFS on your machine. When the procedure is done, you will have completed everything needed to run NFS on your system. This procedure assumes NFS software is installed on your system, as well as all the software utilities on which NFS depends. For information about installation, see UNIX SVR4.2 *Release Notes*.

To access the first menu of the NFS menu interface, do the following:

1. Log in.
2. Type **`sysadm network_services`**.
3. Select **`remote_files`**; then select **`setup`**, and then **`nfs`** to bring you to the following screen:

```
                    Initial Network File System Setup

start       - Start Network File System Operations
share       - Share(s) Local Resources via Network File System
mount       - Mount(s) Remote Resources via Network File System
```

You should execute each of the tasks in the order listed. Continue making interactive menu selections until the job is done. Remember, the HELP function key will provide you with help messages along the way.

Procedure 2: Start/Stop Network File System

This procedure is used to start and stop NFS. It's also used to determine if NFS is running.

1. Type **sysadm network_services**.
2. Select **remote_files**; then select **specific_ops**, then **nfs**, and then **control**. You are now at the following screen:

```
                    Network File System Control

check_status     - Check Status of NFS File Service
start            - Start Network File System Operations
stop             - Stop Network File System Operations
```

Select **check_status** to determine whether or not NFS file service is running.

Select **start** to start NFS, or **stop** to stop NFS.

Remember, the HELP function key will provide you with help messages along the way.

Procedure 3: Local Resource Sharing

This procedure allows you to make your local resources available or unavailable (share/unshare) to remote systems, via NFS. You can arrange this to happen automatically when NFS is started, or immediately during a work session. You can also modify the options by which your local resources are shared. Finally, this procedure enables you to list your local resources that are currently shared via NFS.

1. Type **`sysadm network_services`**.
2. Select **`remote_files`**; then select **`local_resources`**. You are now at the following screen:

```
                    Local Resource Sharing Management

list          - List Automatically-Currently Shared Local Resources
modify        - Modify Automatic-Current Sharing of Local Resources
share         - Share Local Resources Automatically-Immediately
unshare       - Stop Automatic-Current Sharing of Local Resources
```

Select **`list`**, then **`nfs`** to list the local resources currently shared by NFS. Select **`modify`**, then **`nfs`** to modify sharing permissions of local resources via NFS. Select **`share`**, then **`nfs`** to share local resources via NFS. Select **`unshare`**, then **`nfs`** to unshare local resources currently shared via NFS.

Remember, the HELP function key will provide you with help messages along the way. Also see the chapters "Sharing and Mounting NFS Resources Explicitly" and "Obtaining NFS Information" for more information about these tasks.

Procedure 4: Remote Resource Mounting

This procedure allows you to make remote resources available or unavailable (mount/unmount) to your local computer, via NFS. With this procedure, you can specify resources to be mounted or unmounted automatically, whenever NFS operation stops and starts, or you can mount and unmount a resource immediately during a work session. You can also modify the options by which remote resources are mounted on your local computer. Finally, this procedure enables you to list the resources of remote systems that are currently available, via NFS, to your machine.

1. Type **`sysadm network_services`**.
2. Select **`remote_files`**, then select **`remote_resources`**. You are now at the following screen:

```
                    Remote Resource Access Management

list         - Lists Automatically-Currently Mounted Remote Resources
modify       - Modifies Automatic-Current Mounting of Remote Resources
mount        - Mounts Remote Resources Automatically-Immediately
unmount      - Terminates Automatic-Current Mounting of Remote Resources
```

Select **`list`**, then **`nfs`** to list remote resources mounted via NFS. Select **`modify`**, then **`nfs`** to modify mount permissions of remote resources. Select **`mount`**, then **`nfs`** to mount remote resources. Select **`unmount`**, then **`nfs`** to terminate mounting of remote resources currently shared via NFS.

Remember, the HELP function key will provide you with help messages along the way. Also see the chapters "Sharing and Mounting NFS Resources Explicitly" and "Obtaining NFS Information" for details about these tasks.

Setting Up RPC

27 RPC Administration

Introduction to RPC Administration 27-1

RPC Administration Files 27-2
RPC and Name-to-Address Mapping 27-2
System RC File /etc/rc2.d/S75rpc 27-2
The /etc/publickey File 27-2
The SRPC_DOMAIN Variable 27-3

Secure RPC Overview 27-4
RPC Domains 27-5

Secure RPC Administration 27-6
Establishing Secure RPC Domains 27-6
Master /etc/publickey File 27-7
- Adding RPC Users with the newkey Command 27-7
- Network Passwords and the chkey Command 27-8

Troubleshooting Note 27-9

Introduction to RPC Administration

RPC administration consists of configuring administration files that:

- Establish name-to-address mapping relationships
- Start server daemons at boot time
- Prompt users for a network password at login (secure RPC)
- Edit a master machine **/etc/publickey** file that determines who can access secure RPC services (secure RPC)
- Start ypdaemons

Servers are started at boot time by editable system RC scripts. The file **/etc/profile** is edited to call **keylogin** to query for a network password at login time.

NIS is currently the recommended default mechanism for administering secure RPC (see "Network Information Service" for more information).

RPC Administration Files

RPC and Name-to-Address Mapping

Name-to-address mapping must be in effect for RPC (secure or otherwise) to work. Refer to "Name-to-Address Mapping" in "Network Services" for name-to-address mapping administrative procedures.

System RC File /etc/rc2.d/S75rpc

RPC servers can be started at system boot time. When the system comes up in init state 2, all of the scripts in **/etc/rc2.d** are executed. One of these scripts, **/etc/rc2.d/S75rpc**, starts the RPC servers.

The system administrator can edit the script to start additional servers.

The server **keyserv** must also be running for secure RPC to work properly. Administrators may wish to edit the **/etc/rc2.d/S75rpc** script and remove the comment character (#) for the **keyserv** lines so that **keyserv** will start at boot time. If not, **keyserv** will have to be started manually.

The /etc/publickey File

Secure RPC information is kept in this file, which is controlled by a domain master server. For each secure RPC user known to a master, this file contains:

- operating system name
- user ID
- RPC domain name
- public key
- secret key

The triple (*operating system, user ID, domain*) forms a unique key into this database of public/secret key pairs that are required by the RPC built-in security protocol.

The user ID field in `/etc/publickey` may also be a host name. This allows more than one `root` user per domain.

The SRPC_DOMAIN Variable

All machines supporting secure RPC must have what is known as a secure RPC domain name. By default, a machine's secure RPC domain name is null and (because it is null), secure RPC will not work on the machine.

A domain name can be set using the **domainname**(1M) command, but it will not be remembered across reboots. For preservation of the name across reboots, administrators need to edit their **/etc/conf/pack.d/name/space.c** file to set the **SRPC_DOMAIN** tunable to their desired secure RPC domain name. For example, to change a machine's domain name from null to **finance**, the system administrator would find the line:

```
#define SRPC_DOMAIN=""
```

in **/etc/conf/pack.d/name/space.c** and change it to

```
#define SRPC_DOMAIN="finance"
```

After this is done, the kernel must be rebuilt and the system rebooted for the change to take effect. To rebuild the kernel and reboot your system, type:

```
/etc/conf/bin/idbuild -B
cd /; shutdown -y -g0 -i6
```

The above steps will rebuild the kernel, and reboot your system immediately. For more information on the **idbuild** command, see **idbuild**(1M). For more information on the **shutdown** command, see **shutdown**(1M).

Secure RPC Overview

There is a security protocol, based on DES encryption, built into the RPC package. Remote programs that use secure RPC expect client users to have a public/secret key entry in a shared master **/etc/publickey** file. Access to secure RPC programs is controlled by the **keyserv** daemon which accesses the **/etc/publickey** file when users invoke **keylogin**. One **/etc/publickey** database exists for each secure RPC domain.

Secure RPC users must be given entries in **/etc/publickey** by the RPC administrator before they can use secure RPC programs.

In addition, the administrator of every client machine should edit **/etc/profile** to remove the comment character that has commented out the **keylogin** command; in this way, **keylogin** will be invoked for each user at login time. Thereafter secure RPC commands and programs can be used in the same way ordinary commands and programs are used.

Every machine that allows use of secure RPC is a client machine.

One of the secure RPC commands, **chkey**, allows users to change their secure RPC passwords.

The **.profile** files of secure RPC users should be set up to call **keylogout**(1) automatically at the end of a terminal session. For example:

```
# .profile code fragment

trap "keylogout" 0
```

A secure RPC user should *always* execute **keylogout** before logging off the system. Failure to do so is a serious security infraction.

[See **sh**(1) for details on use of **trap** for executing commands at the end of a terminal session.]

NOTE The presence of secure RPC has no effect on remote programs that do not use the secure protocol. Such programs work normally, whether or not the user is also a secure RPC user.

RPC Domains

All machines using secure RPC must have a secure RPC domain name. One machine per domain acts as master server for the domain. The **domainname**(1M) command is used to set a machine's domain name. The machine's **SRPC_DOMAIN** tunable should also be set to the secure RPC domain name. Otherwise, the name is forgotten across reboots. See "The SRPC_DOMAIN Variable" for information on setting the *SRPC_DOMAIN* variable.

Secure RPC identifies users using a triple (*operating system*, *uid*, *domain*). Thus, users may have multiple registrations with RPC, provided all such triples are unique. For example, a user may belong to more than one *domain*, with *operating system* and *uid* identical for each.

Secure RPC Administration

In general, administering secure RPC is accomplished as follows:

1. A domain name is chosen (for multiple domains, more than one domain name is chosen). Secure RPC domain names are set on participating machines, using the **domainname**(1M) command, and the **SRPC_DOMAIN** tunable is set to the secure RPC domain name (See "The SRPC_DOMAIN Variable").
2. For each user or host to be allowed access to secure RPC services, domain master machine administrators add entries to their master **/etc/publickey** file.
3. **keyserv** and NIS daemons are started.
4. Administrators start **keyserv**, either manually or by means of a boot-time script.
5. The system administrators of client machines remove the comment character that has commented out the **keylogin** command from their machine's **/etc/profile** and they direct their secure RPC users to add a trap to their *$HOME*/**.profile** so that **keylogout** will be called when their sessions end.

The following sections detail this procedure.

When slave servers are in use, master servers may have clients as well as slaves.

Establishing Secure RPC Domains

For many networked systems, a single secure RPC domain will suffice. Administrators are notified of the domain name, and they use the **domainname**(1M) command to establish that name as the secure RPC domain name for their machine. For example, to set the a machine's domain name to **research**:

```
# domainname research
```

For networked systems having multiple domains, the process is the same, except that two or more different domains will be in use in the network.

Administrators should also set their machine's **SRPC_DOMAIN** tunable to their secure RPC domain name, as described in "The SRPC_DOMAIN Variable". If this is not done, the domain name will be forgotten across reboots.

A machine can be part of only one domain at any given time. The decision to use single or multiple domains depends on need. In general, the advantages of multiple domains include:

- Duplicate operating system/user ID pairs can be using secure RPC (provided they are in different domains).
- Access to secure RPC programs can be made selective, if some programs are not available to all domains.

The primary advantage of using a single domain is simplified administration.

Master /etc/publickey File

The **/etc/publickey** file is a database of public/secret key pairs. The file contains pairs for users and hosts authorized to use secure RPC. Remote procedures that use the DES authentication protocol (built into the RPC package) expect to find public/secret key pairs (for the processes that call them) in **/etc/publickey**. A system administrator must therefore add an entry to **/etc/publickey** for each user/host to be granted access to secure RPC resources. A single **/etc/publickey** file (on a master server or on a collection of master and slave servers) is used and shared over the network by machines having access to the file.

Secure RPC programs are not required to be hosted by the same machine that hosts the master **/etc/publickey** file. The master **/etc/publickey** machine is not necessarily the server for *any* of the secure RPC application programs or commands.

Adding RPC Users with the newkey Command

On the domain master server machine (only), the system administrator grants a user or host access to secure RPC in that domain by adding an entry to the **/etc/publickey** file. This is accomplished using the **newkey**(1M) command.

The **newkey** command must be executed on the master server machine by the RPC administrator. Furthermore, prior to using **newkey**, the machine's secure RPC domain name must have been set.

For example, to add an entry for the user **alice** the system administrator would enter the following on the master server:

```
master# newkey -u alice
password: password
Re-enter new passwd: password
```

The **-u** option signifies that **alice** is a user ID. The domain field for this entry is the domain of the master server on which this command is executed. This is the only way that user **alice** can get access to this particular secure RPC domain.

The **newkey** command can also be used with the **-h** option to give access to hosts, that is, to **root** users on hosts on the network:

```
master# newkey -h client
password: password
Re-enter new passwd: password
```

Within the domain of secure RPC users having entries in a master **/etc/publickey** file, all user names and IDs must be unique. The **-h** option is provided to allow more than one **root** user to have access to secure RPC. Because **root** users on different machines have the same name and ID, it would be impossible for more than one of them to be a secure RPC user. The **-h** option solves this problem, allowing **root** users to use their unique machine name and address as a user name and ID for RPC purposes.

Network Passwords and the chkey Command

If you are using NIS, client users should be notified of their passwords when they are given access to secure RPC. Their **.profile** files should be modified to execute **keylogout** when they log off.

Users are prompted for their secure RPC passwords when **keylogin** is executed by **/etc/profile**.

For example, a user can set up a password as follows:

```
master$ chkey
New password: password
Retype passwd: password
```

Troubleshooting Note

If all administration procedures have been performed correctly and trouble occurs, suspect that an RPC server daemon process (in particular, **rpcbind**) may not have been started, may have died, or may have been killed.

Setting Up NIS

28 Network Information Service

Introduction to NIS — 28-1

What Is NIS? — 28-1
The NIS Elements — 28-1
The NIS Environment — 28-2
- The NIS Domain — 28-3
- NIS Machine Types — 28-3
- NIS Maps — 28-5

Implementing the NIS — 28-7

Establishing the NIS Domain — 28-7
Preparing the Maps — 28-8
- The publickey Map — 28-9
- Other Maps — 28-10

Making the Maps — 28-12
- The Default Makefile — 28-12
- Modifying the Makefile — 28-14

Setting the Master Server — 28-16
Starting Daemons in the Master Server — 28-17
Setting Slave Servers — 28-17
Starting Slave Server Daemons — 28-19
Setting up an NIS Client — 28-19

Administering NIS Maps — 28-21

Updating Existing Maps — 28-21
- Modifying Standard Maps — 28-21
- Creating and Modifying Non-Standard Maps — 28-22

Propagating an NIS Map — 28-24
- Using crontab with ypxfr — 28-24
- Using Shell Scripts with ypxfr — 28-25
- Directly Invoking ypxfr — 28-26

- Logging ypxfr's Activities 28-26

Adding New NIS Maps to the Makefile 28-26

Adding a New NIS Server to the Original Set 28-28

Changing a Map's Master Server 28-29

Summary of NIS-Related Commands 28-31

Fixing NIS Problems 28-33

Debugging an NIS Client 28-33
- Hanging Commands on the Client 28-33
- NIS Is Unavailable 28-35
- ypbind Crashes 28-35
- ypwhich Displays Are Inconsistent 28-36

Debugging an NIS Server 28-37
- Servers Have Different Versions of an NIS Map 28-37
- ypserv Crashes 28-38

Turning off NIS 28-40

Introduction to NIS

This chapter explains how to administer the Network Information Service (NIS)—a distributed network lookup service formerly known as Yellow Pages.

Information in the chapter includes:

- The NIS environment
- Setting up NIS servers
- Setting up an NIS client
- Creating and updating maps
- NIS-related commands
- Fixing NIS problems

What Is NIS?

NIS is a distributed name service designed to meet the administrative needs of large, diverse, and evolving computing communities. It is a mechanism for identifying and locating objects and resources accessible to the community. It provides a uniform, network-wide storage and retrieval method that is both protocol– and media–independent.

By running NIS, the system administrator can distribute administrative databases (maps) among a variety of machines and can update those databases from a centralized location in an automatic and reliable fashion, ensuring that all clients share in the same databases in a consistent manner throughout the network. Furthermore, the use of the NIS "publickey" map permits running secure RPC and secure NFS across the network of machines.

The NIS Elements

The NIS service is composed of the following elements:

- domains
- maps

- daemons:
  - **ypserv** — server process [see **ypserv**(1M)]
  - **ypbind ypbind** — binding process [for **ypbind**, see **ypserv**(1M)]
  - **ypupdated** — server for changing map entries [see **ypupdated**(1M)]
- utilities:
  - **ypcat** — lists data in a map [see **ypcat**(1)]
  - **ypwhich** — lists name of NIS server [see **ypwhich**(1)]
  - **ypmatch** — finds a key in a map [see **ypmatch**(1)]
  - **ypinit** — builds and installs an NIS database, or initializes a client [see **ypinit**(1M)]
  - **yppoll** — gets protocol version from server [see **yppoll**(1M)]
  - **yppush** — propagates data from master to slave NIS server [see **yppush**(1M)]
  - **ypset** — sets binding to a particular server [see **ypset**(1M)]
  - **ypxfr** — transfers data from master to slave NIS server [see **ypxfr**(1M)]
  - **makedbm** — creates **dbm** file for an NIS map [see **makedbm**(1M)]

The NIS Environment

NIS service is based on information contained in NIS maps. Maps are non-ASCII administrative files, which usually derive from ASCII files traditionally found in the `/etc` directory. Each NIS map has a mapname used by programs to access it. On a network running NIS, at least one NIS server per domain maintains a set of NIS maps for other hosts in the domain to query.

The service is mediated by the daemons **ypserv** and **ypbind**, and updates are facilitated by the daemon **ypupdated**.

The NIS Domain

An NIS domain is an arbitrary name that designates which machines will make use of a common set of maps. Maps for each domain are located in separate directories, `/var/yp/`*domainname*, on the NIS server (see "NIS Servers"). For example, the maps for machines that belong to the domain **`accounting`** will be located in the directory **`/var/yp/accounting`** on their corresponding NIS server.

No restrictions are placed on whether a machine can belong to a given domain. Assignment to a domain is done at the local level of each machine by the system administrator logged in as the NIS administrator. See "Establishing the NIS Domain" for instructions on how to establish the NIS domain.

NIS Machine Types

There are three types of NIS machines:

- master server
- slave server
- client

Any machine can be an NIS client, but only machines with disks should be NIS servers, either master or slave. Servers are generally also clients.

NIS Servers

By definition, an NIS server is a machine with a disk storing a set of NIS maps that it makes available to network hosts. The NIS server does not have to be the same machine as the file server, unless, of course, it is the only machine on the network with a disk.

NIS servers come in two varieties, master and slave. The machine designated as NIS master server contains the master set of maps that are updated as necessary. If you have only one NIS server on your network, designate it as the master server. Otherwise, designate the machine you think will be best able to propagate NIS updates with the least performance degradation.

You can designate additional NIS servers on your network as slave servers. A slave server has a complete copy of the master's set of NIS maps: Whenever the master server's maps are updated, it propagates the updates among the slave servers. The existence of slave servers allows the system administrator to distribute evenly the load implied in answering NIS requests. A stylized representation of the relationship between master, slaves and clients is shown in Figure 28-1:

Figure 28-1: Relationships between Master, Slave(s) and Client(s) Machines

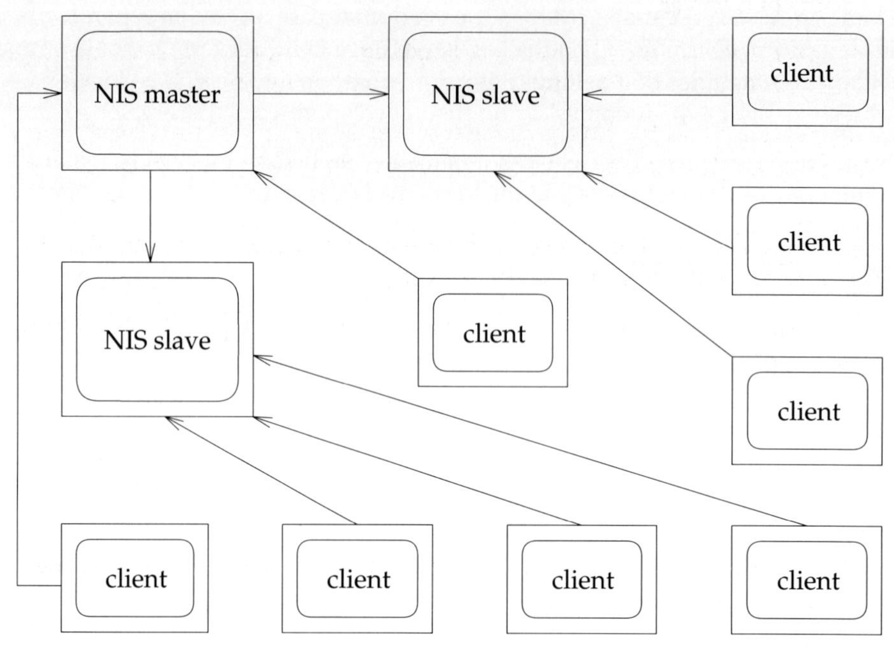

A server may be a master in regard to one map, and a slave in regard to another. However, randomly assigning maps to NIS servers can cause a great deal of administrative confusion. You are strongly urged to make a single server the master for all the maps you create within a single domain. The examples in this chapter assume that one server is the master for all maps in the domain.

NIS Clients

NIS clients run processes that request data from maps on the servers. Clients do not care which server is the master in a given domain, since all NIS servers have the same information. The distinction between master and slave server only applies to where you make the updates.

NIS Binding

NIS clients get information from the NIS server through the binding process. Here is what happens during NIS binding:

1. A program running on the client (that is, a client process) and needing information that is normally provided by an NIS map, asks **ypbind** for the name of a server.
2. **ypbind** looks in the file **/var/yp/binding/***domainname***/ypservers** to get a list of the servers for the domain (see "Establishing the NIS Domain").
3. **ypbind** initiates binding to the first server on the list. If the server does not respond, it tries the next, and so on until it finds a server or exhausts the list.
4. **ypbind** tells the client process which server to talk to. The client then forwards the request directly to the server.
5. The **ypserv** daemon on the NIS server handles the request by consulting the appropriate map.
6. **ypserv** then sends the requested information back to the client.

The binding between a client and a server can change with the network's load as the service tries to compensate for current activity; that is, a client may get information from one server at one time and from another server at a different time.

To find out which NIS server is currently providing service to a client, use the **ypwhich** command

ypwhich *hostname*

where **hostname** is the name of the client. If no **hostname** is mentioned, **ypwhich** defaults to the local host (the machine on which the command is entered).

NIS Maps

NIS maps are one type of implementation of UNIX SVR4.2 administrative databases. (The other implementation is the ASCII files generally found in the **/etc** directory.) Information in NIS maps is organized in a format similar to System V Release 4 **dbm** files. The manual pages for **ypfiles**(4) and **dbm**(3) completely explain the **dbm** file format. Input to **makedbm** must be in the form of *key/value* pairs, where *key* is the first word of each line and *value* is whatever follows in that line. The input can be from a file or from standard input (as when modified through a script; see "Making the Maps"). After passing through **makedbm** the data is collected in non-ASCII form in two files, **mapname.dir** and **mapname.pag**, both in the **/var/yp/***domainname* directory.

The pairs of keys and values are preserved in the NIS maps, so programs can use the keys to look up the values.

The UNIX SVR4.2 package includes a default NIS map, **publickey.byname**, and a default makefile for that map.

Implementing the NIS

Implementation of the NIS service consists of the following steps:

1. Establishing the domain(s) for your machines
2. Writing or preparing the maps in ASCII form
3. Running the ASCII files through **makedbm**
4. Setting the master server
5. Starting daemons in the master server
6. Setting the slave server(s)
7. Starting daemons in the slave server(s)
8. Initializing the clients

The following sections describe each of these steps.

Establishing the NIS Domain

Before you configure machines as NIS servers or clients, you must prepare the NIS domain by:

- Giving it a name.

  A domain name can be up to 256 characters long. However, because your **/var/yp** directory may reside in an s5 file system, and the domain name you select may be longer than the 14-character limit that s5 imposes on filenames, the program **ypinit** makes a shortened domain name and stores it in the **/var/yp/aliases** file. The name of the database directory **/var/yp/***domainname* will correspond to the shortened alias for the domain name.

- Designating which machines will serve or be served by the NIS domain.

  Once you have chosen a domain name, make a list of network hosts that will give or receive NIS service within that domain.

- Determining which machine should be master server (you can always change this at a later date).

- Listing which hosts on the network, if any, are to be slave servers.
- Finally, listing all the hosts that are to be NIS clients.

You will probably want all hosts in your network's administrative domain to receive NIS services, although this is not strictly necessary. If this is the case, give the NIS domain the same name as the network administrative domain.

Log in as the NIS administrator to all servers, whether master or slave(s), and all clients of the NIS domain. There are three ways to establish a domain on your machine. A temporary method is to enter the following command

domainname *name*

where *name* is the name of the domain. A better way is to add

domainname *name*

after the

```
'start')
```

line in the **/etc/rc2.d/S75rpc** file, which initiates NIS service.

A third method is to edit the **/etc/conf/pack.d/name/space.c** file and assign a domain name to the **SRPC_DOMAIN** parameter as follows:

SRPC_DOMAIN="*name***"**

where *name* is the name of the domain.

After this is done, the kernel must be rebuilt and the system rebooted for the change to take effect. To rebuild the kernel and reboot your system, type:

```
/etc/conf/bin/idbuild -B
cd /; shutdown -y -g0 -i6
```

The above steps will rebuild the kernel, and reboot your system immediately. For more information on the **idbuild** command, see **idbuild**(1M). For more information on the **shutdown** command, see **shutdown**(1M).

Preparing the Maps

System V Release 4.2 enables a site to use public key encryption as one of the methods for providing secure networking. If you are planning on running secure RPC or secure NFS, you may use NIS [**newkey**(1), **chkey**(1)] to administer the **/etc/publickey** file.

The publickey Map

This file consists of three fields in the following format:

user name *user public key* : *user secret key*

where *user name* may be the name of a user or of a machine, *user public key* is that key in hexadecimal notation, and *user secret key* is that key also in hexadecimal notation.

Since nobody expects you to be conversant in hexadecimal notation, the program **newkey** is provided to make things easier. Simply become NIS administrator at the master server and invoke **newkey** for a given user by typing

newkey -u *username*

or for the NIS administrator on a given host machine by typing the following:

newkey -h *hostname*

At the prompt enter the appropriate secure RPC or network password. The program will then create a new public/secret key pair in **/etc/publickey,** encrypted with the secure RPC or network password of the given user.

Users can later modify their own entries by using the program **chkey**. The user simply types:

chkey

on the server and then responds to prompts from the command.

The **keyserv** daemon must be running before issuing the **newkey** or **chkey** command. To see if the **keyserv** daemon is running, enter:

```
ps -eaf | grep keyserv
```

and check for output similar to the following:

```
root  2731     1  0 14:20:23 ?        0:00 /usr/sbin/keyserv
```

If the **keyserv** daemon is not running, secure RPC may not be properly set up. See "System RC File /etc/rc2.d/S75rpc" in "RPC Administration" for more information about **keyserv**.

A typical **chkey** session (shown in Figure 28-2) would look like this:

Figure 28-2: Sample chkey Session

```
willow$ chkey
Generating new key for username
Password: user enters password
Retype password: password
Sending key change request to server...
Done.
willow$
```

Note that in order for **newkey** and **chkey** to run properly, the daemon **ypupdated** must be running in the master server. If it is not running at this point, enter the following:

/usr/lib/netsvc/yp/ypupdated

You must also make sure that the **/etc/rc2.d/S75rpc** contains the lines

```
if [ -f /usr/lib/netsvc/yp/ypupdated -a -d /var/yp/`domainname` ]
then
        /usr/lib/netsvc/yp/ypupdated > /dev/console>&1
fi
```

The **ypupdated** daemon consults the file **/var/yp/updaters** for information about which maps should be updated and how to go about it. In the case of the **publickey** map, changes to **/etc/publickey** affected through **newkey** or **chkey** are mediated by **/usr/sbin/udpublickey**.

Other Maps

Other maps do not need the assistance of special programs for their creation or modification. For instance, if you are planning on having distributed automounter files, all you have to do is write the automounter files as they would reside in a machine's **/etc** directory. (For more information on the automounter, see "Using the NFS Automounter".)

A typical **auto.master** map (Figure 28-3) would contain the following:

Figure 28-3: Typical auto.master Map

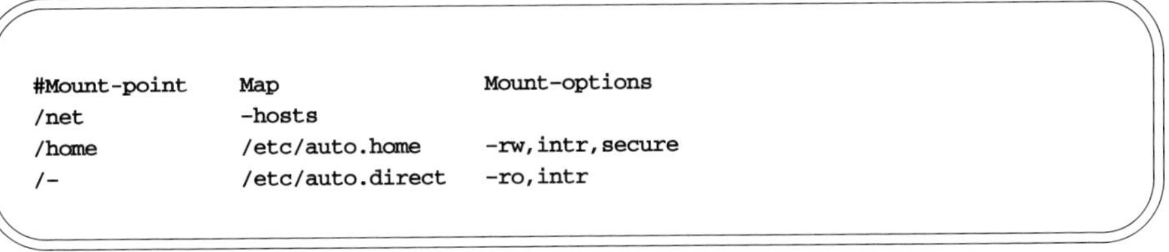

```
#Mount-point    Map                 Mount-options
/net            -hosts
/home           /etc/auto.home      -rw,intr,secure
/-              /etc/auto.direct    -ro,intr
```

A typical **auto.home** map (Figure 28-4) would contain the following:

Figure 28-4: Typical auto.home Map

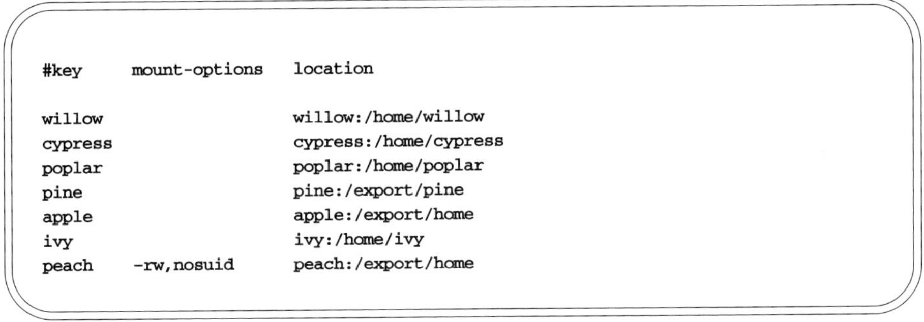

```
#key      mount-options   location

willow                    willow:/home/willow
cypress                   cypress:/home/cypress
poplar                    poplar:/home/poplar
pine                      pine:/export/pine
apple                     apple:/export/home
ivy                       ivy:/home/ivy
peach     -rw,nosuid      peach:/export/home
```

A typical **/etc/auto.direct** map is shown in Figure 28-5.

Figure 28-5: Typical `/etc/auto.direct` Map

```
/usr/local \
                    /bin     -ro,soft   ivy:/export/local/sun3 \
                    /share   -ro,soft   ivy:/export/local/share \
                    /src     -ro,soft   ivy:/export/local/src
/usr/man                     -ro,soft   oak:/usr/man \
                                        rose:/usr/man \
                                        willow:/usr/man
/usr/games                   -ro,soft   peach:/usr/games
/usr/spool/news              -ro,soft   pine:/usr/spool/news
/usr/frame                   -ro,soft   redwood:/usr/frame1.3 \
                                        balsa:/export/frame
```

A full explanation of what these files mean can be found in "Using the NFS Automounter".

Note that these files are all in the directory **/etc**. These are not the maps, these are the files that you will use in order to make the maps.

The automounter recognizes the notation + at the beginning of a line as an indication to consult the corresponding NIS map; this notation is permissible in a client's file in the **/etc** directory.

Making the Maps

Your next step, after creating the maps, is to convert these ASCII files into the non-ASCII files in **dbm** format that the NIS service expects. The prescribed method is to use the **make** program through a permanent Makefile.

The Default Makefile

A makefile is provided in the directory **/var/yp**. It contains the commands needed to transform **/etc/publickey** into the desired **dbm** format and is similar to the following:

```
#       Copyright (c) 1990, 1991, 1992 UNIX System Laboratories, Inc.
#       Copyright (c) 1984, 1985, 1986, 1987, 1988, 1989, 1990 AT&T
#         All Rights Reserved

#       THIS IS UNPUBLISHED PROPRIETARY SOURCE CODE OF
#       UNIX System Laboratories, Inc.
#       The copyright notice above does not evidence any
#       actual or intended publication of such source code.

#ident  "@(#)/var/yp/Makefile.sl 1.4 SVR4.2 04/09/92 2534 USL"
#ident  "$Header: Makefile 1.2 91/06/25 $"

#++++++++++++++++++++++++++++++++++++++++++++++++++++++++++
#       PROPRIETARY NOTICE (Combined)
#
# This source code is unpublished proprietary information
# constituting, or derived under license from AT&T's UNIX(r) System V.
# In addition, portions of such source code were derived from Berkeley
# 4.3 BSD under license from the Regents of the University of
# California.
#
#
#       Copyright Notice
#
# Notice of copyright on this source code product does not indicate
#  publication.
#
#       (c) 1986,1987,1988.1989  Sun Microsystems, Inc
#       (c) 1983,1984,1985,1986,1987,1988,1989  AT&T.
#          All rights reserved.
#
#
#       make.script 1.26 88/10/05 SMI
#
# Set the following variable to "-b" to have yp servers use the domain name
# resolver for hosts not in the current domain.
#B=-b
B=
SHELL=/sbin/sh
DIR =/etc
DOM = `domainname`
NOPUSH = ""
YPDIR=/usr/sbin
YPDBDIR=/var/yp
YPPUSH=$(YPDIR)/yppush
MAKEDBM=$(YPDIR)/makedbm
ALIASFILE=$(YPDBDIR)/aliases
ALIAS=$(YPDIR)/ypalias

all:  publickey
```

(continued on next page)

```
setup:

publickey.time: $(DIR)/publickey
	-@if [ -f $(DIR)/publickey ]; then \
		echo publickey.byname `$(ALIAS) publickey.byname` >> $(ALIASFILE); \
		sort $(ALIASFILE) | uniq > .ypaliases; \
		cp .ypaliases $(ALIASFILE); \
		rm .ypaliases; \
		for i in $(DOM); do \
			sed "/^#/d" < $(DIR)/publickey | \
			$(MAKEDBM) - $(YPDBDIR)/`$(ALIAS) -d $$i`/`$(ALIAS) publickey.byname`; \
		done; \
		> publickey.time; \
		echo "updated publickey"; \
		if [ ! $(NOPUSH) ]; then \
			$(YPPUSH) publickey.byname; \
			echo "pushed publickey"; \
		else \
			: ; \
		fi \
	else \
		echo "couldn't find $(DIR)/publickey"; \
	fi

publickey: publickey.time
```

This makefile first creates an entry in **/var/yp/aliases** which translates the mapname into a shorter name to be used for the **dbm** file name (this is done to accommodate the 14-character limitation that s5 file systems impose on file names.) Then it eliminates all lines in **/etc/publickey** that start with a **#** (that is, comment lines) and passes the rest to **makedbm**. **makedbm** creates the files **publickey.pag** and **publickey.dir**. Both of these files are in the directory **/var/yp/***domain.name*. The makefile then touches a file called **publickey.time** (to keep track of updates) and calls the **yppush** program, if applicable, to propagate the changes to all slave servers.

It is inappropriate to call **make** until you have set the slave servers.

Modifying the Makefile

In order for the makefile to work on the automounter files (or any other files) that you want to propagate through NIS, the following modifications must be made:

1. Modify the line that says

   ```
   all: publickey
   ```

   to say the following:

   ```
   all: publickey auto.direct auto.home auto.master
   ```

   The order is not relevant.

2. Add the following lines at the end of the makefile:

   ```
   auto.direct: auto.direct.time
   auto.home: auto.home.time
   auto.master: auto.master.time
   ```

3. Add the following entry for the **auto.direct** map in the middle of the file, after the entry for **publickey.time** and before the line that reads **publickey: publickey.time**:

```
auto.direct.time: $(DIR)/publickey
   -if [ -f $(DIR)/auto.direct ]; then \
      echo auto.direct.byname `$(ALIAS) publickey.byname` >> $(ALIASFILE); \
      sort $(ALIASFILE) | uniq > .ypaliases; mv .ypaliases $(ALIASFILE); \
      for i in $(DOM); do \
         sed -e "/^#/d" \
               -e s/#.*$$// \
               -e "/^ *$$/d" \
               -e "/^+/d" $(DIR)/auto.direct | \
         $(MAKEDBM) - $(YPDBDIR)/`$(ALIAS) \
               -d $$i`/`$(ALIAS) auto.direct.byname`; \
      done; \
      touch auto.direct.time; \
      echo "updated auto.direct"; \
      if [ ! $(NOPUSH) ]; then \
         $(YPPUSH) auto.direct.byname; \
         echo "pushed auto.direct"; \
      else \
         : ; \
      fi \
   else \
      echo "couldn't find $(DIR)/auto.direct"; \
   fi
```

Create similar entries for **auto.home** and **auto.master**.

Setting the Master Server

The program that helps you establish the master and slave servers, and permits the initial mapping of ASCII files and their propagation, is **/usr/sbin/ypinit**.

You use the shell script **ypinit** to build a fresh set of NIS maps on the master server in the following way:

1. Bring the machine that is going to be your master server to single-user mode, or to a mode that is not defined as running the NIS service, and log in as NIS administrator.
2. Type

   ```
   cd /var/yp
   /usr/sbin/ypinit -m
   ```

3. **ypinit** prompts for a list of other hosts that are to become NIS servers. Enter the name of the server you are working on and the names of all other NIS servers.
4. **ypinit** asks whether you want the procedure to die at the first non-fatal error or to continue despite non-fatal errors.

   If you choose the first option, **ypinit** will exit at the first problem; you can then fix the problem and restart **ypinit**. This is recommended if you are running **ypinit** for the first time. If you prefer to continue, you can try to fix by hand all problems that may occur, then restart **ypinit**.

   Once **ypinit** has constructed the list of servers, it calls up **make**. This program uses the instructions contained in the makefile (either the default one or the one you modified) located in **/var/yp**. It cleans all comment lines from the files you designated and runs **makedbm** on them, creating the appropriate pairs of maps and establishing the name of the master server for each map.

NOTE For security reasons, you may want to restrict access to the master NIS server.

Starting Daemons in the Master Server

The success of the remaining procedures depends on the presence of the **ypserv** daemon in the master server.

If your master server is still in single-user mode or at an inappropriate run-level, bring it to the run-level that is defined as allowing NIS services to run. This entails having the following or similar lines in the **/etc/rc2.d/S75rpc** file:

```
if [ -f /usr/lib/netsvc/yp/ypserv -a -d /var/yp/`domainname` ]
then
        /usr/lib/netsvc/yp/ypserv
        (echo \c ' ypserv') >/dev/console
fi
if [ -d /var/yp ]; then
        /usr/lib/netsvc/yp/ypbind
        (echo \c ' ypbind') >/dev/console
fi
```

Once you have made sure that these lines are in the file, and that there is an executable file called **/usr/lib/netsvc/yp/ypserv** and a directory under **/var/yp** named after the domain name, bring the machine to the multi-user mode.

Setting Slave Servers

Your network can have one or more NIS slave servers. Before actually running **ypinit** to create the slave servers, you should take several precautions.

The domain name for each NIS slave must be the same as the domain name of the NIS master server. Use the **domainname** command on each NIS slave to make sure it is consistent with the master server. Make any necessary changes to the domain name, as described in "Establishing the NIS Domain". Do not forget to set each slave server's host name.

Make sure that the network is working properly before you set up a slave NIS server. In particular, check that you can use **rcp**(1) to send files from the master NIS server to NIS slaves. If you cannot, follow the procedures outlined in *User's Guide* to permit the use of **rcp**(1).

Now you are ready to create a new slave server.

1. Log in to each slave server as NIS administrator and bring the slave server to a run-level, preferably single user, that does not imply running the NIS service. **ypserv** must not be running.

2. Change directory to **/var/yp**.
3. Type the following:

   ```
   /usr/sbin/ypinit -c
   ```

   Enter the names of the NIS servers in order of preference; that is, enter first the names of the servers that are physically closest to the machine in the network. If the client is also a server, enter its name first. This initializes the client and establishes its servers for binding.
4. Type the following:

   ```
   /usr/lib/netsvc/yp/ypbind
   ```

5. Type

   /usr/sbin/ypinit -s *master*

   where *master* is the host name of the existing NIS master server. Ideally, the named host is the master server, but it can be any host with a stable set of NIS maps, such as another slave server.
6. **ypinit** will not prompt you for a list of other servers, as it does when you create the master server, nor will it run **make** again. However, it will stop executing if you have not used **ypinit -c** to initialize the list of servers, and it lets you choose whether or not to halt at the first non-fatal error. **ypinit** then calls the program **ypxfr**, which transfers a copy of the master's NIS map set to the slave server's **/var/yp/***domainname* directory.
7. When **ypinit** terminates in each slave, make sure that the ASCII files in the **/etc** directory direct whichever program reads them to the NIS maps, thus ensuring homogeneity across the network. For instance, if you have added the maps **auto.master**, **auto.home**, and **auto.direct** to the NIS maps, make a copy of each of these files in each slave by typing

   ```
   cp /etc/auto.home /etc/auto.home.old
   ```

   Note that in the particular case of the automounter, if the invocation does not contain the **-m** option, then it will automatically look for a NIS **auto.master** map. You can therefore move the **auto.master** file into another file:

   ```
   mv /etc/auto.master /etc/auto.master.orig
   ```

8. Edit the original files (not those with the **.old** extension) and make them refer to the NIS maps. For instance, the file **/etc/auto.direct** should contain, as its last line, something similar to the following:

   ```
   +auto.direct
   ```

Thus, whenever the automounter reads this file, it will consult the NIS **auto.direct** map upon reaching this line.

9. The preceding procedures ensure that processes on the slave server actually use the NIS services, rather than files in the local **/etc**. In this way, you ensure that the NIS slave server is also an NIS client.

10. Back up copies of the edited files. For instance, you might type the following:

```
cp /etc/auto.direct /etc/auto.direct.bkp
```

Repeat the procedures above for each machine you want configured as an NIS slave server.

Starting Slave Server Daemons

The procedure for starting the NIS daemons in a slave server is exactly the same as that used for starting the NIS daemons in the master server, as explained in "Starting Daemons in the Master Server".

Setting up an NIS Client

To establish a machine as an NIS client, do the following:

1. Edit the client's local files, as you did for the local files in the slave servers, so that processes consulting those files are sent to the NIS maps.

2. Run

   ```
   /usr/sbin/ypinit -c
   ```

   to initialize the client.

3. Bring the client to the run-level defined as permitting the running of NIS services, after making sure that the appropriate file in the **/etc/rc2.d/S75rpc** directory contains lines similar to the following:

   ```
   if [ -d /var/yp ]; then
           /usr/lib/netsvc/yp/ypbind
           (echo \c ' ypbind')     >/dev/console
   ```

4. Type

   ```
   ps -ef | grep ypbind
   ```

   to confirm that **/usr/lib/netsvc/yp/ypbind** is running.

With the relevant files in `/etc` abbreviated and **ypbind** running, the processes on the machine will be clients of the NIS servers.

At this point, you must have configured a NIS server on the network and have given that server's name to **ypinit**. Otherwise, processes on the client hang if no NIS server is available while **ypbind** is running.

Administering NIS Maps

This section describes how to maintain the maps of an existing NIS domain. Subjects discussed include:

- Updating NIS maps
- Propagating an NIS map
- Adding maps to an additional NIS server
- Moving the master map set to a new server

Updating Existing Maps

After you have installed NIS, you will discover that some maps require frequent updating while others never need to change. For example, the **`publickey`** map may change frequently on a large company's network. On the other hand, the **`auto.master`** map probably will change little, if at all.

When you need to update a map, you can use one of two updating procedures, depending on whether the map is standard or non-standard. A standard map is a map in the default set created by **`ypinit`** from the network databases. Non-standard maps may be any of the following:

- A map included with an application purchased from a vendor
- A map created specifically for your site
- A map existing in a form other than ASCII

The following text explains how to use various updating tools. In practice, you probably will use them only if you add non-standard maps or change the set of NIS servers after the system is up and running.

Modifying Standard Maps

Use the following procedure for updating all standard maps:

1. Become NIS administrator on the master server. (Always modify NIS maps on the master server.)
2. Edit the file in `/etc` that has the same name as the map you want to change.

3. Type the following:

```
cd /var/yp
make mapname
```

The **make** command will then update your map according to the changes you made in its corresponding file. It will also propagate it among the servers (see "Propagating an NIS Map" for more information).

NOTE

Do not use this procedure with the **publickey** map. Instead, use the **newkey** and **chkey** commands, as described in "Preparing the Maps".

Creating and Modifying Non-Standard Maps

To update a non-standard map, you edit its corresponding ASCII file. Then you rebuild the updated map using the **/usr/sbin/makedbm** command. (For information on the **makedbm** command, see **makedbm**(1M). If the map has an entry in the **/var/yp/Makefile**, simply run **make**. If the map does not have an entry, try to create one following the instructions in "Making the Maps". Using **make** is the preferred method; otherwise, you will have to use **makedbm** by hand.

There are two different methods for using **makedbm**:

- Redirect the command's output to a temporary file, modify the file, then use the modified file as input to **makedbm**.
- Have the output of **makedbm** operated on within a pipeline that feeds into **makedbm** again directly. This is appropriate if you can update the disassembled map with either **awk**, **sed**, or a **cat** append.

You can use either of two possible procedures for creating new maps. The first uses an existing ASCII file as input; the second uses standard input.

In all cases, if **/var/yp** resides in an s5 file system, you have to create an alias for the map to deal with the 14-character limitation for file names (which, in the case of map names, is actually an 8-character limitation because of the suffixes that **makedbm** creates). To do this, change directory to **/var/yp** and enter the command:

```
echo mapname `/usr/sbin/ypalias mapname` >> aliases
```

Updating Maps Built from Existing ASCII Files

Assume that an ASCII file **/var/yp/mymap.asc** was created with an editor or a shell script on the NIS master (See "Preparing the Maps" for information on creating NIS maps). You want to create an NIS map from this file, and locate it in the **home_domain** subdirectory. To do this, you type the following on the master server:

```
cd /var/yp
/usr/sbin/makedbm mymap.asc home_domain/mymap
```

The **mymap** map now exists in the directory **home_domain**.

Adding entries to **mymap** is simple. First, you must modify the ASCII file **mymap.asc**. (If you modify the actual **dbm** files without modifying the corresponding ASCII file, the modifications are lost.) Type the following:

```
cd /var/yp
edit mymap.asc
/usr/sbin/makedbm mymap.asc home_domain/mymap
```

where *edit* is any editor that will allow you to modify an ASCII file. When you finish updating the map, propagate it to the slave servers, as described in "Propagating an NIS Map".

Updating Maps Built from Standard Input

When no original ASCII file exists, create the NIS map from the keyboard by typing input to **makedbm**, as shown below:

```
ypmaster# cd /var/yp
ypmaster# /usr/sbin/makedbm - home_domain/mymap
key1 value1
key2 value2
key3 value3
<ctl D>
ypmaster#
```

If later you need to modify a map that is not based on an existing file, you can use **makedbm -u** to disassemble the map and create a temporary ASCII intermediate file. You type the following:

```
cd /var/yp
/usr/sbin/makedbm -u home_domain/mymap > mymap.temp
```

The resulting temporary file **mymap.temp** has one entry per line. You can edit it as needed, using your preferred editing tools.

To update the map, you give the name of the modified temporary file to **makedbm** as follows:

```
/usr/sbin/makedbm mymap.temp home_domain/mymap
rm mymap.temp
```

When **makedbm** finishes, propagate the map to the slave servers, as described in "Propagating an NIS Map".

The preceding paragraphs explained how to use some tools. In reality, almost everything you have to do can be done by **ypinit** and **/var/yp/Makefile**, unless you add non-standard maps to the database or change the set of NIS servers after the system is already up and running.

Whether you use the makefile in **/var/yp** or some other procedure, a new pair of well-formed **dbm** files must end up in the domain directory on the master NIS server.

Propagating an NIS Map

When you **propagate** an NIS map, you move it from place to place—most often from the master to all NIS slave servers. Initially **ypinit** propagates the maps from master to slaves, as described previously. From then on, you must transfer updated maps from master to slaves by running the **ypxfr** command. You can run **ypxfr** three different ways: periodically through the root **crontab** file; by the **ypserv** daemon; and interactively on the command line.

ypxfr handles map transference in tandem with the **yppush** program. **yppush** should always be run from the master server. The makefile in the **/var/yp** directory automatically runs **yppush** after you change the master set of maps.

yppush's function is to copy, or "**push**," a new version of a NIS map from the NIS master to the slave(s). After making a list of NIS servers from the **ypservers** map built by **ypinit, yppush** contacts each slave server in the list and sends it a "transfer map" request. When the request is acknowledged by the slave, the **ypxfr** program transfers the new map to the slave.

Using crontab with ypxfr

Maps have differing rates of change. For instance, **auto.master** may not change for months at a time, but **publickey** may change several times a day in a large organization. When you schedule map transference through the **crontab** command, you can designate the intervals at which individual maps are to be propagated.

To run **ypxfr** periodically at a rate appropriate for your map set, edit root's **crontab** file on each slave server and put the appropriate **ypxfr** entries in it [see the manual page for **crontab**(1)]. **ypxfr** contacts the master server and transfers the map only if the master's copy is more recent than the local copy.

Using Shell Scripts with ypxfr

As an alternative to creating separate **crontab** entries for each map, you may prefer to have root's **crontab** periodically run shell scripts that update the maps. You can easily modify these shell scripts to fit your site's requirements or replace them. Here is an example shell script:

```
#! /sbin/sh
#
# ypxfr_1perday.sh - Do daily yp map check/updates
#

# set -xv
ypxfr publickey.byname
ypxfr auto.direct
ypxfr ypservers
```

This shell script will update once per day the maps mentioned in it, as long as root's **crontab** executes it once a day (preferably at times of low network load). You can also have scripts update maps once a week, once a month, once every hour, and so on, but be aware of the performance degradation implied in propagating the maps.

Run the same shell scripts through root's **crontab** on each slave server configured for the NIS domain. Alter the exact time of execution from one server to another to avoid bogging down the master.

If you want to transfer the map from a particular slave server, use the **-h** *host* option of **ypxfr** within the shell script. The syntax of the commands you put in the script is

/usr/sbin/ypxfr -h *host mapname*

where *host* is the name of the server with the maps you want to transfer, and *mapname* is the name of the requested map. If you use the **-h** option without specifying *host*, **ypxfr** will try to get the map from the master server.

You can use the **-s** *domain* option to transfer maps from another domain to your local domain. These maps should be essentially the same across domains.

Directly Invoking ypxfr

The third method of invoking **ypxfr** is to run it as a command. Typically, you do this only in exceptional situations – for example, when setting up a temporary NIS server to create a test environment, or when trying to make an NIS server that has been out of service consistent with the other servers.

Logging ypxfr's Activities

ypxfr's transfer attempts and the results can be captured in a log file. If a file called **/var/yp/ypxfr.log** exists, results are appended to it. No attempt to limit the size of the log file is made. To prevent it from growing indefinitely, empty it from time to time by entering:

```
cp /var/yp/ypxfr.log /var/yp/ypxfr.log.old
cat /dev/null > /var/yp/ypxfr.log
```

You can have **crontab** execute these commands once a week.

To turn off logging, remove the log file.

Adding New NIS Maps to the Makefile

Adding a new NIS map entails getting copies of the map's **dbm** files into the **/var/yp/***domain_name* directory on each of the NIS servers in the domain. The actual mechanism is described above in "Propagating an NIS Map". This section only describes how to update the makefile so that propagation works correctly.

After deciding which NIS server is the master of the map, modify **/var/yp/Makefile** on the master server so that you can conveniently rebuild the map. As indicated previously, different servers can be masters of different maps. This can, however, lead to administrative confusion, and it is strongly recommended that you set only one server as the master of all maps. Actual case-by-case modification is too varied to describe here, but typically a human-readable ASCII file is filtered through **awk**, **sed**, and/or **grep** to make it suitable for input to **makedbm**. Refer to the existing **/var/yp/Makefile** for examples and to "Modifying the Makefile".

Use the mechanisms already in place in **/var/yp/Makefile** when deciding how to create dependencies that **make** will recognize; specifically, the use of **.time** files allows you to see when the makefile was last run for the map.

To get an initial copy of the map, you can have **make** run **yppush** on the NIS master server. The map must be available globally before clients begin to access it.

If the map is available from some NIS servers, but not all, you will encounter unpredictable behavior from client programs.

Adding a New NIS Server to the Original Set

After NIS is running, you may need to create an NIS slave server that you did not include in the initial set given to **ypinit**. The following procedure explains how to do this:

1. Log in to the master server as NIS administrator.
2. Go to the NIS domain directory by typing:

   cd /var/yp/*domain_name*

3. Disassemble **ypservers**, as follows:

   /usr/sbin/makedbm -u ypservers > /tmp/*temp_file*

   makedbm converts **ypservers** from **dbm** format to the temporary ASCII file **/tmp/***temp_file*.

4. Edit **/tmp/***temp_file* using your preferred text editor. Add the new slave server's name to the list of servers. Then save and close the file.
5. Run the **makedbm** command with **temp_file** as the input file and **ypservers** as the output file.

   /usr/sbin/makedbm /tmp/*temp_file* **ypservers**

   Here **makedbm** converts **ypservers** back into **dbm** format.

6. Verify that the **ypservers** map is correct (since there is no ASCII file for **ypservers**) by typing the following:

   ypslave# /usr/sbin/makedbm -u ypservers

   If a host name is not in **ypservers**, it will not be warned of updates to the NIS map files.

   Here **makedbm** will display each entry in **ypservers** on your screen.

7. Set up the new slave server's NIS domain directory by copying the NIS map set from the master server. To do this, log in to the new NIS slave as NIS administrator and run the **ypinit** command:

```
ypslave# cd /var/yp
ypslave# ypinit -c
< enter the list of servers >
ypslave# /usr/lib/netsvc/yp/ypbind
ypslave# /usr/sbin/ypinit -s ypmaster
```

When you are finished, complete Steps 5 and 6 in "Setting Slave Servers."

Changing a Map's Master Server

To change a map's master, you first have to build it on the new NIS master. The old master's name occurs as a key-value pair in the existing map (this pair is inserted automatically by **makedbm**). Therefore, using the existing copy at the new master or transferring a copy to the new master with **ypxfr** is insufficient. You have to reassociate the key with the new master's name. If the map has an ASCII source file, you should copy it in its current version to the new master.

Here are instructions for remaking a sample NIS map called **jokes.bypunchline**.

1. Log in to the new master as NIS administrator and type the following:

   ```
   newmaster# cd /var/yp
   ```

2. **/var/yp/Makefile** must have an entry for the new map before you specify the map to **make**. If this isn't the case, edit the makefile now (see "Making the Maps").

3. Type the following:

   ```
   newmaster# make jokes.bypunchline
   ```

4. If the old master will remain an NIS server, **rlogin** in to it and edit **/var/yp/Makefile**. Comment out the section of **/var/yp/Makefile** that made **jokes.bypunchline** so that it is no longer made there.

5. If **jokes.bypunchline** only exists as a **dbm** file, remake it on the new master by disassembling a copy from any NIS server, then running the disassembled version through **makedbm**:

   ```
   newmaster# cd /var/yp
   newmaster# ypcat -k jokes.bypunchline | \
   /usr/sbin/makedbm - domain/jokes.bypunchline
   ```

   Don't forget that **jokes.bypunchline** should be in the **alias** file too.

After making the map on the new master, you must send a copy of it to the other slave servers. However, do not use **yppush**, as the other slaves will try to get new copies from the old master, rather than the new one. A typical method for circumventing this is to transfer a copy of the map from the new master back to the old master. Become NIS administrator on the old master server and type:

```
oldmaster# /usr/sbin/ypxfr -h newmaster jokes.bypunchline
```

Now it is safe to run **yppush**. The remaining slave servers still believe that the old master is the current master. They will attempt to get the current version of the map from the old master. When they do so, they will get the new map, which names the new master as the current master.

If this method fails, you can try this cumbersome but sure-fire option. Log in as NIS administrator on each NIS server and execute the **ypxfr** command shown above.

Summary of NIS-Related Commands

In addition to maps, NIS service also includes specialized daemons, system programs, and commands, which are summarized below.

`ypserv` — Looks up requested information in a map. **ypserv** is a daemon that runs on NIS servers with a complete set of maps. At least one **ypserv** daemon must be present on the network for NIS service to function.

`ypbind` — Initiates binding. **ypbind** is the NIS binder daemon. It must be present on both clients and servers. It initiates binding by finding a **ypserv** process that serves maps within the domain of the requesting client. **ypserv** must run on each NIS server. **ypbind** must run on all servers and clients.

`ypinit` — Automatically creates maps for an NIS server from files located in `/etc`. **ypinit** also constructs the initial maps that are not built from files in `/etc`, such as **ypservers**. Use **ypinit** to set up the master NIS server and the slave NIS servers for the first time, as well as to initialize all clients.

`make` — Updates NIS maps by reading the **Makefile** in `/var/yp`. You can use **make** to update all maps based on the files in `/etc` or to update individual maps. The manual page **ypmake**(1M) describes **make** functionality for NIS.

`makedbm` — Takes an input file and converts it into **dbm .dir** and **.pag** files—valid **dbm** files that NIS can use as maps. You can also use **makedbm -u** to "disassemble" a map, so that you can see the key-value pairs that comprise it.

`ypxfr` — Moves an NIS map from one server to another, using NIS itself as the transport medium. You can run **ypxfr** interactively, or periodically from a **crontab** file. It is also called by **ypserv** to initiate a transfer.

`yppush` — Copies a new version of an NIS map from the NIS master server to its slaves. You run it on the master NIS server.

`ypset` — Tells a **ypbind** process to bind to a named NIS server. **ypset** is not for casual use.

`yppoll` Tells which version of an NIS map is running on a server that you specify. It also lists the master server for the map.

`ypcat` Displays the contents of an NIS map.

`ypmatch` Prints the value for one or more specified keys in an NIS map. You cannot specify which NIS server's version of the map you are seeing.

`ypwhich` Shows which NIS server a client is using at the moment for NIS services, or, if invoked with the `-m` *mapname* option, which NIS server is master of each of the maps.

`ypupdated` Facilitates the updating of NIS information.

Fixing NIS Problems

This section explains how to clear problems encountered on networks running NIS. It has two parts, one covering problems seen on an NIS client and another covering problems seen on an NIS server.

Debugging an NIS Client

Before trying to debug an NIS client, review the first part of the chapter, which explains the NIS environment. Then look for the subheading in this section that best describes your problem.

Hanging Commands on the Client

The most common problem of NIS clients is for a command to hang and generate console messages such as:

`yp: server not responding for domain` <*domainname*>**`. Still trying`**

Sometimes many commands begin to hang, even though the system as a whole seems normal and you can run new commands.

The message above indicates that **`ypbind`** on the local machine is unable to communicate with **`ypserv`** in the domain *domainname*. This happens when a machine running **`ypserv`** has crashed or is down or unavailable for any reason. It may also occur if the network or NIS server is so overloaded that **`ypserv`** cannot get a response back to the client's **`ypbind`** within the timeout period.

Under these circumstances, every client on the network will experience the same or similar problems. The condition is temporary in most cases. The messages will usually go away when the NIS server reboots and restarts **`ypserv`**, or when the load on the NIS server or network itself decreases.

However, commands may hang and require direct action to clear them. The following list describes the causes of such problems and gives suggestions for fixing them:

- The NIS client has not set, or has incorrectly set, the machine's domain name. Clients must use a domain name that the NIS servers know.
- On the client, type **`domainname`** to see which domain name is set. Compare that with the actual domain name in **`/var/yp`** on the NIS master server. If a machine's domain name is not the same as the server's, the machine's domain name entry in its installation scripts is incorrect. Log in as NIS

administrator, edit the client's installation scripts, and correct the **domainname** entry. This assures the domain name is correct every time the machine boots. Then set **domainname** manually by typing the following:

```
domainname good_domain_name
```

- If commands still hang, make sure the server is up and running. Check other machines on your local network. If several clients also have problems, suspect a server problem. Try to find a client machine behaving normally, and type the **ypwhich** command on it. If **ypwhich** does not respond, kill it and go to a terminal on the NIS server. Type the following:

```
ypserver# ps -ef | grep yp
ypserver# kill -9 pid
```

where *pid* is the process-ID for **ypbind**. Look for **ypserv** and **ypbind** processes. If a **ypserv** process is running, type

```
ypserver# ypwhich
```

on the NIS server. If **ypwhich** does not respond, **ypserv** has probably hung, and you should restart it. Type the following while logged in as NIS administrator:

```
ypserver# kill -9 [ypserv's pid # from ps]
ypserver# /usr/lib/netsvc/yp/ypserv
```

If **ps** shows no **ypserv** process running, start one up.

- If the server's **ypbind** daemon is not running, start it up by typing the following:

```
ypserver# /usr/lib/netsvc/yp/ypbind
```

Notice that if you run **ypbind** and you type **ypwhich** immediately, **ypwhich** will return the error message **not found** in all cases. Run **ypwhich** again; it should now return the name of a server.

- If commands still hang, you may try the following:

  1. Kill the existing **ypbind**:

  ```
  ps -ef | grep ypbind
  ```

  2. Restart **ypbind** with the **ypset** option that permits root to change the server:

  ```
  ypbind -ypsetme
  ```

3. Reset the server to one you know is reliable:

```
ypset servername
```

NIS Is Unavailable

When most machines on the network appear to be behaving normally, but one client cannot receive NIS service, that client may experience many different symptoms. For example, some commands appear to operate correctly while others terminate with an error message about the unavailability of NIS. Other commands limp along in a backup-strategy mode particular to the program involved. Still other commands or daemons crash with obscure messages or no message at all. Here are messages a client in this situation may receive:

```
ypcat myfile
ypcat: can't bind to NIS server for domain <domainname>.
      Reason: can't communicate with ypbind.

/usr/sbin/yppoll myfile
yppoll: Sorry, I can't communicate with ypbind.  I give up.
```

These symptoms usually indicate that the client's **ypbind** process is not running. Run **ps -ef** and check for **ypbind**. If it you do not find it, log in as NIS administrator and start it by typing the following:

```
/usr/lib/netsvc/yp/ypbind
```

NIS problems should disappear.

ypbind Crashes

If **ypbind** crashes almost immediately each time it is started, look for a problem in some other part of the system. Check for the presence of the **rpcbind** daemon by typing the following:

```
nfsping -o rpcbind
```

If the message returned states that **rpcbind** is not running, restart the **rpcbind** daemon or reboot. See **nfsping**(1M) for more information on **nfsping**.

If **rpcbind** itself will not stay up or behaves strangely, look for more fundamental problems. Check the network software in the ways suggested in "Troubleshooting TCP/IP".

You may be able to communicate with **rpcbind** on the problematic client from a machine operating normally. From the functioning machine, type:

rpcinfo *client* **| grep ypbind**

If **rpcbind** on the problematic machine is running normally, **rpcinfo** should produce an output similar to the following:

```
100007    3     tcp  0.0.0.0.12.169  ypbind  superuser
100007    3     udp  0.0.0.0.4.9  ypbind  superuser
100007    3  ticlts  Q 00 00 00  ypbind  superuser
100007    3  ticots   07 00 00 00  ypbind  superuser
100007    3  ticotsord    07 00 00 00  ypbind  superuser
100007    3  starlandg    00 15sfsc.30719?00 20I 00 00 00 00 00 00 10 \
                00j 10 32v376 02  ypbind  superuser
100007    3  starlan   00 15sfsc.;3719?00 20I 00 00 00 00 00 00 10 \
                00j 10 32v376 01  ypbind  superuser
```

There should be one entry per transport; in the preceding example, the entry for **udp** is missing. Because **ypbind** was not registered for it in this case, **ypbind** cannot run on **udp**. As long as there are other transports to run on, **ypbind** should run but the omission may indicate some kind of a problem. Reboot the machine and run **rpcinfo** again. If the **ypbind** processes are there and they change each time you try to restart **/usr/lib/netsvc/yp/ypbind**, reboot the system, even if the **rpcbind** daemon is running.

ypwhich Displays Are Inconsistent

When you use **ypwhich** several times on the same client, the resulting display may vary because the NIS server changes. This is normal. The binding of NIS client to NIS server changes over time when the network or the NIS servers are busy. Whenever possible, the network stabilizes at a point where all clients get acceptable response time from the NIS servers. As long as your client machine gets NIS service, it does not matter where the service comes from. For example, one NIS server machine can get its own NIS services from another NIS server on the network.

Debugging an NIS Server

Before trying to debug your NIS server, read about the NIS environment at the beginning of this chapter. Then look in this subsection for the heading that most closely describes the server's problem.

Servers Have Different Versions of an NIS Map

Because NIS propagates maps among servers, occasionally you find different versions of the same map at NIS servers on the network. This version discrepancy is normal if transient, but abnormal otherwise.

Most commonly, normal map propagation is prevented if it occurs when an NIS server or router between NIS servers is down. When all NIS servers and the routers between them are running, **ypxfr** should succeed.

If a particular slave server has problems updating maps, log in to that server and run **ypxfr** interactively. If **ypxfr** fails, it will tell you why it failed, and you can fix the problem. If **ypxfr** succeeds, but you suspect it has occasionally failed, create a log file to enable logging of messages. As NIS administrator type the following:

```
ypslave# cd /var/yp
ypslave# touch ypxfr.log
```

This saves all output from **ypxfr**. The output resembles the output **ypxfr** displays when run interactively, but each line in the log file is time-stamped. You may see unusual orderings in the timestamps. This is normal – the time-stamp tells you when **ypxfr** started to run. If copies of **ypxfr** ran simultaneously but their work took different amounts of time, they may actually write their summary status line to the log files in an order different from that in which they were invoked. Any pattern of intermittent failure shows up in the log. When you have fixed the problem, turn off logging by removing the log file. If you forget to remove it, it will grow without limit.

While still logged in to the problem NIS slave server, inspect the root's **crontab** file and the **ypxfr*** shell scripts it invokes. Typos in these files cause propagation problems, as do failures to refer to a shell script within **/var/spool/cron/crontabs/root**, or failures to refer to a map within any shell script.

Also, make sure that the NIS slave server is in the map **ypservers** within the domain. If it is not, it still operates perfectly as a server, but **yppush** will not tell it when a new copy of a map exists.

If the NIS slave server's problem is not obvious, you can work around it while you debug it using **rcp** or **tftp** to copy a recent version of the inconsistent map from any healthy NIS server. You must not do this remote copy as root, but you can probably do it while logged in as **daemon**. For instance, here is how you might transfer the map **busted**:

```
ypslave# chmod go+w /var/yp/mydomain
ypslave# su daemon
rcp ypmaster:/var/yp/mydomain/busted.\* /var/yp/mydomain
exit
ypslave# chown root /var/yp/mydomain/busted.*
ypslave# chmod go-w /var/yp/mydomain
```

Here the * character has been escaped in the command line so that it will be expanded on **ypmaster**, instead of locally on **ypslave**. Notice that the map files should be owned by root, so you must change their ownership after the transfer.

ypserv Crashes

When the **ypserv** process crashes almost immediately and does not stay up even with repeated activations, the debug process is virtually identical to that previously described in "ypbind Crashes". Check for the existence of the **rpcbind** daemon as follows:

ypserver# ps -ef | grep rpcbind

Reboot the server if you do not find the daemon. If it is there, type

rpcinfo *yp_server* **| grep ypserv**

and look for output similar to the following:

```
100004    2     tcp  0.0.0.0.12.168  ypserv  superuser
100004    2     udp  0.0.0.0.4.8  ypserv  superuser
100004    2  ticlts  B 00 00 00  ypserv  superuser
100004    2  ticots   06 00 00 00  ypserv  superuser
100004    2  ticotsord   06 00 00 00  ypserv  superuser
100004    2  starlandg   00 15sfsc.2>219?00 20I 00 00 00 00 00 00 00 10 \
                00j 10 32v376 02  ypserv  superuser
100004    2  starlan   00 15sfsc.31319?00 20I 00 00 00 00 00 00 00 10 \
                00j 10 32v376 01  ypserv  superuser
```

Your machine will have different port numbers. As in the case of **ypbind**, there should be one entry per transport. If a transport is missing, **ypserv** has been unable to register its services with it. Reboot the machine. If the **ypserv** processes are there, and they change each time you try to restart **/usr/lib/netsvc/yp/ypserv**, reboot the machine.

Turning off NIS

If **ypserv** on the master is disabled, you can no longer update any of the NIS maps. On the other hand, if there is no **ypserv** daemon running but clients have **ypbind** running, machines may hang indefinitely until they find a **ypserv**.

To turn off NIS services safely, make sure all the clients stop running **ypbind** before **ypserv** in the master and slave servers is turned off.

GL Glossary

Glossary GL-1

Glossary

address
: A unique number that identifies a machine on a network (see *IP address*).

ARP
: Address Resolution Protocol, a protocol that maps an IP address to its corresponding Ethernet address.

ARPANET
: The Advanced Research Projects Agency funded network, for which TCP/IP was originally developed (see *DoD Internet*).

automatic mount list
: A list of remote resources that are mounted on the local system when Remote File Sharing is started. The list is contained in the **/etc/vfstab** file. (See the **vfstab**(4) manual page for the format of the file.) Automatic mount information is added to **/etc/vfstab** using any standard file editor.

automatic share list
: A list of local resources that are automatically offered to other computers when Remote File Sharing is started. The list consists of full **share** command lines placed inside the **/etc/dfs/dfstab** file. The command lines are added to **/etc/dfs/dfstab** using the **sysadm** command or by any standard file editor.

automatic startup
: NFS and/or RFS can be set to start automatically when your machine is booted. This is done by changing the **initdefault** line in the **/etc/inittab** file from **2** to **3**. If you want NFS and/or RFS to start automatically every time you rebuild the kernel, you must change the **initdefault** line in the **/etc/conf/init.d/kernel** file from **2** to **3**. Whenever the kernel is rebuilt, this file is read, and the contents of this file replace those in **/etc/inittab**. See **init**(4) and **idmkinit**(1M) for further information.

binding
: The process by which a client locates the server that shares the information desired, and then sets up communication with that server.

bridge
: A device used at the Data Link layer that selectively copies packets between networks of the same type.

caching-only server
: A domain name server that is not authoritative for any domain. This server queries servers who have authority for the information neeeded and caches that data.

caller
: A process that uses RPC to have another process execute a procedure call.

client
: A machine that uses the resources of another machine; a machine can be both a *client*, utilizing resources that reside on other machines, and a *server*, making local resources available to other machines.

client caching
: The ability of an RFS computer that is using a remote resource to store remote data blocks in its local buffer pools. This technique improves RFS performance by reducing the number of times data must be read across the network.

client list
: When an RFS administrator shares a resource, the administrator can restrict the resource so only certain remote machines can use it. This list of machines is added to the **share** command line when a resource is shared.

client permissions
: When an RFS administrator shares a resource, the administrator can set permissions for the resource. The permissions are assigned on the **share** command line. If the permissions are read-only, the client computers can only mount the resource with read permissions. If they are read/write, a client can mount the resource read/write or read only.

credentials
: Information that is used to prove that something is as it claims to be—for example, an identification badge. (See also "verifiers").

current name server
: When a domain is set up, a primary and zero or more secondary domain name servers are assigned. Only one of those machines is actually handling domain name server responsibilities at a time. That machine is referred to as the current name server. Normally, the primary will be the current name server. However, if the secondary has taken over temporarily, it is the responsibility of the secondary's administrator to pass the responsibility back to the primary whenever the primary resumes running RFS. (See also *domain, name server, primary name server* and *secondary name server*.)

daemon — A program that runs autonomously, performing actions that facilitate more complex operations; for example, the mail service is run by several daemons, all of which work more or less without human oversight.

DARPA Internet
: The Defense Advanced Research Projects Agency Internet (see *Internet*).

Data Encryption Standard (DES)
: A standard cryptography algorithm used to ensure data security.

datagram — Transmission unit at the IP level.

DDN Internet — The Defense Data Network Internet (see *Internet*).

DoD Internet — The Department of Defense Internet, a wide area network to which the ARPANET belongs (see *Internet*).

domain — A domain is a set of computers whose resources are managed by a name server machine(s) in a network (NFS/RFS) environment. A domain name is like a telephone area code, acting as an addressing prefix to attach to a computer name or a resource.

domain information (rfmaster)
: The primary and secondary name server assignments for a domain are stored in the **/etc/rfs/***transport***/rfmaster** file. The primary keeps the definitive copy of this file and distributes it automatically to each computer in the domain when each starts RFS. This file also contains the network address of each name server.

domain member list
: The list of the computers that make up an RFS domain. This list is stored in the **/etc/rfs/auth.info/***domain***/passwd** file on the primary name server, where *domain* is replaced by the name of the domain. Members are added on the primary using the **rfadmin -a** command.

Domain Name Service
: The name service of the Internet Protocol family.

EGP — Exterior Gateway Protocol, a specialized protocol that allows exchange of information with a backbone under a separate administration.

file handle — A key that a client gets from a server to facilitate all further requests between that client and server.

file system type — An implementation of a file system to support a particular file type. The characteristics of a file are determined by its file type. RFS and NFS are implemented as file systems that support files of a type whose characteristics make them suitable for sharing across a network.

forced unmount — To unmount one of your local resources from all remote machines that have mounted it. This has the effect of killing all processes that are currently using the resource on all client machines.

gateway — An IP router (see *router*).

group identification number (GID) — A number that refers to a specific group of users on a system. Each user can belong to one or more groups.

header — Information attached to the beginning of data.Headers usually contain information about the following data to aid in processing it.

hierarchy — A part or all of a file structure. The term "hierarchy" refers to both the directories of the file structure, and the files within the structure.

host — An individual machine on a network.

hung — When a process has been stopped abnormally, with no way to restart that process.

ICMP — Internet Control Message Protocol, which is responsible for handling errors and printing error messages.

ID mapping — To define the permissions remote users and groups have to your shared resources. The tools available for mapping let you set permissions on a per-computer basis and on a global basis. You can then map individual users or groups by ID name or number. When you map IDs for Remote File Sharing, it is easiest to do so with ID numbers since mapping by name requires that you have copies of the remote machines' `/etc/passwd` and `/etc/group` files.

Internet — A wide area network originally funded by the Department of Defense, which utilizes TCP/IP for data interchange. The term *Internet* is used to refer to any and all of ARPANET, DARPANET, DDN, or DoD Internets.

internetwork — A group of networks connected by routers.

IP — Internet Protocol, which allows host-to-host datagram delivery.

IP address — A unique number that identifies each host in a network.

IP network number — A unique number that identifies each IP network (See *net number*).

IP router — See *router*.

local resource (NFS) — Using local resources under NFS allows you to share an individual file. Otherwise, it is similar to using local resources under RFS.

local resource (RFS) — A directory that resides on your machine that you have made available for other computers running RFS to use. You must share the directory (**share**) to offer it to other computers. If a remote machine mounts your resource, it could have access to all subdirectories, files, named pipes, and devices within your directory (depending on file permissions you set up).

map — A file that contains a listing of mount points and their corresponding resources. The maps are used by the automounter program to locate where a file structure should be mounted when it is needed.

mount — The action a client performs to access files in a server's shared directories. When a client mounts a resource, it does not copy that resource, but rather accesses the resource across the network as if it were a local file system.

mount point — A location within the directory tree through which a machine accesses a mounted resource. You need to create and/or specify a mount point when you mount a remote resource. The mount point for a resource is usually an empty directory.

name server — A name server provides a location where lists of resources and network addresses are stored for the machines in the domain. A name server can also provide a level of security via passwords. See *primary name server* and *secondary name server*.

net number — A number that NIC assigns to your network. The net number forms the first part of a host's IP address.

network address — The address by which a computer is known to a particular network. An RFS administrator needs to know the network address of the primary to start RFS for the first time. Address information of other machines is handled internally by RFS.

Network File System (NFS) — A service that enables machines to share file resources across a network.

network listener — The process used by a transport provider to wait for any type of incoming requests from the network. Once a request comes in, the listener directs it to one of the processes registered with the listener. The process represents a service, such as **uucp** or RFS.

network mask — A number used by software to separate the local subnet address from the rest of a given IP address.

network protocols — Sets of rules that explain how software and hardware should interact within a network to transmit information.

network specification — The name that identifies a networking product that is compatible with the Transport Interface (TI). This is also referred to as the transport provider. RFS requires a transport provider to communicate with other machines. The network specification is used to tell RFS the exact device to use for communications. For example, you would enter **tcp** to tell RFS to use the **/dev/tcp** device if TCP/IP is the transport provider.

networking support utilities — A software package that contains the network listener. This package must be installed in order to use Remote File Sharing.

NIC — Network Information Center, a service run by SRI that administers IP network numbers and domain names.

NIC handle — A unique NIC database identifier assigned to a network's administrator and technical contact.

node name — The name you assign to your computer to use for communications needs. Networking software, such as Basic Networking Utilities and Remote File Sharing, use this name to identify your machine. A full RFS computer name is *domain*.*nodename*, where *domain* is the name of the computer's RFS domain.

packet switching
: A concept which states that a network transmits packets over connections that last only for the duration of the transmission.

packets
: A piece of data smaller than a datagram. A datagram is made up of one or more packets.

pathname
: RFS will ask you for a full pathname to a directory in two instances. When you share a local resource, you will need the full pathname of the directory you are sharing. When you mount a remote resource, you will need the full pathname of the directory where the remote resource should be attached.

port numbers
: Numbers used by UDP and TCP to identify the end points of communication.

primary master server
: The primary domain name server for a zone, which maintains all the data corresponding to its domain.

primary name server
: The computer that is assigned to provide a primary location for addressing and information collection for an RFS domain. Information includes a list of domain members, resources offered by domain members, and optional user ID mapping information. Secondary name servers can be assigned to continue limited name service when the primary is down. For example, a secondary cannot add or delete domain members.

process identification number (PID)
: A number that identifies a process to the operating system. Every process has a PID by which it is referenced.

public key cryptography
: A cipher system that involves a published public key and an encoded secret key.

RARP
: Reverse Address Resolution Protocol, a protocol that is the reverse of ARP. RARP maps Ethernet addresses to its corresponding IP addresses.

Remote File Sharing RFS
: A service that enables machines to share resources across a network.

remote server — A machine, which is not the local one, acting as a server for information.

repeater — A machine that indiscriminately transmits data from one segment of a network to another, used at the physical layer (see *bridge*).

RFS daemon (rfudaemon)
: A daemon process that runs when RFS is running. When network connections to remote resources are broken, **rfudaemon** sends a message to **rfuadmin**, which then executes **rmount** to queue the resource for remounting. (See **rfudaemon**(1M), **rfuadmin**(1M), and **rmount**(1M) manual pages for further information.)

RFS password — A password assigned by the primary name server for every computer in its domain. Each computer must enter its password the first time it starts RFS. After that the password is stored locally in **/etc/rfs/***transport***/loc.passwd**. By copying the domain password file from the primary (**/etc/rfs/auth.info/***domain***/passwd**), a computer can verify that a remote machine trying to mount its resource is the machine it claims to be.

remote file sharing state (init 3)
: The special initialization state used to start RFS. When you type **init 3** or set the **initdefault** line in **/etc/inittab** to **3**, your system will start RFS, share all resources in your automatic share list, and mount all resources in your automatic mount list. See *automatic startup* for additional information.

Remote Procedure Call (RPC)
: Procedures that provide the means by which one process (the *caller*) can have another process (the *server*) execute a procedure call as if the caller had done so itself locally.

remote resource (NFS)
: Using remote resources under NFS allows you to mount an individual file. Otherwise, it is similar to using remote resources under RFS.

remote resource (RFS)
: A directory that resides on a remote machine that is available for you to connect to using RFS. You must mount the resource (**mount**) to make it available to users on your system. Once you mount the remote resource, your users could have access to all subdirectories, files, named pipes and devices related to your

directory (depending on file permissions the remote machine set up).

resource — See *remote resource (NFS)*, *remote resource (RFS)*, *local resource (NFS)* and *local resource (RFS)*.

resource identifier — The name assigned to a resource when it is shared. The name is limited to 14 printable ASCII characters. Slash (/), period (.), and white space may not be used.

router — A device that forwards (routes) packets of a protocol family, from one network to another.

run level — A user mode, also called a *run state* or *init state*.

secondary master server — A backup server that takes over for the primary master server, should it become overloaded or inoperable.

secondary name server — A computer designated to take over name server responsibilities temporarily should the primary domain name server fail. The secondary cannot change any domain information. It can, and should, only pass name server responsibility back to the primary when RFS is running on the primary again.

server — A machine that shares file systems or portions of file systems; a machine can be both a *server*, making local resources available to other machines, and a *client*, utilizing resources that reside on other machines. Individual files may be shared if both the server and client are using NFS.

server process — A process that receives directives from a caller process to execute procedures locally.

share (NFS) — The action a server machine performs to allow some or all of its resources (files, directories containing files, subdirectories, devices, and/or named pipes) to become available to other hosts.

share (RFS) — The action a server machine performs to allow some or all of its resources (directories containing files, subdirectories, devices, and/or named pipes) to become available to other hosts.

share table — An internal list of available resources. A share table on each computer running RFS has the name of each resource the computer has made available.

sharing — Making a local resource available to remote machines.

SRI — SRI International, a not-for-profit organization that runs the NIC.

SRI-NIC — See *NIC*.

subnet — An administrative division of a network into smaller networks.

subnet number — The part of an IP address that refers to the specific subnet desired.

TCP — Transmission Control Protocol.

TCP/IP — A term used to refer to the entire Internet family of protocols, consisting of the names of the two most important protocols.

transport provider — The software that provides a path through which network applications can communicate. RFS can communicate over multiple transport providers simultaneously. These transport providers must meet the Transport Interface Specification.

UDP — User Datagram Protocol, a protocol at the same layer as TCP, but without acknowledgment of transmission and therefore unreliable.

unsharing — Making a shared local resource unavailable to remote systems.

user/group name — The names associated with each local user and group that is allowed access to your computer. This information can be found in the first field of the `/etc/passwd` or `/etc/group` files, respectively. Remote users and groups can be assigned the same permissions as the local users and groups by using RFS ID mapping.

user/group ID number — Every user and group name has a corresponding number that is used by the UNIX operating system to handle permissions to files, directories, devices, and so on. These numbers are defined in the third field of the `/etc/passwd` or `/etc/group` files, respectively. Remote users and groups can be assigned the same permissions as the local users and groups by using RFS ID mapping.

user identification number (UID) — A number that identifies a user to the operating system. Every user has a unique number that identifies that user to the operating system.

verifiers	Information that is used to prove that credentials are valid.
virtual circuits	An apparent connection between processes which is facilitated by TCP. A virtual circuit allows applications to talk to each other as if they had a physical circuit.
zones	Administrative boundaries within a domain, often made up of one or more sub-domains (see *domain*).

IN Index

Index IN-1

Index

A

account log (BNU) 2: 119–120
address (A), resource record 7: 28
Address Resolution Protocol (ARP) 3: 2, 5
administrative files, BNU 2: 71
anon, option to NFS **share**(1M) command 19: 4
application gateway *See* gateway 6: 3
application layer, TCP/IP 3: 6–7
ARP 3: 5
ARPANET 3: 2
attradmin(1M) 2: 44–46, 59–63
attribute maps 2: 59–63
  adding an entry to 2: 59–61
  checking and fixing 2: 62–63
  deleting 2: 62
  deleting an entry in 2: 61–62
  displaying information 2: 63
  setting up 2: 59–60
authentication
  DES 23: 3
  ENIGMA 2: 4, 31
  RPC 23: 2
  UNIX 23: 2
authentication scheme, registering client machine 2: 24–25
authentication scheme *See* cr1 2: 23
auto.direct map 28: 15, 18
auto.home map 24: 9, 28: 10–11, 15, 18
auto.master map 28: 10–11, 15, 18, 21, 24
automount(1M) (NFS), 24: 1, 14–16
automounter maps (NFS) 24: 3
  conventions 24: 3
  modifying 24: 17
  preparing 24: 3–12
  specifying multiple locations 24: 9
  specifying multiple mounts 24: 7–8
  using environment variables 24: 12
  using substitution 24: 11–12
  writing a direct map 24: 5–13
  writing a master map 24: 4–5
  writing an indirect map 24: 6–7
automounter (NFS) 24: 1
  debugging 24: 18–20
  hierarchical mounts 24: 8
  how it works 24: 2
  invoking 24: 14
  purpose of 24: 1
  special mount point 24: 2
  updating the mount table 24: 16

B

Basic Networking Utilities *See* BNU 2: 64
binding, (NIS) 28: 4–5
biod(1M) 22: 2, 4–5, 10
BNU
  administration 2: 71–77
  administrative programs 2: 68–69
  check basic information 2: 129
  components 2: 67–71
  daemons 2: 69–70
  debugging 2: 72, 129–131
  escape characters 2: 107–108
  log files 2: 71
  maintenance 2: 125–128
  maintenance (automatic) 2: 126–128
  maintenance (manual) 2: 128
  networking programs 2: 67–70

perflog (conn) 2: 122–123
perflog (xfer) 2: 123–124
poll remote machines 2: 110–111
procedural overview 2: 5–8
process diagram 2: 65
queue jobs for remote machines 2: 111–113
security 2: 69–70, 78–88
security 2: 120–121
security (rexe) 2: 121
security (xfer) 2: 121
setting up 2: 7–8
support files 2: 70–71
unknown calling machines 2: 69–70
user programs 2: 67–68
BNU administrative support files 2: 113–116
(**C.**) work files 2: 114–115
(**D.**) authentication file 2: 115
(**D.**) data files 2: 115
(**LCK.**) lock files 2: 114
(**P.**) checkpoint files 2: 114
(**TM.**) temporary data files 2: 113
(**X.**) execute files 2: 115
BNU database support files 2: 70–71
Config file 2: 70, 90–91
Devconfig file 2: 70, 88
Devices file 2: 70, 91–99
Dialcodes file 2: 70, 110
Dialers file 2: 70, 99–101
Grades file 2: 70, 111–113
Limits file 2: 71, 89
Permissions file 2: 71, 78–88
Poll file 2: 71, 110–111
remote.unknown file 2: 69–70
Sysfiles file 2: 71, 88–89
Systems file 2: 71, 102–110
BNU log files 2: 116–124
account 2: 119–120
command 2: 116
errors 2: 117–118
Foreign (unknown system) 2: 124
perflog 2: 122–124
perflog (conn) 2: 122–123
perflog (xfer) 2: 123–124
security 2: 120–121
security (rexe) 2: 121
security (xfer) 2: 121
system history 2: 116–117
xferstats (transfer) 2: 118–119
boot files (DNS)
creating 7: 11–13
relationship between data files and 7: 12
setting up, for a caching-only server 7: 16
setting up, for a primary master server 7: 14–15
setting up, for a secondary master server 7: 15–16
booting problems, NFS 23: 9
bridge 6: 2

C

cache (RFS)
buffer usage 17: 63–64
client 17: 63–66
consistency overhead 17: 65–66
caching and caching-only servers (DNS) 7: 7
setting up a boot file for caching-only server 7: 16
Canonical Name (CNAME), resource record 7: 30
chkey(1) 27: 8–9, 28: 9
circuit switching network 3: 5
class field record client(s), (NIS) 28: 4, 19–20, 33–35
client-only 7: 6
client(s), setting up DNS on a 7: 6, 8–10
client(s) (RFS), caching 17: 63–66

client/server 7: 6
command log (BNU) 2: 116
common key 23: 3
Config file (BNU) 2: 90–91
configure(1M)
  choices for setting up machine as gateway with 6: 7
  for multiple network cards 6: 8–16
  -i option 6: 8–16
  ifconfig(1M) options with 6: 6
  INET-specific 6: 6–8, 10, 16
  options for generic 6: 8
  protocol-specific requirements 6: 8
connection server 2: 22–30, 65
  application interface 2: 22–23
  auth (authentication scheme file) 2: 27–28
  client machine administration 2: 24–25
  components of 2: 22
  cs.debug (debug file) 2: 29–30
  cs.log (log file) 2: 28–29
  server machine administration 2: 23–24
  setting up 2: 7
  setting up for CS dialer type-client machine 2: 73–74
  setting up for CS dialer type-server machine 2: 74–75
  setting up when CS dialer type not used-client machine 2: 76–77
  setting up when CS dialer type not used-server machine 2: 77
control entry lines 7: 23
conversation key 23: 3
cr1
  administration of 2: 31–40
  bilateral authentication scheme 2: 31–40
  client/server exchanges 2: 32
  command alternatives to 2: 35
  components 2: 31
  cryptkey(1) 2: 7, 35, 37, 39–40, 134
  daemon 2: 37
  identification and authentication facility 2: 3–4
  key creating a master 2: 38–39
  key database 2: 39
  key management daemon 2: 37–39
  keymaster(1M) daemon 2: 7, 31, 35, 37–39
  master key 2: 37
  menu 2: 35
  registering with a port monitor 2: 36
  registering with the connection server 2: 37
  setting up authentication scheme 2: 7
  setting up the key database 2: 39–40
  shared keys 2: 31–32
credentials, in RPC authentication 23: 2
cryptkey(1) 2: 7, 35, 37, 39–40, 134
cs_perror *See* **cs_connect**(3N) 2: 7
ct(1C) 2: 64, 67, 108
cu(1C) 2: 64, 67, 71, 88, 98, 108–109, 129–130

D

daemons
  running route 6: 22
  setting up route 6: 18–19
daemons (network) 2: 69–70
  biod(1M) 22: 2, 4–5, 10
  fingerd(1M) 3: 7, 5: 6
  ftpd(1M) 3: 7
  inetd(1M) 3: 7, 7: 32, 8: 11–12
  lockd(1M) 22: 2, 25: 2, 4
  mountd(1M) 22: 2–4, 7
  named(1M) 3: 7, 7: 1, 4, 6–7, 10–12, 32, 34
  nfsd(1M) 22: 2–4, 8–9

rlogind(1M) 3: 7, 25: 2
routed(1M) 4: 12, 6: 4–5, 7, 18–22, 8: 13–14
rpcbind(1M) 22: 3, 5–7, 27: 9, 28: 35–36, 38
rwhod(1M) 5: 6, 8: 13
statd(1M) 22: 2, 25: 2, 5
telnetd(1M) 3: 6
daemons (NIS)
28: 2
and starting daemons in master server 28: 17
and starting daemons in slave server 28: 19
Data Encryption Standard (DES), authentication 23: 3
data link layer, TCP/IP 3: 5
datagram 3: 5
debugging
named 7: 34
NFS 22: 1–10
NIS 28: 33–39
DES authentication 23: 3
Devconfig file (BNU) 2: 88
Devices
Class field 2: 93
Dialer-Token-Pairs field 2: 94–97
Line field 2: 93
Line2 field 2: 93
Protocol 2: 97–98
Type field 2: 91
Devices file (BNU) 2: 91–99
df(1M) 17: 69
dfmounts(1M) 11: 10, 13: 13–14
NFS 21: 4
RFS 17: 31, 34
DFS Administration 11: 9
commands 11: 10
files 11: 9
menus 14: 1–4
operating states (init states) 12: 4
dfshares(1M) 11: 10, 13: 12–13
NFS 19: 3, 20: 1, 21: 2
RFS 15: 3, 17: 32, 34
dfstab(4) 11: 10, 13: 1–4, 17: 29, 32, 35, 19: 3, 20: 3, 22: 2, 8, 23: 8
used as input to **shareall**(1M) 13: 4, 20: 2
diagnostics
automounter problems (NFS) 24: 18–20
fixing hung NFS programs 22: 9
NFS client problems 22: 7
NFS mounting problems 22: 7–8
NFS server problems 22: 5–6
Dialcodes file (BNU) 2: 110
Dialers file (BNU) 2: 99–101
diff(1) 2: 10
Distributed File System (DFS)
administration 11: 1, 12: 1–4, 13: 1–14
changing default package 12: 3
commands and files 11: 9–10, 13: 1–14
displaying information about 13: 11–14
installing software 12: 2
management menu tree 14: 2
menu options 14: 3–4
mounting and unmounting remote resources 13: 6–10
organization 11: 1–2
overview of 11: 9–10
RFS vs. NFS 11: 5–8
setting a default type 12: 3
setting up 12: 1–4
sharing and unsharing resources 13: 1–5
starting 12: 4
system V file sharing 11: 3–4
distributed file systems, types of 11: 1
DNS data files
creating 7: 11–12
modifying 7: 32
relationship between boot files and 7: 12

setting up 7: 17–21
DNS *See* Domain Name Service 7: 5
domain administrator (DA) 7: 5–6
Domain Name Service
TCP/IP and administrator's role 7: 4–6
TCP/IP and creating boot and data files 7: 11–32
TCP/IP and debugging named 7: 34
TCP/IP and hierarchy 7: 1
TCP/IP and modifying Startup Script 7: 32–33
TCP/IP and name servers 7: 1
TCP/IP and overview of 7: 1–7
TCP/IP and practical example 7: 35–44
TCP/IP and resolver 7: 1
TCP/IP and setting up, on a client 7: 6, 8–10
TCP/IP and setting up, on a name server 7: 6–7, 11–34
TCP/IP and setting up root server for local network 7: 33
Domain Name Service (DNS) 2: 19
configuring a name server 7: 11–34
overview 7: 1
setting up the resolver 7: 8–10
TCP/IP 3: 7
domain NIS/RPC 23: 7, 27: 5–7, 28: 7–8
names 28: 3
domain RFS 15: 2, 4, 16: 8
add/delete members 17: 6
add/delete password for 17: 6
domain share table 17: 34
multiple domain name service 17: 9–10
name server 17: 54–57
primary 15: 4
primary name server 17: 54–57
resource sharing with other domains 17: 8–9
secondary 15: 5, 17: 55–56
setting up domain name 17: 2
share table 17: 34
domain TCP/IP
establishing 4: 5
levels of Internet 4: 5–7
local administrative 4: 7
registering 4: 9
registration form guidelines 10: 1–4
root-level 4: 7
second-level 4: 7
selecting a name 4: 8
top-level 4: 7

E

encryption keys 23: 3
ENIGMA encryption 2: 4, 31
environment variables (NFS) 24: 12
error messages, *See* debugging 2: 7
error reporting routine 2: 7
errors log (BNU) 2: 117–118
escape character 2: 96
/etc/
auto.direct map 28: 11–12
confnet.d/inet/interface(4) 6: 8–10, 13, 15, 8: 9–11
confnet.d/netdrivers(4) 6: 6, 8, 13, 15, 8: 7–9
cs/auth 2: 27–28
dfs/dfstab(4) 11: 10, 13: 1–4, 17: 29, 32, 35, 19: 3, 20: 2–3, 22: 2, 8, 23: 8
dfs/fstypes(4) 11: 9, 12: 3, 19: 3, 20: 1
dfs/sharetab(4) 11: 10, 19: 3, 22: 8
ethers(4) 4: 13, 16–17, 8: 5, 10
hosts(4) 2: 17–18, 26, 33, 134, 4: 1, 12–14, 16, 19, 6: 5–7, 11, 14, 17, 19, 25, 7: 10, 12, 8: 10
hosts.equiv(4) 5: 1–5
iaf/cr1/keys 2: 31

iaf/serve.alias 2: 7, 22, 25
iaf/serve.allow 2: 7, 22, 24, 34, 37, 73, 134
idmap/attrmap 2: 58, 60
idmap/cr1/idata 2: 47, 49, 52
idmap/cr1/uidata 2: 47, 52
inetd.conf(4) 5: 6
inet/inet.priv 5: 6–7
mnttab(4) 11: 10, 22: 3, 24: 16
netconfig(4) 2: 6, 11–18, 4: 24, 7: 8–11
net/ticots/hosts 2: 27
net/ticots/services 2: 26
net/*transport* 2: 6
net/*transport***/hosts** 2: 17, 20–21, 33
net/*transport***/services** 2: 17, 20–21, 33
networks(4) 4: 1, 12–13, 15–16, 6: 5, 7, 17, 19
protocols(4) 4: 13, 17
publickey(4) 23: 7, 27: 1–4, 6–8, 28: 8–10, 12, 14
rc2.d/S75rpc 27: 2, 28: 8, 10, 17, 19
resolv.conf(4) 7: 8–9, 11, 38–39
rexec/services 2: 8, 135, 138
services(4) 2: 17–18, 33, 4: 13, 18
uucp 2: 8
uucp/Config 2: 90–91
uucp/Devconfig 2: 88
uucp/Devices 2: 91–99
uucp/Dialcodes 2: 110
uucp/Dialers 2: 99–101
uucp/Grades 2: 111–113
uucp/Limits 2: 89–90
uucp/Permissions 2: 78–88
uucp/Poll 2: 110–111
uucp/Sysfiles 2: 88–89
uucp/Systems 2: 102–110
vfstab(4) 11: 10, 13: 6–10, 17: 7, 23, 29–30, 37, 19: 5, 20: 4, 22: 2, 7, 10, 23: 8, 24: 1–3, 14, 18
ethernet 3: 5, 4: 16
ethers file (optional), setting up 4: 16–17

F

file system, types defined GL: 4
File Transfer Protocol (FTP) 3: 7
fingerd(1M) 3: 7, 5: 6
Foreign log (BNU) 2: 124
forwarder 6: 3
fstypes(4) 11: 9, 19: 3, 20: 1
changing defaults 12: 3
ftp(1) 3: 7, 4: 18
ftpd(1M) 3: 7
fumount(1M) 17: 30–31, 35–36, 39–41
fusage(1M) 17: 59, 61–62, 67–68

G

gateway 6: 2–3
GID map 2: 58
gid.rules file 17: 14, 18–19, 45–46, 52
Grades 2: 70
Grades file (BNU) 2: 111–113
default 2: 113
ID-list 2: 112
Job-size field 2: 111–112
Permit-type 2: 112
System-job-grade field 2: 111–112
User-job-grade field 2: 111–112

H

hard mounts 20: 4, 22: 6
hardware devices for expanding networks 6: 2–3
hierarchical mounts (NFS) 24: 8
host address database 2: 133
Host Information (HINFO), resource record 7: 28

host number (IP) 4: 3
hosts files, sample 7: 17
hosts files, setting up 7: 12
hosts(4) 2: 18, 26, 33, 134, 4: 1, 12–14, 16, 19, 6: 5–7, 11, 14, 17, 19, 25, 7: 10, 12, 8: 10
hosts.equiv(4) 5: 1–5
  use of + in 5: 3
hosts.rev 7: 12, 19–20

I

ID Mapping
  administration of 2: 41–63
  attribute mapping menu 2: 44
  attribute maps 2: 58–63
  command alternatives to attribute mapping menu 2: 44
  command alternatives to name mapping menu 2: 43
  command alternatives to second level attribute mapping menu 2: 46
  command alternatives to second-level name mapping menu 2: 44
  login maps 2: 46–58
  REXEC 2: 133
ID mapping, RFS 15: 8–9, 16: 9
ID Mapping
  setting up 2: 7
  sub-menu for attribute mapping administration 2: 45
  sub-menu for name mapping administration 2: 43
  user-controlled maps 2: 55–58
ID mapping RFS
  add passwd and group files 17: 18, 48
  components 17: 13, 45–48
  creating **gid.rules** file 17: 18
  creating **uid.rules** file 17: 15–18
  idload(1M) 17: 48
  list current 17: 52–53
  multiple groups 17: 44–45
  remote names 17: 50–51
  remote users 17: 43–53
  rules files 17: 45–53
  run idload 17: 19–20
  tools and files 17: 12–20
  when not to map 17: 11
  when to map 17: 11–12
idadmin(1M) 2: 8, 47–48
idata file
  adding an entry to 2: 47
  administration of 2: 47–53
  checking and fixing 2: 52–53
  displaying information 2: 53
  setting up 2: 48–49
Identification and Authentication Facility, (IAF) 2: 3–4
idload(1M) 17: 48
  -k 17: 12, 20, 52–53
  -n 17: 12, 19, 52–53
ifconfig(1M) 8: 2–3
  options 6: 6–7, 12
IN-ADDR.ARPA 7: 4
inetd(1M) 3: 7, 7: 32, 8: 11–12
inet.priv 5: 6–7
INET-specific **interface**(4) 6: 6, 8–10, 12–13, 15, 8: 9–11
interface file, verifying contents of protocol-specific 8: 9
Internet 3: 2
Internet Control Message Protocol (ICMP) 3: 2, 5, 8: 1
internet network number, obtaining an 4: 2
Internet Protocol (IP) 3: 5, 4: 1
  address creating 4: 4
  address representation 4: 3
  address to hexadecimal notation, converting 4: 22–23
  addresses to network hosts, assigning 4: 3–4

header 3: 6
localhost address 4: 14
number registration form 9: 1–6
internet protocol suite 3: 2
internetwork 6: 4
creating and configuring a router 6: 4–19
creating and setting up router clients 6: 19–22
invocation function, identification and, authentication facility and 2: 3
IP, *See* Internet Protocol 2: 3

K

keymaster(1M) daemon 2: 37
keys *See* encryption keys 23: 3
keyserv(1M) 23: 8, 27: 2, 4, 6, 28: 9

L

Limits file (BNU) 2: 89–90
listen port monitor 2: 2–3
registering cr1 with 2: 36
registering REXEC with 2: 134–135
setting up 2: 6–7
local administrative TCP/IP domains 4: 7
local resource sharing, RFS 17: 32
local resource sharing (NFS) 26: 4
local resource sharing *See also* resource sharing, RFS 16: 6
localhost address 4: 14
local_resources submenu (DFS) 14: 3
lock manager, NFS 25: 1–5
lockd(1M) 22: 2, 25: 2, 4
log files BNU 2: 71, 116–124
account 2: 119–120
cleaning up 2: 127
command 2: 116
errors 2: 117–118
Foreign 2: 124
perflog 2: 122–124
perflog (conn) 2: 122–123
perflog (xfer) 2: 123–124
security 2: 120–121
security (rexe) 2: 121
security (xfer) 2: 121
summary of 2: 129
system history 2: 116–117
xferstats (transfer) 2: 118–119
login maps, setting up 2: 46–58
logins, adding 2: 125

M

Mail Exchanger (MX), resource record 7: 31–32
maintenance, BNU 2: 72
make(1) 28: 12, 18, 22, 26, 31
makedbm(1M) 28: 2, 5, 7, 14, 16, 22–24, 26, 28–29, 31
makefile
adding (NIS) maps to 28: 26
default 28: 12–15
map IDs (RFS)
add **passwd** and **group** files 17: 18–19
complex 17: 10–20
example rules files 17: 49–50
general 15: 8–9
gid.rules 17: 18
how it works 17: 43–44
idload(1M) 17: 12–14
idload(1M) and rules files 17: 45–48
list current map 17: 52–53
multi groups 17: 44–45
remote names 17: 50–51
remote users 17: 43–53
run **idload**(1M) 17: 19–20
uid.rules 17: 15–18

when not to 17: 11
when to 17: 11–12
maps **automount**(1M) 24: 3
conventions 24: 3–4
direct 24: 3, 5–6
indirect 24: 3, 6–7
master 24: 3–5
modifying 24: 17
preparing 24: 3–12
specifying multiple locations 24: 9
specifying multiple mounts 24: 7–8
specifying subdirectories 24: 9–10
using environment variables 24: 12
using substitutions 24: 11–12
maps (NIS)
28: 2, 5, 8–16, 21–27
adding new 28: 26
adding to makefile 28: 26–27
changing master server 28: 29–30
changing server 28: 29–30
creating 28: 22
creating and modifying non-standard 28: 22–24
makefiles 28: 12–15
modifying standard 28: 21–22
propagating 28: 24–26
updating 28: 21–24
updating existing 28: 21
writing and preparing maps
28: 8–15
master key, cr1 *See* cr1 master key
2: 37
master server
setting up a boot file for a primary
7: 14–15
setting up a boot file for a secondary 7: 15–16
master server (NIS)
28: 3–5
map changing 28: 29–30
set with **ypinit**(1M) 28: 16
master servers 7: 6–7
master servers (NIS)
28: 3–4
changing 28: 29
setting 28: 16
starting daemons in 28: 17
MAXGDP (RFS) 17: 71
MAXSERVE (RFS) 17: 71
menus (**sysadm**(1M)), NFS interface
26: 1–5
MINSERVE (RFS) 17: 71
monitoring (RFS) 17: 58–69
client caching 17: 63–66
CPU time 17: 61–62
remote disk space 17: 69
remote system calls 17: 58–59
resource usage 17: 67–68
rfs operations 17: 60–61
server processes 17: 66–67
mount point
automounter 24: 4, 18–19
definition GL: 5
special 24: 2
mount(1M) 11: 10, 13: 6, 8, 14: 3,
24: 1–5, 14, 18
debugging NFS problems 22: 7–8
display mounted remote resources
13: 11
mount remote resources 13: 6–8
NFS 20: 4–5, 22: 2–3, 5, 8–9
NFS parameters 20: 4
RFS 15: 2–3, 16: 7, 17: 9, 23, 26, 37–42
mountall(1M) 11: 10, 13: 6
mount a set of remote resources
13: 9–10
NFS 22: 2
mountd(1M) 22: 2–4, 7
mounting
auotmounter options, 24: 4
automounter options, 24: 5–6
NFS and problems with 22: 1–8
NFS automatic 19: 3, 20: 4–5
RFS remote resource 16: 7, 17: 37–42

mounting NFS resources, explicitly 20: 4–5
mounting *See also* automounter, NFS; remote resource mounting 16: 7
Multi-day technique 2: 128

N

NAA. *See* Networking Applications Architecture 7: 22
name RR 7: 22
name server
  RFS 15: 4–5, 17: 54–57
  setting up DNS on a 7: 6–7, 11–34
name server (DNS), defining 7: 1
Name Server (NS), resource record 7: 27
named(1M) 3: 7, 7: 1, 4, 6–7, 10–12, 32
  debugging 7: 34
named.boot 7: 11–12, 14–16, 32–33
named.ca 7: 11–12, 14, 20–21
named.local 7: 11–12, 15, 19, 39–40
name-to-address mapping 2: 4, 17–21
  connection server and 2: 3
  management menu 2: 9
  RPC 27: 2
  setting up 2: 6
  setting up libraries 2: 18–19
  shell commands for 2: 17–18
net number 4: 3
netconfig(4) 2: 6, 11–18, 4: 24, 7: 8–11
  fields 2: 12–15
  modifying 7: 9–10
  network_id 2: 12
  sample file 2: 15
netdrivers(4) 6: 6, 8, 13, 15, 8: 7–9
netinfo(1M) 6: 6, 8: 7–9
NETPATH 2: 5–6, 11, 13, 16
netstat(1M) 4: 15, 8: 3–7
  6: 15
  -i 8: 5, 22: 10
  -r 8: 6
  -rs 8: 6–7
  -s 8: 4–5
network
  bridge 6: 2
  classifications 4: 2
  configuration database file 2: 12–18
  daemons **in.named** *See also* daemons (network) 7: 1, 34
  definition 3: 2
  files 4: 13
  hardware 6: 2
  masks 6: 23
network address, RFS 15: 6
network address assigning 4: 3–4
network addressing 2: 17–21
  string address providers 2: 20
  TCP/IP 2: 18
network administration, model of 2: 1
network administration *See* BNU 2: 64
network device 2: 12
Network File System (NFS) 2: 5, 4: 19, 11: 1
  administration 18: 1
  automounter 24: 1–20
  clients 18: 4
  debugging 22: 1–10
  DES authentication and 23: 3
  fixing hung programs 22: 9–10
  mounting and unmounting 19: 3, 20: 4–5, 22: 2–8
  network lock manager 25: 1–5
  obtaining information on 21: 1–4
  organization 18: 1
  overview of administration 18: 6
  purpose of 18: 3
  remote procedure call and 23: 2–6
  resource sharing and unsharing 19: 3–4, 20: 1–3
  resources 18: 3–4
  secure 23: 1–10
  secure RPC 23: 3–6

servers 18: 4
setting up 19: 1–5
setting up automatic mounting 19: 5
setting up automatic sharing 19: 3–4
start/stop 19: 2
vs. Remote File Sharing (RFS) 11: 5–8
network ID 2: 12
Network Information Service implementing
establishing domain 28: 7–8
initializing clients 28: 19–20
running ASCII files 28: 14
setting master servers 28: 16
setting slave servers 28: 17–19
setting up clients 28: 19–20
starting daemons in master server 28: 17
starting daemons in slave server 28: 19
writing and preparing maps 28: 8–15
Network Information Service (NIS)
adding slave servers 28: 28–29
binding 28: 4
changing master servers 28: 29–30
clients 28: 4
commands 28: 31–32
daemons 28: 2
debugging 28: 33–39
defining 28: 1
domain 28: 3
elements 28: 1–2
environment 28: 2–6
maps 28: 21–27
servers 28: 3–4
turning off 28: 40
network layer 3: 5
network listener 15: 6
set up 17: 1–2
network lock manager 25: 1–5
network lock manager NFS
locking protocol 25: 4–5
network status monitor 25: 5
overview of 25: 1–5
network number, obtaining an internet 4: 2
network problems
diagnosing 8: 10–11
logging 8: 14
network protocol 3: 2
network security 5: 1
effect of administrative files 5: 2–5
NFS 23: 1–10
.rhosts 3: 1, 5: 1–2, 4–5
Secure NFS 23: 7
username "nobody" 19: 4
network selection 2: 10–21
command alternatives 2: 11
connection server and 2: 3
default search path 2: 15–16
management menu 2: 9
nametoaddr_libs 2: 15
netconfig(4) 2: 6, 11–18, 4: 24, 7: 8–11
NETPATH 2: 6, 11, 13, 16
overview of 2: 11
protocol family identifiers 2: 13–14
protocol name identifiers 2: 14
setting up 2: 5–6
network services
shell command list 2: 9
sysadm(1M) menu 2: 9
network services management menu 2: 9
network specification 15: 6
network status monitor 25: 5
Network Support Utilities (NSU) 15: 6
Networking Applications Architecture (NAA) 2: 2
BNU and REXEC and 2: 5
description and diagram of 2: 2
networking utilities package *See* BNU 2: 64

networks file (optional), setting up 4: 15–16
networks(4) 4: 1, 12–13, 15–16, 6: 5, 7, 17, 19
newkey(1M) 23: 7–8, 27: 7–8
  NIS 28: 8–22
NFS
  booting and setuid problems 23: 9
  menu interface 26: 1–5
  overview of administration 18: 6
  security 23: 1–10
  starting 19: 2
NFS error messages 22: 7–8
NFS lock manager 25: 1–5
NFS mounting process 22: 2–3
NFS resources
  defined 18: 3
  granting root access 19: 4
  mount automatically 19: 5
  unmounting 20: 5
  unsharing 13: 3, 5
  unsharing with **unshare**(1M) 20: 3
  unsharing with **unshareall** *See* **shareall**(1M) 20: 3
NFS resources hard mounted 22: 6
NFS resources soft mounted 22: 6
nfsd(1M) 22: 2–4, 8–9
nfsping(1M) 22: 4
  -a 22: 5
  -o 22: 9, 28: 35
NIS (network information service)
  binding 28: 4–5
  client 28: 4, 19–20
  debugging 28: 33–40
  domain 28: 3, 7–8
  machine types 28: 3
  maps *See* maps (NIS) 28: 2
  master server 28: 16–17
  servers 28: 3–5, 28–29
  slave server 28: 17–19
  steps to implement 28: 7–20
  turning off 28: 40
node name 17: 1
NRCVD (RFS) 17: 70
NRDUSER (RFS) 17: 71
NSNDD (RFS) 17: 70
NSRMOUNT (RFS) 17: 71

P

packet 3: 5, 6: 2
packet switching network 3: 5
parameter tuning (RFS) 17: 70–73
passwords
  add/delete for RFS 17: 6
  assigning 2: 125
  RFS 17: 26–28
passwords and **chkey**(1), RPC 27: 8
perflog (BNU) 2: 122–124
perflog (conn) (BNU) 2: 122
perflog (xfer) (BNU) 2: 123–124
Permissions file (BNU) 2: 78–88
physical layer, TCP/IP 3: 5
ping(1M) 8: 1–2
pmadm(1M) 2: 7–8, 22–23, 36, 74, 77, 135, 4: 19–21, 15: 6
Poll file (BNU) 2: 110–111
  2: 71
port monitor
  listen 2: 2–3
  listen, setting up TCP/IP 4: 19–21
port monitor listen
  registering cr1 with 2: 36
  registering REXEC with 2: 134
  setting up 2: 6–7
primary name server (DNS) 7: 15
primary name server (RFS) 15: 4, 17: 54–56
printers sharing 17: 42
Protocol 2: 97–98
protocols(4) 4: 13, 17
protofamily 2: 13
protoname 2: 13

public key 23: 2
public key cryptography 23: 3
publickey(4) 23: 7, 27: 1–4, 6–8, 28: 8–10, 12, 14

R

RARP 3: 5
RCACHETIME (RFS) 17: 71
rcp(1) (remote copy) 5: 1–2, 6, 28: 17, 38
registering client machine 2: 24–25
relay 6: 3
Remote File Sharing
- automatic startup (init3) 17: 28–31
- computer verification 17: 6–8
- create **rfmaster**(4) file 17: 3–5
- domain name 17: 2
- multiple domain name service 17: 9–10
- network listener 17: 1
- node name 17: 1
- password 17: 26–28
- resource sharing with other domains 17: 8–9
- setting up add/delete password for domain members 17: 6
- start/stop 17: 25–31
- transport provider 17: 3, 20–24

Remote File Sharing (RFS) 2: 5, 4: 19, 11: 1
- administration 15: 1
- design features 15: 9–10
- domains and 15: 4–5, 16: 8, 17: 2, 54–57
- ID mapping 15: 8–9, 16: 9, 17: 10–20, 43–53
- operations 17: 60–61
- organization 15: 1
- purpose of 15: 2
- resource sharing 15: 2–3, 17: 32–42
- restrict resources 15: 7–8
- security 15: 6–7
- sharing printers 17: 42
- transport provider 15: 5, 16: 9
- verify computers 15: 7
- vs. Network File System (NFS) 11: 5–8

Remote File Sharing **sysadm**(1M) interface
- changing configuration 16: 8–9
- domain name servers 17: 54–57
- local resource sharing 16: 6
- monitoring 17: 58–68
- overview 16: 1
- parameter tuning 17: 70–73
- remote resource mounting 16: 7
- setting up 16: 3–4
- start/stop 16: 5

Remote Proceduce Call (RPC), passwords and **chkey**(1) 27: 8
Remote Procedure Call (RPC)
- administration files 27: 1–9
- domains 27: 5–7
- name-to-address mapping 27: 2
- **newkey**(1M) 27: 7
- overview of 23: 2–6
- overview of secure 27: 4–5
- secure administration 27: 6–9

Remote Procedure CAll (RPC), SRPC_DOMAIN 27: 3, 5–7, 28: 8
remote resource mounting
- RFS 17: 37–42
- **sysadm**(1M) interface and 26: 5

remote resources
- automatic mounting of 13: 7
- automatic sharing of 13: 2
- explicit mounting of 13: 6
- explicit sharing of 13: 1
- mounting a set of 13: 9
- unmounting 13: 8

remote system calls 17: 58–59
remote_resources submenu (DFS) 14: 3–4

remote.unknown 2: 69–70, 102, 124
repeater 6: 2
reportscheme(1M) 2: 7, 22, 24–27, 32–34, 74–75, 133
resolv.conf(4) 7: 8–9, 11
creating 7: 8–9
sample 7: 38–39
resolver 7: 1
definition 7: 1
resolv.so library 2: 15, 18–19
Resource Record (RR) 7: 17
address 7: 28
Canonical Name 7: 30
class field 7: 22
control entry lines 7: 23
data field 7: 22
Domain Name Pointer 7: 30
fields for 7: 21–22
Host Information 7: 28
Mail Exchanger 7: 31–32
name field 7: 21
Name Server 7: 27
special characters for 7: 22–23
Start of Authority 7: 26–27
ttl field 7: 22
type field 7: 22
types 7: 24
well known services 7: 29
resource sharing, RFS 15: 2–3
resource sharing NFS
setting up automatic 19: 3–4
sysadm(1M) interface and local 26: 4
using commands for 20: 1–3
resource sharing RFS
automatic 17: 32–33
checking disk space 17: 69
checking usage 17: 67–68
domain share table 17: 34
forced unmount 17: 36
in use 17: 34
local 17: 32
local share table 17: 33–34
remote resource disconnected 17: 40–42
remote resource mounting 17: 37–42
security and 17: 33
unsharing 17: 35
with other domains 17: 8–9
Reverse Address Resolution Protocol (RARP) 3: 2, 5
REXEC
adding services 2: 136–137
administration 2: 133–134
authentication scheme 2: 133–134
connection server 2: 133–134
host address database 2: 133
ID Mapping 2: 133
linking services to 2: 138
purpose of 2: 132
registering, with port monitor 2: 134–135
removing services 2: 137
rl 2: 132
rquery 2: 132
rx 2: 132
services defined by 2: 132
setting up 2: 8
REXEC listing defined services 2: 138
rfmaster(4) 17: 3–5, 23–24
create 17: 3–5
RF_MAXKMEM (RFS) 17: 72
RFS
active 17: 25
auto start init 17: 28–31
enter init 3 17: 28–29
initial start 17: 25–26
mode scripts 17: 30–31
See Remote File Sharing 17: 72
starting 17: 25–31
stopping 17: 31
tunable parameters 17: 70–73
RFS resources
auto remote mount 17: 37
auto share 17: 32–33

identifier 15: 2
local mount table 17: 39–40
local share table 17: 33–34
local sharing 17: 32–36
local unmount 17: 42
mount guidelines 17: 37–38
mount rules 17: 38–39
remote disconnect 17: 40–42
remote mounting 17: 37–42
shared in use 17: 34–35
sharing 15: 2, 17: 42
unmount remote 17: 36
unshare 17: 35
RFTMO_TIME (RFS) 17: 72
rfuadmin(1M) 17: 36, 40–42
rfudaemon(1M) 17: 30, 40–41
RFUD_DISCONN 17: 40
RFUD_FUMOUNT 17: 40
RFUD_GETUMSG 17: 40
RFUD_LASTUMSG 17: 41
.rhosts file 3: 1, 5: 1–2, 4–5
rlogin(1) (remote login) 2: 2, 132, 3: 7, 5: 1–3, 6, 6: 4, 8: 10, 22: 7, 23: 9, 28: 29
rlogind(1M) 3: 7, 25: 2
root server for local network, setting up 7: 33
route daemon
running 6: 22
setting up 6: 18–19
routed(1M) 4: 12, 6: 4–5, 7, 18–22, 8: 13–14
router 6: 2
router clients, setting up 6: 19–22
router files, sample 6: 17
router(s)
configuring a 6: 4–22
purpose of 6: 2–3
specifying a default 6: 20–21
using specific 6: 21
RPC authentication 23: 2
RPC *See* Remote Procedure Call 2: 138
rpcbind(1M) 22: 3, 5–7, 27: 9, 28: 35–36, 38
rquery 2: 138
RR *See* Resource Record 2: 138
rsh(1) (remote shell) 3: 7, 5: 1–2, 6
rwhod(1M) 5: 6, 8: 13
rxservice(1M) 2: 135–138

S

sacadm(1M) 2: 6, 8: 11–12, 17: 2
sar(1M)
-C 17: 65–66
-D 17: 58
-Db 17: 63–64
-Dc 17: 58–59
-Du 17: 61–62
-S 17: 66–67
-x 17: 60–61
secondary name servers 15: 5
RFS 17: 55–56
secret key 2: 4, 23: 3
secure NFS 23: 1–10
Secure NFS
administering 23: 7–8
NIS 28: 8
Secure RPC 23: 1
secure RPC 23: 3–6
Secure RPC, NIS 28: 8
security 15: 6–9
maintaining TCP/IP 5: 1–7
map IDs 15: 8–9
NFS *See* network security 23: 1
restrict resources 15: 7–8, 17: 33
RFS 17: 33
verify remote computer 15: 7, 17: 6–8
security issues 5: 6
security logs (BNU) 2: 120–121
(rexe) 2: 121
(xfer) 2: 121

security RFS 15: 6–7
semantics 2: 12
sender/receiver interaction 3: 3
server(s), NFS 22: 5–6
servers, (NIS) 28: 3–5, 16–19
server(s)
  processes 17: 66–67
  See also master servers; slave servers 22: 5
  setting up a boot file for a primary master 7: 14–15
  setting up a boot file for a secondary master 7: 15–16
  setting up DNS on a name 7: 6–7, 11–34
server(s) (DNS), setting up a boot file for a caching-only 7: 16
Service Access Controller (SAC) 2: 6
Service Access Facility (SAF) 2: 3
  menu 2: 36
services(4) 4: 13, 18
setuid problems, NFS 23: 9
share(1M) 11: 10, 13: 1–2, 11
  in **dfstab**(4) file 19: 3
  NFS 19: 3–4, 20: 1–2, 21: 3
  RFS 17: 32–33
shareall(1M) 11: 10, 13: 4–5, 20: 2–3
shared/sharing resources
  as a set 13: 4
  automatically 13: 2
  browsing 13: 12–13
  displaying a list of 13: 11–13
  displaying resources mounted by remote systems 13: 13–14
  explicitly 13: 1
  through NFS 20: 1–3
sharetab(4) 11: 10, 19: 3, 22: 8
Single-day technique 2: 128
slave server, (NIS) 28: 3–5, 28–29
slave server (NIS)
  set with **ypinit**(1M) 28: 17–19
  start daemons 28: 19
slave servers 28: 3–4
  adding 28: 28–29
  debugging 28: 37–38
  setting 28: 17–19
  starting daemons in 28: 19
soft mounts 22: 6
SRPC_DOMAIN 27: 3, 5–7, 28: 8
Standard Resource Record Format 7: 17, 21–32
Start of Authority (SOA) resource record 7: 26–27
  class field 7: 26
  expire field 7: 26
  minimum field 7: 26
  name field 7: 26
  origin field 7: 26
  person in charge field 7: 26
  refresh field 7: 26
  retry field 7: 26
  serial field 7: 26
  SOA field 7: 26
Startup Script, modifying 4: 12
startup script, modifying 7: 32–33
statd(1M) 22: 2, 25: 2, 5
straddr.so library 2: 15, 18, 20–21
subnets
  changing to a system without to a system with 6: 25
  examples of 6: 25
  number 4: 3
  setting up 6: 23–25
support files, BNU 2: 70–71
sysadm(1M)
  basic_networking 2: 78
  DFS 14: 1–4
  menu interface 2: 9
  name_map 2: 42
  network_services 2: 9
  network_services/cr1 2: 35
  NFS 26: 1–5
  ports 2: 35
  RFS 16: 1–9

Sysfiles file (BNU), 2: 71, 88–89
system administration menus *See also* **sysadm**(1M) 14: 1–4
system history log (BNU) 2: 116–117
System-name field 2: 103
Systems
  basic management menu 2: 102
  Class field 2: 104
  Login field 2: 106–108
  Phone field 2: 105–106
  Time field 2: 103
  Type field 2: 104
systems file, checking 2: 130
Systems file (BNU) 2: 71, 102–110

T

TCP or TLI-conformant provider 2: 88
TCP/IP 2: 5, 3: 2–5
  application layer 3: 6–7
  converting IP address to, hexadecimal notation 4: 22–23
  creation of 3: 2
  data link layer 3: 5
  disabling service commands 5: 6–7
  Domain Name Service and practical example 7: 35–44
  Domain Name Service and setting up, on a client 7: 8–10
  Domain Name Service and setting up, on a name server 7: 11–34
  establishing a domain 4: 5–9
  ethers file (optional) 4: 16–17
  hosts file 4: 13–14
  installing network media 4: 10
  installing software 4: 11
  maintaining security 5: 1–7
  network layer 3: 5–6
  obtaining an internet network number 4: 2
  physical layer 3: 5
  protocol layers 3: 3–7
  protocols file 4: 17
  services file 4: 18
  setting up as a preferred network 4: 24
  setting up assigning IP addresses to network hosts 4: 3–4
  setting up files 4: 13–18
  setting up listener 4: 19–21
  setting up networks file (optional) 4: 15–16
  setting up overview of 4: 1
  starting 4: 25
  top-level domains 4: 7
  transport layer 3: 6
  troubleshooting commands 8: 1–9
  troubleshooting improving system performance 8: 13
  troubleshooting logging network problems 8: 14
  troubleshooting restarting 8: 12
  troubleshooting running software checks 8: 10–11
  use of the term 3: 2
  Domain Name Service and overview of 7: 1–7
TCP/IP expanding
  creating an internetwork 6: 4–22
  hardware devices for 6: 2–3
  setting up subnets 6: 23–25
tcpip.so library 2: 15, 18–19
telnet(1) 3: 6
telnetd(1M) 3: 6
Time field 2: 103
TM. (temporary data file) (BNU) 2: 113
/tmp_mnt, special directory (NFS) 24: 2
transfer log (**xferstats**) (BNU) 2: 118–119
Transmission Control Protocol (TCP) 3: 2, 6

transmissions, debug 2: 130–131
transport layer, TCP/IP 3: 6
Transport Level Interface (TLI) 3: 4
transport provider 15: 5
  set name 16: 9, 17: 3
transport provider RFS
  setting up 17: 3
  setting up multiple 17: 20–24
transport provider (TRANSPORT), RFS 15: 5–6
tunable parameters, RFS 17: 70–73

U

uidadmin(1) 2: 54–55
uidata file
  adding an entry to 2: 56
  administration of 2: 54–58
  checking and fixing 2: 57
  deleting an entry in 2: 57
  enabling and disabling user-controlled mapping 2: 55–56
  setting up 2: 55
uid.rules file 17: 15–18, 45–46, 49–50
umount *See* **mount**(1M) 11: 10, 13: 6, 8
  NFS 20: 5
  RFS 17: 42
umountall *See* **mountall**(1M) 11: 10, 13: 10
UNIX System, authentication 23: 2
unshare(1M) 11: 10, 13: 3
  NFS 20: 3
  RFS 17: 35
unshareall *See* **shareall**(1M) 11: 10, 13: 5, 20: 3
User Datagram Protocol (UDP) 3: 2, 6
user programs, BNU 2: 67–68
user-level services 2: 4–5
username "nobody" 19: 4
/usr
  /include/netconfig.h 2: 12
  /lib/laf/crl 2: 41
  /lib/cron/log 2: 128
  /lib/iaf/crl/scheme 2: 31
  /lib/uucp/remote.unknown 2: 69–70
uucheck(1M) 2: 68, 129
uucico(1M) 2: 65, 69, 125
uucleanup(1M) 2: 68
uucp(1C) 2: 51, 64, 67–69, 75, 78–79, 85, 88, 106, 114–116, 118–120, 125, 130, 17: 18, 38
  logins 2: 125
uudecode *See* **uuencode**(1C) 2: 68
uudemon.admin 2: 127
uudemon.clean 2: 127–128
uudemon.hour 2: 126–127
uudemon.poll 2: 126
uuencode(1C) 2: 68
uuglist(1C) 2: 68
uulog *See* **uucp**(1C) 2: 68, 129
uuname *See* **uucp**(1C) 2: 68, 129
uupick *See* **uuto**(1C) 2: 67
uusched(1M) 2: 69
uustat(1C) 2: 68, 129
uuto(1C) 2: 64, 67, 69
Uutry(1M) 2: 68, 129
uux(1C) 2: 68
uuxqt(1M) 2: 65, 69

V

/var/
  adm/log/cs.debug 2: 29
  adm/log/cs.log 2: 28
  iaf/crl 2: 31
  spool/uucp/.Admin/account 2: 119–120
  spool/uucp/.Admin/command 2: 116
  spool/uucp/.Admin/errors 2: 117–118

spool/uucp/.Admin/Foreign 2: 124
spool/uucp/.Admin/perflog 2: 122–124
spool/uucp/.Admin/security 2: 120–121
spool/uucp/.Admin/xferstats 2: 118–119
spool/uucp/.Log 2: 116–117
verification, RFS computer 17: 6–8
verifiers, in RPC authentication 23: 2
vfstab(4) 11: 10, 13: 6–10, 17: 7, 23, 29–30, 37, 19: 5, 20: 4, 22: 2, 7, 10, 23: 8, 24: 1–3, 14, 18

X

xferstats (transfer) log (BNU) 2: 118–119

Y

Yellow Pages 28: 1
ypbind *See* **ypserv**(1M) 28: 2–5, 31, 35–36
ypcat(1) 28: 2, 32
ypinit(1M) 28: 2, 16–20, 28, 31
ypmatch(1) 28: 2, 32
yppoll(1M) 28: 2, 32
yppush(1M) 28: 2, 31
ypserv(1M) 28: 2–5, 31, 38–39
ypset(1M) 28: 2, 31
ypupdated(1M) 28: 2, 32
ypwhich(1) 28: 2, 5, 32, 36
ypxfr(1M) 28: 2, 24–26, 31

Z

zones, administrative 7: 1–4

What do YOU think?

USL values your opinion. Please indicate your opinions in each of the following areas. We'd like to know how well this document meets your needs.

Book Title:____________________________________

	Excellent	Good	Fair	Poor
Accuracy - Is the information correct?	❑	❑	❑	❑
Completeness - Is information missing?	❑	❑	❑	❑
Organization - Is information easy to find?	❑	❑	❑	❑
Clarity - Do you understand the information?	❑	❑	❑	❑
Examples - Are there enough?	❑	❑	❑	❑
Illustrations - Are there enough?	❑	❑	❑	❑
Appearance - Do you like the page format?	❑	❑	❑	❑
Physical binding - Do you like the cover and binding?	❑	❑	❑	❑

Does the document meet your needs? Why or why not?

____

____

____

What is the single most important improvement that we could make to this document?

____

____

____

Please complete the following information.

Name (Optional): ____________________________

Job Title or Function: ____________________________

Organization: ____________________________

Address: ____________________________

____

Phone: (   ) ____________________________

If we need more information may we contact you? Yes ❑ No ❑

Thank you.

BUSINESS REPLY MAIL

FIRST CLASS MAIL PERMIT NO. 199 SUMMIT, NJ

POSTAGE WILL BE PAID BY ADDRESSEE

UNIX System Laboratories, Inc.
Director
USL Documentation Department
Room F–313
190 River Road
Summit, NJ 07901-9907